About the Author – Gordon Moir

Born in Fraserburgh North-East Scotland, I left school in 1975 to work on the family farm. A keen golfer I accepted an apprenticeship at Fraserburgh Golf Club and began there in February 1976. I attended Elmwood College, Cupar where I gained my City and Guilds qualification in Greenkeeping and was awarded the St Andrews Links Trust Award for the best student in year three. Promoted to Head Greenkeeper at Fraserburgh GC in 1980, I remained there for a further eleven years. In September 1991 I began a twenty-seven-year career with St Andrews Links Trust when I accepted the position as Head Greenkeeper of the Eden Course. In October 2000 I was promoted to the role of Links Manager, responsible for all turf related matters on the six golf courses managed by St Andrews Links Trust. This title subsequently changed to Links Superintendent, then again to Director of Greenkeeping. Alongside overseeing the construction of the new Castle course in 2005 I led the greenkeeping department at three Open Championships, two Women's British Opens, a Seniors' British Open and a Curtis Cup along with numerous European Tour events and other championships. From an early stage in my career I was a consistent supporter of the British and International Golf Greenkeepers Association, becoming President of BIGGA in 2022.

St Andrews
The Greenkeeper's Tale

With best wishes,

Gordon Moir

Published in the UK in 2022 by

Copyright © Gordon Moir 2022

Gordon Moir has asserted his right under the
Copyright, Designs and Patents Act, 1988, to be identified
as the author of this work.

Paperback ISBN: 978-1-7396059-0-2

eBook ISBN: 978-1-7396059-1-9

Cover design and typeset by SpiffingCovers

St Andrews
The Greenkeeper's Tale

Gordon Moir

Acknowledgements.

I had often thought of writing a book about my experiences working at St Andrews Links after I retired but life got in the way, then came Covid 19 and lockdown!

Even then, without the encouragement and support of many friends, my idea would never have come to fruition. In particular, without the help and advice of Dr David Hamilton, my notes would still be gathering dust, or whatever the equivalent of a word document on a laptop is. I received considerable assistance from the following: Jim Allison, Davie Anderson, Peter Mason, Roger McStravick, Gillian Stewart, Jon Wood and Sir Michael Bonallack, along with various past colleagues who confirmed facts and provided pictures. I'm indebted to them for their help along with St Andrews Links Trust.

I'd also like to acknowledge the help I received from SpiffingCovers in getting the book to print.

I'm especially appreciative of my editor-in-chief, namely my wife Pauline, who helped turn my words from a rambling manuscript into a product that is actually readable, along with putting up with me during the process.

I'm also eternally grateful to an anonymous R&A member for supporting me, which allowed for the book to be printed.

While the majority of the photographs are mine, many should be credited to the following:

St Andrews Links Trust.

Jon Wood, course manager at the Castle course.

Jared Nemitz, a seasonal greenkeeper at the Links in 2005.

Various other greenstaff, unknown, who added pictures to our shared drive over the years.

The Toro Company

Contents

Foreword by Sir Michael Bonallack OBE

S T ANDREWS is 'The Home of Golf'. This is a fact recognised by practically every golfer who has ever played this great game.

It therefore follows, that to have the responsibility for looking after the seven golf courses operated by The St Andrews Links Trust is one of the most important positions in the world of golf.

Gordon Moir had this responsibility for eighteen years, firstly as Links Manager, then as Links Superintendent and finally, in recognition of the proper title for such a crucial position, Director of Greenkeeping.

To read of Gordon's appointment in 1991 and the conditions he found waiting him, make it a miracle that he survived the primitive and totally inadequate staffing arrangements and almost total lack of the necessary equipment to enable him to do his job.

He not only survived, but by the time he retired in 2018, the St Andrews Links were all in pristine condition and managed in a highly efficient and professional manner. A tribute to his professional skills as both a technician and as a manager of people.

Preparing The Old Course for an Open Championship brings even added pressures, but Gordon very successfully oversaw three Championships, all of which were praised by the players, the spectators and the world's media.

In addition, he has found time to play a leading role in BIGGA and in January 2022 will take over as President of this great association, which is so important in ensuring that the highest possible standards of care are possible for every golf course in the land.

It is very easy for golfers to forget that the greatest asset of any golf club is not its clubhouse or membership, but its golf course.

Gordon has our respect and enormous thanks for reminding us of this and for the outstanding contribution he has made to the game we love.

Sir Michael Bonallack
St Andrews

Introduction

W E WERE standing in the locker room of the Royal and Ancient Golf Club, assembling into position prior to leaving for the presentation ceremony at the close of the 2015 Open Championship, when Peter Dawson, CEO of the R&A, reminded us to, "Check your mobile phones are switched off and your zips are pulled up." Good advice. We climbed the stairs and passed through the Clubhouse, where five-times Open Champion Peter Thomson joined the line-up, before exiting the building and walking down the steps onto the Old Course. As soon as we arrived in our positions, I realised I was going to be standing immediately behind where the Champion Golfer of the Year would be presented with the Claret Jug and from where he would be making his thank-you speech.

While I was standing waiting for the presentation to begin, I thought to myself, "A've deen nae bad for a loon fae 'i Broch." Translate – "I've done well for a young boy from Fraserburgh." This is from the Doric dialect, the language spoken in the north-east of Scotland

As soon as Zach Johnson began talking, I could feel my mobile phone vibrating in my pocket. 'Friends' from around the world, who were either watching the ceremony on television or were in the actual crowd, were sending me text messages and pictures of Zach standing there with the trophy. Gordon McKie, Course Manager of the Old Course, and I were standing either side and slightly behind him in our blazers and ties, looking every inch like we were his bodyguards!

This book is a selection of stories, factual and sometimes irreverent or downright bizarre, of 27 years working at St Andrews Links.

It charts my career at The Home of Golf, from arriving there in 1991, where I discovered to my surprise, the most famous golfing complex in the world wasn't exactly how people would expect it to be, through to my retirement in December 2018.

It includes my reflections on five Open Championships, three of which I led the greenkeeping team through. I go 'behind the scenes' revealing some of the more unusual events which took place during those championships, and the numerous other tournaments staged during my time as Director of Greenkeeping.

It's certainly not a technical book on greenkeeping and was never intended to be although it does contain aspects of the work we undertook, explained in laymen's terms.

It explains the complexity of the Links Trust, its management and governance. It also charts the changes, at times controversial, to the Old Course and some of the more significant changes to the other courses managed by the Links Trust, along with my experience as part of the team constructing the Castle Course.

In my position, I was fortunate to have the opportunity to visit, and play, many of the greatest courses in the world and meet some extraordinary people. Throughout the book are stories of the educational, interesting, unusual, humorous incidents and friendships I made over the years. Things the reader will never have heard of elsewhere or would have imagined could happen. These range from being part of the cast in a Hollywood movie to causing the local police concerns prior to an Open Championship, and from being heckled by the spectators at a US Open, to being chased through the grounds of Augusta National at the Masters.

Gordon Moir, St Andrews 2022

Chapter 1. Starting at St Andrews

An aerial view of the Links

P ILMOUR HOUSE, that was where I was looking for, a strange name I thought and wondered if it had been a misprint or typo and it should have been Pilmuir but no, Pilmour it was. It was just outside town and was the offices of the St Andrews Links Trust. It was the last Sunday in July 1991 and I had an interview at 4pm for the head greenkeeper's position on the Eden course at St Andrews. I'd been to St Andrews a few times, mostly in the late 1970s/early 1980s when I attended nearby Elmwood College studying for my City and Guilds in Horticulture with the turfgrass option, and played both the Old Course and the Jubilee once in that time. I'd also attended the Open Championships for a day in 1978 and again in 1984. At the 1990 Open I was part of the British and International Golf Greenkeepers

Association (BIGGA) involved in the bunker raking for the tournament where a greenkeeper was allocated to accompany a group of players inside the ropes and rake any bunkers the players went into. But more about that later.

In 1985 I'd attended the Ransomes International golf tournament held in St Andrews which also involved seminars and a competition on the Eden course. It was my first experience of attending a large BIGGA meeting outside section level and over the four days I met many greenkeepers who went on to be lifelong friends. I could remember a few holes on the Eden from that day, the par 3s, the 18th and a few others and I remember my golf was terrible. I'm sure a few of my 'friends' would say there's nothing new in that, but it was quite strange that I was now back here for a job interview some six years later.

Since 1976 I had been working at Fraserburgh Golf Club, the 7th oldest golf club in the world and a superb links course in the north-east of Scotland and had been head greenkeeper there since 1980. There were various reasons I decided to look for an alternative position in the greenkeeping industry and after discussing things with my wife in early 1991, I started actively applying for other jobs. I'd already had a few interviews for jobs in England and had even been offered a couple of positions but felt they weren't the best ones to take at that time. When I saw the post at St Andrews advertised, I thought there was no harm in applying, although I had no great expectations of getting the job. I was sure there would literally be hundreds of greenkeepers wanting to work there, but I did think there was an outside chance of getting an interview. I'd been involved in the North section of SIGGA, (the Scottish and International Golf Greenkeepers Association, the precursor to BIGGA), for some time and was the secretary/treasurer, attending the regional meetings held quarterly at Haggs Castle GC in Glasgow. Walter Woods, who was Links Supervisor at St Andrews at the time, was also heavily involved in SIGGA and I was hoping, because we had known each other for some time, it might help me get to the interview stage. Walter was probably the best-known person in the greenkeeping industry in the UK from when he arrived at St Andrews in 1974 until he retired in 1995, and perhaps even until he died in 2018. He was the first chairman of BIGGA when the different associations amalgamated in 1987/88 and helped set up the education programme for greenkeepers at nearby Elmwood College.

To many greenkeepers, Walter might have been a daunting figure but due to the fact I had often been in his company at meetings and different BIGGA events, coupled with the fact he was very down to earth and sociable, I didn't feel nervous or uncomfortable in his company, job interview apart. I also felt I had made massive improvements to the course at Fraserburgh and in particular to the greens in my time in charge there, and had confidence in my ability to present a golf course to a high standard.

And so it transpired. There I was sitting nervously outside Pilmour House at 3.55pm on a Sunday afternoon. If I'd known who was going to be interviewing me, I would have been ten times worse! I was invited by Alex Beveridge, Secretary of the Links Trust, into his office. It was quite a dark room with a large table. As well as Walter and Mr Beveridge there were three others present: Robert Burns, Chairman of the Links Management Committee (LMC), Ian Bunch, Chairman of the Green Sub-Committee (GSC), and George Malcolm, a member of the Green Committee. The names didn't mean anything to me at the time, but as I went on to discover, they could be described as 'heavy hitters' in the St Andrews golfing community. Robert Burns was a gentleman farmer near Elie and a well-respected member of the Royal and Ancient Golf Club (R&A). He was also involved with the Scottish Golf Union. Ian Bunch was also a member of the R&A and a Past Captain of the New Golf Club in St Andrews. Ian was the Managing Director of the Swilken Golf Company, which was a well-known golf club manufacturing company in the UK and after its demise he went on to be Secretary at Prestwick Golf Club until his retirement. George Malcolm worked for Scottish Agricultural Industries, which was later taken over by ICI, and as I recall, he was a fertiliser salesman although he would have been in a senior position. George was also a member of the New Golf Club and well known in town. It's well recognised in greenkeeper circles that fertiliser salesmen, especially agricultural ones, and greenkeepers are not a good mix!

Some thirty years on, it's no surprise that I don't remember too much about the interview. It didn't last much more than thirty-five to forty minutes and although I was initially a little nervous, I felt reasonably comfortable by the finish. At one point we discussed the salary and the other conditions which were much improved from what I was currently getting, which one would expect. The only question I can remember being asked was, "Had I been for a walk around the Eden course and what did I think of the it?" Well, you would never dream of going for a job interview these days, even for a basic greenkeeping position, let alone any kind of promoted post, without a thorough walk around most of the course and taking a few notes. I would normally have done this on every occasion but circumstances prevented me on this one. As I explained to the panel, we had an 18-hole Open tournament at Fraserburgh that day and I had to prepare the golf course for play in the usual manner as we only had three of a staff. It was then over a three-hour drive to get to St Andrews and, unfortunately, I never had the time to get even a quick look at the course before the interview. I had played the course some years earlier, (although there had been substantial changes in the late 1980s) and it was my intention to go and walk part of the course after the interview before heading home. What I omitted to tell them was that I had also played, badly, in the competition at Fraserburgh before setting off for the interview!

They seemed to accept this and after the interview I duly set out to have a look at the Eden course. Because of the aforementioned changes, the Eden now started and finished at Pilmour House rather than beside the Old Course Hotel as it once did. The first two and last two holes had been lost as part of a grand master plan for the entire Links and the area which previously was those four holes was now the practice ground. Although they lost four excellent holes, all the best golf destinations, even by the 1990s, needed good practice facilities.

When I did step onto that 18th green, I got the shock of my life. To say it was in poor condition was an understatement; there was more bare soil than grass and the green just looked terrible with weeds present throughout the grass sward which mostly consisted of Poa Annua, (annual meadow grass). I was nervous of coming to work at St Andrews because I was anticipating to have to keep a course in the pristine condition one would expect but that feeling suddenly evaporated as I thought to myself, "God, a blind man could improve the state of this." I was later to find out it wasn't quite as simple as that!

I walked a few more holes and for the main they weren't much better. The 18th was a relatively new green having come into play in 1988 as a result of the changes and the older, more established ones, were a lot better but they still weren't that good. As I walked off the 18th again on my way back to my car, I was met by Alex Beveridge the Secretary who said, "I'm glad you went to have a look at the course and that I managed to catch up with you. You were the last person to be interviewed and we'd like to offer you the position."

I remember a range of emotions hitting me, the main one being shock, quickly followed by jubilation and I blurted out a thank you and also there was something they should know. "I suffer from rheumatoid arthritis. It's a condition I've had for around seven years and although it was difficult initially, it's now under control. Apart from attending hospital for a check-up every six months, I haven't missed a day's work because of it in over four years. I didn't want to disclose that at the interview as I didn't want it to influence any decision." Mr Beveridge was as sharp as a tack, "It will all be subject to a medical of course," he replied. I was happy with that because other than restricted movement in some of my joints, it hadn't really affected me for a number of years because of the medication I was taking.

There were no mobile phones in those days and I can't even remember if I called home, probably not as I never was good at that kind of thing, but while I might have taken over three hours to drive down, I was a lot quicker in getting home. Let's put it down to the fact there was less traffic on the roads on a Sunday evening.

When I got home, Pauline was excited for me but there was also a bit of trepidation as well. She'd been to St Andrews with me in 1985 for the conference and golf tournament and knew it was a beautiful place. It would be a great area to bring up our three children, (Andrew was just starting school, Shirras our daughter was three and a half and Bruce had not long turned one), but it meant leaving all our friends. My parents had both died a number of years beforehand, we had a great support network in Fraserburgh as it was my home town and we had lived there since we got married in 1983, Pauline moving there to work in 1980. The other factor was her elderly parents lived in Elgin which was little more than an hour from Fraserburgh but over a three-hour drive from St Andrews. The following Sunday, we arranged for the children to stay with friends and headed off to have a look at the place we would soon call our home. It was all very hush hush. Other than Pauline's friends, we never told anyone what was happening. I'd seen people make big announcements like these before and they'd fallen through, plus I didn't particularly want my employers at Fraserburgh GC to know and I most certainly didn't want it circulating around the greenkeeping industry before it was signed and sealed. While greenkeeping is a great industry, it's terrible for rumour and speculation, especially when a new position comes up and who has got it.

When we arrived in St Andrews, we couldn't have wished for a better day, calm, warm with the sun splitting the sky. At one point we were up on the hill at Kinkell looking down on the town and the view was amazing, one I still never tire of. The only down-side was the house prices which scared the life out of us, but we knew this was where we wanted to be.

I made an appointment with the doctor for my medical which went fine. The letter of employment duly arrived and when everyone was happy and it was signed and accepted by both parties, I began letting people know. St Andrews wanted me to begin as soon as I could but I still had to give a month's notice to Fraserburgh Golf Club so the start date was set for Monday 16th September, my grandmother's birthday. I've said I'd played things really close to my chest regarding the move and when the news spread round the greenkeeping industry there was quite a bit of surprise, but not in the manner you, or I, might have expected. More than one person was shocked that I'd taken the position.

Neil MacDonald, a good friend who was a rep selling industry products for Stewarts of Edinburgh at the time, was in complete disbelief. "You've done what?" he exclaimed, "Do you know what you've let yourself in for?" I just couldn't understand where he was coming from. "But it's St Andrews, the Home of Golf, the R&A, the Old Course, the most famous course in the world. It's brilliant," I replied. "Have you seen the sheds and the equipment?" he asked. "And do you know what it's like to work for Walter?" "No, I haven't seen the sheds or the machinery, I've only seen part of the Eden course," I said. "It wasn't in that good a condition but that's okay, I can only make it better. The machinery can't be that bad, there's got to be loads of money available and Walter's fine, I've known him for years." "Well prepare yourself for a shock," he said. "It's not all it appears from the outside." How right he, and many others, were.

I wasn't due to start until the middle of September, but I did visit one day beforehand. Pauline came with me so we could do a recce on houses and I had made arrangements to call in past the Jubilee sheds which was where I would be based, just for a look around and to meet Walter and some of the staff. The Jubilee was the only maintenance facility then and served all the courses. There were only four courses at that time, the Old, New, Jubilee and Eden.

The Strathtyrum course and the 9-hole Balgove course had been built and seeded as part of the grand plan, but they weren't due to open until 1993. There was a temporary, and very rough, 9-hole Balgove course laid out on some of the mature fairways of the Strathtyrum for children etc. to play on, which the Eden team looked after. The Jubilee sheds were situated between the 1st and 18th holes of the Jubilee course and were quite a distance from the 1st tee of the Eden, not to mention the fact you had to cross one hole of the Jubilee, two holes of the New and two holes of the Old to get to there. Bad enough first thing in the morning but frustratingly time consuming if you had to go back to the sheds for anything during golf, plus you had to constantly alter your route across the Old Course to avoid tracking the fairways and rough. Still, at the interview they promised they were going to build a new maintenance facility to serve the Eden, Strathtyrum and Balgove courses.

When I arrived at the Jubilee sheds, I began to understand what Neil MacDonald was talking about. To say they were dire was being kind, a series of single-brick walled buildings which had been built in the 1950s. They were tiny and dark, if you don't include the fact you could stand inside and see the daylight outside through the cracks in the walls! The roofs were corrugated asbestos with numerous holes in them caused by errant golf balls meant for the 1st green or 18th fairway of the Jubilee. I used to joke that we would open the doors in the morning to let the water out from the overnight rain. The machinery was in equally dilapidated condition and there wasn't that much of it. When greenkeepers from America visited and saw the equipment they would say, "We like the museum, now where are the mowers you use today?" Just outside the doorway there was a small section of concrete and another square of concrete by a hose where the equipment was washed down. The remainder of the yard consisted of a fine red gravel. When dry it was dusty, when wet it was muddy. Behind the sheds there was an area part concreted, part soil, where sand and topsoil were stockpiled and kept for divot mix, construction projects and topdressing. There was also a large shed which housed the tractors and some of the other bulky pieces of equipment.

Walter Woods with the greenkeeping team circa 1980. I swear some of these tractors and mowers were still there in 1991. Many of the staff certainly were!

I fully expected to find one of these overgreens to use for mowing the greens.

It's only fair that I point out at this time that the Links Trust in 1991 had little in the way of money. While the golf travel industry was beginning to take off, they were still selling green fees on the Old Course to tour operators at the standard rate of, from memory, £33 per person. The tour operators were then marking that up by who knows what. I've heard it said that Fergus McCann, the Canadian business man who saved Celtic Football Club from going bankrupt, was one of many people who made their money selling Old Course tee times in Canada and America. More about the complicated set up, structure and management of the Links Trust later.

Walter had arranged that I was shown round by Mark Brunton who was head greenkeeper of the New Course. Mark explained that each course had its own head greenkeeper, team and everyday equipment such as mowers, utility vehicles and tractors while the larger items of kit were shared. There were systems of a kind in place of who got what equipment and when, and Mark said that I would soon get into the way of things. He must have forgotten to say that the Eden was at the bottom of the pecking order and usually last to get anything! The mechanics were also based there in their own little space, best described as a hovel! They were headed by Dod McLaren who it seemed had been there for ever but was a great mechanic and who was Walter's right-hand man. He could fix anything and often had to. He was also responsible for keeping the irrigation system going, including the boreholes for the abstraction of the water and for maintaining all the drainage across the Links. People will be surprised at the extent of the drainage systems, including some pumped ones which are in place throughout the courses. Dod was a Godsend, and I don't think the committees of management fully appreciated his role in keeping things operating. He was always available any time of day or night to help out and fix things, his only faults being that he kept all his knowledge in his head and he could be a grumpy individual at times, but given how most of the greenkeepers spoke to him, that was understandable.

The 'bothy' or mess room/canteen and toilets for the staff were in another similar sized shed at right angles to the machinery one. It had another section at the rear for housing seed and other sundries and this building was in just as poor condition. Everyone would eat at the same time and there would be around twenty-eight staff crammed into the mess room if everyone was present. The first time I went in, I immediately clocked two guys sitting in the corner as far away from the door as possible and thought to myself, "They look like trouble." Something which turned out to be an accurate assessment. Break times could be 'boisterous' but it was unusual for everyone to be at work most days. The outside door was always open and the first thing which greeted you as you entered was the toilets or, in particular, the shower curtains, which were constantly black with oil and dirt and flapping in the wind. Needless to say, no one ever took a shower but instead the staff would use the showers to wash their hands rather than the sinks. Next door was where the four head greenkeepers shared a room which was our 'office', with each of us having our own desk. No laptops or computer-controlled irrigation systems back then.

The original Jubilee sheds with staff and equipment. Circa 1958

Davie Wilson, who was on the Jubilee Course, was the longest serving of them having started in 1968 with a short hiatus of eighteen months around 1971/72 when he left to go on a fishing boat. Mark on the New Course and who was showing me around, was in his late twenties and had been there since leaving school. Eddie Adams was acting head greenkeeper on the Old Course as the previous one had retired between me accepting my job and by the time I started. Eddie would have only been in his early twenties and went on to be appointed head greenkeeper shortly afterwards. The job was advertised and although both Davie and Mark applied for it, I never did. I didn't think it right applying for another role within the organisation when I had literally just accepted one. I was never aware of any interviews taking place and remember saying to Walter one day that he must have received a huge number of applications. I was quite surprised when he told me there were hardly any but reached my own conclusions on that comment at a later date.

Shortly after I began, we were joined by a fifth person in the office as Roddy Barron, another long serving member of staff, was appointed head greenkeeper of the Strathtyrum course which was due to open shortly while the responsibility of the 9-hole Balgove was given to me. Roddy is just slightly older than me and is a real character. He was an extremely observant greenkeeper, very skilled practically, real 'old school', and even in those days he was very environmentally aware. He had been what was classed as a chargehand on the New course before being seconded and given his own small team to complete work outstanding from the large-scale alterations to the Jubilee and Eden courses from 1987/88. This involved building tees, which for some reason had never been done by the contractors, and rebuilding a number of greens on the Jubilee course of which the contractors had made a complete mess. Roddy's skills were ideal for this type of role as he had a great vision of the finished product and good attention to detail. Despite never having played golf, he knew exactly what he was looking to achieve. His team on the other hand left a lot to be desired as quite often one or more of them either wouldn't turn up or be late. Roddy's punctuality wasn't that good either, unless being five minutes late every day can be classed as being consistent. Roddy was very well known in and around town as he was an excellent piper, one of the best in Scotland. He taught a few different pipe bands such as the Boys' Brigade and Madras College and still teaches the bagpipes today to bands and individuals. Surprisingly, back in 1991, more of the greenstaff at the Links played in pipe bands than played golf!

Last, but not least, next to our office was Walter's which was a Portacabin with a room at the back for his secretary, who also assisted the head greenkeepers by typing up our GSC reports and any memos or letters we required.

After visiting the sheds, my wife and I went house hunting where the prices in St Andrews were shocking compared to Fraserburgh. So much so, that we thought it was more than likely we would have to stay in some of the outlying towns or villages even though we very much wanted to stay in St Andrews. As luck would have it, we were able to find somewhere in town as one of the ladies in an estate agent said that her house was going on the market and if we were interested, we could see it before it was advertised. We finished up buying that house and I now play quite a bit of golf with the husband of the couple we bought it from. It was much smaller than the one we were leaving behind in Fraserburgh but a lot more expensive. Entry wasn't going to be until December and I ended up staying as a lodger with a couple, literally around the corner from our new house, for three months. My landlord, Jimmy Atkins and his wife Paula were great company. Jimmy was a caddy on the Links and full of tricks, with a sense of humour similar to mine. I had a great time staying with them during the week as I would normally drive down on a Sunday evening for the 6am start Monday morning and then leave after work on a Friday at 2pm which got me home around 5pm. Jimmy told me one night that when he was younger, he played for Arsenal Football Club, even making a couple of appearances in the first team. Although he hailed from London originally, I had a hard time believing this, given his stature and physical condition even though he was now in his fifties but Paula assured me it was true and, therefore, I fell for it hook, line and sinker. It was some time afterwards before Paula told me it was a wind-up.

How the position on the Eden course came about and how I ended up getting the job was quite a series of events and strange coincidences, although when one position comes up in the greenkeeping industry, it does turn into a bit of a merry-go-round. In March 1991 I had applied for the head greenkeepers job at The Nevill Golf Club in Kent, not far from Tunbridge Wells. The course had a good reputation and was where a couple of Tour players were members. I flew down to Gatwick on the last Saturday of the month and stayed with friends nearby who drove me to my interview the following morning. It had snowed overnight and the course was still covered when we got there. I couldn't see much of the grass when I walked a few holes but could tell the ground looked heavy and wet. There was a house with the job but it didn't look too smart and neither did the greenkeeping sheds. A couple of tractors sat outside and were quite rusty, while there were also bags of fertiliser sitting out in the snow. I didn't have a good interview, partly because by the time I went in, I had made up my mind I didn't really fancy the job based on what I'd seen. As I was leaving, I met the next candidate waiting to go in, a fellow Scot by the name of Bruce Cruickshank who was at Crail Golfing Society at the time. Bruce got the job and his position at Crail was taken by Alan Purdie who left the Eden Course at St Andrews, thereby creating that opening for me.

I arrived back in Fraserburgh on the Sunday night and the very next day got a letter for another job interview, this time at Royal Eastbourne GC, and they wanted me down by the end of the week. By Thursday I was back on the first flight out of Aberdeen to Gatwick again and was interviewed in an airport hotel by the Captain and Greens Chairman. That interview went well and we proceeded to drive down to Eastbourne so I could have a look at the course and continue the interview. I really liked the set up and what I saw of the course and the area. The weather from the earlier Sunday was very different, it was a beautiful sunny day. They drove me back to Gatwick and I was back in Fraserburgh by midnight. A letter offering me the position arrived the following week but Pauline was nervous and reminded me our children would grow up with English accents! In the end I turned their offer down, a decision which was to have a profound effect on my life. I met Bruce Cruickshank a few years later at the British Turf Managers Exhibition (BTME) at Harrogate and asked him how the job at The Nevill was going. He said I was lucky that I didn't get it as he was finding it tough due to a mixture of staff and committee problems.

After the Eden and Jubilee course had been redeveloped in the mid to late 1980s the decision had been made to put a head greenkeeper in charge of each of the four courses and also give them their own team. From what I gleaned from the staff, until then there were only different teams for each task, with each team having what was termed as a chargehand or foreman. That meant one team would cut greens, another team would cut tees and another cut fairways and so on. Davie Wilson would tell me how, in the summer, he used to start at the 1st tee of the Old Course on a Monday and cut tees until finishing time, moving to another course once the Old was complete. Then on the Tuesday he would go back to where he finished and carry on, until he eventually arrived back at the 1st of the Old again before repeating the process. When they did go down the route of appointing head greenkeepers, three of the four appointments were from people already on the staff. Donald Dewar was given the position on the Old, Davie Wilson on the Jubilee and Mark Brunton on the New. Alan Purdie was the only one of the four to come from outside the Links having previously been at Silverknowes Golf Club in Edinburgh. None of the teams had deputies and that position didn't come into being until 1994.

Chapter 2. The First 100 Days

I'VE NAMED this chapter the first 100 days and it is mostly about my experiences of that time but it also includes some of the things that happened over probably the first year or two. I do have diaries from that time but can't always read my scribbles and the details are more about the work that was carried out on the course rather than what happened. Once you've read the following stories, you'll understand why they've stayed in my mind.

My very first day didn't exactly turn out as I expected. Monday 16 September 1991 and I turned up shortly before the start time of 6am to meet with Walter. After a brief, "Hello, how are you?" opening bit of chit chat, Walter suggested that I head over to the Eden course and have a look around and to be back for 9am when he'd introduce me to my staff and the other head greenkeepers. I thought it a bit unusual that he couldn't just introduce me to them there and then and we could organise the morning's work programme. He went on to explain this was the third and final week of the R&A Autumn meeting. They had a Medal on the Old Course all week and therefore all the staff from the other courses were seconded to the Old Course for the first three hours to prepare the course for play which started at 7am. He also asked me to get the previous weeks' time sheets collected from my staff and check them over ready for submitting as they needed to be in by 9am. He advised me the person who had been acting head greenkeeper would likely have them. So off I set in search of someone whom I'd never met, to get the time sheets organised before I headed over to the Eden course.

Now it's fair to say my first encounter with him didn't go particularly well and a good part of the blame lies with me. When I did catch up with him, I was probably abrupt, which was partly my nature. I never was one for small talk in a work situation when there were plenty of things to be done and my broad north-east accent would have made that sound much worse. In my defence, I could say that I was probably a bit apprehensive about my new surroundings and also taken by surprise with the news that I wasn't going to have any staff for the first three hours.

Anyway, my recollection was that I got the timesheets which had been signed off and I checked them over, even though I didn't know for sure that all the guys had been there the previous week or what they had done. Then I headed over to the Eden Course. I just drove round the course in the order the holes are played to get my bearings, moving the tee markers into a fresh area of the teeing ground and looking things over as I went. I don't think I changed the holes and the reason I say that is because all the staff on the courses at St Andrews were still using the old 'bogey' style hole cutter which I hadn't seen for a long time. Even at Fraserburgh we had switched to the Supacut hole cutter shortly after I started in 1976. The Supacut took the hole plug out in one piece which usually fitted in the old hole perfectly, whereas with the bogey, the plug would be in three pieces. This inevitably meant the operator had to mess around with the pieces and soil to get the old plug level with the surface of the green. It was so much slower.

A young, and in many ways, naive head greenkeeper begins at St Andrews Links.

16

Golf started at 6am on the other courses and there was the odd single player out. It felt a bit strange to me that they were playing and we hadn't cut the greens or raked the bunkers in front of them. Around the hole looked quite scruffy as the hole cups hadn't been moved for a few days, probably since the Friday of the previous week.

At 9am I was back at the Jubilee sheds and met with Walter who introduced me first of all to the other head greenkeepers, Eddie, Mark and Davie. I had met Davie previously either at Elmwood or perhaps a BIGGA event but didn't know him. Davie was one of the first greenkeepers to go through the education system at Elmwood, something which Walter and a few of his peers were instrumental in setting up. There was a brief meeting where each of them told Walter their plans for the next day or two and then we went to meet the Eden course staff.

The Eden had a team of six with varying skill levels plus me.

The most senior and most skilled had the title of first-class greenkeeper. He had worked at the Links since 1981 and was originally from the town. He had been very hopeful he was going to get the job which was now mine, so wasn't particularly happy that I had arrived on the scene. Although he classed himself as a qualified greenkeeper and being highly skilled, he would have struggled to select a suitable fertiliser or make up a suitable mix from the raw ingredients and then calculate the rate of application. I remember an occasion early in my time where he had borrowed a small tractor from the contractors working on the Strathtyrum to pull a set of trailed gang mowers to cut the mounding on the right of the 1st hole on the Eden course. He was struggling to get the tractor to pull the mowers up the hill and had the wheels spinning and the engine revving like crazy. "This is impossible with this tractor," he said. As was often the case with the staff, it was everything else's fault, the tractor was s**t, or something else was wrong, it was never their fault. I jumped on the tractor, selected the correct gear and engine revs for the situation, put my foot on the differential lock pedal and the tractor and mower climbed the mound comfortably. It wasn't something I did to show off or to belittle him, it was simply a skill I'd learned when working on the family farm back in Fraserburgh, but it certainly annoyed him that I was able to do something he couldn't.

Next was a young lad who would have only been in his early twenties, again, from the town. He could do most tasks but was a bit unreliable as he was often late, often by an hour or more, and some days wouldn't come in at all. There was a group of guys on the staff who hung about together and there was gossip that they enjoyed the occasional smoke of something stronger than cigarettes. I never saw any evidence of that, not that I would have known what to look for! This lad and I would have many a battle when he did come into work.

Then there was a slightly younger lad who stayed in town (are you sensing a theme here?) who hadn't long finished his apprenticeship and could also do the main tasks. He was an excellent drummer and played in a pipe band which competed in, and often won, the World Pipe Band Championship. He was a clever guy who I had a lot of time for and he could have done well in the industry, but he seemed to lose his interest in greenkeeping before leaving the Links after a few years.

There were also three older team members. One would have been well into his fifties and was a big gentle giant who stayed with his elderly parents and seldom went out. He was a very quiet and nervous individual, incredibly slow when processing instructions. He had very little practical skills and did not have the ability to operate a ride-on greens mower or some of the other items, probably because prior to 1988, the staff only did one or two tasks. There was no job rotation or learning new skills. Basically, all he could do was cut tees with a pedestrian mower, operate a pedestrian rotary mower, use a strimmer, rake bunkers, drive a tractor and trailer, (although reversing with the trailer on was still a challenge), and labour when doing construction jobs. Everything he did was carried out at a slow pace, not because he was lazy or spent his time skiving like some of the other staff, that was his only speed.

Another guy was older still and he had been there since the 1960s, maybe even the 1950s. His main skill was as a tractor operator so he would spend almost all his week in the summer cutting fairways and roughs with the different gang mowers. There were no dedicated ride-on fairway mowers back then, although in 1990 the Old Course team had begun cutting their fairways with the three-reel Ransomes 180 tees mowers and collecting the cuttings. I don't know where this idea came from, possibly Walter or the Sports Turf Research Institute (STRI) who advised the Links on agronomy matters, but it was a great idea. Certain fairways or areas suffered badly from worm casting in the wetter weather but by collecting the clippings and sanding the fairways, this improved them ten-fold over the years. As well as cutting fairways and semi-roughs on the Eden, he was also given the task of cutting these on the new Strathtyrum and Balgove courses as they 'grew in', along with the landing area of the practice range. As a result, I would hardly see him as, like painting the Forth Rail bridge, this never-ending job kept him going all week. He took everything very slowly, which in some regards was a good thing as he was careful and didn't 'scalp' the top of any humps unlike many of the other staff, but he would make each task last longer than was always necessary. In the winter he would switch to doing aeration work or driving soil/sand to construction jobs. He was an awkward individual and could be very twisted with everyone. You could describe him as the archetypical Fifer in that he never gave much away. He would remember everything and have no hesitation in casting it up or using it against you at a later date if things weren't going his way. There's a saying in Scotland that 'It takes a lang spoon to sup (eat) with a Fifer' which means they are hard to know, suspicious to the point of paranoia. It could also refer to the fact that you'd need a long spoon to share a Fifer's food because if you ask them they'll say no, so you would use a long spoon to steal their food when they're not looking!

The last member of the team, was another guy in his fifties and who had been in my class at Elmwood in the late 1970s, even though he would have been in his forties at the time. He was a reasonably big, strong guy although not the fittest and had been at the Links since 1974. He told me on many occasions he was the last person employed by John Campbell who was Walter's predecessor and then always follow up with the fact that Roddy Barron was the first person employed by Walter. Yet here he was on the Eden course some seventeen years later and the extent of his abilities was still just to rake bunkers, cut tees with a Ransomes Marquis, use a strimmer and a walk behind rotary and drive a tractor, all of these with difficulty. To give you an example, despite raking the bunkers on the Eden course most days in his working life, he still struggled to remember the best route to take. You would often see him walking from one set of fairway bunkers back to a group that he had already raked, just to check he'd raked them. I know you're thinking I'm making this up but I promise I'm not. He was an incredibly clever person, well read and educated and had received a private education. He lived on his own and never had a television. His late father owned a haulage business which he joined at one stage but couldn't cope, hence why he ended up working at the Links. He had no coordination and despite many people trying to teach him, he simply couldn't get to grips with operating a ride-on greens mower. Trying to think of a few different things at the one time was just beyond him. Sometimes when you didn't see him, you would still know where he was as you'd hear him shouting and swearing at the tees mower or strimmer because it wouldn't start. Of course, because of these things, the staff on all the teams would constantly wind him up although they made sure they always had a safe escape route in case he went for them, which on occasions he did. When I was working on my own with him then we would often have some good conversations (that was dependent on his mood as if I'd picked him up on something he had done wrong, then he would be quiet for a few days). He had a broad range of knowledge on many subjects other than sport and often he would fill me in on the things which had happened on the Links over his time there, providing background knowledge on some of the staff. He never brought any food to work and he would go the entire day without eating though he claimed he had a cooked breakfast before he came to work each morning. Occasionally, some members of staff would offer him a half sandwich or a piece of cake and he would devour it as if he hadn't eaten for a week.

I could lay claim to the fact that I come from a fairly unusual family, but it was nothing compared to this dysfunctional group. The Eden team didn't have the monopoly as all the teams had some 'special characters'. It soon became apparent they all based how good a greenkeeper a person was on two things, you had to cut a green, tee or fairway in a straight line and you had to be able to build a revetted bunker in the style they could. If you couldn't do these two tasks then you were classed as being 'f***ing useless', even though on many of the bunkers they built, the top layer of turf would sink shortly afterwards.

As far as equipment goes, on the Eden course we had the following:

- One Ransomes 171 ride-on greens mower, with one set of units for the greens and another set for the tees. (Even Fraserburgh had a mower for both operations back in the 1980s). Ransomes was the preferred supplier at the Links at that time but because we only had the one machine, I couldn't cut greens and tees, or greens and surrounds at the same time. We would usually cut greens in the morning and then go out after break and cut tees and surrounds on alternate days. The alternative was to use the three pedestrian Paladin mowers to cut greens but that took three staff and I only had three, plus myself, who could operate the ride-on and the pedestrian mowers. Frustratingly, the Eden mower always seemed to be parked at the back of the shed.

- Two Ransomes Marquis 18-inch tees mowers which everyone could operate to some degree but to cut all the tees with them would take well over half the day. When cutting greens or tees by hand we had to walk from site to site as there were no trailers for the pedestrian mowers, although to get them across to the Eden course we would load them onto the back of the utility vehicle.

- Two Ransomes Cushman utility vehicles for carrying the hole cutter, strimmers etc. therefore the chances were, if you were on bunker raking duty, then you were walking. Although we would go round the course with the Cushman when moving the holes and markers, the greenstaff didn't empty the litter box on each tee or fill the ball washer since that responsibility fell to another department. I could never understand why there was another person in a vehicle practically following you most mornings and leaving another set of wheel marks. It was apparently the result of criticism of the ball washers not being topped up often enough, so Walter persuaded the committee he was short of staff and they hired someone just to fulfil that role. It took me a long time to get that changed so that the greenstaff took responsibility for emptying the bins and filling the ball washers.

- A couple of old Ford tractors for pulling the gang mowers, driving sand for bunkers, soil for construction work or turf for rebuilding bunkers and any other repair jobs.

That was most things, with other pieces of equipment such as a Ford digger, a loader tractor, Vertidrains* for aeration work and other items being shared. Teams would often 'borrow' things from other teams if they could.

---

* Vertidrain is the brand name for a piece of equipment which can aerate the ground up to a depth of 16 inches to ease compaction to the soil. It was invented in Holland in late 1960s or early 70s. Since then, other machines which do a similar job have been developed.

Because it was mid-September by the time I started, the growing season was beginning to wind down but it was still my objective to cut the greens every morning before golfers went out. The greens on the Eden were quite large, measuring over a hectare if you included the putting green and it would take a person close on four hours to cut them with a ride-on mower. At first, I couldn't understand how the staff managed to do it in three hours at a weekend but on a weekday it would take nearer four. It was only in my second season I discovered the reason was because, on a Saturday, when the three greens cutters had finished cutting the Old Course greens, they would split up, one going to the New, one to the Jubilee and one to the Eden to help these teams out. The fact the Old Course mowers might have been set at a different height of cut seemed irrelevant. Because the Old Course was closed to golf on a Sunday, the staff didn't come in as there was no requirement to set up the golf course and cut the greens. As a result, none of the other head greenkeepers would cut the greens on their course on a Sunday. On a few occasions over my first couple of years, if one of the Old Course ride-on greensmowers broke down, then a member of their staff would come over and take our one, even if the we were only halfway through cutting the Eden greens at the time and our mower was set at a different height of cut. We would get it back once they were finished so we could complete our greens cutting. I also discovered the staff would cut each green in a manner which minimised the number of times they had to turn, which could bring the task down to under three hours and thirty minutes. They did this by altering the direction of cut by the tiniest of a fraction each time, rather than go round the 'hands of the clock' as was normal practice, and a method which was better for the turf and for ball roll. Because we were near the end of the growing season, I never noticed that the greens weren't being cut on a Sunday those few remaining weeks of 1991, even though I'd left instructions that it was one of their overtime jobs. This was because the staff couldn't get the job completed in the three hours they worked and they would never consider working longer to complete the task. On a Monday they would either tell me they had cut the greens or that the mower had broken down.

Since I was still travelling home at weekends, I would leave instructions for what my staff were to do on Saturday and Sunday mornings. Staff would only work three hours each day on a weekend, being paid overtime rates of time and a half for Saturday and double time on a Sunday. After only a few weekends I began to wonder what was actually being done because of how the greens looked on a Monday, and because of the stories of the mower always breaking down. I would always ask on a Monday morning if everything had gone okay and other than any aforementioned mower problems, the answer was always a yes. Another thing I noticed was that the areas between the tee markers were always very worn, but only in one place. I was unable to tell where the markers had been on the other day.

So, before I left one Friday and once everyone else had gone, I placed a couple of broken golf tees under some of the discs that acted as tee markers, noting the colours. It was a weekend when my most senior member of staff was left in charge and when I came in on the Monday I asked if everything went okay and got the normal "Yes." But I had already checked as I had seen from a distance that the markers hadn't been moved since Friday, so I asked him to come with me out on to the course. As we walked towards the first tee, I asked him again if the staff had moved the markers each day and again he replied, "Yes." I told him what I did on the Friday, what colour of tee peg I placed under each marker and if they were still there, then he was lying and the staff hadn't done their job. The broken tees were there and at that moment I knew what kind of people I was dealing with. There was no disciplinary action taken but I don't think it happened again.

My first 100 days would have taken me up to Christmas 1991 and here are of some of the things I encountered in that period.

The first large tournament which took place was the Dunhill Cup in October which was an international team event back then. Three-man teams played medal match play in a knockout format from Thursday to Sunday. With sixteen teams they would play 36 holes a day in a round robin format and the four group winners would qualify for the semi-final on the Saturday and then the final on the Sunday. Initially when it began in 1985 the top players in the world would come and compete. Australia, with Greg Norman in their team, won the first two years. The semi-final and final would attract large crowds and there would be a great atmosphere, especially if Scotland or Ireland won through to that stage.

In 1991 the tournament was held from 10-13 October which was late in the season for this part of Scotland and the weather had been quite wet in the lead up to the event. Sweden won the final which was reduced to 18 holes by 2 matches to 1, beating South Africa who were competing for the first time and had Gary Player in their team. It was Player's match which decided the competition as, after tying with Mats Lanner, he lost at the first extra hole of the play-off. I remember the South Africans had a large following with many of their supporters in the crowd waving their national flag. I was present when one of the Swedish players, Per-Ulrik Johansson, who lost his match against David Frost, was penalised on the 5th hole for taking either a free drop or a preferred lie from a worm cast. He had been used to this ruling when playing on the US Tour and had automatically lifted his ball to clean it when just off the green and, as such, was penalised. Whether this affected his mindset or his game, then only he can say, but he went on to score 74 to David Frost's 69. Still at least his team won, as Anders Forsbrand beat John Bland 68 to 69 in the top match and Lanner won that play off against Gary Player. At that time some areas of fairways were badly affected by wormcast but Walter had initiated a programme a couple of years earlier of collecting the grass clippings along with applying sand from the beach and deep aerating them annually. After six or seven years this led to a dramatic improvement in their firmness and general condition, with the worm casting greatly reduced. By the mid-1990s the other courses were following the same procedures.

Funny how I remember so much about the golf, but I can't remember what I was actually doing at work during that week. I might have been cutting fairways or something but I suspect it was more likely I stayed back on the Eden course. Most, or all, of my staff helped on the Old in the morning before they came to the Eden for a spell, then went back to the Old Course in the evening to divot fairways and clean up in preparation for the next day's play. Although I wasn't expected to help out in the 'late' shift because I was in a salaried position, I would often go across to assist with the divoting as it would allow me to meet with the staff and get to know them, along with having some banter.

What I do remember was the European Tour used to give vouchers to the value of £5 each day for the greenstaff to get food, etc. at the hospitality tents. What disturbed me, however, was not every member of the greenstaff got one, the reason given being the Tour never provided enough. This never went down particularly well with those who missed out. They knew many of the staff got more than enough to buy food each day and still had plenty left over to get completely plastered on the Sunday afternoon, and they had no problem rubbing it in the noses of those who missed out. By the same token, back in 1989 I had asked a golfing friend in Fraserburgh if he fancied going down for the weekend to watch the Dunhill Cup. I thought I might be able to get entry tickets through knowing Walter, which I did, so we booked ourselves into a B&B and off we set early on the Saturday morning. We planned to get down for 9am, just before golf would start and Walter had suggested that would be ideal as he would be back home from the morning set up and we should come to his house to collect our tickets. We duly did and he was the perfect host, inviting us in and his wife Caroline cooked us breakfast. As well as the entry tickets, Walter gave us some £5 vouchers for the food outlets which I thought was brilliant, reckoning he would have received loads of these to give out. It was only some two years later that I realised whose vouchers we were given!

The Links Trust, being a public body, had to be accountable for certain things and one of those was to hold a public meeting every year. This would take place in the Town Hall on a Thursday evening each November and was open to anyone to attend. Being in town and looking for a reason to go out, I thought it would be a good idea to go along and see the kind of things that were discussed. I didn't really know anyone so I thought I'd just sneak in, sit at the back of the hall and watch the proceedings. There would have probably been over two hundred people present and they were out for blood! The main complaints were the cost of a season ticket for local golfers, access to the courses as an increasing number of visitors were turning up to play the Old Course, the 'Grand Plan', (many people didn't like or understand the need for a practice ground and hated the fact they now had to walk a further 400 yards from their Golf Club to get to the 1st tee of the Eden) and the general condition of the courses. The Old Course could have been described as being in good or reasonable condition but the other three were all pretty dire in many areas, including the greens. The Chairman of Trustees chaired the meeting, flanked by Alex Beveridge, Secretary to the Trust, along with some of the other Trustees and some of the members of the LMC. The meeting was dominated by three or four individuals who were intent on giving the chairman, Alex Beveridge, and the committee members in attendance a hard time, and they weren't holding back. Walter, or no one else from the greenstaff, was present and the meeting became quite heated at times but I felt quite relaxed just sitting there taking it all in. Then, near the close of the meeting, one individual who hadn't spoken up previously asked the Chairman what he was going to do about the condition of the newer greens on the Eden course, which he said were dominated by weeds. In fact, he suggested the weeds outnumbered the grass. There was no one more taken aback than I was when the Chairman replied, "Well, we have the head greenkeeper of the Eden course in the audience tonight, perhaps he would like to give the answer to this one?" F**k me, speak about a hospital pass, how did he know I was there? I didn't even know the Chairman of the Trust, I'd never met him. I stood up and blurted out some type of answer, along the lines of agreeing the greens were in poor condition but I'd only been here a matter of weeks. Although I had assessed what was required, it was now too late in the season for particular tasks, but I was looking forward to making improvements in 1992. I think I got away with it.

If I thought that Public Meeting was a riot, apparently it was a walk in the park compared to the previous one in 1990. On the morning of that one, the then Chairman of Trustees, turned up to be briefed by Alex Beveridge on what to expect. He became so concerned, he resigned his position and headed back to Edinburgh immediately. The Trustees then had to meet beforehand, where they elected John Lindsay-Bethune acting chairman and he chaired the meeting that evening.

Soon it was 30th November, St Andrews Day, and in 1991 it happened to land on a Saturday, plus it was my landlord, Jimmy Aikin's birthday. Jimmy suggested I should stay down that weekend and we could have a game of golf on the Old, go for some food then have a few beers. I thought that would be a good idea as I'd been at the Links for some ten weeks and had never taken my 'share' of weekend overtime as I had gone home every weekend other than the Dunhill one. This idea was endorsed by the other head greenkeepers and it proved to be an eventful weekend on a number of fronts.

By that time of the season, growth had stopped so there was only a handful of staff in, one greenkeeper each on the New, Jubilee and Eden while there would have been three on the Old Course. Their role was simply to walk or take a buggy round their course, move the tee markers and rake the bunkers. If there happened to be any dew lying on the greens then tough, the golfers would just have to put up with it. My brief from the other head greenkeepers was just to open up the sheds, check everyone came in and then maybe have a wander around the courses checking all was okay with them; simple. With the darker mornings it would have been a 7.30am start so I would come in about 7.20am. No point in being too early as the staff would only come in bang on start time, except one didn't - the person scheduled to be the duty greenkeeper on the New course that weekend. One of the younger 'gang' was a good practical greenkeeper and a scratch golfer, probably the best on the staff at the time, as well as one of the best golfers in town. I hung around the sheds not sure what to do when he eventually turned up just before 8am, no apology, no excuse. He immediately jumped on a vehicle and headed out of the complex, but not to start work as I anticipated. Instead, he headed over to the Eden course to book a tee time for the following morning. He was quite matter of fact about what he did when he came back in; he didn't seem concerned or try to hide the fact. On the Sunday, after again being fifteen or twenty minutes late and offering no excuse, he collected a rake and off he headed, walking towards the New course. There were no Old Course staff in on the Sunday as the Old was closed for golf, so I only had the three staff to 'look after'. I did some paperwork or planning in the office for a spell then thought I'd have a walk out and see how things were going. Starting on the New course, I noticed the bunkers on the 17th, which were the first bunkers he would have encountered, hadn't been raked. That's okay, he'll get those at the finish I thought, he's probably started at the first hole to keep in front of the golfers. Then when checking the first and second holes, the bunkers on them hadn't been raked either. I continued to walk out the course in hole order and none of the bunkers had been raked, and the greenkeeper in question was nowhere to be seen. By that time some early golfers were out playing and one of them asked me what I was looking for, to which I replied, "A greenkeeper." "You'll find him in the shelter by the 15th tee," was their response! How did they know that? I wandered out and from a distance I could see the smoke from a cigarette drift out of the shelter in the clear morning air. I watched for a while, then the greenkeeper emerged from the shelter and started walking down the 15th. I stayed well back, just watching and he walked the 15th, 16th and 17th holes, passing several bunkers but never bothering to rake any. Then he took a sharp left back to the sheds, he didn't even bother going to the 18th. By the time I got back to the sheds, I was just in time to catch him leaving in his car, despite the fact he hadn't been in for anything like the three hours allocated. I managed to stop him and ask where he was going. "I've got a tee time on the Eden in fifteen minutes," he said. I told him he hadn't even raked any bunkers and that he should go back and do that rather than play golf, to which he just shrugged his shoulders. It was obvious that he wasn't going to stay so I told him I would just give his boss a rundown on Monday morning of what exactly he did, or rather didn't, do over the weekend. Another shrug of the shoulders and off he went to golf.

Next morning, I gave his head greenkeeper chapter and verse, including how many hours he worked. Nothing happened and he was recorded on the timesheet as having worked three hours both mornings.

That was work, Jimmy's birthday was another story. We had a fine game of golf over the Old Course in the afternoon. The weather was good, my golf probably not so good. We went home and changed then went out for a Chinese meal. We went to a bar, which at that time was frequented by locals rather than golf tourists, and we began playing darts. At one point a guy who Jimmy knew came into the pub and I was introduced as the new head greenkeeper of the Eden course. "That's the last f***ing thing we need here, another outsider telling us how to run our golf courses," was his reply. I wasn't too bothered given the course was in a terrible condition, or maybe I was just in shock, but Jimmy wanted to knock his head off and he might have done if others in the bar hadn't intervened. I can never remember the guy's name but I still see him around town to this day although I can't recall ever seeing him play golf. Quite a weekend!

It was around this time that I was getting extremely frustrated with different things I was discovering, on what seemed like a daily basis. These all related to the behaviour of the staff and the lack of interest they showed in their work or the condition of the course, and their general apathy and demeanour. I could understand why some of this could be, given the poor standard of working conditions such as the mess rooms, along with the poor provision of personal equipment like workwear and waterproofs, or even the machinery. But to me, there appeared to be no enthusiasm for improving things. I had never encountered this in my eleven years at Fraserburgh where everyone took a pride in their work and would be willing to help one another or come up with ideas to either improve a working practice or suggest an improvement to the course. We would have disagreements within the team at Fraserburgh at times but they would be worked out and we would move on. This was something which I didn't see at St Andrews, with part of the reason being greenstaff on the other teams constantly stirring things with their snide comments such as, "Why are you doing that?" or, "I wouldn't be doing it that way," etc. I would have expected healthy competition between the teams to get their course to be the best, but there was nothing like that. Staff would much sooner put another course or team down rather than try to improve the course they worked on.

It was this frustration which led me to ask all my team to come for a meeting with me in the head greenkeepers' office at finishing time one Friday before I headed back home. I was fairly blunt with my words, (I didn't know any other way then, and some would say I've never really changed, although I'd like to think I did over the years!) I let them have both barrels with what I saw was wrong and where I wanted to see improvements. At one time I told them they were all thieves and one team member in particular took exception to this, which was ironic as there were always stories circulating about what he and a colleague used to get up to away from work.

There was quite a bit of stealing taking place within the department although that was not necessarily them*.The theft I was accusing them of was stealing time, as all of them, with perhaps the exception of the one who was just naturally slow, would string out every little job they could at every opportunity. As an example, they knew it would take over an hour to get from the golf course back to the sheds then back to the course so they would 'forget' things, or 'break' things to waste time, especially if it was a job they didn't like. I discovered two favourite tricks. One was to pour the petrol for the strimmer under a bush so they had to go back to the sheds for more. The other was to remove the spark plug and knock it on a stone, thereby closing the gap and preventing the strimmer starting, which meant they had to get one of the workshop team to come out and repair it. To report this, they would either walk back to the shed or, sometimes, they might have been able to radio back. It never took the workshop staff long to find the problem but it was a waste of everybody's time and of course the work wouldn't be done. The meeting descended into a bit of a shouting match and never improved or resolved anything. They left and probably had a good laugh at my expense while I got something off my chest. It was another quick journey back to Fraserburgh that afternoon! I often asked myself throughout my career, especially as I gained experienced, what I could

---

* One Christmas period in those early years I was the only head greenkeeper on duty and was alone in the office doing some paperwork. Immediately after Christmas, a member of the New course staff came in, fully aware his head greenkeeper was still off. He knew his boss had won a half bottle of whisky in a staff raffle and was looking for it. I said I didn't know where it was and he'd probably taken it home but the guy then went and broke all the locks in his boss's desk until he found the whisky before going off with it. I later pleaded ignorance of what happened.

have done differently to get a better result. Other than not having the meeting, I still honestly don't know.

Other than the young member of my team who was constantly being late or not coming in at all, there are two other things that stick in my mind that happened during the first 100 days. Firstly, was when I was going around the course one morning and I came to the 6th tee, in front of which is a hollow the golfers have to carry. Standing from an elevated position, I could clearly see someone had written the words, "THE EDEN IS S***E," in big, three feet high letters with spray paint. I've still no idea who did it but some of the Old Course staff were suspects.

Second, as all greenkeepers will know, autumn is aeration time and I was a great believer in aeration, especially deep tine aeration using a Vertidrain and we had a couple of them at St Andrews which we shared. The only thing was that Walter decreed no aeration was to take place before the beginning of November.

Deep aeration on the greens with the vertidrain.
Note the large holes behind the machine.

As I'd come to expect, and I understood the reason why, the Old Course got to use it first but their greens were huge so they took quite some time to complete the work. After the Old it was the turn of the New course, then the Jubilee. I was the new kid on the block so I was last, add the obligatory break downs and repairs and I remember it was the week leading up to Christmas before the greens on the Eden were completed. That was bad enough, but Walter had also instructed I use three-quarter inch diameter tines. This left the surface of the greens in a condition which resembled putting on a gravel road. It was too late in the year to try and fill the holes up with topdressing for fear of causing disease and they remained in that condition well into April, until there was growth and we could apply some topdressing.

Using a tees mower to roll the greens after vertidraining.

I couldn't leave this chapter without mention of the infamous greenkeepers' Christmas party held in the Jubilee sheds, usually on Christmas Eve, which in hindsight wasn't the smartest idea. Organised by Walter, it followed the same pattern for many years where he would provide all the alcohol, the majority of which came from companies he dealt with through the year. His wife would make stovies for everyone and they would be gracefully dished up by Dod, the workshop manager, as if he were a blacksmith shaping a horse shoe at the anvil. Starting at 2pm, an hour before the normal finishing time, some people would stay in their work clothes, while others would take a half day and come back dressed for the occasion. There were darts and dominoes competitions which seldom reached a conclusion, as by the later stages, those still in the competition were too far gone to participate with either accuracy or competency. A stranger walking into the mess room at 4pm could be excused for thinking he had stumbled across a film set where they were shooting the bar room scene for a Star Wars movie. Even though there was still plenty of booze left, by around 5pm everyone would leave and head to some of the local bars. This was after it was dark and if the Jigger Inn was the pub of choice, inevitably someone would fall into a bunker when crossing the courses to get there. By the end of the night, sometimes even before they left the sheds, there would always be a fight between some of the staff as they settled old scores. Once Walter retired, the party continued for a couple more years with the head greenkeepers organising it, until the new Jubilee Maintenance facility opened. We brought it forward from Christmas Eve so not everyone's Christmas dinner would be ruined, bought pies to replace the stovies and had a short quiz instead of the darts and dominoes. But the result remained the same: carnage.

Chapter 3. The Links Trust

I THOUGHT THIS might be an appropriate point to introduce some history and explain what the St Andrews Links Trust is about, its role in running golf in St Andrews and how it operates. Despite all the facts being out there and well documented across various mediums and platforms, it's astounding that a large part of the golfing public still thinks the Royal and Ancient Golf Club own and manage the Old Course. Even people from outside town who I've known for years, still have this impression that the R&A calls the shots and that I worked for them. I guess the fact they have their clubhouse directly behind the 1st tee of the Old adds to that belief. When people think of St Andrews and the Old Course, they think of the R&A, as it's a much larger 'brand', due to them running the Open Championship and being the governing body for golf around the world (other than the USA and Mexico). Put in those simple terms, it becomes understandable why golfers form this impression.

The following paragraphs are very much an abbreviated history of the Links Trust and the Act. There is a wonderful book written by the late Tom Jarrett entitled, 'St Andrews Golf Links, the first 600 Years' which explains in depth the full history of the Links.It tells the story from the time in 1123 when the land was granted to the Burgh of St Andrews by King David, most likely to use as a source of food, (rabbits), peat for fuel and turf for roofs, right through to the 1974 Act. It includes episodes such as the rabbit wars, the Links Road war, the caddies and many other interesting aspects.

The Links Trust is the body entrusted by an Act of Parliament to run the courses. Prior to 1974 the management of the Links had been jointly shared by the Town Council and the R&A under the title of the Joint Links Committee. They controlled who had access to the courses, was responsible for hiring the staff and setting the price of playing golf. At the end of each year, the cost of maintaining the operation was split between the Council and the R&A. With the proposed changes there were well founded fears within the town that control of the courses would be handed over to a larger local authority and that the rights of the townsfolk, (and the R&A), would be badly eroded. As a result, the R&A along with the Town Council and with the support of the other golf clubs in the town, put forward a motion to repeal or amend the existing Act and try to establish an independent Trust to carry out the work previously done by the Joint Committee. This was successful and the result was The St Andrews Links Order Confirmation Act 1974. Subject to the provisions of the Act, Trustees are required 'to hold and maintain the Links as a public park and a place of public resort and recreation for the residents of the town of St Andrews and others resorting thereto....'

The only golf club with any 'rights' in the Act is the R&A, while the other main beneficiaries are the residents of the town of St Andrews. Since 1974, through ongoing discussions with all stakeholders, this has been relaxed to allow members of the other golf clubs much more access than the original concept as there was no real provision for what would have been classed as 'country members' back in 1974. Today, thanks to the Links Trust, all the golf clubs in the town are thriving with more than an adequate number of members, bucking the trend of many clubs around the UK. Golf in St Andrews is still one of the best deals in the world, with the season ticket price for a resident of the town only £230 per year until the Covid-19 crisis in 2020. This gives unlimited access to all seven of the St Andrews courses, subject to availability, which is not too difficult to obtain with the exception of the Old Course. Still some residents are unhappy because the older ones remember when it was free.

Prior to 1946, golf on the courses actually was free to residents of the town. From 1946 until 1974 it was an additional cost of circa £10/ year on your rates if you chose to play golf.

The rights of R&A date back to the time when the New course was built as it was the R&A which paid for it. There was a time when they also paid 50% towards the cost of running the Links. However, ticket holders aren't necessarily aware of these facts. As a result, it does occasionally cause a bit of tension locally.

The R&A have the following:

- Sole use of the Old Course for their Spring meeting the first week of May.

- Sole use of the New Course the first week of September for their Autumn meeting.

- Sole use of the Old Course for the second and third weeks in September for their Autumn meeting.

- One hour of tee times on the Old on Saturday morning between 8am and 9am in August.

- One hour of tee times each afternoon through August.

- The right to every second tee time on the New Course throughout the year. Over time this has been more flexible and led to less confrontation as now the porter normally calls down from the clubhouse to advise that some members will be down in twenty to thirty minutes and looking to play. This gives the Starter time to advise any waiting golfers when they are liable to get off as, previously, the R&A members often just turned up and 'bumped' the golfers next due on the tee. The other benefit is that an R&A member, wherever in the world they stay, only pays the same yearly ticket price as a resident, whereas out of town members of the other Clubs, (and you have to be a member of a Club to obtain a Links Ticket), have to pay double or treble that price depending on where they live. Plus, you would have to pay your annual Club Golf membership fee. Of course, the R&A members would still have to pay their own club membership fees above the cost of their season ticket.

A further statute conferred on Trustees by the Act 'shall be deemed to be exercised in the furtherance of the use and enjoyment of the Links by the public'. The Links Trust is classed as a charity and this is part of the reason that the Old Course is closed for play on a Sunday, with the exception of five or six Sundays a year when it is hosting either the last day of a tournament or a specific event.

There was one individual, or family, who retained certain rights to the Links after the 1974 Act was passed. This was whoever was the proprietor of the neighbouring Strathtyrum Estate. Back in 1797 the Town Council were in what could be described as financial difficulty and were looking at ways to reduce their costs and raise some money, (sound familiar?). As a result, they struck a deal with two individual businessmen to borrow some funds and used part of the Links as security with the proviso that the lawyers could sell this land off if the Council defaulted on the loan, which they did by the end of that year, selling it off to another local businessman. He saw this as an opportunity to improve his income by introducing rabbits, which he bred and then sold as food and pelts. Rabbit was a staple diet of the working classes at the time. I guess he didn't have to work too hard in the breeding part of the process. This led to the episode mentioned earlier that came to be known as 'the rabbit wars' as the rabbits did what they do best and began digging, leading to a deterioration in the course, much to the discontent of the golfers. The situation wasn't resolved for some twenty-four years when James Cheape, the Laird of Strathtyrum which was a neighbouring estate bought the feu off the links from the individual concerned. The family later sold the land back to the R&A for £5,000 which in turn sold it to the Council, having been threatened with a compulsory purchase order.

They did retain two rights: The first was the right to extract cockleshell from the Links to use on the driveways of their own estate. They couldn't sell it on although they could stockpile it, but to retain this right they had to extract some every so often. I never witnessed this, but many of my original staff had and you can still see where they extracted the cockleshell today on the approach to the 3rd green and the carry of the 4th hole of the Eden course. They usually gave the Links some warning they would be coming, which allowed the greenstaff time to strip the turf from the area before coming in and excavating the shell. Then they had to use other material to return the ground to a similar level as they found it. On the 3rd and 4th of the Eden now, different sections are clearly visible where grass growth is really strong because of the rich soil underneath, while other areas are dry with poor grass cover as it sits on pure sand.

The area set aside for golf was demarcated by 'March stones', most of which are still visible today. A number of them are actually on the fringes of the New and Eden courses as well as on the Old Course. Some March stones on the Old Course are actually in the middle of fairways which indicates how the course has changed over the centuries. Quite how the rabbits knew which area was theirs and which area for golf I've never figured out. Perhaps the rabbits were smarter 250 years ago!

A March stone marking what was the land set aside for golf.

The other right they had was to six tee times on the Old Course every day to use as they wished, except when the R&A had their rights. These were seldom taken up, but it prevented the Trust selling these times as they couldn't do so in advance and golf tourism was picking up, putting all available tee times on the Old Course at a premium. In 1993, the Links Trust reached an agreement with the owner of Strathtyrum Estate at the time, Gladys Cheape, to purchase back the Rights at a cost of £245,000 payable at £35,000 a year for seven years. The principal reason for her selling was because there was a possible inheritance tax liability. That might appear to be a lot of money for six tee times per day but even back in 1993 they could have been worth £2,400 per day. The approximate green-fee on the Old then would have been around £40, so a tour operator might have got £100 per golfer, 4 x £100 x 6 times per day. By 2020, that could be worth over £20,000. Mrs Cheape was in her eighties or nineties and died shortly afterwards and her heir, who as far as I can recall was a nephew, was extremely unhappy and explored every avenue open to him to try to get the times back.

Aside: The large fairway bunker on the left of the 2nd hole of the Old Course which can catch a wayward drive, is called Cheape's bunker after James Cheape, for purchasing back the land from the rabbit farmers and returning it for the playing of golf.

Cheape's bunker which protects the left side of the 2nd fairway. Named after James Cheape.

The Links Trust is quite a complicated organisation to explain and the manner in which it was set up in 1974 was probably very relevant then, given what preceded it, and would have worked quite well initially but even by the time I started at the Links in 1991 it was becoming outdated. Basically, this was because everything was expanding at such a pace and it was mostly run by volunteers who did not have the time to commit to run such a diverse and ever-growing operation.

There were two tiers of management put in place. The main duty of the Trustees is to make sure the Links are run in accordance with the Act and for the main beneficiaries, the residents of the town. They take the lead in being responsible for setting the strategy and direction the Trust moves in and looking at the long-term issues, while the Links Management Committee (LMC) sit underneath them and are more to do with the day to day running of the Trust which is still the structure today. Back in 1974 they had a Secretary and a few people in Admin while the bulk of the employees were the greenstaff, a few Starters to control the tees and a number of Course Rangers who patrolled the courses on mopeds, checking that golfers had season tickets or had paid green fees.

The eight Trustees comprised three members of the R&A and three from the new Local Authority which was, at that time, North East Fife District Council but following more Local Government changes in 1996, it became part of the larger Fife Council. The other two Trustees were a nomination from the Secretary of State for Scotland and the Local Member of the UK Parliament. It's interesting that this is still the case, even though we now have a Scottish Government with much devolved powers.

St Andrews Links Trustees circa 2011. Chairman Peter Forster, front centre, went on to be Captain of the R&A in Sept 2021.

The eight members of the LMC are four nominations (members) from the R&A and four from North East Fife District Council, (later from Fife Council) and both Boards elect a chairman from within the eight members who is in place for a year but can be re-elected as long as they remain on their respective Board. Over time, both the R&A and Fife Council have given up places on both Boards to representatives from Local Clubs*. They both give one place on the Trustees board and two on the LMC board. Trustees sit for a three-year term and can be re-elected for a further three years, while the LMC term is four years with the option of a further four. All members are instructed to act with the best interests of the Trust at all times and not to represent their nominating body, (they sign a letter to that effect every January). It was obvious at many of the LMC Board meetings I attended that some of them struggled massively with that and quite often there was a 'conflict of interest' which led to some dubious decisions at times as they considered what might be the best outcome for the Local Clubs. Sometimes it felt like taking three steps forward then two back. We often got there but not always as quickly as it might have been.

As already stated, these people were all volunteers. The Councillors were elected officials while the R&A members and representatives of the other clubs were simply that, club members taking on a post on a committee as they would in most golf clubs. This was a particularly onerous task as they were heavily involved in the hiring and firing of staff, who had access to the courses, fees, setting caddy rates, start times, settling disputes between the Local Clubs and the Links and many other aspects that are associated with running a golf club, only on a much larger scale. They also provided the members of the Green Committee from their eight members, but that's a chapter in itself. Running the Links in this manner might have been satisfactory in 1974, although even with a full-time secretary and admin assistance it must have been a considerable workload for these volunteers. By the time you get to the 1990s, with the growth in golf tourism and golf in general becoming as much a business as a leisure pursuit, this was becoming far too much for these well-intentioned volunteers, who in

---

* There are nine Local Clubs who use the St Andrews courses as their 'Home' course. The R&A, The St Andrews Golf Club, The New Golf Club, The St Andrews Thistle Golf Club, The St Rule Club, The St Regulus Golf Club, The XIXth Hole Golf Club of St Andrews, Leuchars Station Golf Club and The University Golf Club. (There is also the Children's Holiday Golf Club and the Ladies Putting Club). To recognise the role these Local Clubs play in the fabric of golf in St Andrews, when I mention them throughout the book, I'll use capital letters to reference them.

many cases lacked the relevant skill set and business acumen. Many of them were often still more concerned with what was best for their golf club or the local ticketholder. I should add, however, that as a head greenkeeper this didn't cause me any huge issues or problems and, on the whole, they were fairly supportive. I had far greater challenges to overcome.

Things changed around the late 1980s when three like-minded R&A nominees came onto the board of Trustees, Kit Blake, Air Marshal Sir Peter Bairstow and John Lindsay-Bethune. John Lindsay-Bethune went on to be chairman in 1991 and 92 and again in 1996-98 while Sir Peter was the chairman from 1992-95. Word was that Sir Peter only became involved after complaining in the clubhouse one day about the condition of the courses after a round of golf and was met with the response, "Why don't you go onto the Trust and improve things?" The 'grand plan of improvements' had been agreed and much of it initiated by then, including the changes to both the Jubilee and Eden courses which were more or less complete, but the Trust was still desperately short of funds, despite an interest free loan from the R&A, along with a loan from the Trust's bankers.

Very briefly, the grand plan included the alterations of the Eden and Jubilee courses. The Jubilee changed from a short holiday course into a championship layout and was still considered the toughest test for the amateur golfer from the normal medal tees until the Castle course came into being in 2008. The Eden was redesigned with seven new holes to allow for the building of a good practice ground/driving range. Although some fine details were still required to complete the changes, (forward tees mostly), these two redesigned courses opened in 1988. There was now a practice area but people still had to use their own golf balls and pick them up afterwards. Neighbouring land had been purchased for the Strathtyrum and updated Balgove courses and these were duly built and open for play on the same day as a proper driving range, (now known as the Golf Academy), in 1993. The Strathtyrum is a relatively short course, only measuring 5,000 yards when it opened, but over a number of years new tees were added to stretch it to 5,600. With raised and challenging green complexes, it is also great for sharpening up your short game. The Balgove is basically a Par 3 course with holes of varying lengths, ideal for juniors, seniors and beginners.

Sir Peter was to oversee the final pieces of the plan which were:

a. A Clubhouse for visiting golfers playing the Old, New and Jubilee courses in particular, to change in and relax after their round with a good food and beverage service. Up until then visiting golfers playing had no facilities near the courses and had to change their shoes in the car park or come dressed and prepared from their accommodation. There was a small building with a toilet and that was it. After the round they had to go back into town for a drink or to eat. They couldn't buy things such as golf balls or other accessories at the courses.

b. Build a proper covered Driving Range/Practice facility where golfers could buy a bucket of balls which would then be collected. This was built and opened in 1993 and has since been expanded. It's an excellent facility with a number of teaching professionals, a club fitting centre and the 'Trackman' system in 50% of the bays. There's also an indoor room for fitness training, putting lessons and which can host small seminars. It didn't come without its issues however; it wouldn't have been St Andrews without objectors. The local golfers took umbrage with having to pay for hitting the practice balls provided, even though their discounted price was very reasonable. The Links didn't employ their own professionals initially but there were a number of coaching professionals based in town, who the Links charged a nominal fee to use the facility which they immediately passed onto their client. The professionals weren't too happy as they thought they should run the facility. Because the facility was open into the evening, there were objections from locals because of light pollution in the winter months, therefore lighting was sourced to reduce the glare to a minimum. Now, over 25 years later, tens of millions of balls are hit each year and local children get free golf balls.

c. Build two new greenkeeping facilities, one to service the Old, New and Jubilee courses and the other for the Eden, Strathtyrum and Balgove courses along with the Practice Centre. This was done with the Eden Greenkeeping Centre (EGC) opening close to the 1st tees of those three courses in 1996. The new Jubilee Greenkeeping Centre (JGC) opened in

1997 on the site of the former Jubilee sheds to service the three Championship courses. It included a new workshop and both facilities were built to a high standard as should be expected at the Home of Golf. Although it was almost five years from when I was promised new facilities, it was well worth the wait as it made a tremendous difference, especially being so much closer to the actual golf courses.

d. Upgrade the greenkeeping equipment. A much-improved fleet of equipment began arriving shortly after the completion of the Eden Greenkeeping Centre in 1996 and the continual upgrading of this has continued since, with the greenkeeping staff having some of the best equipment available.

e. Build a Clubhouse to service the Eden, Strathtyrum and Balgove courses at the other side of the complex, along with expanding and improving the offices for the increased number of managers and admin staff the Links Trust were employing. The Eden Clubhouse finally opened in 2000.

As part of the plan, there had to be a change in the management structure and a much larger, professional, management team put in place. The Trust was growing at a considerable rate as the popularity of golf tourism increased and the size of the operation was becoming far too large to be run by volunteers. Still this was met with resistance in local quarters and it took a while to finally achieve it but the Trustees stood firm and eventually won the day. It's alleged Sir Peter was advised by one of his fellow Trustees, "The locals won't like this, there will be trouble," to which he replied, "I'm accustomed to dealing with 50,000 service personnel so I'm not going to be too bothered by some local golfers!"

However, the part of the plan people really objected to the most was the deal the Trustees agreed with the Keith Prowse company, a corporate hospitality group to which the Trust sold a number of guaranteed tees times on the Old Course at a premium price. This gave the Trust some essential guaranteed income to allow them to progress the other developments. The number of times wasn't that many and they came from those which would normally have been sold directly at the basic green fee value to tour operators whether they were local, Scottish or based anywhere else in the world. The local tour operators were protected, but as you could imagine, the tour operators elsewhere were less than happy at this move as it reduced the amount of times they could get at a minimum price which they would then mark up. Now their only route was through the Old Course Experience, a subsidiary company set up by the Keith Prowse Group, and they had to pay a set price for their times. The tour operators weren't going to take this lying down and managed to whip up a storm, convincing many local golfers it was they who were losing out as the Trust would soon use their 'local preferential' tee times as they chased this additional income. Every week there would be letters or articles in the local, Scottish and UK papers as well as many golf magazines about how the Trust were selling the birth rights of the St Andrews people to an overseas corporate conglomerate. It was original 'Fake News' which many people believed.

The new Management Team came into operation in 1993 with Nicky James replacing Alex Beveridge as Secretary. He had a supporting team of Euan MacGregor as Finance Manager, Ian Forbes, who already worked for the Trust, as deputy secretary and project manager to some of the changes. Soon, John Lindsay, previously of the Professional Golfers Association, arrived to oversee the golf side of the operation. To this day, some members of the LMC at times still struggle a little with their actual role now there is a full time, professionally qualified management team in place to run what, by the time I retired in December 2018, was a business with a £20 million turnover. Their role now should really be to act almost as scrutineers and to oversee that the day-to-day business is being run properly and fairly in the interests of all stakeholders but they face continual pressure from the members of the local golf clubs and others who all think they deserve a larger piece of the pie whether that be greater access to the Old Course or cheaper golf. Local golfers contribute less than 8% of the Trust's annual income yet still some golfers and the Clubs expect more. Amazingly, there are still some people in the town who think the Trust is too big and would like to see it fail despite the massive improvements made in all areas of the facilities over the past 30 years

Now to get back to the more interesting experiences of my early years at the Links and some of the other staff on the different teams or 'squads'. I have felt it necessary to give an explanation of the structure and how the Links Trust operates.

Chapter 4. Working with Walter Woods

W ALTER WOODS had been the Links Supervisor at St Andrews since 1974, the change coinciding with the new Links Act coming into operation. Walter replaced John Campbell, who I believe retired at that time. John was a competent greenkeeper and well respected through the industry and I have no information about the condition of the four courses at that time, but as mentioned elsewhere, the Trust were not financially well off*. Until then, the greenstaff had all been employees of the Town Council and because similar-graded staff looked after the parks and gardens in the town, the Links greenkeepers were allowed to finish five minutes early each day to allow for the additional distance they had to travel to get back into town. This was a practice which, although I understood the reason for, I could never quite fathom why it continued until well after I became Links Superintendent in 2000.

After working at the Links for a period, Walter became more well-known and respected throughout the turf industry than John Campbell had been, particularly in America and Canada as well as in the UK, and rightly so. He was very supportive in assisting Elmwood College introduce the recognised City and Guilds qualification for greenkeeping to their portfolio. This is something which had been in existence since the late 1960s, having previously been included with horticulture. Charlie Crossan, the head of horticulture at Langside College in Glasgow, had worked closely with notable Scottish greenkeepers Bob Moffat from Douglas Park GC, and Cecil George from Lenzie GC to create a suitable syllabus. Cecil was actually on the short list for the job at St Andrews when Walter was appointed Links Supervisor in 1974,

---

*   Over the years I've seen various television programmes and films of previous Opens and other events such as Shell's Wonderful World of Golf played over the Old Course in the 1960s and 70s and was always interested in how the course looked. It's difficult to judge accurately because of the grainy pictures, but the greens never looked in particularly good condition although they were probably acceptable to the players and what they were accustomed to at other venues at that time.

or so he always told me. Cecil often said to me that Sandy Rutherford, one of the committee members interviewing for the position and who, as well as being a member of the R&A was also a member at Lenzie GC, told him he thought he was actually the best candidate but didn't vote for him. "Thanks a f***ing bunch," was Cecil's reply.

Walter was also more responsible than anyone in amalgamating the three greenkeeping organisations that existed in the UK in the mid-eighties into the British and International Greenkeepers Association (BIGGA), which has given a voice to greenkeepers and grown to be the professional association it is today. He was able to get the R&A to support the initiative through his friendship with Sir Michael Bonallack, who was their Secretary, and along with providing funds to help the fledgling association, the R&A were able to help with legal advice while also bringing the Home Unions to the table. Walter was the first chairman of BIGGA in 1987 and fought hard to establish and grow the association, as there were many other organisations within the game who would have been quite happy to see BIGGA fail and keep greenkeepers subservient. Greenkeepers today, not just in the UK but around the world, owe a great deal to Walter Woods who sadly passed away in 2019.

Walter was awarded the British Empire Medal for his services to the industry and in 2002 was awarded the Old Tom Morris award from the Golf Course Superintendents Association of America, (GCSAA), whose previous recipients include Arnold Palmer, Bob Hope, Gerald Ford, Dinah Shore and Tom Watson.

Walter was also a very good golfer, playing to a scratch handicap for many years, and reached the final of the Eden tournament one year, a competition which attracted many top-class players at that time, including some who represented their countries on the international front. One of my favourite golfing stories about him, which he never spoke to me about but I have heard from his peers, was when he was head greenkeeper at the Notts GC shortly before he moved to St Andrews. He had been selected to play for the county in an inter-county match and played in the No.1 Singles against a young Mark James who was representing Lancashire. Walter beat him 5 & 4. Fast forward a few years when Walter had moved to St Andrews and Mark James had turned Pro. There was a professional event over the Old Course and the players had been notified that in their practice rounds they shouldn't hit more than a couple of balls to the greens to minimise divot damage to the fairways. Word got back to Walter that someone was on the 17th fairway hitting multiple balls and he immediately jumped in his Daihatsu truck to confront him, (Walter had what could be described as a short fuse on occasions). He raced down to the 17th and as he approached the golfer, recognised it was Mark James. Having been asked what he thought he was doing Mark James asked, "Who the hell are you?" Walter replied, "Son, if someone had whipped my a**e 5&4, I'm bloody sure I'd remember who he was."

Although I'd known Walter since the early 1980s, I only actually had him as my boss for just over four years, as he retired in December 1995. It just seemed a whole lot longer. Don't get me wrong, I had a lot of time for him and he was a great guy to be with when we travelled to any BIGGA events. He was very sociable with a good sense of humour and always had plenty of stories, sometimes greenkeeping related, but often about his other life experiences or football, (he often claimed he supported Dundee although his real team was Glasgow Rangers). But he was bloody difficult to work for!

One of the aspects which frustrated me about him was his reluctance to make a decision, particularly a tough decision if it didn't materially affect him. Particular examples often related to disciplinary matters as Walter never wanted to discipline people. His default position was usually to give them a memo or a stern talking to, rather than making anything official. The staff knew this and that nothing severe would happen, so many of them basically did as they wanted, knowing very little would come of it.

A case in question was the incident I'd described earlier about the first weekend I covered the overtime rota. The employee's head greenkeeper did nothing, so when a similar incident happened later, I went to Walter and explained the situation to him. The response I received was to go back and talk to his head greenkeeper which basically didn't result in anything changing.

The hardest battle for me however was with one of my own members of staff, a guy who was late more days than he was on time, if indeed he came in at all. Despite many requests to Walter over many months there was always a reluctance to go down the disciplinary route. I had a notebook full of evidence on days he was either late or wasn't in, weekdays and weekends, along with other indiscretions while at work. Eventually I was able to issue him with verbal and written warnings but actually firing him was another story. There was even one day where I had just come out of a meeting at 9.30 with Walter where I'd mentioned this lad wasn't in and Walter's advice was to 'give him a roasting' when he does come in, even if it's tomorrow. Just then, the lad turned up, over three hours late. Taking Walter's advice, I shouted loudly at him in the yard finishing with the instruction, "Get your f***ing Wellington boots on and go down and help the guys clean the burn." The source of the irrigation water at that time was from a borehole just off the premises which was then pumped into the Swilcan burn that runs across the 1st and 18th of the Old Course. The burn was then dammed just before it exits the course into the sea and the water pumped from the burn back to a holding tank at the Jubilee sheds. An ongoing issue was algae which would bloom in the burn in the warm weather and block the suction valve so, almost weekly through the summer, each team would send one member of staff to rake out the algae. Sitting in my office shortly after this confrontation, I could see the lad heading over the dune and assumed that he was off to do as instructed. It was only at the end of the day I discovered he'd actually just gone home.

Clearing the burn of algae is a routine task on the mornings of tournaments, as shown here. It used to be a punishment for misbehaving!

I thought that would be the final straw as, since he had walked out of work, it would be an automatic dismissal but when I reported it to Walter, it was me who got the rollocking for shouting at him in front of the other staff!

So, this employee had walked off the job without telling anyone and didn't come back for a few days, yet amazingly, no action was taken against him and his absences and lateness continued as if he was immune. Then, at one point when Walter was on holiday, he didn't come in for a few days. He never got in touch to say he was ill and by that time he had some disciplinary points on his record. I went 'up the ladder' to Walter's line manager and explained the situation where the decision was made to dismiss him. A breakthrough at last. Walter then came back from holiday and, while I got the impression he wasn't very pleased, life went on. Then, just over a week later, one of the staff told me that this lad was going to be coming back to work the following Monday.

Some of the greenkeeping staff, circa 1994.

The said Monday came and sure enough he turned up and was back on the payroll as if nothing had happened.

His return didn't last that long, however, as by then it appeared he had a drug problem and was arrested one night and spent some time in the cells before finally being found guilty and sent to prison. His absence did cause some consternation though as when he was arrested, we discovered he had borrowed a pedestrian mower from the Links to cut his own grass and it was in his garage so there was a bit of a panic to get it back.

Ironically, I remember one incident when on a Saturday afternoon Walter had arrived at the first tee of the New course to play in a St Andrews Golf Club medal and there were no medal markers on the tee. Someone had stolen them or thrown them in the bushes overnight and the greenkeeper on duty that morning hadn't noticed because he hadn't bothered going down to the first tee to move them, which would have been a standard task. We discovered later that he had been late and so the entire field in the medal played the 1st hole without tee markers. This would have made Walter feel stupid or inept in front of a lot of people he knew, so when he came in to work on the Monday morning this would still have been at the forefront of his mind. Once he established the greenkeeper responsible, he gave him the full Alex Ferguson hairdryer treatment in the yard in front of the entire staff.

The four head greenkeepers along with Dod the workshop manager, Arlene the secretary and Walter used to meet every Monday, Wednesday and Friday in Walter's office to discuss what each of us was doing or planning and Walter would pass on any information he thought might be relevant. These meetings could last from between five minutes to over an hour, depending on what was coming up, maybe a tournament or a GSC meeting. From my point they were mostly a royal pain in the behind as it took me some considerable time to make my way back over from the Eden course to attend and there was often little to discuss. On odd occasions Walter wouldn't even turn up, leaving a message with Dod to let us know the meeting was cancelled.

In 1992, as spring arrived and temperatures began to rise, my thoughts turned to applying fertiliser. I always liked to follow the advice of Jim Arthur* and apply a small amount of sulphate of ammonia along with sulphate of iron at some point in March. You would always get a decent window of opportunity for a week or so, when it would be warmer before the east winds came along and slowed growth right down again. It was very much a case of being ready to go as soon as that window occurred. This would help the grass get through the following four to six weeks until the main spring feed, especially since it was coming under increasing pressure as more golfers came out of their winter hibernation. Walter didn't believe in this, which I always considered strange, as he was also a great disciple of Jim Arthur. The greens on the Eden, especially the newer ones, were particularly poor that spring, partially as a result of the delayed vertidraining back in December and partially because they had been starved of fertiliser the previous year, leaving them very thin on grass. I played in a match for BIGGA against the club secretaries at Dunbar in late March or early April that year and the greens there were in great shape for the time of year, particularly compared to all the courses at St Andrews. I spoke to the head greenkeeper, asking what he had been doing to get them in that condition. It was no surprise when he answered he had given them a little boost of nitrogen some two weeks earlier when it was relatively warm. The following day at our 9am meeting, Walter asked me how the golf had gone, I mentioned the greens at Dunbar were quite a bit ahead of the ones at St Andrews. It was an innocent remark, a throw-away line almost, not meant as a comparison, just a statement. Walter didn't comment so I forgot about it immediately. Shortly after the meeting I was back in the office having my break with some of the other head greenkeepers when Walter came to the door, (he seldom came into our office). Standing there by the door he asked me why I thought the greens at Dunbar were so good, to which I replied one of the reasons

---

*   Jim Arthur was a well-known and respected agronomist from the 1950s through, and into, the 70s. Working for the Sports Turf Research Institute, (STRI), he was the agronomist at many Open Championships and his book, Practical Greenkeeping, is considered a bible by many people. He could be quite controversial at times, though I thought his views were often misinterpreted. His mantra was, "Don't apply phosphates and limit the amount of water," which people often read as no fertiliser and no water. His basic principles are sound, especially avoiding overwatering, but things are very different these days. Mid-20th century, very few people played golf through the winter when the grass is at its most susceptible. Now, taking daylight hours into consideration, tee sheets can be as full in the winter as they are in summer. Many courses are seeing well over 50,000 rounds per year, while weather patterns are also changing. Grass needs some assistance to survive, whether that's through more aeration, better nutrition or by using other products. Or, as Old Tom Morris would say when asked why the Old Course was closed on a Sunday, "The golf course needs a rest, even though you may not."

was they had been given a little fertiliser a couple of weeks previously. "Well, you'll no be f***ing putting fertiliser on here in March," he said. He then turned on his heel and walked away.

The third week in April was when we fertilised on the Old Course, the third Sunday to be exact, as with the course closed to golf, it was an ideal opportunity. It didn't matter what the weather was like unless it was torrential rain. I personally would always hold off as long as I could for the main spring feed until I could see the weather was potentially going to pick up. At Fraserburgh I would mix up my own fertiliser as it was much cheaper. A few days before applying it, I would mix up different quantities of sulphate of ammonia, dried blood, hoof and horn, sometimes adding sulphate of potash and sulphate of iron. I'd measure each ingredient by weight to suit the area of each individual green then add the required amount of sand for that green size. Then it would be put into bags and I'd mark which bag would cover a particular green, applying it by hand in two different directions.

At St Andrews, Walter would purchase the fertiliser for us from an agricultural firm called Central Farmers and it would arrive in 25kg bags but there was nothing on the bags to say what the 'ingredients' were. All the turf industry suppliers had multiple, suitable products available to use, all with application rates of how large an area a bag would cover at different rates. But there was absolutely no information on these bags. By looking and smelling it, I could tell there was sulphate of ammonia in there along with iron and it had been bulked up with dry sand, but I had no idea of what percentages. I asked Walter what was in the bags and what quantity should be applied, or how large an area a bag should cover. "Bulk it up with some beach sand and spread it on the greens two directions, if you want to add more, do it a third way." Hardly scientific, so I ended up finding out how much sand Eddie was using to bulk it up with when applying it in two directions on the Old Course and following suit. I never did find out the rate I was applying it. To see some of the staff spread the sand and fertiliser mix from a hopper was impressive, especially on the Old Course when there could be six or seven men working in a line to cover the size of the greens. As in all things, some were better at it than others but pity the person who couldn't do it or made a mistake. Fortunately, I had applied fertiliser by this method before.

Staff working on the Old on a Sunday was a bugbear of my staff, and those of the other teams because it resulted in a similar scenario to that with the Dunhill lunch vouchers. The Old Course team would usually only come in on Sundays for tournaments, to apply fertiliser or to topdress the greens. This meant they didn't get the opportunity to accumulate as much overtime as those in the other teams as it was double time on a Sunday. However, because the Old Course staff usually worked more Saturdays, over the course of a year the number of hours or the money each member of staff would accrue, would be very similar. What everyone had issue with was the Old Course team might only work three or four hours until the task was complete but would get eight hours added to their timesheets. That this was being done and being openly authorised was bad enough, but once again the Old Course team took great pleasure in rubbing their colleagues' noses in it.

Two stories from those early years involve the Dunhill Cup. On one occasion friends came to stay for the weekend to follow the golf. It's always good to go out around town in the evening and catch a bit of the atmosphere and on the Saturday night we found ourselves in the Dunvegan Hotel, less than 100 yards from the Old Course. As to be expected, it was busy but we managed to get a table. Ernie Els and Steve Elkington came in immediately behind us and there were only two seats available which happened to be at our table. After the drink had been flowing for a spell, I asked Ernie Els if he had ever played at Dornoch or some of the other courses in the north of Scotland. When he replied in the negative, I began offering to be his tour guide for a week!

I would usually cycle to and from my work in those early days and the shortest route was by crossing the 1st and 18th fairway of the Old Course over Grannie Clarks Wynd. This is a one-way road with the 'correct' direction being from the town towards the beach, but every day, myself and others would cycle against the one-way system. Going across one evening after a late shift at work, a policewoman stepped out in front of me waving her arms and shouting, "This is a one-way street." I swerved onto the fairway to pass her before shouting back, "I'm only going one way."

Chapter 5. Greenkeeping Work in those Early Years

I FOUND MY first four years at St Andrews difficult in so many ways, the practices that were carried out, the behaviour of many of the staff and their 'couldn't care less' attitude to work and their employers in general, along with the lack of discipline and real leadership.

It wasn't only the Eden team who had all the difficult or poorly skilled staff, there were under performers in every team. The Old had the best people as they were generally young, fit and had the better skills in the main but they were also very aware that if they didn't perform, then they were liable to be moved off the Old Course to another team. Alongside that, if any of them were to consider moving to another job away from St Andrews, then the fact they worked on the Old would be to their advantage. In saying that, there were very few staff who ever seriously thought of moving, especially those who came from the town itself. They often spoke about it but it was mostly bravado. In most cases I felt they lacked confidence and key skills, particularly in the field of machine maintenance, as they had a workshop team who did everything for them. In many cases they were short of knowledge in different areas, including drawing up fertiliser programmes, irrigation systems and man management because they were never trained in these areas. They were all proud of how many Dunhill Cups or Open Championships they had worked, despite the fact they were only ever cutting greens or raking bunkers rather than help run the tournament or organise any part of it. Likewise, they thought because they could cut a really straight line when cutting greens or were good at building bunkers then they were good greenkeepers. Many of them were excellent at these skills, although some weren't as good as they thought they were.

One of the most common phrases I would hear was, "That's not how we do it at St Andrews," which used to get right up my nose. Especially as they were still doing things which wouldn't have been out of place in the 70s.

Revetting bunkers with strips of turf is a skilled job.
Note the sandy profile of the ground behind the bunker face.

I used to tell my team there was more than one way to skin a cat, and as long as the end result was as good or better, then it didn't really matter how you got there. But as soon as I turned my back, they returned to their old methods. They would often choose the way that made it easiest for them, even if the result was substandard, rather than put in that little extra effort to make things better. Or they would do it in a manner that wasted time rather than saved time. Something which didn't help this situation was the fact that all the teams would assemble in the sheds each morning to go through the day's work plan and staff would be too busy listening to what other teams were going to do. A member from another team would come over to my team after the briefing and say, "What the f**k are you doing that for, I wouldn't be doing that or doing it that way." One of the worst culprits was an older guy who behaved like an old sweetie wife. He had been a greenkeeper, then as he grew older, he moved to controlling the rabbits across all the courses. He would go around the courses all day, gassing rabbits by putting a powder containing cyanide down their burrows which would turn to gas when it became damp. Because the Links was common land, we couldn't set traps or snares as it was a popular area for dog walking. He did a lot of gassing and not just of the rabbits as, when walking around the courses, he would constantly stop to chat to the greenstaff, telling them all this wasn't how he would have done it. Or he would bad mouth guys in another team which again wasted thirty minutes of everyone's time, not that anyone was bothered about stopping for a spell. One of his favourite sayings was that you should go home from the Links at the end of the day weary but never tired. He knew I didn't have much time for him so I was one of his favourite people to bad mouth.

When there was a 'project' happening which might have affected multiple courses such as clearing the burn on the Old Course of algae, then it was common for each of the teams to send a member of staff to assist. Invariably what then happened was each would send their least skilled person or the one who caused them the most problems. That inevitably meant the work would take longer or was poorly done as many of the guys who were sent just messed around, knowing there would be no consequences for their actions. We weren't allowed to discipline someone from another team. That was up to their head greenkeeper and I'd already discovered that was never going to happen.

There was an old roadway called Mussel Road which was a right of way from the town down to the edge of the Eden estuary where in the past the townsfolk would have been allowed to dig for mussels. This ran diagonally through the centre of the new practice area and was an aggregate-based road sitting a foot or so higher than the surrounding grass. The Links were able to get this right of way diverted and because it was nearest the Eden course, I was to get help from each team to remove and level the old roadway and turf over where it had been. After a few hours had passed on the first morning I went down to see how things were progressing, only to discover there had been next to nothing done as the four staff had spent most of the time chatting. There was a bit of a stand-off but ultimately there wasn't much I could do and had to accept the fact this was going to take as long as they wanted to make it. One of the individuals was the good golfer who didn't complete his overtime the first weekend rota I worked and, as luck would have it, when the draw came out for the competition to find the Match Play Champion of St Andrews, I was drawn to play against him. I practised hard for that game and on the night I played well, winning at the 1st extra hole although I got a fortunate break near the finish. One up on the

18th tee, he found a fairway bunker off a good drive which allowed me to square the game. That was sweet.

Topdressing* the greens, or any area, was difficult as it wasn't easy to get good quality topdressing. Sometimes there was a product called Fensoil bought in which was mixed with sand taken from the beach. It was a terrible product to work with as it would clag and remain in lumps if it got wet or damp and the resulting mix would be inconsistent. On other occasions we used some soil which was from old bunker faces or other areas which had been allowed to break down over time. Sometimes Walter would be offered topsoil from a building site nearby. These materials could vary tremendously from sandy material to a much heavier soil type and it all had to be screened and mixed with the beach sand. If the material was wet at all, then this was a laborious process. The large screen we used would let some sizeable particles through, especially seashells. Alternatively, the small screen was exceptionally slow if the material had the smallest amount of moisture in it. Then the topdressing had all to be applied by hand using wheelbarrows and shovels as there were no topdressing machines.

Topdressing greens wasn't quite as easy as this in 1991.

---

* Topdressing is essentially lightly applying a material, usually either pure sand or a sandy loam, to the surface of the greens, (or other areas). It has various benefits for the grass which includes; smoothing the surface, diluting the build-up of organic matter caused by the grass decaying, keeping the surface firm and aiding drainage.

Applying topdressing evenly across an area by this method was a skill which not everyone could master but fortunately I had done this at Fraserburgh when I started greenkeeping although, by the time I left there, we had our own walk-behind topdressing machine. If another team was using the screens, or if everything was wet, I often found it quicker to just mix the different materials with the tractor and front loader. We'd then spread it across the greens, before removing all the stones, shells and other debris from the surface using brooms or lutes.

At St Andrews we have always been allowed to take a certain quantity of sand from the West Sands beach to use on the courses. We had been allowed to take from the East Sands beach as well at one time but this was stopped before 1991. There was a protocol to follow in that the sand could only be taken from below the High-Water mark, so we had to wait until the tide was out and it had to be taken from a certain area of the beach. We could only scrape a few inches from the surface over a large area. We couldn't simply dig a hole as this could cause a danger for other beach users such as horses galloping in the shallows. After the tide had come and gone, then it was impossible to see where the sand had been taken from. We had to call up the Local Authority each time prior to taking sand and make them aware as they would often receive a call from a member of the public, (I suspect it was often the same person) concerned that we were causing coastal erosion. Taking a quantity of sand from the beach for use on the courses used to be considered as 'accepted practice' but from around 2007, due to a change in legislation, we had to apply to Marine Scotland for permission every three years. We were limited to the amount taken per year and, as previously, had to contact Marine Scotland each time prior to extracting, then contact them afterwards with the quantity taken. We had to have the beach levels surveyed every year and undertake a larger survey to accompany a full report at the end of three years when re-applying for the licence. A team would drive in a few hundred tonnes at a time to an out-of-play area in the middle of all the courses where it was piled up and left to dry. Coming from below the High-Water mark, the sand was saturated. Because it had such a fine particle size it was very prone to wind blow, therefore sometimes when my team went to use it, they could find that a lot had blown away or another team had used most of it. The sand can only be used on the courses and was used in the bunkers, topdressing or for mixing with material for construction jobs and divot mix.

*Where the sand and soil were stored with the large screen used to mix
topdressing, construction material and divot mix.*

Over time we began buying in sand for topdressing greens though we
still used the beach sand on fairways. In later years, we bought in most
of our divot mix and changed the sand over in all the bunkers other
than on the Old Course, buying in a sand which had a heavier grain and
didn't blow as badly. What is taken from the beach today is only used in
the Old Course bunkers, topdressing fairways and to bulk up material
for construction jobs.

There was a reluctance by the staff to help each other, either
between teams or even within a team itself. Yes, everyone would assist
the Old Course in times of competition or they would help another
team out if they had an event on. The Eden tournament, held over the
Eden and New courses was an example, although another team would
only send one or two staff for this. But this was more a case of being
told to do it or 'expected' to do it. No one would go out of their way to
help anyone in a general sense, in fact they were more likely to stand
and laugh as someone struggled with something or simply walk on by.

As regards everyone helping on the Old at tournaments, e.g. the
R&A meetings, things came to a head in September 1992. Walter had
left an envelope on my desk which was a memo from Alex Beveridge

the Links Secretary. He had received a complaint from some golfers asking why the greens on the Eden hadn't been cut that morning, nor the bunkers raked. I went over to see Mr Beveridge and explain that I only had time to move holes and markers as I was by myself. The rest of my staff were all helping on the Old Course until 9am. He wasn't aware this practice was taking place and after that I was able to retain two people plus myself to carry out the minimum of maintenance deemed acceptable whenever competitions were taking place on the Old. This didn't go down well, especially with Walter and Eddie, but also many of the other staff who weren't too happy they had to work on their own course rather than the Old. I found that quite bizarre and while I wouldn't put it as strongly as to say I was ostracised because of it, people were very cool towards me for a while and it was something I suspect was never forgotten.

I've already mentioned that the greens on the Eden were in poor shape which was true for all of them but for different reasons. The eleven original greens, those on the front nine and numbers 11 and 13 had a high percentage of a coarse, agricultural type ryegrass in them, especially through the centres. These greens dated from 1914. The grass would have been indigenous to the Links and would have likely had some ryegrass in the sward. But a lot of the ryegrass stemmed from a period through the 1970s and early 1980s when Walter undertook a strategy to remove the ryegrass from the Old Course greens. This fact was often spoken about by many of the staff, including those who worked on the Old Course at the time. This was attempted by taking plugs of turf, referred to as 'heading', from the Old Course greens and replacing them with plugs of the finer grasses from the centres of the greens on the Eden and New courses. The result was that both the Eden and New course greens were then also infected with the ryegrass while it never was completely eradicated from the Old Course greens! I can only surmise this was because the plugs were never taken deep enough to remove all the roots of the ryegrass and over time it grew back up to the surface through the plugs. No one could ever tell me why the Jubilee greens weren't included in this programme, and it is still noticeable today that there is less ryegrass in the original Jubilee greens compared to those on the New and Eden.

The problem with the new greens on the Eden was completely different. They had been seeded in the mid-1980s when the course was redeveloped and were probably brought into play too early as there would have been pressure to get the course open. As a result, the new grass wouldn't have had a decent time period in which to mature. As soon as the pressure from regular close mowing and the continual foot traffic from golf hit them, the greens would have deteriorated. Add the fact that Walter didn't believe in applying much fertiliser, even to newly-seeded grass at a time when it really needed it, simply added to the problem. As a result, the coverage was very bare which allowed for Poa Annua, (annual meadow grass) to fill the gaps. In its early stages the Poa is very 'clumpy' until it matures and becomes more refined after a few years.

By adding a little more fertiliser and giving them adequate water, I was slowly making progress with these new greens and they were gradually improving, with the Poa becoming a little more refined, when Walter decided we should returf six of them. Without prior discussion with me, he raised this at a GSC meeting where I was very much opposed to it. I had never seen an occasion where returfing a green, especially with turf bought in from another site, was successful. The turf bought in has inevitably been over-fertilised to speed up the production process and while it looks great initially, as soon as the height of cut is reduced, experiences pressure from golf and the amount of fertiliser is reduced, the grass goes backwards, quickly. My argument was, a year down the line we would be back where we currently were, or even worse as the Poa would then be at the 'clumpy' stage again. My view was I'd be better carrying on as I'd been doing, increasing the overseeding programme as well as ensuring the greens were getting sufficient nutrients and water. I must have put up a solid case as my views won over the GSC. The next day, I ordered additional grass seed and the following week my team and I began to heavily overseed the new greens through shallow aeration, scattering seed, and brushing it into the holes. I kept Walter updated on the progress we were making at the morning meetings on the Wednesday and Friday and I was even able to persuade a couple of the staff to work on for a couple of hours on the Friday afternoon to complete the final green. When I got back to my office there was an envelope sitting on my desk. I opened it up to find a letter from Walter telling me that, at the LMC meeting on the Wednesday that week, the LMC had reversed the decision to overseed the greens and they should be turfed instead. To say I was livid would be an enormous understatement. I can only surmise that Walter had been instrumental in getting the LMC to change their minds, (head greenkeepers didn't attend LMC meetings) as I couldn't see why the members of the LMC would have gone against the GSC recommendation of their own accord without someone speaking against it. What made it even more galling was the fact Walter knew what had happened, yet he didn't have the decency to say, letting me carry on with the overseeding for two days. Later that year we did returf four of the greens, which meant golfers had to play to temporary greens for the rest of the year. The following year when they came back into play, they immediately went backwards as I had predicted, while the two which weren't returfed continued to improve. To those reading this and who play their golf at St Andrews or know the course, the two Eden course greens which weren't returfed were 12 and 17.

The 16th green is a story on its own. When the course was first altered in the mid-1980s the 16th green was part of a double green with the 12th, the two of them being back-to-back rather than side-by-side. Immediately in front of the green ran Mussel Road, so any ball landing short on the approach could bounce in any direction and as the hole played down the prevailing wind, landing short was what you wanted to do. Add to that, there was a cavernous bunker on the front left where the sand in it would always be blown to one end of the bunker, or blown out completely, due to the direction the bunker faced. By the time I arrived at St Andrews there was already a new green built at the same side of the old railway line as the fairway, (the old railway line had also to be crossed when playing to the existing green). This made the hole considerably shorter but still a Par 5, reachable in two, which wasn't a bad thing. However, Walter had arranged for the contractors who were building the Strathtyrum course to build this new green, with the same rootzone mix used on the Strathtyrum greens, which was very different from the mix on the other greens on the Eden. As such it needed different management, especially in regards to what topdressing it received. Because topdressing compatible with that green wasn't always or readily available, it meant I couldn't topdress that green or the ones on the Balgove most of the time. Comparing that with what Roddy Barron did on the Strathtyrum course, it was a good decision. He decided to go with what Walter had advised and use the sand off the beach to topdress his greens. The beach sand had a much smaller particle size and after a few years this caused a thin layer of material which prevented any rain water or irrigation applications from percolating below it and this led to 'black layer' where the soil became anaerobic. It was the same with the grass roots which just stopped when they reached that layer. It took Roddy and his team a lot of hard work in the 2000s to cure this situation, with constant vertidraining and coring, followed by brushing as much sand as possible down the holes to allow the water and roots to penetrate through the rootzone.

That 16th green opened in 1992 or 93 but over time it began to suffer from black layer as well. It was never a great green and it wasn't very inspiring, one gradual slope from back to front with a very unnatural looking mound up both sides and along the back. There were bunkers left and right guarding the front. The only thing going for it was a decent player could reach in two, even under calm conditions and saw it as a good birdie opportunity towards the end of their round. Eventually in around 2005, Graeme Taylor, who was head greenkeeper on the Eden at the time, was granted permission from the GSC to build a new green. The new green was built immediately behind the existing one thereby adding some forty to fifty yards to the hole and Graeme sourced a rootzone mix from elsewhere on site consistent with the other greens. He designed it himself and based it on the 5th green of the Old Course where a similar dip ran across the approach. The green was made larger than average with a hollow on the left and a run off to the right and resembles many of the original greens on the front nine of the Eden, designed by Harry Colt. There aren't any greenside bunkers and one of the two bunkers which guarded the old green was moved to make them offset. They are now in the landing area for the second shot. As I've discovered over the years, golfers don't like change and this one was no different. I still feel the biggest issue was the hole was no longer the birdie chance it used to be, especially when a new tee was added to stretch it to over 600 yards, making it a beast if it was into the wind. I quite like the hole other than the mounding up the right of the fairway which the contractors built in the 1980s to separate it from the Strathtyrum course. It can still be reached in two from the normal tees in the prevailing wind, even by me, and the cross bunkers make players think about their second shot under normal conditions, or if they haven't hit their best drive.

One of the reasons those new greens, and indeed the other ones, began to improve before I ended up returfing them, was because of some action I took through the early summer of 1992 which I kept secret from people for quite some time. It was early May and I was golfing on the New course in a Club competition on the Saturday afternoon.

As the round progressed it seemed as if the greens were drying up as I went, with the grass positively wilting in front of me. As soon as I finished, I made my excuses to my playing partners and headed across to the Eden to see if the greens there were in a similar condition as they had been perfectly fine when I had left on the Friday afternoon. I was shocked to find they were equally dry with the grass looking very sickly. What made it worse was there was no rain forecast and I couldn't access my irrigation controller as Walter had deemed we couldn't irrigate until he said so and he had the keys to the controllers. It was his opinion that the method to combat poa annua, or annual meadow grass, was by droughting it out. I went home and told Pauline I was going to bed for a sleep as I decided I needed to do something and the only thing I could think of was to go in at night and water the greens by hand, which is what I did on alternative nights for the next two to three weeks. I was lucky in that I could divide the Eden up into three sections of six greens each and I would walk around a section putting each green sprinkler on, then going back around turning them off before heading to the next section. Then I would do the Balgove greens before heading home. The fact that no one else was watering meant there was plenty of pressure and as I was only watering greens, no one noticed how much water was being used. The only people who did notice were golfers who wondered why the greens on the Eden and Balgove were looking healthier and performing better than those on the other courses. I did the same thing the following spring and no one was any the wiser.

To the best of my knowledge the Links have used the Sports Turf Research Institute, (STRI), since at least the 1950s to give them agronomic advice on the courses. Established in the early 1920s to carry out research and give advice on golf courses the length and breadth of the UK, they were initially part-funded by the R&A along with subscriptions from the clubs they advised. I used to deal with the STRI when I was at Fraserburgh so I was well used to the format. My agronomist at Fraserburgh was one of their top people, Dave Boocock, an archetypical Yorkshireman who wore a flat cap, a tweed suit and heavy leather brogues and who called a spade a bloody spade. He really knew his stuff and I got on extremely well with him, learning a lot about grasses and fertiliser over the years I worked with him. He followed Jim Arthur as the agronomist to St Andrews but by the time I arrived at St Andrews it was Peter Hayes, the Director of STRI at the time, who would come and carry out the visits himself, one in spring and another in autumn. The normal format for these visits was for the two of us to walk the course and discuss the general fertiliser programme and any other work required, in particular to the greens but covering all the other areas of the course as well. If there were any areas or aspects of the course that I was concerned about, then I made sure we looked at these and came up with a solution to try and improve them. However, I soon discovered what happened at St Andrews didn't always follow that pattern. The other head greenkeepers would drive Peter around their course in a Cushman utility vehicle and take him to a few greens, tees and fairways. They made sure to stay well away from any poor or weak areas of turf. When the reports came in a week or two later, there were always much more objectives to work towards on the Eden than on the other courses. In fact, the report could be quite critical of the condition of the Eden and the other head greenkeepers thought this was very funny. Walter even made light of it on one occasion, but I didn't see the point in paying someone for advice and not covering the areas which were requiring the most attention. A head greenkeeper even told me of an earlier occasion when Peter visited and because the weather on the day was terrible, he and Walter wrote the reports without even going outside.

Peter was succeeded by Steve Isaac which was an improvement from my perspective as Steve was much more on the ball regarding more modern techniques, newer products and the latest developments. He spent more time out in the field than Peter did and was in constant dialogue with greenkeepers around the country. Steve subsequently went on to work for the R&A as part of their Golf Course Committee and latterly was their Director of Sustainability.

Steve's replacement was Richard Windows and Richard became a firm favourite with the course managers. As well as being a first-class agronomist, Richard is an excellent public speaker and would often give presentations to both the full-time and seasonal staff about golf course maintenance in general and the work undertaken on the Links in particular. If his visit happened to coincide with a GSC or LMC meeting then I would sometimes ask him if he would give a quick presentation to the committee on the recommendations he would be making. He excelled at this as his enthusiasm always came to the fore and the committees would generally love it. I remember one committee member saying afterwards, "I can't believe anyone can get that excited about grass".

I have always valued the STRI's work and looked forward to their visits. The fact that they visited so many golf courses and met such an array of head greenkeepers or course managers each year in the course of their job, gave them a great insight into what was happening throughout the industry. The access to research papers available to them along with the conversations they could have with their counterparts in the US Greens Section or elsewhere in the world, gave them a broad spectrum of knowledge. I often heard the comment that they weren't value for money as the reports they submitted were often what the course manager would have done anyway or what he would have recommended. In my experience many course managers, myself and others at St Andrews included, were unable to get these suggestions through committee, but when the advice came from the STRI agronomist it was accepted without much resistance. To have that support alone made it worthwhile as far as I was concerned. The only area in which I didn't always agree with them was when they made suggestions to make a significant change to a hole or some other aspect of the course, as I didn't feel it was their place and weren't qualified golf course architects.

Just as I would use their visits to influence the committee into doing things I wanted to do when I was a head greenkeeper, I was equally aware that the course managers used the same tactic when I was Director of Greenkeeping to try to influence me. Nine times out of ten I wasn't too concerned with this approach; it was only when they used the agronomist to instigate architectural changes or it involved capital expenditure that it became a problem. We had budgets and to go and buy a piece of kit wasn't something that could happen immediately on the recommendation of the agronomist. Equally, material changes to a golf course require a lot of discussion with various stakeholders before it can be progressed. The starting points for any change being, what significant improvement would the alteration bring to the hole both strategically and, to a lesser extent, visually.

I often reflected why Walter behaved in the manner he did in a lot of the incidents I've written about and I can't come up with definitive answer. He told me on more than one occasion his fear of a disgruntled employee, or ex-employee returning and doing some serious damage to the courses, which was a distinct possibility. I think many course managers share that concern, myself included, but I don't believe it's a valid reason for not taking the necessary action when an employee has been found to act inappropriately. Even though I later fulfilled a similar role myself, I don't know all the different pressures he might have come under, either from any committees or individuals such as a chairman or Alex Beveridge, Secretary to the Links Trust. Perhaps it was an ongoing lack of funds which prevented him improving the courses to the condition, or as quickly as he wanted to. Or that the condition of the sheds and the equipment were slowly deteriorating frustrated him.

When it was announced he was retiring and going to be replaced by Ian Forbes, (a person with no greenkeeping experience), Eric Clark, a past captain of the St Andrews Golf Club and a strong critic of the Links, put his name to a letter published in The St Andrews Citizen, the local weekly newspaper, stating quite categorically that St Andrews needed a figurehead such as Walter to lead the greenkeeping department and not simply a 'manager'. Under this new structure, each of the head greenkeepers would be given more responsibility for their respective course or courses and we reported to Ian. A couple of years after the letter appeared in the Citizen, Eric Clark, who I knew reasonably well, approached me and said he was wrong to have had that opinion as the courses had all improved in the intervening period. I thought it was very honest of him to admit he had been wrong.

To put these previous comments into perspective and some type of context I would add the following observations. How Walter managed the staff would have been typical of the time and many of his peers would have managed their staff in a similar fashion. In fact, it would have been common across the turf industry. The money available, I've already said, was tight. Add to that, the vast improvements in equipment which occurred over the following ten years, made things much easier for those of us coming afterwards.

As I say elsewhere in the book, away from the work environment I had a good relationship with Walter and he was great company. We wouldn't normally socialise and apart from meeting him when he was playing golf, most conversations I had with him were at BIGGA or other industry events.

Chapter 6. The Green Sub-Committee

THE GREEN Committee was a sub-committee of the Links Management Committee and in my early years usually consisted of three members. Later that increased to four when the chairman of the LMC would also attend the GSC meetings. The higher number was an advantage as it meant anything decided at GSC could be considered as agreed and greenstaff could begin the work rather having to wait for up to a month or more for the LMC to confirm an action. The members were all golfers, something you might think would be obvious, but I say that because often the two local authority members on the LMC didn't play golf. Fortunately, when GSC matters did go to LMC for final approval, they would generally support the recommendation.

In the early days of my career at the Trust there used to be ten GSC meetings a year and items were discussed much more thoroughly than they were by the time I retired. That was because in 1991, the members of the committee were still very much involved in the running of things. We had to take items such as when trollies were allowed on the Old Course, when we could begin vertidraining the greens and other standard procedures to the committee for agreement annually. Eventually, as Director of Greenkeeping, I was able to get agreement that all these items were practically set in stone. We would simply advise the committee when they were taking place and communicate them to the Local Clubs and golfers. By 2013 we were down to four or five meetings per year and the course managers and I would only raise matters which could be considered as making a material difference to the courses or significantly impact the local golfer. The best examples of these would be any winter work programmes that were proposed, such as building a new tee, moving or filling in a bunker or other alterations.

Looking back, it seems amazing that each year we had to ask the committee for simple things such as permission to have preferred lies from 1 November. This was Scottish Golf Union guidelines and we had to bring it to the committee in August so it could be discussed and agreed by the LMC before brought into operation in November. They would debate these subjects every year, with new committee members sometimes proposing another idea. I wouldn't say these meeting became heated or voices were raised, but they were often keenly debated.

Certain items, such as the alterations made to the Old Course for an Open Championship, were different and required much more debate. That was especially true in 2012 when the R&A requested quite a few changes which became very controversial, but not necessarily within the town or the local golfing community. Earlier changes which really only added length to the Old Course by adding tees, didn't have the level of consultation the 2012 changes did. As expected, there was some press coverage about them which caused mixed reactions both locally and around the world, the new championship tee at 17 for the 2005 Open in particular, but coverage died down shortly after each championship.

For my first few years, the GSC meeting used to take place in the Garden Room of the Scores Hotel as the Trust had no suitable place to host them. The four, (eventually five), head greenkeepers along with Walter would attend and we would each submit a report in advance then talk to it. Walter would go first and we would follow in order, the Old, the New, the Jubilee, the Eden, then when the Strathtyrum came into play Roddy Barron would finish with his report. We had standard headings in the report and this basic format continued right through until I retired with only some minor changes. There was much more involvement and discussion in what Walter had to say and what was happening on the Old Course. It was a bonus being last and reporting on the Eden or Strathtyrum as by then the committee's interest had waned, unless there was a particular issue they wanted to raise or had been asked to raise by a golfer about a specific course. In most instances these would have been something minor which affected a player during their round of golf.

The first GSC chairman I had was Ian Bunch, one of the people who interviewed me for the job on the Eden. Ian is a really nice guy, very well spoken who took a keen interest and great pride in his role. When I reflect back, those members of the GSC would have had a really tough time from the local golfers, including many of their friends, as the courses weren't in very good condition and many of the comments would have been blunt and straight to the point. There would have been little consideration in phrasing things in a polite manner.

One of Ian's habits was that he would often finish his sentences with the word "what", something he maybe never noticed or was particularly aware of. We greenkeepers however picked up on it and so, before the meetings, we would have a sweep between us on how many times he would say it. We would be sitting there and let's say I would have twenty-five while someone else had twenty-two. Once Ian said "what" twenty-four times I would find a way to signal the person who said twenty-two. Maybe give him a kick under the table or even just a smile and so it went on. It was always good to have a high number and, although childish, it added a bit of fun to the meetings.

There's one particular incident I remember from a GSC meeting at that time and it involved Ian Bunch, Walter and Davie Wilson from the Jubilee course. It was winter or early spring and would have been in 1992 or 1993. The GSC meetings were always on a Wednesday afternoon and we had our normal morning meeting with Walter at 9am. Davie had been turfing the immediate approach to the Jubilee 11th green where the grass had all died. He had previously discussed with Walter where he would source the turf to replace it, but on this morning he reported to Walter that the turf they had agreed to use was equally as poor. Walter just told him to carry on and use it anyway, so after the meeting Davie told his staff to carry on as planned. That afternoon before the GSC meeting, a site visit had been arranged to look at a specific area. This didn't happen prior to every meeting but maybe every alternative one, and on this day we were visiting the 9th of the New course and had to walk across a part of the Jubilee course to get there. This took us right past the 11th green of the Jubilee where Davie's staff had just finished laying the turf and the committee stopped to have a look. Once back at the meeting we were going through the agenda and came to the Jubilee course. After Davie gave his report, the chairman asked what they were doing on the 11th approach to which Davie said they had just returfed it. Ian then turned to Walter and asked why they had used turf which looked dead to carry out this work. Walter replied, "I don't know, you had better ask Davie that!". Davie had no answer and his face was a picture. It was a classic and although the other head greenkeepers and I thought it funny because it didn't happen to us, I thought to myself that if it did ever happen to me, then I wasn't going to sit there with my mouth shut and take it like Davie did.

Once Walter retired, Ian Forbes took over his role and after the Links Clubhouse was opened in 1995 the meetings moved there. Ian's reports were based more on project work and golf matters. He was responsible for project managing both new greenkeeping facilities when they were being built at the Eden and Jubilee complexes and he was also responsible for tournaments, while we head greenkeepers very much stuck to reporting on our own courses. Approximately every three or four years the chairman and committee members changed as new committees were formed. Over my twenty-seven years at the Links, including my time as a head greenkeeper, I had eight GSC chairpersons, and I would like to think I had good relationships with all of them. I almost always felt they were very supportive; they would rightly question things but usually we could work matters out. Between myself and the course managers, along with the support of our agronomists at the STRI, we could get them to understand the reasons why it was necessary to carry out specific practices at particular times. It was more challenging to get approval for course alterations, but again, by providing good reasons and information, these would usually be passed, although it might take a little longer and we didn't always get what we asked for. It was important to understand that some of the resistance they put up came, not necessarily from the committee, but from their clubs or the members of their clubs. It wasn't an automatic step, but quite often the GSC chair would go on to become the chairperson of the LMC. This was a benefit for the greenkeeping department as they had a good understanding of how we operated. From my personal perspective, I built up a good working relationship with them due to mutual trust and respect.

One additional meeting I seldom looked forward to was meeting with the Inter Clubs Liaison Committee*, (ICLC). They were a different proposition completely from the GSC with a very different agenda. The ICLC was set up initially as a method where the Local Clubs could meet and raise matters of a common interest to them. They would then take these to the Trustees or LMC as a group with a consensus, rather than each club bringing their own individual points of view. Although each Club was represented on the Board of Trustees or the LMC, they still felt that the 'local voice' wasn't being heard or listened to. The principle of the ICLC was good and initially it revolved around items

---

* The ICLC comprises of only six of the clubs who play on the courses. The R&A, The St Andrews GC, The New GC, The St Andrews Thistle GC, the St Rule Club and the St Regulus GC. The other clubs don't have representation in any group. Of the above six, only the R&A have men and ladies as members. St Rule and St Regulus are ladies only clubs, while the others are men only.

such as start times on the courses where ticket holders got preference, or the price of season tickets and similar issues, but it wasn't long before they began to get involved in course matters. In the early stages, and with the agreement of the LMC, they would send two of their members out to 'inspect' a course each spring. For example, the R&A might send two people to inspect the Old, the St Andrews Club, send two to the New and one of the Ladies Clubs, send two to the Eden etc. Then we would have a meeting when the representatives would come along and table their reports to us, the head greenkeepers. Walter had retired by this time and Ian Forbes, although attending the meeting, didn't have enough greenkeeping knowledge to answer many of the questions. At the very first meeting we had been given no prior warning what they were going to raise but subsequently they submitted their reports to us in advance, so we had at least some time to prepare our answers. We five head greenkeepers would sit in our office a few days prior to the meeting and discuss the reports. This would generally involve quite a lot of swearing at most of the points they had written! At the actual joint meeting which was held immediately after a GSC meeting, quite often the person who wrote the report wasn't the same person attending the meeting. Therefore, if at any time a head greenkeeper asked for some clarity on a particular point, the person raising it may not know the answer. That could be extremely frustrating for both parties, just like many of the issues they raised which we considered very minor in the grand scheme of things.

At one meeting, one attendee went through their report on the New course on a hole-by-hole basis, noting everything they thought was wrong with each hole. On the first they thought the rough immediately behind the 1st green, where every golfer walked to get to the 2nd tee, was too short, (it wouldn't grow as it was literally trampled to death). Then they went on to holes 2, 3 and 4 where they had different complaints. When they got to hole 5, it was that the rough immediately behind the green was too long. The head greenkeeper of the New course just blurted out, "Could you make up your damned minds, it's too short here, too long there, what is it you want?" Even the GSC chairman laughed.

When I was Director of Greenkeeping there was a meeting, where I'm embarrassed to say, I let their chairman get to me and there was a real dingdong of exchanges throughout the meeting which also included the GSC chairman, who had a short fuse of his own at times.

From my point of view, I was getting really frustrated as the chairman of ICLC would ask at every meeting, (and we had moved to two meetings a year by then) about the angle, (steepness), of the bunker faces and also the height of the step into the bunker from the rear. Both had become too severe over time which was something we had acknowledged and had agreed a standard with the GSC and LMC of what these should be. This had been relayed to the ICLC along with the information that, as we repaired the bunkers over a period of four years, we would rebuild the bunker faces to the new agreed angles. These were fifty-five degrees for fairway bunkers and sixty-five degrees for greenside ones with the exception of three or four key bunkers on the Old Course, such as Road Bunker on 17 which would be seventy degrees. We would also reduce the step into the backs of bunkers wherever the surrounding area would allow us to do so without having to significantly alter said area. The drops into the bunkers had naturally grown higher over the years through sand blow and golfers carrying sand out on the soles of their feet. This resulted in many older members having great difficulty physically getting in to, and out of, some of bunkers, let alone being able to hit their golf ball out. This work had been ongoing for a couple of years at least and I reached the stage where I would ask the course managers to provide information in advance of the meeting. This would include how many bunkers they had altered to meet the new standard and how many were in their immediate plans to be completed by the end of that current winter. Having passed on all this information to ICLC, along with the fact we had explained our plan to do it over a period of years, their chairman would repeatedly raise the matters and it just got too much for me that day. As well as the bunker issue there were the other 'standard' items on their agenda, none of them relating to the actual turf:

- The condition of the roads around the courses, which were always at their worst in the winter due to the weather and the heavier traffic using them as we trailed turf and materials around.

- The fact we were changing some roads from aggregate to tarmacadam to reduce maintenance.

- The severity of the rough. One of the two meetings was usually in early June when the rough was always at its thickest.

- The type or condition of mats on Par 3 holes in the winter. Across all the courses we only had five tee mats on Par 3s. Three of them were on the New Course, one on the Jubilee and one on the 8th of the Old and we had them because there was a lack of room to build a winter tee in these areas. We also tried many different types of mats over the years including the same ones we use in our Golf Academy which are acceptable there, but it appeared weren't acceptable on the courses.

- An ongoing request to increase the use of trollies on the Old Course.

Looking back now, it appears to me that my fractious relationship with this chairman was a combination of two things. One was the points above, some of which I felt were personal items he pushed rather than the collective view of his committee. The other was his tone of voice and the air of superiority I sensed from him, giving the impression that because of his education and profession, he thought he was better and knew more than any greenkeeper. While I could accept that it was only proper these meeting took place and, as their chairperson, he had every right to raise these matters, I would still get irritated with the fact he raised the same points every time.

There would be two meetings per year, one in February or early March, and another in June, where two representatives from each of the Local Clubs would come along to give their points of view on the courses as they saw things. At the February meeting, the course managers and I would begin with a PowerPoint presentation of all the winter work that had been done on the different courses and when we would expect any outstanding projects to be completed. In the early years I tended to give the presentation myself but as time went on I did less and each course manager would talk about their own course, while I concentrated on more general points. I would cover environmental matters, along with trying to give explanations or answers to questions which I thought might be raised. Like getting my retaliation in first! Although there was always an agenda, the GSC chairman, the chairman of ICLC and I would meet a few days beforehand to go over things. This would allow me to clarify any points I didn't quite understand and help in our responses, meaning there would be no surprises for either party come the meeting. I wanted to be sure we had good, robust answers to questions they might ask. At the end there would be AOCB where we were liable to get a fast ball from some of the representatives of the different clubs. Despite my best efforts to take AOCB off the agenda, and I did stop putting it on, our chairperson would still ask the question.

The June meeting was different in two aspects. Again, we would begin with a PowerPoint presentation where we would show the work we had planned for the coming winter along with the reasons. This might take the form of course changes, gorse management, drainage, or which tournaments might be coming up and their impact on course closures. Like February we might pre-empt some of the points we knew they were going to ask. Then came the course reports which, eventually, we managed to change from 'inspection' to 'visit'. Also, by then, each Club was asked to make contact with the relevant course manager beforehand so the representatives and he could go on a joint visit. Sometimes the course manager would take his deputy or third-in-charge along and there would be a lot of explanations about the different tasks the greenstaff carried out and why. From that point of view, it was a beneficial learning experience for all parties. The golfers would understand about course maintenance, which in many instances they would relay back to their friends, and the staff would get experience of talking to committee members. This proved very successful as an exercise in public relations as the members of the ICLC were constantly changing. The people who carried out each visit would then come to the meeting to discuss the contents of their reports, where, because they had already covered all the matters with the course manager, it usually ran smoothly. At the completion of each meeting, everyone was invited to stay for a glass of wine or a soft drink and where the chat would be about the Links in general or some of the topics from the meeting. Some of the course managers didn't care much for this part, especially the ones who didn't play golf. While I appreciated they had been in at work since before 6am that morning and it was now after 6pm, I thought it was important that they stay and mix with what was essentially our local 'customers' and build a relationship with them.

It took a while but all these changes were for the better and worked particularly well latterly. The fact the courses were in much better condition than when these meetings began probably helped.

At the time of writing this book, most of the points I listed earlier are still on the agenda some three years after I've retired!

Chapter 7. John Daly and Sherry
for Tea, the 1995 Open

T HE FIRST Major tournament I was involved in was the 1995
Open Championship. This made the Dunhill Cups played over
the Old Course each autumn pale into insignificance as regards
infrastructure and spectator numbers and of course it was held in July,
meaning growing conditions and how the golf course was presented
and played were completely different.

I'd experienced a number of Opens previously as either a
spectator or as a member of the BIGGA support team, where we would
be allocated a group to follow round and rake any bunkers the players
went into. At some venues the BIGGA team would also help with divot
repairs and pick up the old divots in the evenings after golf was finished.
As it happens, I was on the support team at St Andrews in 1990.

When I began at St Andrews in September 1991, the damage
caused by the temporary infrastructure used for the 1990 Open was
still visible in places, some fourteen months after the tournament.
On the Eden course the worst affected areas were the fairways and
roughs to the right of the 2nd and 3rd holes where vehicles had driven
to deliver everything required to build and dismantle the spectator
stands and catering tents. At that time there was no route from a main
road to get them to the 11th, 12th and 13th greens of the Old Course
without driving on these Eden course fairways and roughs. Access to
the holes up to the 10th could be gained by using the roadway which
separated the Old and New courses via the Jubilee maintenance facility.
Alternatively, the traffic could travel out the West Sands Road then
along a roadway crossing the Jubilee and New to the 9th green of the
Old. During the tournament there were service vehicles driving these
two fairways as well as thousands of spectators trampling them and
it took a couple of years to repair the damage to the Eden. Before the
1995 Open I was able to convince Walter and the GSC that we should

build a new road to join the one which ended adjacent to the 1st green of the Eden. This would run along holes 2 and 3, then on past behind the large double green at 7 and 11 on the Old Course to join the road which stopped beside the 8th green of the New, just to the side of the Old Course 7th green. This was a distance of some 1,200m, much of it through heavy gorse which was a good thing as it was hidden and mostly out of play from golf. After getting approval to go ahead, Eddie Adams and his team on the Old worked alongside myself and the Eden team to get the road completed in time for the Open infrastructure build to begin in April. This made an unbelievable difference in reducing damage to those 2nd and 3rd fairways on the Eden, not just through the time around the Open Championship but throughout the year. We greenkeepers now had a route to use when driving trailers of turf, sand etc. rather than drive on the fairways or semi-roughs. It also helped cut down on wear on the Old Course as, although it was much longer, all vehicular traffic would go by this route rather than cut across the Old at various points. We had to leave the finish as aggregate topped off with crushed cockleshell to appease the golfers but still many of them complained, unwilling to see the improvement to the main play areas. These aggregate roads constantly required maintaining as they became full of potholes following wet weather, especially in winter when greenstaff were transporting heavy trailers around them. Cockleshell was becoming increasingly expensive as it had to be transported from the south of England. It would also cause numerous punctures to our ride-on mowers for the first few weeks as some shells could be sharp until they broke down further. Oh, and it smelt of fish! This improvement gave me the idea to add more roads around the courses to allow better access for greenkeeping equipment and where possible get them finished in tarmacadam. It was always an ongoing battle to achieve this but by the time I retired I did manage to get a lot of roadways completed and left a sizeable amount of money in the 2019 budget to tar a significant section which my successor completed in 2019 and 2020.

As the head greenkeeper on the Eden, my involvement in the maintenance and daily set up of the Old the week of the Open was limited. As it was July, the grass was still growing and the Eden was closed for only nine days. It closed at the end of play on the Saturday prior to the Open and opened again at 9am on the Monday, the day after the tournament finished. There was provision to delay opening until the

Tuesday if the tournament ran over to the Monday. Therefore, we had to continue to cut greens through Open week though that was reduced to every second day, as well as cut tees, surrounds and fairways at least twice through the course of the week. We also had to rope off many of the greens nearer the Old Course to prevent vehicles from being driven over them by the contractors working for the TV companies and other organisations which support the Open. It's amazing how many people involved in that type of work have no idea about golf and couldn't tell a green from a field. Of course, we had to take all these fences down again first thing on the Monday morning along with putting out the tee boxes, markers and pins, rake bunkers and cut greens so we could get the course ready for play at 9am. To help, we cut new holes along with cutting the green surrounds on the Sunday before players began their final round of the Open.

All the greenstaff on every team helped out at the Open as it was such an important tournament and as soon as they were finished on the Old, they went back to their respective courses to get as much done as they could before play started. This was to avoid noise interfering with play although there are certain areas of the Links far enough away from the Old Course where it was possible to carry out some work without causing any disturbance. I can't recall exactly the task I was given in 1995 but the idea I was cutting fairways each morning seems to be lodged there in the back of my mind and I came back in the evenings to help with divoting fairways.

What I do remember from that Open wasn't related to the course which was in good shape and well received by the players. Most of us knew that this was going to be Walter's last Open and he delegated a lot of his responsibility over to Eddie Adams, the Old Course head greenkeeper. I remember that early on the Thursday there was an incident with Mark O'Meara who, when he arrived at the 15th green, thought the hole was not completely round and suggested it was too small. There was a bit of a panic and Eddie came to me and asked if he could borrow my cup setter. In 1995 I was the only head greenkeeper at the Links who had, and used, a cup setter to make sure the hole cup was set at the correct distance below the surface of the green. As the new cup was sunk down, this tool also ensured the hole was perfectly rounded and prevented the new hole being 'crowned'. On the other courses the staff would just bang the metal cup down with a cleek until they thought it was at the correct depth. This sometimes left it too shallow, meaning the ball could hit the rim and bounce out. More often than not, it was sunk too deep and the hole would quickly look scruffy. Eddie went off with my cup setter which fitted into the hole perfectly, proving the hole was the correct size and Mark O'Meara was mistaken. Crisis averted. It did cause Eddie to be as upset as I had ever seen him, concerned over the fact it was his first Open in charge, and this was all it would be remembered for. All I could say was that in the minds of anyone who mattered, it would never be given a second thought, especially since there was nothing wrong, and by the Friday it would be completely forgotten about.

In 1995, I was fortunate to be the chairman of the Scottish Region of BIGGA and as such, had a number of duties to undertake away from work. The association always had a hospitality unit in the tented village for the support team to relax in and also act as a place for greenkeepers attending the golf to meet and socialise. In 1995 they were very fortunate to be allocated the new Madras Rugby Club clubhouse near the 17th green of the Old Course. The most memorable task I had to do was present Arnold Palmer with a crystal tankard in recognition of what he had done for the greenkeeping profession throughout his career. It was going to be Arnie's last Open and it was something the Scottish Region had agreed to do as a way of getting some publicity to raise the profile of the association. The only thing was that Barry Heaney, the chairman of BIGGA at the time and who was attending the Open, wanted to get in on the act. Therefore, after we made the necessary arrangements with the R&A, the two of us met with Palmer on the first tee prior to his practice round on the Wednesday to present him with the tankard. There were official photographs taken and, at a later date, I was fortunate to have Arnold sign one of them.

Presenting Arnie with a gift at the 1995 Open.

That Open was the first time I heard the name Dr Rich Hurley* and although I never met him that week, my friend Iain MacLeod, head greenkeeper at Tain GC in the north of Scotland, met him in the BIGGA hospitality area where they began chatting. They went on to be good friends and Iain asked me to host Rich and his friend Joe O'Donnell on the Old Course when they were over from America a couple of years later. Since then, Rich and I have met almost every year, either here or in the States, and together have played most of the links courses in the UK. That chance meeting between Iain and Dr Hurley led to what was to become one of the most positive influences in my career, in fact I'd go as far as to say that Rich had a bigger influence on my career than any other individual. My subsequent friendship with him became invaluable when I was promoted to Links Superintendent in 2000. His knowledge of the turf industry, in particular the seed and turf business, was vast. His advice, support and the contacts and experts he was able to put me in touch with, gave me the ability to carry out my role far better than I could ever have achieved alone. This was a huge help not only for me, but my staff, my employers and all those who golfed at St Andrews. Together we've had the opportunity to play some of the greatest golf courses in the world.

The turf industry is full of individuals and organisations who are willing to help others in different ways and I've been fortunate throughout my career to have many of these people support me. Whether it was other course managers, agronomists, architects or people in the equipment, fertiliser and other areas of the industry, almost everyone I've met , in some small way, assisted me in my career.

But the 1995 Open was special for a completely different reason which was nothing to do with my job but the fact my wife Pauline was driving the courtesy cars. We sent the children to their grandparents for the week and she set off on the Sunday morning with her new Rover to pick up her first player. I'd asked her on the Saturday who she was to pick up and she replied, "I've got to collect a Tiger Woods, whoever he is!" Tiger of course was still an amateur, albeit the reigning US

---

* Dr Rich Hurley was initially a superintendent but went back to college before becoming involved in breeding new grass varieties. Some of the grasses he helped develop, (especially the bentgrasses), are used on some of the top courses around the world and he'll advise on managing these grass types. He has consulted at many of the top clubs, including Augusta National, where he worked as a volunteer on the greenstaff for thirty consecutive Masters. He also worked as a lecturer at Rutger University in New Jersy on their turf programme for many years. Rich occasionally caddied for Australian Bruce Crampton while at university in the early 70s, when Crampton was near the top of the PGA money list.

Amateur Champion, and this was his first Open but the golfing world had heard all about his arrival. He'd been playing in the Scottish Open at Carnoustie the week before and Pauline had to pick him and his father up from Carnoustie and drop him at Rufflets Hotel on the edge of town where they were staying as guests of Jack Nicklaus and Tom Watson.

All the talk was of his rivalry with the top UK Amateur of the time, Scotland's Gordon Sherry. Sherry had won the British Amateur earlier that year and had also been runner-up in 1994. He had just finished 4th in the Scottish Open, while he had a hole in one at the 8th in a practice round at St Andrews playing with Jack Nicklaus and Tom Watson, so he was on form. The press was all over this fight for the Silver Medal as leading Amateur but ironically, Englishman Steve Webster scored a final round 73 to Sherry's 76 to pip him by a shot. Still, Sherry won a £1 side bet off Tiger by finishing two ahead of him, Tiger scoring 78 in round 4.

Pauline drove Tiger again in one of the practice rounds, taking him and his father from their hotel to the course. They waited ages in the car for his father, Tiger at one stage saying, "You'll have to excuse my dad, he's as slow as molasses." She also drove Seve as she was the only driver in the courtesy car waiting room one afternoon who knew the area when Seve came in with his children and wanted to go to a playpark. When they arrived at the park, she even gave them her umbrella as it was starting to rain, then forgot to get it back! It was great for me and my friends, as when she wasn't busy, she gave us a lift down to a pub in town a couple of times and we could imagine the people peering at the darkened glass wondering which 'star' was in the car. If only they knew!

When Pauline came home from driving on the Monday evening, I asked her who all she had driven that day. One of the players was Gordon Sherry and when they were chatting he was lamenting the fact he was having to stay in Cupar, some ten miles away and was missing out on all the action. I jokingly said that he could stay with us as the children were away and the next morning at work, I thought it wasn't actually that stupid an idea. Once I'd completed my tasks for the day, I went off in search of him practising. The first person I approached was his caddie and I said I'd heard he was looking for somewhere in town and that I might have somewhere. He called Gordon over and I explained my wife had driven him yesterday and that they could stay with us. I think they smelt a rat in that I would rip them off, so when they asked the price I said £20 per night, (my wife had told me they were paying £25 in Cupar). We arranged to meet when they finished his round and I would take him and show him where we stayed, then I called Pauline who thought I was joking. When she realised I was serious, all she could think about was we hadn't tidied up the house since the children left and where was he going to sleep exactly because he was 6' 7" tall. We ended up turning our daughter's toy-box upside down, adding it to the bottom of the bed and putting a pillow on top of it while his caddie slept on one of the boys' bunks. They were great company to have around the house for the week and on the Saturday evening, Gordon's mother and father came round for a cup of tea. He was eight shots off the leader Michael Campbell but wasn't far off second place and realistically thought there was no reason he couldn't finish second or if he scored really well, actually win the Open. It wasn't arrogance or big headedness but the thoughts of a golfer who was very comfortable and confident in his game at that time.

House guest Gordon Sherry with his caddy and Pauline (standing on a wall) beside her courtesy car.

When he left on the Sunday, he left behind a whole lot of signed hats and other goodies for the children who were so jealous they'd missed out.

Of course, he didn't win and John Daly beat Constantino Rocca in a playoff after Rocca holed that outrageous putt on the 72nd hole to tie. What many people forget is that Daly holed a much longer putt with multiple breaks on it at the 2nd hole of that play-off. There was a fairly stiff breeze blowing across the course from right to left coming down the closing holes and only one player broke 70 in that last round, Steven Bottomley scoring 69 to move into a tie for third. Daly scored a fine 71 and for all that people talk about his long driving, it was his deft touch around and on the greens that won him the title 'Champion Golfer of the Year'.

After the presentation ceremony Pauline's last drive of the day was to take Constantino Rocca back to his hotel. Once in the car he asked her to take him for some cigarettes first, so they drove to the Shell garage in town where there was a lengthy queue waiting to get snacks, soft drinks etc. Pauline said they all parted like the waves and applauded Rocca to the front of the queue. Scottish hospitality.

Me? I went out for a few beers with the greenstaff and can't say for certain what time I got home but I was back in at work for 5am on Monday morning to get the Eden course ready for play.

Chapter 8. My First Visits to America and The Masters

AFTER WALTER retired there was a significant difference in the greenkeeping department as things began to change. With each of the head greenkeepers given more responsibility on how we managed our own courses and do things we thought would benefit them, there was an overall improvement in many areas. Meetings between the head greenkeepers and Ian Forbes, although held less often than previously, became more structured and valuable. Ian could be approached directly and a case put forward requesting a particular product or other small items. There was more discipline within the teams although there were still things going on which some head greenkeepers kept hidden from him.

Even before Walter retired, a change in the department resulted in a huge improvement to my team in particular. That was the introduction of deputy head greenkeepers to each team. While most teams were content to go with one of their existing staff for the position on their team, Roddy Barron and I were allowed to take someone from outwith the existing workforce. We both felt strongly there was no-one in any of the teams we thought capable of filling the role. We each had a greenkeeping student from Elmwood College coming in one day per week as a volunteer to gain experience. Their work ethic and enthusiasm compared to the existing staff was like night and day. The person I had helping on the Eden was a mature student called Richard Barnham who was changing career. Richard had a college degree and background in agriculture and had done a bit of travelling, at one stage managing a sheep ranch in New Zealand. He was fast tracking through the college system with the knowledge and experience he had already gained and had a lot of sound, practical ideas with the theory to back them up. He also wasn't scared of hard work or what the full-time staff thought of him. He thought nothing of putting a strimmer over his shoulder and walking over thirty minutes from the Jubilee sheds out to the middle of the Eden course, just to strim down an area he thought was looking untidy. The permanent staff wouldn't even have noticed something like that was needing to be done and if they'd been instructed to do it, they would have needed a vehicle to get there and probably suggested it was a two-man job. Even though he'd only worked with me one day per week for a few months, I knew he had the drive, skill and knowledge to do a good job. Roddy also went with his volunteer who had an agricultural background along with a good work ethic.

On the Old, New and Jubilee courses, they simply gave the positions to the three longest serving members of their existing team. The three individuals concerned had no management experience or skills and they were never encouraged to change or improve. It was very much carry on as you were in those teams other than they now had a 'deputy' and it allowed a couple of the head greenkeepers to spend even more time in their office or, in one case, away from work. Of the three selected, they all went back to the position of greenkeeper over time because they never acquired those key skills and weren't fulfilling the role.

Richard was ambitious and hanging around as deputy on the Eden was never going to be a long-term plan, in fact it wasn't even a mid-term one and within a very short period of time he secured a full-time job in the south of England which was nearer home for him. I again went outside the Links for a replacement and after interviewing several candidates, I offered the job to Gordon McKie. Gordon had completed his apprenticeship at Tain Golf Club in the Highlands of Scotland under a friend of mine, Iain MacLeod. I also knew him from his attendance at BIGGA outings and conferences and he had recently come on to the committee of the North section. Although I had moved into the Central area, I still retained my membership of the North section for a spell as it allowed me to get away from St Andrews and to meet up with old friends a couple of times a year. Being a close-knit industry, when looking around for staff it doesn't take much to make contact with someone you know and trust to get sound advice on a potential employee if you don't know that person yourself. I already knew Gordon reasonably well and to get the reassurance from his boss about his qualities just gave me confidence in my decision. Gordon went on to fulfil many roles at the Links over the following 25 plus years and became course manager of the Old Course in 2007.

April 1996 saw the opening of the Eden Greenkeeping Centre, (EGC), which was a milestone as far as both Roddy and I were concerned as it allowed us to operate much more efficiently being nearer to our respective courses. It was built at a cost of over £500,000 and opened by one-time Home Secretary, The Right Honourable Willie Whitelaw. A keen golfer and a member of the R&A, he was President of BIGGA from 1988 until 1998.

The Right Honourable Willie Whitelaw opening the EGC with some of the Eden and Strathtyrum teams.

Roddy and I had a lot of input into the design, along with the Links' Health & Safety advisor Douglas Shearer from Elmwood. This meant there was plenty of room for everything, other than the very largest pieces of equipment, to be kept under cover. There were separate, secure buildings for fertiliser and seed, storage under cover for topdressing materials, underground petrol tanks and a dedicated wash down area.

The move also helped raise the morale of the staff of the two courses as, for the first time, they had good facilities to work from and take their breaks. There were proper showers and drying rooms for any wet clothes, as well as individual lockers for their everyday wear, while the canteen and toilets were cleaned daily by the Links cleaning team.

A new fleet of Ransomes equipment had been recently purchased and while we allowed room for a 15% increase in the equipment fleet, this was taken up a lot sooner than we anticipated! The only thing which didn't go down particularly well was something introduced across all the Links buildings and that was the 'No Smoking' rule.

The new Jubilee Greenkeeping Centre, (JGC), was opened the following July in the same place as the existing sheds were but in a completely different layout, the difference between the new and old sheds were like chalk and cheese. At over twice the size of the Eden Greenkeeping Centre, which it needed to be, it was probably the largest greenkeeping facility in Europe. Costing over £1 million and with all the same attributes and additional outbuildings as the Eden had, it was a facility worthy of the Home of Golf. The JGC had a fully-fitted workshop where the mechanics were based and as such, all the larger repairs and all the reel sharpening* took place there with only basic servicing and small repairs taking place at the EGC. It also had a meeting room where teams could meet or carry out training and we moved the GSC meetings there. Both the JGC and EGC projects were overseen by Ian Forbes as was the Links Clubhouse which opened prior to the Open in 1995.

The new Jubilee maintenance facility

---

* Reel sharpening. This is when the cutting blades of the mowers are placed onto a machine specifically designed to sharpen them. On greens mowers, this process is usually carried out approximately monthly through the growing season and is a skilled, technical task.

With the new facilities, better equipment and more money available, course conditions began to improve across all the courses, although perhaps less so on the Old which had always been slightly better than the others. Within the greenkeeping department there were a few new members of staff beginning to gradually appear as existing ones left for various reasons and we were also able to increase staff numbers. I had certainly managed to build a much better team although it was still far from ideal while Roddy, now that the Strathtyrum had been up and running for a few years, had a larger team than he started with. He needed the additional staff as he undertook a fairly large programme of improvements to the greens surrounds, along with building more tees to lengthen the course. The Strathtyrum had been built on very flat farmland, most on a very nice sandy loam. To give it character all the greens were raised. It's a relatively short course, originally only measuring 5,004 yards with a par of 69. It was built to suit the older golfers, ladies, juniors and beginners and it quickly became popular. With its raised greens, it's a great course for sharpening up approach shots from inside 100 yards and for improving a player's overall short game, irrespective of ability. As there was plenty of room available, Roddy was given permission from the LMC to build new medal tees on almost every hole and increase the overall length to over 5,600 yards. A much larger project was the improvement of the greens' surrounds. Although the greens had been built to a very loose UGSA specification[*], the surrounds were built with any material the contractors could lay their hands on. If any building work was going on locally, then any unwanted rubble from the site was taken down to the Links for this purpose. There was also a great deal of material taken from the new pond installed between the new 14th and 15th holes of the Eden. The pond was built for drainage purposes as well as being part of the design but the material had poor drainage qualities. Add the fact the contouring and mounding of the surrounds were really sharp which made it impossible to aerate most areas. On the parts that could be aerated, the machine would bounce off the rocks etc. that were just under the surface. It was even difficult to cut some parts as they were so acute. Even though he wasn't a golfer, Roddy had a great eye for this type of work and over a number of winters he and his team rebuilt

---

[*] USGA specification. A method devised by the USGA of building a green which conforms to certain criteria, particularly drainage. As a very basic principle, above any drainage channels there is a layer of gravel followed by 300mm of compacted sand, both fitting into precise size bands.

something like 16 or 17 of the 18 surrounds. In most green complexes this would have involved digging out 75% of the surround to a depth of over two feet where they literally did find things like kitchen sinks, parts of toilets and numerous huge rocks. The majority of this was done by hand where staff would dig out the old material with spades as there wasn't always a digger available. The area was then filled with a good sand, soil mix and the mounds made much softer, allowing them to be aerated and more easily cut. To break up the open look of the holes, some of what was taken out of the surrounds was used to mound parts of the rough between holes. This aspect of the changes wasn't as successful as the material was too rich leading to excessive growth. The mounding, like the original surrounds, was too sharp so the team went back at a later date and softened them, covering them with a sandier material to reduce growth.

Prior to Walter retiring, he arranged for the Links to rent a 10-acre field from a neighbouring farmer so we would have enough turf for rebuilding the bunkers. Up until then this was a challenge as, following the changes to the courses, there was hardly anywhere we could take turf from. The field in question was three miles from the courses on the main road towards Cupar and Dundee, which wasn't ideal as it was a busy commuter route. Through the winter, car drivers could get frustrated being held up by two or three tractors and trailers running in convoy at under 30mph. The soil wasn't a typical sandy links profile as it was the same silty material as the lower holes at the far end of the Eden and Strathtyrum courses, but it was okay for revetting* bunker faces.

The good thing about this field was, being next to the estuary, it didn't suffer much from frost and often on a winter's morning when the courses were frozen, staff could go there and still be able to lift the turf. Through the worst periods of the winter the staff would often go and fill trailers of turf in the afternoons and leave them inside overnight so they could start building the following morning. Every time we removed turf, we also took around two inches of soil so we were always on the lookout for developers starting new building projects to see if there was excess topsoil, providing it was decent quality, to build the ground

---

* Revetting. The process of building or rebuilding the face of a bunker by stacking rows of turf on top of each other in a manner similar to building a brick wall. Each piece of turf would be approximately two feet long by six inches deep and two inches thick. How much the next row is laid back from the face of the one beneath determines the steepness of the face.

level back up. We would often acquire this for free or for the cost of the transport as the developer would otherwise have to pay for the its disposal. It wasn't long before we began renting another ten acres in the next field and we ran a pipe from the far end of the Eden course, out along the edge of the old railway line so we could get water to any newly seeded areas. Around that time, the Links agreed to give up a strip of their land within the tree belt which separated the Strathtyrum course from the main A91 road. This was to help the local authority build a cycle track from St Andrews to Guardbridge. They did this with the proviso that Links staff could use the track to get tractors and other vehicles to the turf nursery, thereby keeping them off the main road. Any topsoil going to the nursery had to run along this track for the last 100 yards and the size of the lorries caused us a few surface repair bills over the years.

1995 until 2000 was a relatively quiet time on the Eden, most of it being spent simply trying to improve the course as best I could. It was bliss being away from the other three teams and some of the nonsense which went on. There was a small turnover of staff which strengthened the team but work on the course was uneventful until nearer the end of the decade. There wasn't too much movement on the other courses and as a whole there wasn't a large turnover of staff during my first ten years. Many of the staff had little intention of moving, since few of them had much ambition to move up the career ladder. In 1997 Eddie increased the size of his team to help prepare for the 2000 Open as one of the requirements was to construct new tees on Holes, 3, 7, 10, 13, 15 and 16 adding a total of approx. 170 yards to the overall length of the course while the 6th tee was extended slightly to the right. He brought in five experienced people on a fixed-term contract from around the country. All of them stayed beyond the length of their contract and after leaving they went on to have successful careers at other courses, with one eventually moving into golf club management.

With having more responsibility and control in how we managed our own courses, some of us began trying new products that had either come on the market or which we were unable to obtain previously. One such product was grass seed and we would look at the annual STRI quality listings and purchase the seed which came top of their lists rather than a cheaper mix that used poorer performing varieties. These were invariably varieties produced by a Dutch company named Barenbrug and after a year or two it was suggested we enter an agreement with them. Ian Forbes did all the background work and in late 1997 we signed an agreement that we would only use Barenbrug seed on the courses which is still the arrangement to this day, albeit the contract has been renegotiated and changed a few times in the intervening years.

One of the bonuses of the deal was that the head greenkeepers and Ian were invited over to Holland to the Barenbrug headquarters in Arnhem, where they had one of their research stations along with a production plant. In mid-April 1998, the week after I had returned from being at The Masters, a group of us set off for a three-day trip which we found interesting in more ways than one. Our host was their European Manager, a larger-than-life personality, and we learned about producing a new cultivar and the qualities required. This was through a mixture of presentations and visiting their breeding and trial areas. Most people will be unaware that it's a fifteen-year process to take a new seed from first development to get it to the market, and many varieties fail to make it to that final stage. After two days and one night at their HQ, the final night was spent in Amsterdam prior to our flight home the following day. It's probably best I end the story there and leave the rest to your imagination other than to say our host left us to our own devices after dinner, telling us he was off to see his 'aunt' who lived in Amsterdam. Aye, right! As well as more alcohol, I seem to remember our night involved window shopping, cake, table tennis balls and bananas although not all at the same time or in that order.

Ian Forbes with some of the head greenkeepers and Barenbrug managers in 1998.

ılly we would visit Arnhem every alternate year but in smaller
ually a mixture of head greenkeepers and deputies. This
...as an opportunity for different people to increase their knowledge
as our staff was gradually changing over time. It then tailed off to
more infrequent trips, not always to Holland, as we visited some of
the trial grounds Barenbrug had in Ireland and England. In 2007, with
Barenbrug's help, we set up our own trials at both the Castle course and
the Links

The Trustees approved a plan to replace the entire Links irrigation
system with the latest 'state of the art' one from Toro, featuring the
Sitepro computer control system. This was going to be a project costing
over £1million and was to be completed over two winters. Phase 1
was going to cover the Eden, Strathtyrum and Balgove, and the Golf
Academy. This would be carried out in the winter of 1998/1999 with
the second phase taking place after the 2000 Open on the Old, New
and Jubilee courses. This was the first time I met Adrian Mortram who
worked for Robin Hume of Robin Hume Associates, the company who
designed the system.

A young Adrian Mortram training me on the new Toro Sitepro irrigation system.

Adrian went on to take over the company after Robin retired and became a good friend, carrying out all the irrigation upgrades on the Links after that. He is one of the best in his field.

There had been irrigation on the Old Course for much longer than people would have imagined, possibly before the 1950s. There are a couple of small circular depressions behind the 12th green which seem to sink every few years giving rise to the thought they were wells at one time. The next water source was a reservoir some two miles away on the outskirts of St Andrews at Cairnsmill which is on the way to Leven on the A915. As this reservoir was at a much higher elevation than the Links, it ran by gravity from there through the town to the courses in pipes. In the late 80s the Links Trust then sank a borehole on ground belonging to the University on the North Haugh, depositing the abstracted water into the Swilcan burn. Staff would then dam the burn just before it left the 1st fairway and headed out to sea and would pump the water back to the holding tank by the Jubilee sheds. The irrigation system being replaced dated from the 1970s and was constantly bursting. The pipework was PVC plastic of six metre lengths glued together at each join, where it would come apart. This pipework was linked throughout all the courses and it was very difficult to isolate any particular area which meant when there was a burst, the entire system had to be shut down. If that happened on a large pipe, or through the night, then we usually had to wait for the water level to recede before digging out the area to find the burst, which the workshop staff would come and repair. Sometimes we had to wait a couple of days for the water level to drop which meant no-one could irrigate their courses. The sprinklers were a mixture of the impact head type and some gear driven ones made by Toro, but they were so old and had been damaged so often, the coverage was very poor. When I discovered I was coming to a course which had an irrigation system that covered greens, tees and fairways I was ecstatic, but the reality was it proved nothing but a headache initially.

First up was the building of a new storage tank beside the existing one which would give a total capacity of just under one million gallons. The new water source was four new boreholes at the other side of the complex. The first one was on the corner of the Balgove course with each subsequent borehole approx 400m along the boundary of the Balgove and Strathtyrum course, running parallel with the main A91 road. These were all sunk to a depth of around 55m to find the aquifers, and from each location the water was pumped back to the holding tank at the JGC. A considerable trench was required to lay these pipes into as it crossed the Balgove, two holes of the Strathtyrum, the 1st fairway of the Eden, the 15th and 4th fairways of the Old Course, one hole of the New course then behind the 16th green before crossing the 2nd fairway of the Jubilee. We employed the services of local drainage contractor John Meiklem who carried out all our drainage work as he had the expertise to lay it at the depth required to prevent accidental damage in the future.

Next was the installation of the new pipework and sprinklers to the Eden, Strathtryum and Balgove courses which were installed by TIS Sandbach over the winter. This was mostly mole-ploughed in to reduce surface disruption, the new pipe being MDPE which was fusion welded at each joint. There were enough gate valves fitted throughout the system that if there was a burst, each individual fairway could be isolated without disturbing the flow to any other area. The sprinklers were the latest available models and each normal sized green would on average have four, each one being individually controlled. This meant the amount of water used could be managed much more efficiently. Everything was linked to a computer in each head greenkeeper's office and the sprinklers could be turned on and off via a hand-held radio.

Laying the transfer for the new irrigation system from the boreholes back to the JGC. Seen here passing behind the 16th green of the New course.

Once all courses were complete there would be over 4000 sprinklers across the Links and more than seventy miles of pipework and cable.

Until then the Links had seldom used seasonal staff other than the occasional one on the Old Course. In 1998 the Toro Company and the Canadian Superintendents Association started the 'Future Superintendent's Award', part of which was a trip to Scotland to take in some greenkeeping courses at Elmwood College, followed by a couple of weeks working at St Andrews. The other head greenkeepers weren't interested in being involved, therefore the first winner of the award, Kerry Watkins, came to help on the Eden for two weeks. The drive and enthusiasm he brought with him was a breath of fresh air although it didn't go down particularly well with the full-time staff. He was more than a little surprised by their attitude, given they were working at arguably the most famous golf complex in the world. Like me when I first arrived, he couldn't understand why they didn't use the opportunity they had to secure better jobs within the industry rather than continually complain about the conditions at the Links. We continued to host the winner of this award for over fifteen years until the winning students began to make it more of a golf trip than a work based one.

1998 was the start of me travelling to some memorable places around the world although my first trip wasn't work related. It was a holiday trip to the Masters at Augusta combined with golf, and it happened through contacts in the industry. My friend Iain McLeod from Tain met Dr Rich Hurley in the BIGGA pavilion at the 1995 Open in St Andrews and they got chatting at the bar. Rich mentioned he was heading to Dornoch to play golf after the Open and as Iain worked just along the road, he invited him to Tain for a game. In return, Rich invited Iain to the 1996 Masters where Rich worked as a volunteer on the greenstaff for the tournament for a number of years. Rich, along with his company and Rutgers University, had developed the seed used at Augusta each year in their overseeding programme. He would rent a house in Augusta where the company would invite clients and take them to the tournament, so Iain had a base and off he went. In 1997, Iain called me to ask if I could arrange some golf in the St Andrews area for Rich and his friend Joe O'Donnell which naturally would include the Old Course. This I did, joining them for their game on the Old. Of course, I knew the story of Iain and the Masters so on the 5th hole, when Rich invited me over to Augusta the following year, I didn't hesitate in saying, "My flight's already booked!"

Joe stayed in Atlanta and was also in the seed business, managing Sunbelt Seeds, a distribution company affiliated to Lofts and this was the company which actually supplied Augusta. They said to bring a friend and we could stay at Joe's and play some golf beforehand. You could get entry to the Masters in those days through being a member of the GCSAA, so along with my former apprentice Charlie MacDonald, head greenkeeper at Crieff GC, we set off on a twelve-day trip to play golf and take in the Masters. Our time there could fill a book on its own and we were like rabbits in the headlights, country cousins gone to town. Joe and I really hit it off, having a similar sense of humour and although I don't see him as often as I do Rich, we still remain friends to this day. Through his contacts in the industry, Joe arranged for us to play some great golf courses in the Atlanta area. My very first game of golf in America was at the famed Peachtree GC where we played with the course superintendent, William Shirley. Now, I only consider myself a reasonable golfer while Charlie was very handy in his day, playing off scratch at one time. It still came as a shock when William stood up on the 1st tee and knocked his drive onto the front of the green some 360 yards away.

It was on that trip Joe christened me with the nickname Rooster. It came about when we played at The Farm, an excellent course at Dalton just outside Atlanta with the course superintendent Tim Kinnelly who also played off scratch. (What is it with these American superintendents?) Tim was at the top of his backswing on one tee when his assistant came on the radio for him and he still striped it 280 yards down the middle of the fairway. We came to the 12th hole, a mid-length Par 5 with a burn, or creek as the Americans call it, running across the front of the green. The three of them were winding me up by saying how, being the short hitter, I wouldn't get on the green in two while this was a great birdie opportunity for them. It turned out I was the only one who did carry the burn, hit the green in two and make birdie. Then on the next hole I sunk a long putt across the green for a second consecutive birdie. When I looked up, Joe was busy discussing some blemishes on the green with Tim and they never even commented on my putt so I said something along the lines of, "I've just made back-to-back birdies and no one even said well done." Being as sharp as a tack, Joe used that opportunity to change the facts to his version which was that I was strutting around the green with my chest puffed out like a cockerel or rooster, (which I probably was), and the name has stuck ever since.

There was one day we were rained off completely but that wasn't a problem as we both had 'shopping lists' from our wives of things we had to buy, so we headed off to a mall. After a full day shopping, (I bought so much I filled the extra suitcase I brought plus had things in Charlie's golf bag which put it overweight on our return flight), I fancied a beer or rather a proper pint to be more precise. I asked a guy on the checkout of a store where there might be a bar, as he looked as if he liked a beer. He suggested we go to one called Oasis which we recognised as we'd seen the signs for it a few times from the Interstate on our regular route back to Joe's. It was still pouring with rain and by this time it was dark, but we soon found it and pulled into the car park. Within seconds of getting out of the car we heard a gunshot and made a quick decision to run for the entrance. We were so naïve we just thought it strange there was a cover charge to get in, and again when I got a pile of single dollars back in my change from a $20 note for two beers. It had been an interval and it was only as we were finishing the beers the dancing girls arrived. We had been sent to a lap dancing bar and for fifteen minutes had been blissfully unaware that's what it was!

Attending the Masters was an eye-opening experience, even though we were only there for two days. My abiding memory is from first walking in and looking over the course from the area beside the first tee and how I was struck by the 'green-ness' of it all. It's surprisingly hilly, an aspect the tv pictures don't convey. Joe had arranged for us to visit the maintenance facility where we saw more equipment than there would be at an exhibition. There were mowers from all of the large manufacturers as Augusta wasn't tied to a single company though some of them were painted battleship grey with no logos. We were able to talk briefly to Marsh Benson, the superintendent, but as he and everyone else was busy, we didn't want to overstay our welcome. We had planned to watch the Par 3 event on the Wednesday but it was cancelled due to thunderstorms. This meant we couldn't take any pictures as cameras weren't allowed on tournament days. We decided to ignore that rule but were very careful not to show our cameras when play was underway. When play was on the back nine, we decided to go and walk the front nine to have a better look at the golf course and perhaps see them cutting the fairways in formation. A greenkeeper was cutting the fourth green and I thought it worthy of a picture but as I was taking it, he went straight onto his two-way radio and we could hear him reporting us, even describing what we were wearing! We ran off into the nearby trees, carrying the bags of merchandise we'd purchased earlier, while stripping off our waterproof jackets and sweaters to change our appearance. We escaped unscathed.

A greenkeeper cutting the 4th green at the 1998 Masters.
Just before he spotted us taking his picture.

Due to work and flights we had to leave Augusta on the Saturday and flew home overnight on the Sunday via Amsterdam therefore we didn't know who won. Sitting in Schiphol airport I caught a glimpse of a European newspaper and could see a headline featuring Fred Couples and we assumed he was the winner as he had been leading after each of the first three rounds. When we arrived at Edinburgh, the family told me it was Mark O'Meara. I didn't believe them at first but the newspaper in Schiphol and its reference to Couples had been the previous day's newspaper!

Being my first trip to America, I was blown away by the condition of the courses we visited and played, and not just Augusta. Even allowing for the fact every one was what could be described as 'high end', there was little to find fault with. Listening to Joe discuss things, such as fertiliser requirements and maintenance programmes with each superintendent was a learning experience in itself, especially the fine detail and margins they spoke of. If there was anything we saw which we thought unusual, then Joe was brilliant at providing an explanation. Two other things I learned, or found surprising, were that most of the courses were built on clay, therefore drainage was an issue on them. Atlanta is in what they call the 'transition' zone, which means that both cool and warm season grasses find it difficult to grow at particular times of the year. The winters are too cold for warm season grasses and the summers too hot for cool season ones, although bent grass greens will survive the summer with careful management and skilled watering. In September, the courses either overseed their fairways with ryegrass or the members have to play off dormant Bermuda grass through the winter. Most of the courses we played had chosen to overseed and Joe told us we'd become 'overseeding snobs'. Augusta National closes around the end of May, reopening in October once the newly overseeded ryegrass has established. A process which takes only a few weeks, how I wished that was the case in Scotland!

The week prior to travelling to the Masters was a very unusual one. It began with Steve Isaac calling to ask if I would mind meeting two gentlemen and showing them around the EGC as they were building a golf course and wanted to get a feel for the size of maintenance facility they might need. Their names were John Ashworth and Dave Thomas, but not the well-known ex-professional golfer who went on to have a second career as a golf course architect. This Dave Thomas was an Australian developer who lived in Bali, and the two of them had bought property immediately adjacent to Muirfield in East Lothian where they were going to build a 36-hole complex. I arranged to meet them on the Friday and after showing them around the building, we sat and had a chat in the office afterwards. It was only when I asked if there was anything else they wanted to know about the building they told me the reason for their visit wasn't just to look at the sheds but to find out if I'd be interested in the job of course manager, building and growing in their new development. I was interested but I was leaving for America on Tuesday which meant I didn't have any time to find out more about the project and they would be gone by the time I returned. They persuaded me to visit the site on the Sunday with my wife so we managed to arrange baby sitters and headed down. We spent the entire day looking at the property, called Archerfield, and seeing all their plans. During lunch in a café in the neighbouring town of Gullane, I was left alone for five minutes with John when I said, "I've only ever heard the name Ashworth once before, and that's the golf clothing company."

"Yes, that's me," he replied. Doh!

I didn't have to make my mind up immediately but thought a lot about it during my trip away. It was very appealing as the site had great potential and the areas we walked had good, sandy soil. Their plans were for a high-end complex which included accommodation in the very grand Archerfield House within the estate. After a lot of soul searching, I decided to turn it down and stay in St Andrews. It proved a wise decision as after initially starting the project, they sold it on during construction and the new owner dismissed the course manager they had hired and replaced him with his own man. It's turned out to be an excellent facility in a great area for golf.

It was a hectic three weeks between that, the Masters and then Holland.

In my time from 1991 to 1999, the majority of our grass cutting machinery and all our greenkeeping utility vehicles were manufactured by Ransomes, a UK based company from Ipswich. The only exception being the pedestrian greens mowers, (a walk-behind mower), which were Lloyds Paladins. There was no contract with Ransomes, the reason we used their equipment, (along with cost), would have evolved through good relationships developed between Walter, Dod McLaren and the local dealer.

Towards the end of the 20th century, management thought it would be beneficial if we looked at entering into a contract with one of the four main machinery companies, Ransomes, Toro, John Deere and Jabobsen, (Jacobsen didn't purchase the Ransomes company until 2003). Toro, Ransomes and Jacobsen were well established in grass machinery market whereas John Deere, who were renowned in the agricultural market, were only recently making inroads in the turf sector.

A local company based in Cupar, Double A, had become the John Deere dealer in the area and the company owner and managing director, Sandy Armit, invited two of us from the Links to go on a John Deere feedback trip to their global HQ in Illinois. Ian Forbes selected myself and workshop manager Dod McLaren to attend, and in October we travelled to Moline, Illinois for five days. It was a huge event with seventy turf industry professionals from the UK, quite a few of them greenkeepers I knew from around Scotland. The purpose of the trip was to operate some of their latest pieces of equipment to provide feedback of things we liked and what we thought could be improved upon before the equipment went to final production. We were treated extremely well as they organised trips to various places around the area known as the Quad Cities. They also provided every person with $200 cash on arrival to pay for any meals or other incidentals we might incur, although it turned out all meals throughout the trip were included. As well as visiting their Corporate HQ we were shown their museum and one of their production plants. An external tour was to the Rock Island Arsenal Museum, the second oldest Army Museum in the US, while we also visited the area's largest indoor venue for exhibitions and rock concerts. The day we were there we noticed Cher was playing a rearranged concert at the venue that night and I asked Sandy if he fancied going. When we enquired, we discovered there had been tickets returned as people couldn't make the new date, but Sandy thought them expensive. I had visited the local casino the first night we were there and had turned my $200 into over $800 and said I would treat him and bought a couple of tickets. The only thing was, we had an organised dinner with John Deere at 5pm that evening but one of their team said he would drive us from the dinner to the concert as soon as it finished. There was one other thing, the dinner was formal and we had brought our kilts. That didn't bother me but Sandy wanted to go back to the hotel and change so the driver dropped me at the concert, took Sandy back to change before dropping him back at the concert. We didn't realise that the support act was Cyndi Lauper and although I missed the beginning of her performance, Sandy missed it all. Our seats were about ten rows back from the front of the stage and I had the end seat on an aisle. At one point near the finish of her set, Cyndi Lauper came down from the stage and into the audience. I'm not sure if I was lucky or unlucky that she chose the other aisle to walk up! 3,000 people were there but I was the only one wearing a kilt, I think she would have noticed. Sandy arrived back at the interval and we had a great night. I think he secretly wished he hadn't gone back to change beforehand.

The only thing I found strange about the trip was they left the feedback part until the final morning by which time we were all a bit jaded. We were up very early and off to a nearby golf course where John Deere was given the use of part of their 9-hole course, but being October it was frosty so we were delayed a short while. When we were finished it was a quick lunch, then back on the bus for the three hours plus trip back to Chicago where we had an overnight stay and time to see some of the city the next morning before flying home.

Another Scot on the trip was Ronnie Bunting, head greenkeeper at Kilmacolm GC and chairman of the west section of BIGGA at the time. Ronnie had asked BIGGA for 100 business cards beforehand but ended up with 1000 which cost him a small fortune. On the flight back, after a few drinks, he went down the plane giving every single passenger a business card.

February 2000 saw me back in America, this time to the GCSAA show in New Orleans. In August 1999, I persuaded Ian Forbes that it would be good from an educational point of view to go to the American show where I could also check out the latest mowers from the major manufacturers. I suggested that it might be better if two of us went and it would be good to take a deputy rather than another head greenkeeper. The one Ian thought would be best was a very good golfer but wasn't much of a socialiser. A few weeks before we left, I was watching a programme on TV about New Orleans and Pauline hoped I had a great time. I told her I would, even though the person I was going with didn't drink or socialise much. Pauline replied I'd likely just leave him in the hotel and go out on my own.

We travelled out on the Saturday and Joe O'Donnell had arranged golf for us at English Turn on the Sunday with a friend of his, Dennis Hurley of The Turf Drainage Company of America. Our flight was late in landing at Atlanta and by the time we got through immigration we missed our connecting flight so it was after midnight before we got to our hotel, well over 24 hours since we left Scotland. We had a great round of golf on the Sunday and Dennis drove us back to our hotel through a thunderstorm. I asked him if he could recommend somewhere to eat and he said everywhere in New Orleans would be good. When we got back to the hotel and the rain had stopped, I suggested we go out and find a place to eat. My companion said he just wanted to go to MacDonald's to which I replied, "I wouldn't eat in MacDonald's in the UK, I'm damned if I'm going to eat in one here." Off we went and began looking at menus in restaurant windows but when I started to suggest various ones looked good, every suggestion was met with a, "No I don't really fancy this one." I finally quizzed him on what he didn't like about the different places when he told me that he didn't like music. S**t, I was going to be spending a week in New Orleans with a guy who didn't drink and didn't like music, what fun! We eventually found somewhere to eat which wasn't playing music. When we left the restaurant, I suggested going on somewhere else but he just wanted to go back to the hotel. I decided I would just go for a look around by myself but he didn't know how to get to the hotel, even though it was only three blocks away, so I ended up walking him back. The next day I sent Pauline a postcard which read, "Dear Pauline, having a good time. You were correct, first night by 9pm I'd dropped my fellow traveller back at the hotel and I'm OUT!". I only went for a scout around that night as we had a class the following morning but did discover why everyone had a fascination with beads.

We were able to walk to the convention centre where I had enrolled us both on a full day management course which started at 8am. I usually always preferred the management classes to the technical ones as they were more interactive and the presenters are generally better since that is their forte. Techie ones on soil science or fertilisers are more suited to American conditions and the products they use mightn't be available in the UK, plus they are sometimes delivered by a sales person or scientist whose skillset isn't presenting. As an ice breaker, the presenter asked us to take a few minutes to come up with something to say then we would each have to stand up and introduce ourselves to the other fifty or so students in the class. While doing this we could go for a coffee or a comfort break. I'd deliberately suggested the two of us should split up within the class as it's good to meet and chat with other greenkeepers but when we resumed after the break, I noticed he hadn't returned. I thought nothing of it but after thirty minutes he still hadn't reappeared, nor was there any sign of him at lunch. When I arrived back at the end of the day, he was back in the room and said he had been feeling unwell although he hadn't been sick and was now feeling a bit better. I asked if he had had something to eat and he said he hadn't so I suggested we go out as he must be starving but he said he was fine, he didn't fancy eating. As I was getting ready to go out myself, I noticed two sandwich wrappers and an empty Coke can in the bin. I never questioned him about them but I reckoned the thought of standing up in front of a group and telling them who he was had freaked him out and it was easier to leave.

It didn't stop me though and off I went to Bourbon Street. After eating I came across Preservation Hall and had a great hour in there sitting on the floor listening to the jazz. Then I discovered Pat O'Briens and their piano bar where I found a seat at the corner of the bar and ordered a Budweiser. I was curious about the large red drinks most people were buying so I asked the barman what they were. He told me that it was the famous Pat O'Briens Hurricane and they were $6 or $4 if you returned the glass. I thought was better value than the Bud at $2.50 so I ordered one up. Drinking it through a straw, the first sip almost blew my head off as it tasted like pure rum and I asked him what the record was for drinking these. His reply was, "You keep drinking and I'll tell you when you've broken the record." After eight or nine drinks he hadn't said a word, so I thought I'd better quit while I was ahead and it was only when I stood up I realised I wasn't actually ahead at all!

The next day, Dennis Hurley had invited us to his company golf day and when I told some of the guys what I'd done the previous night they were amazed I'd even made it to the course. I actually played brilliantly the first eight holes or so as I didn't give a damn, but as I sobered up the golf went to pieces. Every night I would end up at Preservation Hall then Pat O'Briens on the Hurricanes, only fewer of them. I even took some of the powder mix they sold back with me to make Hurricanes at home, just adding the rum and Dennis went on to supply me with the mix every year I visited the show. I also brought back shirts for the kids, whose words when they saw them were, "Oh dad, what were you on when you bought these?"

Between the time difference and no mobile phones in 2000, it was very difficult to keep in touch with those back home when in America, especially as Pauline was working full time. Finding a phone box which worked and having enough change to pump into it was a challenge, therefore I never actually managed to call home at any point. Imagine my surprise when, after being in New Orleans for almost a week the phone in my hotel room rang while I was in, as I'd literally only nipped back for five minutes to change clothes before heading out for the evening. On answering I got a bigger surprise to discover it was Pauline whose opening line was, "Oh, you've arrived safely then?" "Yes," I replied,"someone would have been in touch if anything had happened to me." All week our friends had been asking Pauline, "How's Gordon getting on?" Understandably, having to answer that she didn't know had become too much for her.

The show itself was amazing, I'd never seen anything like it. It was much bigger than I could have ever imagined and I really enjoyed it. Between the education, the golf and the show I met a lot of people who would go on to provide help and advice over the years as well as become friends.

We stopped off in Atlanta on the way back as we had to travel through there anyway and again stayed with Joe O'Donnell. I'd arranged a car hire and fixed up a visit to Augusta through superintendent Marsh Benson. It was brilliant to get a 'behind the scenes' tour of the course and facilities and find out all that could be achieved, although certain details weren't divulged.

Alan McGregor and Ian Forbes had visited Augusta back in 1998 on a tour to benchmark with the top facilities and get ideas on where the Links could improve and understand the standards they needed to reach. As Marsh showed them around, every question such as, "What height are the greens cut?" "What speed do they run?" or, "What is your maintenance budget?" Were all met with the same answer from Marsh, "I'm sorry but I can't disclose that." This frustrated Ian and having a mischievous streak he said to Marsh, "Do you know what a good idea for the club would be?" When Marsh asked him for his thought he replied, "Wouldn't it be a good thing for the club to open up their Par 3 course for the children of the local neighbourhood to play on?" Given the demographics of the surrounding area, Ian knew that was never going to happen.

Chapter 9. The Millennium Open and a Tiger Win

T
HE MILLENNIUM Open was the largest Open held up until that time and the scale of the event was considerably larger than anything any of us had experienced at St Andrews before. Crowds of over 230,000 for the week were a record for the Open and the extent of corporate hospitality far exceeded that of 1995. The event had been hyped up tremendously by the media, in particular the fact that Tiger Woods was at the top of his game having just won the US Open by fifteen shots some five weeks earlier. Victory at St Andrews would have made him the youngest player to have achieved the Grand Slam of winning all four Major Championships.

It was an eventful tournament and not all for the best of reasons, the most significant for us at the Links Trust being the fact that Ian Forbes, our Links Manager since 1995 had been diagnosed with cancer back in late 1999. Ian had put in a tremendous amount of work in the years leading up to the event but by the time the Open came he was too ill to attend the tournament. He subsequently died in September 2000 at the age of forty-five and his passing was a great loss to everyone at the Links where he had been very well respected by the staff. Ian had been strongly influential in the numerous improvements which had taken place over the previous decade which have gone on to enhance St Andrews Links as a premier place to come and play golf.

Other factors which had a negative impact on the week was the course itself, particularly the condition of the greens and how the bunkers were presented. The greens weren't particularly good and although the R&A didn't say so publicly, they did convey disappointment at their condition to Alan MacGregor, Secretary to the Links Trust, afterwards.

The bunkers were another issue, in fact they caused a few issues before and for a lengthy period after the tournament. In the winter prior to the Open, Eddie wanted every bunker, all 112 at the time, rebuilt so they would look their absolute best. This was a massive task and to achieve it, through the preceding winter, some staff were seconded from the other courses to assist. As well as reducing the work the other teams could carry out on their respective courses that winter, only the 'best' bunker builders were selected to work on the Old, even though they often ended up just labouring rather than actually building the bunkers. They were given the opportunity to work a considerable amount of overtime. If people are given this, many will slow down the speed at which they work to gain as much extra income as they can. Some of the staff ended up with an annual wage over 50% higher than they normally would earn. This made a significant variation to the labour budget as the additional expenditure had never been flagged up in advance. The R&A have subsequently informed all the host venues they don't want every bunker at a course rebuilt in the winter prior to the Open as it makes the course look unnatural if every bunker is pristine.

The other aspect was how the bunkers were built that winter. All the faces were made extremely steep, almost vertical in fact, and when the sand was replaced following the rebuild, much less sand was put back than was taken out initially. This caused two problems, the step down for a golfer to physically get into the bunker was much greater and, with the face being so steep, the sand wouldn't stay up, or on, the face. That meant when a ball went into the bunker, nine times out of ten it would come to rest only a couple of inches back from the face and the golfer couldn't get the ball out, or certainly not in the direction of the pin. If they tried, they would hit the revetted face with their follow through, taking a lump out of it. This meant the bunker would deteriorate more quickly and require replacing sooner than planned. I have no idea where this idea or directive came from, it was never raised or agreed at a GSC meeting and I never heard anyone within the greenkeeping department talk about it.

The Open week started off as it normally did when an event like this is taking place. I was allocated to follow the teams cutting semi-rough and fairways and see that everything was okay behind them. We were going through a dry spell so there wasn't much grass to cut as most of it had gone into a summer dormancy since it was getting next to no water.

If fact at one point Eddie measured the 9th fairway on the Stimpmeter* and it was running slightly faster than the greens! Then on the Wednesday morning, after having been allocated our jobs, we were hardly out of the sheds when those of us cutting the fairways and semi-rough, myself included, received a message to drop what we were doing. We were to collect rakes and shovels, then meet Eddie and the bunker raking team at Cartgate bunker by the 3rd green. It was explained to us that we had to go to every bunker and shovel the sand up the face and leave the base of the bunker 'bowl' or 'saucer' shaped so the ball would roll back from the face a little more.

Prior to this, for the practice rounds on Monday and Tuesday the bunkers were what we would have described as being 'flat raked', in that there was no low point in the centre of the bunker which would be the normal method.

*Craig Parry in Strath bunker during the 2000 Open practice days.
Note how flat the bunker base is.*

---

*   A Stimpmeter is a bar used to measure green speeds and was invented in 1935 by Edward Stimpson. While he invented it to show the greens at the US Open played at Oakmont that year were too fast, its most helpful purpose is to achieve consistency across the greens on the course. While Stimpson's bar was made of wood, it has since been redesigned and is now made of aluminium and engineered to a high standard. It was first used by the USGA at the 1976 US Open and became available to superintendents in 1978. Unfortunately, over time it has too often been used by both committees and course managers or superintendents to try and impress others that the greens at their club are faster than those at neighbouring ones. In the long term this can have a detrimental effect on the turf as it's put under undue stress for prolonged periods.

Apparently, at the Past Champions dinner in the R&A Clubhouse on the Tuesday evening it was alleged one of the Past Champions had remonstrated strongly with the R&A that if they played the Open with the bunkers as they were, then the Championship would be a lottery.

Past Champions photocall at the 2000 Open.

At a much later date, I had it on good authority there were a few players who voiced their concern. It worked out well for me however, as I then headed down to begin on the four bunkers which guarded the 2nd green. By that time, it had gone 6am and Tiger, who was renowned for being the first out in the practice rounds to avoid most of the crowds, was already on the course. As he approached the green, I asked one of his four personal security guards if it he would autograph a piece of paper for me as he was well known, even at that stage of his career, for not signing too many autographs. They couldn't promise but said as long as he didn't have to stop walking there was a possibility he would. After he drove off the 3rd tee, I walked alongside him and he duly signed. I just thought my kids would be so excited I got his autograph. Then, as Tiger approached the 4th green, Eddie had just driven up to help his deputy finish the work on Ginger Beer bunker and had forgotten to put the handbrake on his buggy. As it rolled down the small incline towards the bunker, Tiger turned to his caddy Steve Williams and said, "Look, the fairways are so fast and firm you can't even stop a cart on them!"

It turned out that the four tournament days were played under clear blue skies and, even more remarkable for St Andrews, there was not a breath of wind at any time. Tiger won by eight shots and never went in a bunker in any of the four rounds. His score was the lowest 72-hole score achieved in relation to par at −19, which was a record for any major championship at that time.

What happened subsequently was, after the Open, all the teams then started building the bunkers on their own course to the same style, but no one ever spoke about it or checked this was how they were to be built; staff just took it upon themselves to do it this way. By the winter of 2000, when this started on the other courses, I had been promoted to Links Manager but was never aware it was happening and I certainly never gave a directive that this was how they should be built. In fact, it was the complete opposite and it's still a disappointment to me that it wasn't until I started getting comments from golfers and committees that I even noticed. This went on to cause me endless hassle for several years with committees and local golfers as it took quite a few years to get the bunkers returned to anything like they previously were. Readers might be thinking I couldn't have been paying attention that I didn't notice this, but the R&A Championship committee didn't notice either until it was pointed out to them two days before the Open.

Another memory from the 2000 Open is Vijay Singh, known for practising prolifically, caused a bit of a stir at the chipping area on one of the practice days. He turned up and cut his own hole on the practice putting green which would normally be the 18th green of the New course. It was one of those extra small holes, just large enough for a golf ball and which the pros often use, but he then proceeded to throw the plug he removed into the rough. The head greenkeeper happened to be there but wasn't prepared to deal with it so he went and reported it to Alan MacGregor the Links Secretary. Alan went down and approached Vijay only to get a tirade of abuse. Alan didn't reply but instead went to Hugh Fraser, Chairman of the Championship Committee who had to go down and remind Vijay that they were here as guests of the Links Trust and to be mindful of his behaviour.

To celebrate the Millennium, the R&A had the brilliant idea of staging a small event over holes 1, 2, 17 and 18 on the Wednesday afternoon, featuring all the previous Open Champions who wanted to play, putting them out in teams of three or four. Twenty-two Past Champions took part and although Arnold Palmer wasn't amongst them, 88-year-old Sam Snead made the journey to participate. It was a marvellous event for the spectators to watch, all very light-hearted with the players interacting with the crowds while it also raised over £40,000 for charity.

Although we never take on many volunteers for a tournament because we have a large enough staff of our own to prepare the course, a Canadian greenkeeping friend of mine came over to help out that year. In 1998 Kerry Watkins won the inaugural Canadian Future Superintendents Award, sponsored by Toro, part of which was a trip to Scotland where he worked on the Eden for two weeks. In 2000, he came back for a month to work on the Eden as well as be a volunteer on the Old for the Open. Although the R&A hadn't requested it, Kerry asked Eddie if he could go and stand by Road Bunker at the 17th green and rake the bunker if any player went into it. It was a smart move by Kerry as he got one of the best views of the action. Imagine his surprise when, as he was walking around town the following day, he passed the local newspaper office and in the window was a large picture of Sam Snead putting on 17 and right behind him in the centre of the frame was Kerry.

The day following the Open, after work I played golf on the Eden with Kerry Watkins, Rich Hurley and Marsh Benson, superintendent at Augusta. That game allowed Kerry the opportunity to work as a volunteer at The Masters in 2002 and he has completed a career 'Grand Slam' having worked the US Open in 2001 at Southern Hills and the 2003 US PGA at Oak Hill. In the group behind us that day was a Mr George Wislar, a member at Augusta and well known to both Rich and Marsh. It turned out George was my route to playing Augusta in 2006.

As well as being Peter Dawson's first Open as Secretary to the R&A, 2000 was also Alan MacGregor's first as Secretary to the Links Trust and he had a lot on his plate with Ian Forbes being gravely ill. I probably didn't help the situation when I asked Alan if a greenkeeper friend of mine, Brian Finlayson from Kilmarnock Barassie could stay in a caravan in the yard of the Eden greenkeeping facility through the tournament along with his brothers, who were also greenkeepers. They had tickets but they had nowhere to pitch their caravan as all the nearby sites were full. Alan agreed to this so I made arrangements for Brian to call me on the Wednesday evening when he arrived and I could get them 'through the gates' to show them where to park up. I was out on the course working when Brian called me to say they had arrived so I met them and got them settled in before heading home. The next morning, we were in to begin work at 4.30am, and because everyone was working out of the Jubilee greenkeeping sheds, I just headed there. Being his first Open, Alan had decided to come in for 5am and parked over at his office at Pilmour House, right beside the Eden sheds. When he saw me his first words were, "Gordon, there's a group of guys lying sleeping on the 1st tee of the Eden."

"Oh okay," I replied, "They'll be the greenkeepers I spoke to you about staying over." They had brought their own drink and after their meal got completely hammered and fell asleep on the tee! They were (slightly) better behaved the rest of the week.

One of my favourite things to do when we were off duty was to go to the practice area and watch the players up close, as our staff passes allowed access inside the ropes. As well as watching them on the range, I could get down to the 18th green of the New course which was divided in two with the back section used for putting practice and the front for chipping and bunker shots. The bunkers around that green weren't an ideal replica of those on the Old as the faces weren't nearly as high but Tiger found a way of making them more comparable. He would take the rake and stick it upright in the sand at the front of the bunker then play his shots so they went over the rake. I also worked out his routine and where he went when he came down to practice. Therefore, on the Sunday afternoon I brought my children down to watch Tiger prior to him going out in the last group. Things were more relaxed in those days and with Andrew, who at fourteen was the eldest, wearing one of my staff polo shirts, I was able to take them all inside the ropes. We went down to the greenside and they sat down on a banking, tucked in at the edge of a gorse bush. There were a few players coming and going but it wasn't long before they got bored and started asking why we were there. I told them to be patient and to just wait and see. Then Tiger arrived and after five minutes of chipping practice, he came into the bunker less than five yards from where they were sitting. I had moved myself back a little and was able to take a photograph of the three children sitting having a picnic, with Tiger playing bunker shots in the background.

The Moir children having a picnic with Tiger at the 2000 Open.

As the tournament was coming to its conclusion, the crowd following Tiger coming down the closing holes in the last match was massive and spilling onto the fairways behind the players. Eddie had anticipated this and, in an attempt to protect the greens, had organised some of us to go out with rope and the metal posts, referred to as 'stabs', to rope off the greens as soon as practical after the players had completed the hole. I was in a group sent to rope off the 16th, each of us having three stabs with one person carrying the rope. As soon as the players had teed off on 17, we each ran across the front of 16 green and pushed a stab in after every four paces while the guy with the rope came behind and quickly looped it around the hook at the top of the stab. The process ran like a well-oiled machine and kept the spectators off the green when, just as we were leaving, I turned around to see a guy on one of the tv camera buggies get off his buggy and start taking the rope down so they could drive across the green. Needless to say, the air turned blue and that was the first of a long list of encounters I had with contractors driving buggies where they shouldn't at different tournaments over the next eighteen years.

*An aerial view of the tented village from the 2000 Open. The contractors'
compound is bottom right on part of the Balgove course.*

There's also a large amount of work required after an Open. Tents and
grandstands which have been up for sometimes four months can badly
damage the grass and a lot of effort is required to return the areas to a
good condition.

Damage to the 11th tee caused by a grandstand.

Pauline was driving the courtesy cars again, this time it was Saab who provided the vehicles. It was still fun getting a lift down to the pub some evenings and she had an array of well-known players during the week including John Daly the 1995 champion. She found a few of them to be a bit 'tetchy', but like golfers of all abilities, it could most likely be linked to the fact they had had a bad round. Oh, and she was consistent. After the presentation ceremony she had to take Ernie Els the joint runner-up, back to his hotel!

Chapter 10. Landing the Top Position in Greenkeeping

I AN FORBES sadly passed away shortly after the 2000 Open and a few weeks after his death, I returned to my office at the EGC to a voicemail message from Alan McGregor asking to see me. My first thoughts were, "What has happened or what has someone done?" When I called back, Alan asked if I could come over straight away which I did. You could have knocked me over with a feather when he told me they were looking for someone to take over part of Ian's role and become the Links Manager, responsible for all turf related matters, the workshop team and the gardeners. Alan explained that Ian had spoken to him at length about the future when he became aware his cancer was terminal. Of the existing head greenkeepers, I was the one he thought most suitable for the job, often feeling some of the others took advantage of his lack of greenkeeping experience, as he didn't have the underpinning knowledge to question them in depth. While obviously delighted to be asked, my immediate thoughts were what the other four head greenkeepers would think if I was just given the job without any type of process or interview. Alan confirmed, however, the job would be advertised internally and proper interviews conducted, therefore it wasn't a certainty I would get it. Four of us applied and three were selected for interview. We were interviewed by Alan and Alistair Nicol, the then Chairman of LMC, who was there to represent the committee and satisfy everyone the process was open and transparent. Given what I knew, I would have started favourite but did feel a lot of pressure as I could have messed it up badly. The others would have also felt they had a good chance of being successful. In the end my interview went well and I was appointed at the beginning of October, just in time for that year's Dunhill Cup. When Alan confirmed I had the job, I referred back to a question they asked at the interviews about what things I'd do if successful and said I had something to add to the answer I gave then and said, "I'll catch your thief."

It was quite a baptism of fire as, immediately, three of my direct reports were pretty unhappy that I'd been successful ahead of them, especially as I'd been there considerably less time than them.

With the Dunhill Cup taking place that week it was a bit awkward, but all the preparation had been done beforehand, so I thought it easiest and best to just let Eddie carry on as he normally would have done. There was no point in me taking any kind of role as he had all the experience required. Therefore, other than meeting officials from the European Tour who ran the event, I stayed very much in the background apart from going around with everyone when they were selecting the pin positions and setting the course up some of the days. I also had to find a replacement for my old position on the Eden and we again advertised internally. There was only one choice as my deputy on the Eden, Gordon McKie, was head and shoulders above the other deputies or anyone else on the staff.

There was a strange story brought to my attention within weeks of my appointment as Links Manager. The Irish Superintendents Association had their annual conference where one of the speakers was Jim Arthur. A friend of mine who attended the conference called me afterwards to tell me Jim Arthur made the comment during his presentation that St Andrews had appointed a monkey to the role of Links Supervisor and they'd get what they deserved. If true, why he would have said this I have no idea. As I've already said, I was a supporter of Jim Arthur and his policies having previously asked him to consult when at Fraserburgh Golf Club, and although things have moved on over the last forty years, his basic principles are still sound. He had been retired for some time and I hadn't met him for years so why he made a comment like that I thought bizarre. I can only surmise whoever provided him with any information about me was obviously unhappy with my appointment, but I think history has proved them both wrong.

While some working practices could be altered fairly quickly by introducing or changing standard operating procedures, to change the staff culture which had been so deeply embedded was not something which was going to happen overnight and patience was going to be a key requirement. I had to get buy-in from the head greenkeepers and that was always going to be easier with some than it was with others. An ethos had been allowed to build up over many years where there had been no guidance or proper discipline. The normal punishment to adopt when someone had messed up badly or upset their manager was to give them a more laborious job for a week or so, usually putting them on bunker raking duties or similar, rather than have them cut greens or fairways. The other 'punishment' for any minor mistake, whether it was accidental or even something out of your control, was often ridicule, both by your peers and your manager. By the time the person involved in the mistake arrived back at the sheds, they could guarantee everyone would know and they would get a barrowload of humiliating comments. I never thought either approach was very helpful as both just led to resentment from the staff and weren't exactly effective as they didn't change anything. In my opinion it would have been far better for instances where staff were clearly not carrying out their work in a proper and timely manner to issue them with a verbal or written warning. It would have only taken one or two staff members to be fired before the message that inappropriate behaviour wouldn't be tolerated to ensure the others stepped more into line. The methods being practised showed a lack of leadership but there was no real appetite to change, which compounded the behaviour of the staff. To avoid ridicule when a machine broke down, not only through misuse but even accidently, the operator would return it to the shed but wouldn't tell anyone it was broken. This meant when someone else went to use it next, they had to change all their plans until it was fixed and if that machine was an important part of a larger operation, it could hold half the team up. Of course, there were some people on the staff who were quite happy to see that happen. Covering up machine damage was an ongoing battle all twenty-seven years I worked at the Links, although it did become better over time. We would constantly put the message out that accidents happen and if it was purely an accident, then that was fine and everyone could learn from it, but the problem persisted. To wind the newer or seasonal staff up, some of the longer serving staff would continue to tell them they would be fired, so it was something I had to keep repeating. It was worse with the equipment that was shared and we put procedures in place to try and record who used what and when, but if the process was too time consuming, then it wasn't worth it.

The title Links Manager caused some confusion in certain quarters and after a while I persuaded Alan and the committee it should be changed to Links Superintendent, (Walter's title had been Links Supervisor which had also caused confusion). Links Superintendent sounded very grand as well as American and it wasn't ideal, but there was a very simple reason behind it. We were constantly being contacted by visiting greenkeepers, particularly superintendents from the US, who wished to speak to the person in charge of the golf course and my secretary would say she would put them through to the Links Manager. They would tell her they didn't want to talk to a manager, they wanted to talk to the greenkeeper or person in charge of the golf course (incredibly, many people still don't know there is more than one course) and she would have to explain everything before putting them through. It was a title which was well recognised within the industry throughout the world and remained until shortly before Alan retired at the end of 2010, when he managed to get the Trustees to change everyone's title to better reflect the professionalism of the organisation. His own title changed from Secretary to the Links Trust to CEO while the others in the management team all became Directors of their respective departments. It didn't come with a salary increase unfortunately, or not for me at least!

After a few months in the post, I began to move staff around between teams which wasn't something that had happened in the previous ten years. If a new employee was placed on a particular course on the day they began at the Links, then that was 'their' course. One of the reasons I began doing this was driven by a few staff asking to be moved because of friction between themselves and their head greenkeeper. Some of this was due to the creation of a new position I introduced called Senior Greenkeeper which was basically the third in charge on a course. Prior to that, staff were graded based more on their length of service as opposed to their skill levels. There was a correlation of sorts, as the ones who had been there the longest could do more of the tasks, but they didn't necessarily do them better or accept more responsibility. From early on in my time at St Andrews, I always thought the new staff coming in gave more than most of those who were there prior to me arriving and I continued to think that until I retired. New staff, whether it was for a permanent position or just a summer job nearly always came with more enthusiasm, a greater desire to learn and a better work ethic. When selecting people for the senior roles, I wanted staff who would show more desire and ambition, who wanted to continue to improve, whether that was at the Links or elsewhere. I was never hung up about staff moving on to a better job, I'd far rather someone came and worked for us for a short time and did a good job rather than simply turning up every day and going through the motions. Don't get me wrong, you need staff from both groups but we had far more in the 'I'm going to be here until I retire' camp than we did in the other. I wouldn't have called most of the staff greenkeepers either, even though they had their basic qualifications. While some could and would spray pesticides, apply fertiliser and such like, most required their head greenkeeper to tell them the quantities of the product each time they went out, or if they were to use a new or different product. It wasn't intentionally planned, but what transpired with the creation of this role of a senior greenkeeper and the choice of people selected, along with some of the other moves, turned out to be a light bulb moment for many. Some of the younger staff saw there might be more opportunities for them either at the Links or elsewhere. At the same time, I was encouraging them and investing more in education for those members of staff who showed willing. I always took the view skills could be taught, whereas attitudes and behaviours were more difficult to change.

One of the first to be promoted was Graeme Taylor, who I moved from the New course over to be the senior on the Strathtyrum. Bizarrely, this was something many people considered a demotion rather than a promotion purely on the basis he was moving from a Championship course like the New to a much smaller one, despite the fact he was getting more responsibility and a higher salary. They didn't see he was going to learn more under Roddy and the fact he was being given more opportunities. Funnily enough, the same staff thought they were more deserving of promotion based purely on the fact that they had been at the Links much longer. My answer to them was, it was a pity they hadn't shown more willing before the position became available.

Graeme had only been at the Links since 1998 where he started in a role classed as a grade two greenkeeper on the New course. This meant he had acquired the basic greenkeeping qualification although he had much more than that. He had a university degree in chemistry and as a keen golfer, found a temporary job at his local club in East Kilbride after leaving university and loved it. He then moved to Wales to be head greenkeeper on a small 9-hole course before deciding to come back to Scotland to further improve his knowledge and the Links supported him through his HNC in greenkeeping.

That initial move started something which acted as a wake-up call for many of the staff as over time, they saw him go much further. In 2003 he went on to become deputy on the Eden, initially on a temporary basis which was made permanent at the end of 2003. He retained that position until taking over from Gordon McKie as head greenkeeper at the beginning of 2005. Two years later he became head greenkeeper on the Jubilee and in 2009 became course manager of both the Jubilee and New courses when the structure of the teams changed. With his background, Graeme has a very different skill set, using a more scientific approach to managing turf, soaking up technical knowledge on all aspects like a sponge. He was also much more computer literate than any of the rest of us, and we benefitted from this.

Another notable change was Kevin Muir who, along with another person, asked if they could be moved off the Old Course. Kevin came from a farming background and had started at the Links soon after leaving school. Because he was an excellent tractor operator his role was mostly restricted to that and although he was a qualified greenkeeper, he wasn't given much opportunity to develop his greenkeeping skills. I moved the other person to the Jubilee where he stayed until he retired in 2020 and Kevin to the Eden where he soon began progressing. First, he replaced Graeme as senior on the Strathtyrum, then became Graeme's deputy on the Eden. When Graeme moved to become head greenkeeper on the Jubilee in 2007, Kevin was appointed his successor on the Eden. His was a completely different route to Graeme and it was great to see someone, who in his own words, had been at the Links for over ten years and going nowhere, begin to fulfil his potential. Quickly, he climbed the ladder to success through the smallest of changes as he saw an opportunity which he took with both hands, applying himself through hard work and dedication.

A process I changed in 2003 was the closures the Old Course enjoyed for two weeks every March and November. This was for a mixture of resting the course and carrying out maintenance such as aeration and topdressing. (The New course also used to close for one week prior to the Old closing in March and one, or sometimes two weeks, after the Old in November). The November closure basically ended the visitor season two weeks earlier that it might have done. Both periods could be affected by frost in the mornings, preventing the planned maintenance taking place until mid-morning. Initially I scrapped the New course closure completely and reduced the Old Course to just one week in both March and November, then in 2005 the committee agreed the Old would only close each Monday in November and the first Monday in December and then again in the last Monday in February and the first three in March. This would still allow the greenstaff plenty of days in which they could get their principal tasks done, especially if they utilised the Sundays as well when the course was already closed. These weeks were prime off-season golfing times and with reduced green fees, many Scottish and UK golfers were willing to play then and take a chance the weather would be okay. It was good business for local accommodation providers and tour operators. From 2000, golfers were expected to play from little fairway mats* throughout the winter months to reduce divots, thereby protecting the courses. Also, with the advances in aeration equipment, it was easier to deal with the wear and compaction caused by foot traffic.

Fairway mats were introduced through some winter months to the courses other than the Old where they'd been used previously.

---

* Fairway mats. These are small pieces of Astroturf, measuring approx. 300mm x 120mm. The golfers carry one around with them and, if their ball finishes on the fairway, they place it on the mat before playing. This prevents divots being taken at a time of year when there is no recovery or when seed won't grow, leaving the fairways in a much better condition in spring than they would otherwise be. We first used them at St Andrews on the Old Course the winter prior to the 1995 Open. It was 1999 before we began using them on the other courses. Although their introduction initially met with some resistance from local golfers, over time it has become more acceptable to most. The time they are in use has increased from two months to four months, while their use has also become widespread on other links courses around Scotland through winter.

Simultaneously, I introduced a day each autumn when each of the other courses were closed for one day to allow them to deep aerate their greens. That mightn't seem much in comparison to the closures the Old enjoyed, but the course managers could set up all five Vertidrains we had (usually with 8mm or 12mm thick tines to a depth of 250mm) and easily blitz their course in a day. They would roll the greens immediately afterwards with a tees' mower or, from 2006, a turf iron[*].

Turf irons were first used on the St Andrews courses at the 2005 Open. We would also use them to roll the greens after vertidraining.

[*] A turf iron is a ride-on machine on rollers and is used to roll the surface of the greens. Their principal use is to help increase green speeds without lowering the height of cut, thereby reducing the stress put on the grass plant. Their secondary use is helping smooth the greens in winter, either after aeration as mentioned, or instead of mowing because there's no growth. We first used them during the 2005 Open although they had been widely used in Australia for many years prior, but hadn't really taken off in the UK, or more surprisingly, in America. The majority of golfers wrongly assume if you want to increase the speed of the greens then you simply cut them closer, but cutting too close or maintaining a low height of cut for too long a time period has the opposite effect. The desirable grass species such as fine fescue and colonial bentgrass can't withstand continual close cutting and will die out to be replaced by poorer species such as annual meadow grass, (Poa Annua). Poa can be a great surface through July, August and September but it creates a lot of thatch, making the greens softer and prone to ball marks and footprinting. It's a costly situation to get into as applying more fertiliser causes increased growth, leading to more and closer cutting. The roots remain near the surface resulting in the plant drying out more quickly and needing additional irrigation. All these factors cause higher disease incidences requiring greater use of fungicides, which even back in 2000, were beginning to be withdrawn from the market due to their negative impact on the environment. Usually in the autumn when the greens are still in good condition, they need to be aerated to remove the excess thatch the extra fertiliser and water has produced so they can recover prior to winter. It soon becomes a vicious circle. I often joked with visiting American superintendents about our approach to greenkeeping in Scotland by telling them the following. "A long time ago in Scotland we discovered that applying fertiliser and water made the grass grow quicker which led to spending more time cutting it. This just created more work for ourselves and in turn meant we had less time to play golf and drink whisky, so best to just keep everything minimal." Many a true word is spoken in jest.

The dates were staggered so golfers always had a choice and didn't have to play on greens recently aerated, even though the surface disturbance was minimal. With a good operator, a well set up machine and favourable ground conditions, it's difficult to tell the greens have been aerated by the following day. We would begin on the Eden during the practice days of the Dunhill in late September or early October, then follow on with the New being aerated the week after the Dunhill finished. The Jubilee greens would be aerated the following week and the Strathtyrum a further week after that. It was a practice which continued after I retired and with much better results than in 1991 when I was aerating the week before Christmas.

At a later date, the committee agreed to allow the other courses to have what we referred to as a 'maintenance morning' through the main playing season, where each course could carry out disruptive maintenance such as verticutting* or topdressing without interference from golfers. This didn't mean the course was closed, but before 9am greenstaff had the 'right of way' and we communicated this to all golfers suggesting they switch to another course for that morning. We standardised it in a manner that the same course would have its maintenance morning on the same day each week, tying it in to avoid competitions. It was very much based on the American model where many courses are closed on Mondays and it worked fairly well, although there were limitations. If it was raining on the day a course had 'their morning' that might prevent them topdressing so they would miss the opportunity and if they had an additional competition scheduled, they'd again miss out. This provided them with a better opportunity than they had previously and avoided, or at least reduced, any conflict with local golfers. Like many things and as equipment and turf conditions improved, it was used less often as the course managers found ways to fit in this type of work when they felt the course needed it most.

Another of the things I was keen to change was how vouchers were distributed to staff at events such as the Dunhill. What I thought important was that everyone should be treated equally, we were one department all doing the same job. It didn't really matter to me if staff were working on the Old at the tournament or on their own course, my

---

* Verticutting is a mechanical operation to the turf which does as it says, namely using blades on a machine to cut vertically into the turf. This removes a small amount of thatch and prevents the grass growing latterly. It 'lifts' the grass blades up to get a cleaner cut and all these things refine the turf. It is similar to scarifying, only not as disruptive as the blades don't go as deep into the turf.

view was that everyone was contributing. I approached IMG who ran the event, but they weren't prepared to provide me with the number of vouchers I required each day. They would only give me 40 vouchers to the value of £200 per day for the four tournament days so I asked if I could bill them for the £800 total and rather than receive vouchers, I would provide food for the staff by another method. IMG were okay with this and I borrowed the large gas barbeque the clubhouse used and bought food locally to provide breakfast for all the staff each morning from the Monday of tournament week through until the Sunday. A couple of the greenstaff would cook the food or I would sometimes help out with that myself. There was usually enough money left at the end of the week to allow me to buy a few extra things such as bottles of wine which I would keep and, periodically, give to individuals for their contribution during the year. That first year was a challenge as the weather the entire week was terrible with rain and mist almost every day. The tournament even ran into the Monday but staff improvised and were able to cook the food under the canopy at the front entrance to the JGC. It just smoked the sheds out!

Prior to the 2000 Open the Trustees had agreed to stage an event entitled the Millennium Shotgun where on 21st June (the longest day in the northern hemisphere) golf clubs around the world would stage a grand competition. The Links Trust did all the arrangements for a competition on the courses which involved members from all the local clubs, followed by a function in the evening which was held in a large marquee on Station Park, the playing fields owned by the local authority adjacent the Old Course Hotel. During the construction and removal of the marquee the contractors had damaged the surface of the playing fields on an area used for athletics and hockey, leaving some deep wheel ruts in the turf. Although this was staged in June, it was after the Open when the greenkeeping department were asked to repair the damage rather than pay the local authority to do so. This request received a very cool response from the other head greenkeepers who, because it didn't affect their course, simply weren't interested. Unlike them, I saw it as an opportunity to help the Links in another area while also getting my staff some additional money through overtime. Perhaps my willingness to help was just one of many things which had a bearing on my promotion a few months later?

Chapter 11. The Joys of Seasonal Staff

THE LINKS had never employed many seasonal staff to work over the summer months other than one or two who came to work on the Old occasionally, perhaps through a friendship Walter had with another greenkeeper or superintendent.

The arrival of Kerry Watkins in 1998 planted a seed in the back of my mind that this was something which could be developed and be of benefit to the Links in the future. Kerry brought an enthusiasm with him, as did the Canadian student who came the following year, and I thought there must be a lot of young greenkeepers out there who would love the opportunity to come and work at St Andrews for a summer as it would be a positive addition to their CV.

When becoming Links Manager in 2001, it was something I wanted to try but it was a slow beginning as it wasn't something which had been budgeted and I had other priorities initially. It was only when Rich Hurley told me he had a student at Rutgers who was interested in going overseas to work for the summer that I even took anyone on in 2001. It was a difficult thing to organise with work permits and other requirements, especially for Americans, as the person coming to work had to still be enrolled at college. This wasn't ideal as their college season didn't finish until at least mid-May and started again in August, while we would prefer people to arrive before the end of April and be able to work until at least the end of September. As a favour to Rich and as a trial for myself I agreed to have him from the end of May for fourteen weeks, using the experience to evaluate how it would work. A work permit was arranged through an organisation called BUNAC*. The other stumbling block was accommodation which, as well as

* BUNAC - British Universities North America Club is an organisation which helps young people to travel and work overseas if they meet the visa criteria. It helps UK citizens to travel to North America as well as allowing North Americans to come over and work in the UK. Due to changes in immigration laws, BUNAC has evolved since I began working with the organisation. There is also now BUNAC Australia and other destinations.

being expensive, is never easy to come by in St Andrews due to the high student population. However, because the students leave at the beginning of June until September, getting somewhere to live for those three months was easier. It wasn't quite as difficult in 2001 as it became latterly and the individual, Peter Crowl, was able to get himself a room for the season. I placed Peter on the Eden as there was already another American coming to work on the Old Course.

It worked out well for the summer as both students were keen and helpful, but we got a surprise afterwards. The lad who had worked on the Old, when he returned to America wrote an article for an industry magazine where he was very critical of his time working on the Old Course. When we saw the article, a lot of guys on the staff were annoyed with him, although I was more philosophical as most of what he had written was accurate. I saw it as proof there was still a lot of improvements required.

In 2002 we only hired a few local summer staff who had been in the greenkeeping class at nearby Elmwood College. Again, lack of budget was the main issue, and I decided if any full-time staff left over the course of the year, rather than replace them, I would try harder to recruit summer staff for 2003. For every full-time employee, I could afford three seasonal staff which would allow us to carry out more maintenance through the main playing season, including cutting the greens more often with pedestrian mowers, something we were unable to do outside of tournaments because we didn't have the staff numbers.

2003 saw me take on twelve summer staff, a mixture of overseas and local people. Rich Hurley had another student he recommended very highly to me and who was keen to come over. Lauren Giordano from Rutgers joined another girl on the staff, Stacey McCullough from Canada. We already had one girl training as a mechanic in the workshop but to my knowledge, Lauren and Stacey were the first female greenkeepers to be working on the courses with Lauren coming back in 2005 to work at the Open.

The idea of recruiting summer staff went from strength to strength after that and we began employing people from literally all around the world. As I was building up more contacts, we were getting young greenkeepers from America, Australia, New Zealand and Europe along with students from many UK greenkeeping colleges as word spread of this opportunity. Once the Castle Course began construction in 2005, we would be looking to employ as many as 20 seasonal staff. At first, many of the greenkeepers at the Links weren't too sure about all these different people arriving. Some of it was just change but some was because they were being shown up by the enthusiasm and work ethic many seasonal staff brought. The seasonals would question senior staff why they were doing certain tasks or why they were doing them in such a manner and many of them were more confident in their own ability and knowledge than the full-timers.

In March 2002, one of our full-time staff, Peter Stewart, asked to take a year out and went to Australia to work at Royal Melbourne. When he returned, he became really helpful when it came to assisting the new arrivals settle as he had experienced the same difficulties and anxieties they were experiencing when he first went to Australia. He also put me in contact with Jim Porter, the then superintendent at Royal Melbourne, and we set up an exchange programme which would take one of their staff over to St Andrews for our summer and one of ours would go to work at Royal Melbourne during our winter. Although that sounds simple to set up, we had to do it in such a manner that those going on the exchange had to resign from their employment for the six months they would be away and we would guarantee to hire them again on their return on the same contract. It was also up to each individual to arrange their own work permits, flights and accommodation and pay for all of these. That would limit the number of people who wanted to take advantage of the opportunity, while it also made it unlikely any of the married staff would be interested. Finally, neither of us would send someone who wouldn't be a good representative of our organisations, our personal reputations were on the line as well as that of our respective companies. I then began a similar arrangement with Steve Marsden at Cape Kidnappers in New Zealand although we were only able to keep it going for a few years. It was another indication to St Andrews staff that there were many different opportunities available for them. Both Royal Melbourne and, to a lesser extent, Cape Kidnappers continued to send us people for a number of years afterwards.

Although I didn't attend the Golf Industry Show, (GIS), in America every year once I'd gained promotion, there was more to the show than simply an equipment exhibition. The education accompanying it was superior to what was available in the UK and I always fitted in at least one day of classes. I would also use the trip as a means of trying to recruit summer staff, whether that was when visiting other golf facilities or at the show itself where all of the colleges have stands, or booths as they're called in America. This led to an influx of Americans coming over for a few years. When I returned to the GIS over the years, many of those people came up to say hello on the show floor or at education seminars and many went on to be superintendents. As time went on it became more difficult to obtain work permits for them, especially as they had to still be studying while I also began insisting they needed to come from early April until at least the end of September. These changes eventually led to the numbers coming over dropping off.

Another good market I was able to tap into were the young UK greenkeepers who had been in the US on the Ohio State Programme and were looking for a job on their return to the UK. This was a great programme run by Irish-American Mike O'Keeffe, who took youngsters in the turf industry from all around the world to America for anything between six and eighteen months. There wasn't a huge amount of formal education involved, sometimes none, but Mike would get these kids work experience on the very best courses in America. They would generally spend the summer months in the northern part of the country, then spend the winter down in the southern states working with warm season grasses, or sometimes spend a full year in places like California. How much they learned would depend on the superintendent at the facility where they were placed. No one went there for a holiday; the days were long and the students were expected to put in over eighty hours per week at most facilities. If you didn't cut the mustard then you were out, or at best, your second six months would be at a lesser facility or with a boss who was a tough taskmaster. I'd known Mike for a number of years as he would regularly visit Elmwood and other UK colleges, as well as BTME, looking for students. It was expensive to get on the programme although the students could make their money back once over there. Mike would complete all the paperwork for the work permits etc and the American courses usually had accommodation for the students or would help them find a place to live. He was also willing to help find them work when they were returning to the UK or wherever they were going back to and would often recommend people to me. Sometimes we would take on an overseas student who was looking for another experience before returning to their home country. The best things I found about these youngsters was they had a great work ethic from their time in America and had good skills in different departments as they were given a lot of responsibility, being entrusted to run entire crews on projects or left in charge of the facility at weekends. In fact, they often found the work back here much less demanding given what they had experienced and the hours they were used to working in the States.

We had some great people come back and work for us from that programme. Many were able to pick up full-time jobs with us before the year was out through people moving on and vacancies opening up. If there was someone really good, then I would try everything I could to find a way of keeping them and some of them went on to good careers both here and at other clubs in the UK. There are too many to name them all but some such as Gavin Neill, Phil Hind and Gary Semple all gained promoted posts with us at the Links, the former two still working there. Jon Wood who is now course manager at the Castle is another, although he didn't come to us directly from the Ohio programme.

I always made a point of explaining to everyone who was coming for a seasonal position that the role they were coming to wasn't a supervisory one. They would be expected to carry out all the tasks associated with being a greenkeeper, from cutting greens to divoting fairways. They wouldn't be allowed to spray pesticides as this was regulated. What I could offer them was to experience a different culture if they were coming from abroad, learn a little about maintaining a Links course and get some tournament experience as there were always events where the courses were prepared and set up as the Old would be. This might not be to Open Championship standard, but something very similar. Likewise, we would always rebuild the faces of a few bunkers towards the end of the season just so they could see how it was done, even though they might never have to do that when they returned home. To add more value to their experience, I'd arrange different educational events for them. These ranged from seminars by different companies who provided our fertiliser or seeds, to a tour of the R&A Clubhouse, a visit to the R&A club and ball testing facility and the British Golf Museum. Sometimes they would visit nearby courses including the one at Hill of Tarvit which is maintained as it would have been back in the 1920s and where they would get the experience of playing with hickory clubs. They would have to do all this in their own time but as they were generally finished by 1.30 in the afternoon, it gave them something to do.

Agronomist Richard Windows delivering a seminar to the seasonal students.

If you're stuck in a foreign country with only your fellow workers for company, then it was important there was something to do when away from work. As a result, I was successful in securing them a golf pass to let them play any of our courses Monday to Friday apart from the Old, although I would always try to get them one game on the Old during the time they were here. I had to spell it out to them that it would likely be at the end of the day and it was better if they took their opportunity before the end of May when the Old Course was a little quieter. There were always a few who left it until August or September and I had to tell them they had missed their chance.

I felt it was important to be up front with them as much as I could, almost to the extent I might have put some of them off coming. Two other things I always explained were, the difficulty in finding accommodation in the town and that not every one of them could work on the Old Course. I was able to compromise on the latter a little by introducing Sunday working on the Old and splitting the seasonals into two groups, coming in on alternate Sundays. In previous times, other than coming in for tournaments and another few Sunday mornings to topdress greens, then the Old Course team didn't work on a Sunday. Imagine being in the golf course business and your prize asset had no customers on a Sunday, wouldn't it be bizarre not to have your team in to carry out as much maintenance as possible while there are no customers to disturb? But that was the culture and people weren't willing to change, driven I suspect by the fact many of them enjoyed their Saturday night out. If someone was fortunate enough to be working on the Old Course, then I think that was the price they had to pay. The greenkeeping department is the only one at the Links who don't work a shift pattern where staff work five days on and three off or something along those lines. They still class it as a Monday to Friday job with only course preparation carried out on Saturdays and Sundays unless there was a tournament on. The HR department put pressure on us to change, but it was something I resisted as there would inevitably be Local Club competitions on Saturdays and Sundays, and I didn't want staff working through the competitions as it would only lead to complaints from the Clubs.

By far the biggest stumbling block in attracting students from outside the area was accommodation and that became more difficult as time went on. It was more the availability than the expense, although it wasn't cheap. While they wouldn't go home with a lot of savings, they were generally able to have a good time whilst here and visit other parts of the UK or Europe during their time off. Trying to explain these difficulties to them over the telephone, by Skype or in an email wasn't easy. In the early days, I would offer some of them a room with me for a few days until they found somewhere but eventually I had to stop that as it was becoming too much. To obtain a bank account and a National Insurance number they needed a permanent address and I would let many of them use my home address so they could get these. That generally worked out well other than they would often forget to close their bank account when they left and I continued to get statements and other mail for them long after they'd gone. Only one seasonal, who worked with us in 2007, caused a real problem when he left without clearing his debts at different places and I would get debt collectors' mail for him for years afterwards from different companies. I had a folder which took up a drawer in my desk with letters for him on which I'd written every telephone conversation I'd had with each company. This went on for nearly ten years!

After a succession of Americans stayed with us, who all seemed to have unusual names, my youngest son said to one, "How did you get a job with my dad? Was it because you have a strange name?" Then, when it was mostly Europeans who were staying, as I was trying to explain something to one of them in my broad Scottish accent he said, "Dad, he's Italian, not deaf!"

Guelph University in Ontario was another establishment I was able to link with through the Canadian Toro 'Student of the Year' award and we had a few candidates from there for a spell but like the American students, they eventually began to tail off. Being in the Commonwealth, it was much easier to obtain work permits for Canadians, Australians and New Zealanders.

Through Elmwood College, we could have quite a diverse workforce at times as they had students coming from all parts of the world. A large contingent of young greenkeepers would come to Elmwood from Iceland and we employed a few of them over the years. They were all great workers, always very keen to learn. At the other end of the spectrum, we had very few Norwegians or Swedish students as they preferred to go back to their own countries. I would get a lot of requests from South Africa but it was extremely difficult for them to get a work permit. We had only two or three from South Africa over the years and they had dual citizenship. We had one Argentinian who was here studying in the UK, but he had to leave at the end of his studies despite the fact he appeared to have good contacts in the Argentinian Embassy. One Elmwood student came from Nepal and after working as a seasonal, worked full-time with us for a couple of years while completing his studies online. He eventually left to work in India and still keeps in touch.

Elmwood began working with a Chinese university at one time and had a considerable number of Chinese students come over for a few years. We did take on a couple of them, but it wasn't a success for a variety of reasons. Perhaps it was the culture or what they wanted to achieve from being in Scotland, but there never seemed to be a connection with them.

Latterly, many of our summer staff were coming from different European countries. It felt like the United Nations as, over the years, some came from Germany, while we also had people from the Czech Republic, Slovakia, Italy and Spain. Some came through Elmwood while others were recommendations from people I knew. The one thing they had in common was that they were studying greenkeeping and wanted to experience working at St Andrews.

Of course, everyone wanted to work on the Old Course but that wasn't practical. They would also have very different levels of competency based on their practical experience. Those coming from Royal Melbourne or Cape Kidnappers, for instance, could have been in greenkeeping for a decade or more, while some of the Elmwood students might have only worked on a golf course for a year or less. If it was someone coming from an established venue with a strong recommendation, then I would always place them on the Old Course. Through looking at their CVs and asking questions during their interviews, I had to try and balance each team with a mixture of experienced and inexperienced staff. While many were disappointed they weren't working on the Old Course Monday to Friday, they often realised later they were getting a more varied experience on the other courses and actually learning more than their colleagues on the Old Course were. Due to how the Old Course is laid out with the double greens and shared fairways, allied with the fact it is crammed with four golfers teeing off every ten minutes from 6.30am until dusk, there is less opportunity and time available to spend training staff. That time pressure isn't as bad on the other teams, plus there are more opportunities to 'experiment' on the practice greens or out-of-play areas on the other courses.

While it was great to have these people come from all over the world to work here, I was also acutely conscious that I had a responsibility to look to the local job market and, with Elmwood on our doorstep, this was the main source of recruitment. I was fortunate as Elmwood would ask me through every September to talk to the new intake of students where I would explain all the various opportunities the turf industry had to offer. I would use the opportunity to try to recruit students to come for the following summer once they completed their course. Part of their course was they had to volunteer at a golf course one day per week over the winter and we were always willing to take students who wanted to do this. From our point of view, this was a great way of finding out about them before committing to offering them a job. Over the years we had many good students who came through Elmwood and some of them went on to get good jobs with us or at other clubs. Many of the best ones had already built a successful career in another field such as finance or IT and they had reached the stage where they wanted a change and a better work-life balance.

Not every seasonal worker we employed was a great success. When employing as many as we did, over the years there were always going to be a few who didn't work out but the vast majority were an asset. Generally, those from abroad were the best as they had made a significant commitment to move away from home to progress their career and although there were a few who suffered from homesickness, there weren't many who left for that reason. Regrettably, we had to fire one or two over the years. There was a Canadian who came in drunk one day. He shared a house with three American staff and had been drinking heavily the previous evening. In the morning, the Americans didn't wake him, thinking it better they leave him where he was. I actually saw them come in and noticed he was missing and commented on it but they covered for him by telling me he was ill. Unfortunately, a short while after they had left their house he woke up and rather than miss work decided to come in, albeit twenty or thirty minutes late. His head greenkeeper, not noticing he was still a little under the influence, sent him out to help the divot fillers who happened to be on his course that day. Once with them, he took over the role of driving their tractor between holes and went over some slopes at an inappropriate speed and scared them. At this point they contacted the head greenkeeper who, before he even spoke to the guy, contacted the HR Department. Once HR knew about it there was only one outcome unfortunately, which was dismissal, meaning the individual had to pack up and leave, get himself a flight back to Canada and explain things to his family, friends and University. It might have been better if the head greenkeeper had just taken a little time to think the consequences through as the lad had proved himself to be a good asset in the time he had been with us and this was a 'first offence'. If it had been someone who had been a poor employee and had required talking to a few times then I would have agreed with the course of action. On this occasion though it might have been better for all concerned, if he had just told him to b****r off back to his bed and not let it happen again!

We also had two cases where the police were involved and led to arrests. The first one concerned a fight in a night club where the greenkeeper was charged with serious assault. The first we knew was when he didn't turn up for work on Monday as he had been locked in a cell all weekend and was appearing in court. This was completely out of character as he'd been an excellent employee, well above average knowledge and skills. Immediately they heard, our HR Department wanted to fire him, (they seemed to have forgotten the phrase, 'presumed innocent until proven guilty'). There had been absolutely no problem at work and if we fired him, because he came from overseas and the court had taken his passport, he would be left homeless and without an income. HR agreed we could keep him on until his trial but unfortunately, that was delayed until after his work permit ran out, at which time BUNAC found out about the incident. I hadn't realised that part of the BUNAC agreement was if a student was in trouble with the authorities, I had to inform them and end the contract. I still feel that leaving someone in that position, with no income and rent to pay was the wrong thing to do, provided they weren't a threat to their fellow employees. After he left our employment, two of his fellow employees kindly took him in until his case came to court. This didn't go well as the Judge appeared to have a previous grievance with the defence lawyer who was the duty solicitor the police had provided for the lad at the outset. He was found guilty which was bad enough, but to compound the situation the judge took an age to pass sentence which she wanted to be a spell in custody. While being a serious offence, it would be unusual for a first offender to be given a custodial sentence under the circumstances, especially as the defence had offered compensation to the victim. Despite that, the judge did send him to prison. He lodged an appeal and fortunately, after over four months in, the sentence was substituted for a fine. The Appeal Court ruled the original sentence was excessive based on him having no previous criminal record and that he had a constructive life. While the ordeal will have impacted his life to an extent, fortunately it hasn't prevented him having a successful career in the turf industry. But it does show how one moment has the potential to hugely alter a person's life.

The second criminal incident involved another overseas employee who was accused of sexual assault. As with the previous incident, our HR Department wanted him to be fired, but again this would have left him with no income and unable to leave the country as the court had taken his passport. This might have been a more difficult situation as he was working in a team with some female greenkeepers. However, they didn't have a problem, having often been out in his company previously. When I met with him after his court appearance to determine his version of what happened, I realised that he'd been appointed the same duty solicitor as the person in the assault case and strongly advised him to get a better lawyer. His English wasn't the best and I helped him find a lawyer who immediately picked up on mistakes the duty solicitor had made, along with a lack of urgency, confirming my assessment of the duty solicitor. As well as having his passport removed, he was placed under a curfew where he had to be in his accommodation between the hours of 9pm and 5am. In Scotland, in cases such as this, the prosecution has up to a year to bring the accused to trial and his contract was due to finish at the end of November so rather than have him unemployed, I budgeted to keep him on through the remainder of the winter and the following summer. It was a full year after the event before he was scheduled to go to trial. It was further delayed and eventually didn't take place for another five months. The outcome on this occasion was more positive.

Every year when the seasonal staff begin, they are given a full induction. This has been company-wide at times but sometimes staff could be employed for more than a month before that would take place. From the time we began employing summer staff I made a point of giving everyone an induction, if not on their first day, then by the end of their first week. I would cover points about the Trust and the Links in general, as well as many aspects about the greenkeeping department before each person would receive a more detailed induction on their specific golf course.

Two aspects I always covered were:

- To be careful of the law in the UK.

- To be wary of bullying within the workplace

You might think the second point was a strange one to have to inform new employees about but unfortunately it was an issue that cropped up time and again. Only I seldom knew about it until after the person being bullied had left at the end of their contract. It was only one or two people who were responsible for it, but the fact many of the staff were aware of what was going on yet chose to remain silent, was every bit as disappointing to me. It still amazes me how some individuals in our workforce could sense vulnerability in another person and manipulate the situation to make their time at work a misery, always being smart enough to do so at a time when a supervisor or manager wasn't around. It wasn't always the shy person, or the one you would have thought most susceptible who was the 'victim'. It might have been someone who simply had different ideas, values or beliefs from the majority.

A change I introduced for the beginning of the 2005 season caused a real stir, although it turned out to be a storm in a teacup. Since long before I begun working at the Links, the divots were repaired by a group or groups of elderly guys referred to as 'sandpatchers'. This was because their job was to go around the course(s) and fill any divot holes on the fairways with sand which had been taken from the beach. My understanding was that this had started under Walter's tenure, although it's possible it went back further than that. When I arrived in 1991 there were two teams, one only worked on the Old Course while the other team rotated around the other three courses. Then, when the Strathtyrum came into use, a few more staff were employed and one team worked on the Eden and Strath while the other covered the New and Jubilee. Almost all of them were over seventy years old while some were into their eighties. A Links employee in another department even begged me not to give his father a job one summer as he was eighty-three! They would usually work five hours per day, five days per week, 6am until 11am and would have a fifteen-minute break at the nearest on-course shelter. If it was raining heavily the arrangement was they either wouldn't come in or would leave early. Then, when there were competitions such as the R&A Medal week taking place, they would spend their time tidying up the roadways and filling in the potholes. I never fully understood why they only used beach sand since most of it would blow out of the divot holes when it dried and I began adding a small amount of soil and fescue seed to the mix once Walter retired. While most of them did a satisfactory job, there were a few who were up to every trick in the book. When golfers arrived on the tee, they would 'stand aside' to let them play which was important from a Health and Safety aspect but some of them would head into the bushes to look for golf balls, often only coming out when the next group came on the tee. I also began to notice when driving around the courses that their fifteen-minute break was turning into one more resembling forty-five minutes. As well as talking to them myself on occasions, I'd asked the other head greenkeepers to have a word with them when it was something they saw and while there was a small improvement for a period after each 'talking to', between that and the increasing age of most of them, I decided it was time to try something different.

The first thing was to come up with a plan which I could implement with the same or a lesser budget. Latterly, the older guys worked what equated to 275 manhours per week. If I could get six people working eight hours per day, six days per week that was 288 manhours. It was becoming common to employ Eastern European labour, although it was better to do so through an agency as they had the experience of handling all the paperwork. My thought process was that this group could work as one team and do one of the five courses each day, covering the Old Course on a Sunday when there was no golf being played. On the sixth day they could concentrate on heavily used landing areas and the practice grounds. It would suit them to work six days per week as they were here to make money and would have little else to do being so far from home.

I engaged with a local agency who dealt mostly with people from Estonia to discuss the arrangements and the terms and conditions. It was the agency's responsibility to complete all the necessary paperwork for visas etc and to find them accommodation as well as to find a replacement if, for any reason, one or more of them left. For that we had to pay the agency a fee of £15 per person each week for each employee but paying them the minimum wage meant I was still within budget. The idea was all agreed prior to the end of 2004, then I got a telephone call from the agency to ask if it mattered if the people were all men or if there could be a mixture of male and female. I'd never considered the matter but the agency suggested it would be easier from an accommodation aspect if they were couples which made sense. We went through early 2005 and I hadn't heard much until a week or so before the group were due to start when the agent called one day to tell me he had six people and that they were all women. The thought was a shock initially, but in reality it shouldn't make any difference as both greenkeeping centres were equipped with separate locker rooms and toilets. The biggest concern was these women were coming from a country with little history of golf and they probably wouldn't understand the concept of the game or know the etiquette, when to stand still, move to the side etc. It would be a challenge for them to find their way around the courses and learn where to drive the tractor to avoid greens, bunkers and slopes. We agreed it was best if one greenkeeper from each team took a turn to work with them when they were on each course to show them what to do and make sure they were safe. I asked everyone to refer to them as divot fillers as opposed to sandpatchers as it was more reflective of what they did. Now, the greenstaff at St Andrews hadn't filled divots for some twenty years or more and many thought it was beneath them to carry out such a mundane job, so I was anticipating some resistance from the staff. That was all forgotten about on the first morning when the girls arrived. All of a sudden, there was an army of greenkeepers keen to help! While initially their English was poor, some of them had a good enough grasp of the language to communicate reasonably well. They were here to work and save money to send back home and although the work was boring and mundane, they just got on with it with no complaints.

Seasonal greenkeeper Lauren Giordana (3rd from left) with the divot fillers at the 2005 Open.

That wasn't the case with the old guys who had previously done the job. When they weren't contacted about coming back, one or two of them called me and weren't best pleased when I told them they wouldn't be required for the coming summer. Once they found out the job had been given to Estonians, they went to the local press to cause a bit of a stir. As is usual in these situations, the Links wouldn't get involved in any discussion through the newspapers and simply ignored the matter. The men didn't let go after a couple of weeks and a couple of them must have persuaded friends and family to write in, as periodically another letter would appear from 'a concerned local'. While showing sympathy for the old guys, the tone of some letters left a bit to be desired and came close to verging on racism.

It was important from my point of view that the courses didn't suffer from the change of direction and it was pleasing there were never any negative comments from committee, or golfers, regarding the job the divot fillers did through the entire season. The only disappointment was discovering the agent was taking money from each of them every week as well as from the Links.

I thought what we tried in 2005 worked well enough to merit continuing with that format in 2006 so the agent found me another six people, who again were all women. It meant we had to begin the training all over again, showing them the courses etc, but they were equally hard workers. Towards the end of the season, I was getting more confidence in them and asked what their plans were longer term. Now they had their work permits, I made them an offer that if they wanted to come back in 2007, I would employ them directly. The money I was paying the agent each week, I would give to them while they would also be able to keep the money they paid the agent. The only thing they would have to do was find their own accommodation and their own transport to get to and from work. They were all keen for that, so we agreed terms for the following season and they came back in April 2007. Of those six, two are still working at the Links some thirteen years later. While one is still working as a divot filler, the other, along with a girl who came for the 2008 season, came to me with a request - if they went to Elmwood over the winter and gained their National Certificate in Greenkeeping, would I employ them as seasonal greenkeepers in 2009? I said I would, provided they could find me suitable candidates to take their place in the divot team. They were able to do that and when they passed their college course in April they started back as seasonal greenkeepers. One moved to Germany to work but the other, Natasha Repinskaja, continued to do well and secured a full-time position after a couple of seasons. Over the years she has continued to develop and has shown a great interest in the ecology aspect of greenkeeping. A regular attendee of BIGGA events, for which she won the Central section's Patrons award in 2018, she represented St Andrews Links at the 2019 Open Championship at Royal Portrush. All done while undertaking an Open University course in psychology, pretty impressive for someone who travelled to a foreign country at 17 with only a limited grasp of English.

Natasha Repinskaja became the first full time female greenkeeper to work on the Links.

Shortly before the 2010 Open, a Sunday Red-top heard about these divot fillers and asked if they could do a feature on them along with some pictures of them on the Swilcan bridge wearing swimsuits. I said no! The journalist then suggested they wore evening dresses, which I again refused. They did finally get their story with some picture of the girls on the bridge wearing their normal every day, casual clothes.

Another divot filler who arrived later followed a similar pathway of attending college in the off season, getting his qualifications and working his way up to a greenkeeping position at the Links.

Over the years, some of them began dating some of the greenkeepers and a few of them married. As some left, we were always able to find replacements and this arrangement carried on for another ten years when it came to the end of its shelf life. As with the old guys, some of them had been in the role too long and were beginning to pick up bad habits. Four of the team were from one family and when one requested a day off, they all wanted off, and only one of the four could drive. At the end of 2016, after some discussions, the course managers decided to do the divoting on their respective courses using their own staff.

As time went on, it was more difficult to find staff who only wanted to work the summer, which wasn't a problem exclusive to St Andrews. Talking to contacts in Australia and America, they were facing similar problems. Ohio State were having difficulties enrolling students for their programmes, not just the turf programme, but where they ran similar ones in other industries. The two main UK colleges at Elmwood and Myrescough, were recruiting more students who were in employment and doing their courses on-line. Accommodation was becoming more difficult to find and the competition from Scandinavia in particular was strong, as the working conditions there were better and where there was accommodation on site. I thought there might be a lot of interest from local people who had taken early retirement and were looking for something to fill a few hours each day and, if they were golfers, would find it interesting. We were willing to train them up to a competency where they could cut tees, surrounds and fairways rather than just having them rake bunkers and fill divots. I wrote to all the golf clubs within a twelve-mile radius and asked if they could advertise these positions to their members. While I got a decent response, after explaining the hours would be 5.30am until 9.30am a lot of the interest disappeared. We did get a few who took the opportunity and while some were happy to try different tasks, others were content to only do the more mundane jobs. Some only did it for a season but others came back for three or four years which was good for us as we didn't have to retrain them.

Over the seventeen years or so we used seasonal staff in this manner, I would describe it as very successful in the main for a variety of reasons. We were able to carry out more greens pedestrian mowing which was the original reason for going down that route and we were also able to do all the little extra things the additional bodies allowed.

It was a challenge at times as the occasional person would change their mind at the last minute and not come, while some weren't as good as they claimed at their interview, but overall, the pros outweighed the cons. Having some of the better qualified and more experienced ones come and work with us, even for a season, allowed our own staff who had ambition to see what was achievable if they worked hard. Many of the seasonal staff and our own full-time staff, have gone on to have excellent careers in the industry and I'm delighted that working at St Andrews and the experiences they gained here had a part to play. I'm pleased to consider many of the people who went through the programme as my friends and we still keep in touch.

One funny incident before I finish this chapter concerned three seasonals who decided to mark their last day by donning swimming trunks and jumping from the Swilcan bridge into the burn. This despite there only being four inches of water in the burn at the time, which resulted in one of them having to attend A&E. It happened in October when Gordon McKie and I were both on holiday and we didn't become aware of it until nearly Christmas when someone told us about pictures of it being on Facebook. I found the pictures and printed one off as one of the guys, a student at Elmwood, was keen to return the following summer. When he came for his interview, I spoke solemnly at length about responsibilities, how our social media policy had tightened up and employees had to be very careful not to post things which might bring the Links into disrepute. He agreed all this was important and he would never do such a thing. I then pointed to the picture that I had pinned to the board behind me and which he hadn't noticed. The look on this face was priceless and he was really worried I wouldn't take him back as I carried on about the seriousness of his actions for a minute or two. But I did hire him.

It's not a good idea to go diving from the Swilcan bridge!

Chapter 12. Challenges and Changes

BEING APPOINTED to the position of Links Manager was obviously something which made me extremely happy and excited but it also presented me with some major challenges and took me to areas I had never experienced before. It was one thing being a head greenkeeper and reporting to committees or a manager but I was only responsible for a small number of staff and dealing with a small budget and one golf course. To suddenly having to deal with over fifty staff, five golf courses and a budget which was considerably larger than I'd previously experienced was a completely different ball game. As well as the five greenkeeping teams reporting into me, I also had the workshop team and the property and gardening departments to manage. Fortunately, there were various procedures in place and guidelines to follow while the other senior managers in the organisation were there to offer a lot of invaluable assistance and advice until I began to find my feet.

I had picked up on the key points on the history of the Trust during my nine years working there through reading books and articles and I had a decent knowledge of the Tom Morris era and the role Allan Robertson and Old Tom had on the Links. Most of this I learned through attending various functions where David Joy, a local artist and actor who played Old Tom Morris, performed. But I wasn't fully aware, or understood, what all the different departments within the Trust did and how they all contributed to the success of the business as a whole. Moving into my position and attending Trustees and LMC meetings along with discussing management issues and overall budgets gave me a much greater insight and understanding of the Trust.

When I first moved into the role, I kept the same hours as the greenkeepers as I wanted to spend time with them on the courses. I wanted to keep abreast of all that was happening and have an input into the condition of the turf. I also wanted to know how the head greenkeepers were going to react to the change of management. I had four head greenkeepers who used to be my peers but were now having to report to me, three of whom had applied for the role I now held. I was well aware what they were like, how they behaved, managed their staff and exactly what they thought of the organisation, which in many instances wasn't the most positive view. Over the previous four years we had attended a lot of management classes of one form or another as the Trust looked to achieve the Investors in People accreditation to improve people's management skills. I was always enthused by these as I was always keen to learn and willing to try things to improve my own management skills. Inevitably, we would leave these seminars or workshops and the comments from the others would be along the lines of, "What a heap of rubbish, I'm not going to do any of that crap." Most of them were very comfortable just doing as little as they could to get by, reacting to situations when they arose rather than being proactive and looking at continual improvement. They didn't like or embrace change, although some were more receptive than others to at least carrying things out when instructed.

The two immediate challenges I faced were the completion of phase two of the irrigation system to the Old, New and Jubilee courses over the winter of 2000-2001 and finding the cause and a solution to the appearance of a disease called Take-All*, which we were increasingly seeing more of on all the courses. The irrigation project was mostly a logistical challenge. To mole plough the amount of cable and pipe required for the fairways, greens and tees on three golf courses busy with golfers was a substantial task. Even in winter, the courses can still be extremely busy and the health and safety of the contractors and our own greenstaff was a major consideration.

Work began initially on the New course, progress was good through the sandy ground and the late autumn weather was favourable. Links greenstaff would work ahead of the contractors and remove the old sprinklers which, as we did, and with the ones from the Eden and Strathtyrum, we sold on or gave away to many smaller golf clubs around Scotland. This allowed the contractors to proceed undisturbed and they

---

*   Take-All disease. Circular shapes varying in size from side plates to dinner plates appear in the turf where all the grass inside the area dies off, except the fescue grasses, making the name a little bizarre. Although it can happen on any finely maintained turf, its effect is worst on greens and surrounds. There is no effective cure, making prevention the best course of action. The suspected cause is a continual change taking place on the surface between acidic and alkalinity influences. For example, applying acidic fertilisers followed by alkaline irrigation water.

would simply plough through the old pipes as removing them would create an unnecessary mess. When installing the new pipe and cables, it was important to ensure both were buried to a minimum depth of 400mm to prevent them being damaged by any aeration work in the future as the deepest a Vertidrain could go was 350mm. While it was possible to close one or two holes on the New or Jubilee course for a day or more to allow work to carry on undisturbed, with the numbers of green-fee paying golfers booked on the Old Course, that wasn't possible. However, we did still have the advantage of the two-week closures in both November and March along with Old Course being closed on Sundays.

After completing a few holes on the New, the contractors moved to the Old for two weeks in November while the course was closed and managed to get four holes finished. When they went back on the New course, Adrian Mortram, who was working on behalf of the Links, went out to check the pipes and cables were deep enough and discovered they were only 300mm below the surface. The contractors had brought a new mole plough on site just before they moved across to work on the Old Course and hadn't noticed that the blade on it wasn't set at the correct depth. That was two weeks of work wasted which would have to be done again, with the new pipe which had just been laid also having to be left in the ground. Fortunately, the contractors did manage to make up the time lost by working on Sundays and were able to complete the project before the main golfing season commenced.

The increase in disease activity and why it should suddenly appear was a more difficult one to solve. It first became noticeable on the Strathtyrum and Balgove courses. We knew that Take-All was more prevalent on newly constructed greens, in particular if they were sand based as in a USGA construction but these greens were ten years old. We then began to see outbreaks on the newer greens of the Eden course which weren't built to a USGA specification and were nearly 15 years old. Eventually it was appearing on almost every green to some degree or another, including on the Old Course and in the strangest of places. It was generally worst in areas near to the sprinklers which led to the theory it was in some way linked to the irrigation water but it was also appearing on slopes which cast doubt on that theory. The STRI were consulted for advice and they felt it was water related but couldn't come up with a definitive reason. I had asked Rich Hurley in America for advice and he also advised it could be water related and put me in touch with Dr Bob Carrow who specialised in irrigation water quality. After much discussion with Dr Carrow and the STRI it transpired that the issue was the high pH of the irrigation water. When changing source from the borehole on the university's land to the four new boreholes on ours, no one had thought of checking the water quality. Lesson learned, when drilling for water in future, get the quality tested. It was determined that the application of this high pH water, (approx. 8.1), to a turf surface consistently using fertilisers of an acidic nature, resulted in a fluctuation of the pH at the turf surface, causing the Take-All. Resolving it was another matter, to which the STRI didn't have an answer, so again I enrolled the services of Dr Carrow and Rich Hurley. The result was in February 2001 I headed to the GIS show in Dallas and met with George Frye, the original superintendent at Kiawah Island and who had installed a number of sulphur burners on golf courses around the US. They worked on the principal that poor quality water would pass through the device which burned elemental sulphur, and the pH could be lowered to whatever was required, within reason. It was more commonly used to reduce bicarbonates in the water, allowing the water to penetrate the surface more easily as bicarbonates form a crust on the surface. Whilst at the show I took a couple of days out to visit some courses where sulphur burners were used and understand how they worked. At one of the courses, I met John Harmon, who developed the SO2 generator, (a sulphur burner). The big difference was these usually operated in a large irrigation pond while we only had a holding tank but John was confident that, as our tank held just under one million gallons, it would work fine. The alternative would have been some sort of acid dosing of the water using sulphuric acid which had considerable H&S implications in the delivery, storage and the addition of it to the tank. The beauty of the sulphur burner was that it was completely safe. It worked by heating raw organic sulphur and converting it into a gas, (sulphurous dioxide) which, mixed with water, becomes sulphurous acid, (H_2SO_3).

The result is that the treated liquid, with an acidity level similar to lemonade, is then added to the water in the holding tank, reducing the pH to the level required depending on the rate you burn the sulphur. We chose to bring the water down from over 8 to a neutral position of between 6.3 to 6.5.

Not everyone was convinced of the safety in going down this route however, particularly Alistair Nicol, a former science teacher and current chairman of the LMC. Alistair was convinced this had the potential to burn all the grass across the courses if it went wrong, not something he particularly wanted to happen on his watch. To alleviate his concerns the AquaSO2 company, when they came over to install the burner, showed him a simple experiment. They ran the burner for a spell and collected some treated water with a pH of 2.1 from the outlet. One of the team then took a cup of this and drank it in front of us which was enough to satisfy him, and anyone else watching, that it was safe! And no, he didn't go behind the sheds and throw up afterwards.

Within a matter of weeks, we began to see less Take-All disease and that has been the case since, other than some occasional outbreaks on areas near sprinklers when the burner has been off line for a period for repair. No grass has been burned by the low pH and no one has died or been injured! It's economical to run with the only cost other than the electricity to power it being the elemental sulphur which has to be 99.9% moisture free and imported from the US.

Dod McLaren and me with the AquaSO2 team at the installation of the sulphur burner. George Frye, ex-superintendent at Kiawah Island is third from the right.

Another project which was taking place at this time concerned coastal erosion work on the Eden Estuary, although the planning for this began a few years earlier. There has always been erosion on the Estuary, going as far back as the 1870s as there are records of Tom Morris taking measures to protect the 11th green of the Old Course. Over the decades those defences have been added to, initially by a wooden sea wall constructed from railway sleepers which is still visible, and in front of this wall, some 700m of vertical gabions, (stone filled baskets). Behind the 8th green and along the 9th of the New course are a further 450m of sloping gabions. In the estuary, adjacent to the 9th green of the New, remains of barriers can still be seen where, in days gone past, attempts were made to stop or slow the movement of silt and sand from leaving the estuary.

It was Davie Wilson who first noticed that the dunes which ran parallel with the 8th hole on the Jubilee course were beginning to erode from the end of the gabions by the 8th tee out towards the mouth of the estuary. In late 1997 he installed a number of posts along the dunes and measured the distance from them to the estuary, allowing him to measure the rate of erosion. In the first 18 months, this was around six metres and there was no sign of it slowing down.

The Estuary has been well monitored over the years by the university, particularly by Professor Jack Jarvis of the GeoScience department and it was his view that, as the course of the River Eden changes as it makes it way out to sea, it causes erosion in different areas of the estuary. Over the forty years he had been studying it, the dunes now being eroded had at one time been accumulating.

In autumn 1999 the Trust, through Ian Forbes, applied for planning permission to erect more gabions along the next 400m stretch to protect the 8th of the Jubilee. The planning process was slow as the Eden estuary was designated a Site of Special Scientific Interest, (SSSI). The Trust commissioned an independent study to find the best method of protecting the coast which, in turn, would preserve the golf courses. Invited to participate in the study were Fife Council, Scottish Natural Heritage, Fife Council Ranger Service, the Royal Society for the Protection of Birds, the Scottish Environment Protection Agency, the Sea Mammal Research Institute, The Ministry of Defence, (they had similar problems on the opposite shore of the estuary at RAF Leuchars) and HR Wallingford, an engineering company who had expertise in this field.

The result of the consultation was published in the autumn of 2000 and it allowed the Trust to install a further 100m of sloping gabion baskets, which was referred to as 'hard engineering', with further permission to add 12,000 cubic metres (approx. 24,000 tonnes), of sand over the next 300m, a process called 'soft engineering'. It was made clear at the time that this 100m of gabions was the last time permission would be given to install a solid structure within the boundary of the Estuary. The project was to cost in the region of £200,000.

Installation of the gabion baskets began in November 2000, shortly after I was appointed Links Manager and by which time the erosion had taken another three metres of coastline.

Gabion baskets being installed to reduce the erosion
to the 8th hole of the Jubilee.

The soft engineering part of the project had to be delayed until September 2001 to avoid any disturbance to the seal breeding season. This was the first and only scheme of its kind in Scotland and the first in the UK to be applied to a site of international importance for both golf and wildlife. At low tide, six large dumper trucks would drive over 300m offshore where a 13-tonne excavator would load them with wet sand. They would then drive back and deposit the sand at the base of the dunes where a couple of bulldozers would shape it up in the form of a false beach.

Sand recharge taking place to reduce erosion to the left of the 8th on the Jubilee.

After completion, we arranged for a class of primary school children to come and transplant Marram and Sea Lyme grasses to stabilise an area of the 'beach' which we then fenced off to protect it. The theory behind the soft engineering was the shallow slope of the false beach would replicate the natural process of the Estuary and reduce the power from the waves before they hit the base of the dunes, while at low tide the loose sand would blow onto the dunes in the prevailing wind, thereby building them up. This process is often referred to as beach nourishment.

The completed project after the sand recharge.
Fenced and with dune grasses planted to stabilise the sand.

The results were exactly as predicted as sand blew over the dunes in the prevailing wind, raising their height, while some of the sand was slowly washed out towards the mouth of the estuary by the tide. The speed and extent of the sand movement depended on the weather, the strength of the wind and tides.

We had to repeat the soft engineering process again in the autumn of 2007 but haven't had to do it since, although I suspect it will be required sometime in the early 2020s. By 2007 the Eden estuary had been designated a Special Area of Conservation and a Natura 2000 Site. The increase in the height of the dunes between 2000 and 2020 was significant. As they slowly eroded and fell, they replenished the false beach to an extent. Over the past few years, the original datum posts and the fencing installed to protect the transplanted grasses have begun to reappear as this windblown sand dune has collapsed.

In early 2001 we embarked on arranging a deal with one of the three major equipment suppliers, Toro, John Deere and Ransomes, or Textron as they had become by then, following the merger of Ransomes and Jacobsen. This included visits to their UK bases along with visits to each company's local dealer or distributer and presentations by the companies to the senior management team at the Links. Each company put in some of their mowers and utility vehicles for greenstaff to trial and evaluate for a period. Up until then there had been no 'official' supplier of equipment and we had a mixture of different mowers with Ransomes supplying the pedestrian and fairway mowers along with the Cushman utility vehicles, while Toro supplied the greens ride-on mowers.

After much debate between the head greenkeepers and myself, then discussions with Alan McGregor, Euan MacGregor the finance manager, and me, the Trust signed its first deal with Toro to be the official supplier to St Andrews Links for 'Fine Turf Equipment'. It was signed during Dunhill week in October 2001 and included all pedestrian and ride-on greens and tees mowers and was to run for five years. The head greenkeepers preferred the Jacobsen fairway mowers they had been using for several years and we also decided to stay with Cushman for our utility vehicles.

There had always been problems at the JGC with golf balls coming into the yard from both the 1st and 18th holes of the Jubilee course and hitting the buildings. The holes in the roof of the old buildings and the marks on the front wall of the new facility were testament to that.

The head greenkeepers, Alan McGregor and me
after signing our first deal with Toro.

Although some tee shots from the 18th tee would come in, by far the worst problem was second, or subsequent shots, from the 1st hole. The 1st was a 465 yard par four with the green situated at the bottom of a banking which separated it from the main building of the new complex on the other side. A hole of that length is difficult at any stage of the round but being the 1st and playing into a prevailing wind coming slightly from the left, made for a tough start. Many golfers of all abilities, after slicing their tee shot, would then attempt a blind or 'miracle' shot over the banking to a green which they probably couldn't reach. Even good golfers from the centre of the fairway were liable to see their second shot drift right in the wind and into the complex. I could be sitting in my office and think a bullet had hit the frontage and neither the windows of the building or cars parked in the yard were safe. The first attempt to reduce the damage was to install six-metres high nets on top of the banking at the point where most balls were coming from. As well as being unsightly they were only partially effective, as golfers would still attempt to go over them and golf balls continued to hit the building.

The alternative was to move the 1st green further to the left, shortening the hole by some 100 yards. This was the proposal I put to the GSC and LMC, basing the reason for the change on staff safety. To compensate for the loss of 100 yards the plan included lengthening the 2nd hole some 30 yards by moving the tee back on to the site of the old 1st green. A bonus to this change was, it moved the green out into the open more as in its previous position it was shaded from the winter sun, and was the last to clear of frost in the morning. After selecting the site, the task of designing the new green was left to Davie Wilson and his team, subject to approval by myself and the LMC. The work was completed by Christmas 2001 using the turf from the original green and the new holes came into play for the 2002 season.

At the beginning of November 2000, I found myself heading off to the US again, this time to Pebble Beach in California. Alan McGregor and his wife were in that area on holiday and, because Pebble Beach had many similarities with St Andrews, (multiple courses with large numbers of vising golfers), Alan thought it would be a good idea if I flew out and visited. We would meet their greenstaff, benchmark, and pick up ideas from their operation we could use and, of course, squeeze in a game of golf. I felt it was also an opportunity Alan used to get to know me better. It was a flying visit and an eventful trip for me as I flew out on the Sunday to San Francisco, picked up a hire car and drove down to Pebble where we were staying, courtesy of the Pebble Beach company. On the Monday we were given a tour of the facilities and the different courses, meeting the different course superintendents and some of the departmental managers. On the Tuesday at 7am we had the first tee time at Pebble Beach but when we got to the Par 3 seventh hole the heavens opened and although we hit our tee shots, by the time we got to the green the course was unplayable and we had to come in. After a change of clothes, we made our way back out but not to play golf, just to look at the other holes! In the afternoon I walked Spanish Bay with the superintendent there. The sun was shining and there was hardly a golfer on the course, which looked tremendous, but at no point did he suggest I go and fetch my clubs!

The following day we played Cypress Point which remains one of my favourite courses in the world. We played with a member who did some work for the USGA called Tom Loss, who went by the name of Total Loss, (his words, not mine). He was a very accomplished player and while I played badly, I did par 15, 16 and 17 before resorting to type and taking an 8 up the last.

*At Pebble Beach. We didn't quite make it to the green here
before the rain began and halted play!*

Thursday saw me head back to San Francisco and home which was a bittersweet experience. Now I was classed as senior management I was allowed to fly business class which was wonderful. This was the only time I ever flew business class as an employee of the Links Trust. Thereafter, it was always standard class as I was always flying with some of my team and I didn't like turning left when entering the plane and leaving them to turn right. When I arrived home, I discovered my suitcase had been broken into and all the items I'd bought at Pebble and Cypress had been taken. Although I was reimbursed by the insurance company for the Pebble items, Cypress was a cash only facility and I had to bear the loss as I'd no receipts.

In February 2019, just after I retired, I returned to California to say a few goodbyes to friends at the GIS in San Diego. As part of my retirement gift the Links kindly arranged for two nights' accommodation at The Lodge at Pebble Beach. My wife and I were to make a holiday of it and through friends I was able to fix up golf for myself at both Pebble and Cypress. Unfortunately, the day we arrived at Pebble the wind was blowing over 50 mph, trees and power lines were falling down everywhere and all their courses were evacuated an hour before I was due to play. It continued to blow and pour rain overnight and Cypress Point was closed the following morning, although it's debatable if I could have got there because trees and powerlines were blocking the roads. I guess some things are not to be.

Christmas time 2001 was a breakthrough moment for me when I was able to fulfil my promise to Alan McGregor that I would 'catch the thief'. Although I had never set out with the sole purpose of doing so, I kept my eyes and ears open in the hope I might discover something to help me at some point. That moment came through unusual circumstances via a disgruntled member of staff. The annual pay increase always came at the end of the year and in 2001, I had refused to give one of the staff an increase. As a result, he came to see me in my office on 21 December, the Friday before we broke off for Christmas, to complain about my decision. I explained my reasons and promised that if he improved sufficiently through 2002, I would give him a raise which would put him back on track. Although he wasn't entirely happy, he accepted my decision, then, as he was leaving my office, he turned around and came back in, closing the door behind him. I wasn't quite sure what was coming next when he said, "Do you know you have a thief?" I replied that I did but I didn't want him to tell me who it was as I was confident I already knew. What I didn't know was when it was happening and was told it usually took place first thing in the morning and I had just missed him today. What he had stolen that morning was diesel which apparently was a common item for him to take. I thanked him for the information and he left. I contacted Alan McGregor and told him my news along with a plan which might catch him.

It had to be someone who had access and also be able to get things off the premises as most staff weren't allowed to take their cars into the yard. The individual I had in mind was going to be the duty head greenkeeper on Christmas Eve and Boxing Day before going off on holiday for two weeks and, with only a skeleton staff working those two days, might prove to be my best opportunity. Early on Christmas Eve and well before starting time, I arrived at the courses, parked my car at the other side of the complex and walked across to the JGC. Although still dark, I hid myself down in the banking behind a gorse bush and from where I could clearly see the diesel shed. After around twenty minutes the staff came in and I watched them head out onto their various courses to carry out their tasks. I gave it another twenty minutes and nothing happened so, disappointed, I left and went home. I called Alan to tell him what happened and said I would try again on Boxing Day. On Boxing Day, I did the same thing and again, I saw the staff head out to work. I was just about to give up again as I thought everyone had left the sheds when I heard an engine start up and a Cushman truckster appear and park at the door of the diesel shed. The person had six 25litre drums which he filled with red diesel then drove off towards the front of the building. I gave it another ten minutes when he appeared again and headed out onto the courses. Emerging from my hiding place I went to the front of the building where his own truck was parked. In the back, I could see the shape of the drums covered with a piece of carpet. After considering my options, I decided that to confront him myself could result in him managing to talk his way out of things as there would be no witnesses and it would end up being my word against his so I thought it best to just call the police. They arrived shortly afterwards where I explained what I'd witnessed and they asked if I could call him back to the sheds. I contacted him through our radios and just said someone wanted to see him back at the JGC. When he arrived, I simply pointed him out to the police and said, "That's him, call me when you're finished with him."

When the police called back, I then had to telephone the individual and explain he was suspended on suspicion of theft and that we would be in touch. He gave a reason why he had diesel in his vehicle which following an investigation, proved to be incorrect. After a disciplinary hearing he was fired because of his actions and although he did appeal, at the meeting it wasn't his dismissal he appealed against but rather, because of the time he had worked at the Links, he thought he should receive some severance payment for his long service. Although it was a good outcome, I was left disappointed by one aspect. At least one of the other head greenkeepers would have known what was going on, as would many other staff. Yet, until I upset the particular individual who tipped me off, no one had the desire to do anything about it.

If this hadn't happened and things had carried on as they were doing, I doubt if I would have stayed at St Andrews because I would have found the ongoing difficulties insurmountable. That's how big a deal it was.

This episode allowed me to recruit someone into the organisation who could bring a new enthusiasm and fresh ideas to the Links. I saw no point in simply promoting someone internally as I didn't see a candidate with any of the necessary qualities although many of them thought they should get the position. There might have been an opportunity to move Gordon McKie across from the Eden but he'd only been in that post for 15 months which would have left me with two teams with new leaders. I decided it better to leave Gordon where he was at that time until the team was more established. There was a great response to the job advert and we interviewed seven candidates.

Although most of those interviewed had a lot of experience working on a links course, in the end we decided on giving the job to Euan Grant. I first met Euan Grant at the BTME back in the 90s shortly after he had won the Toro Student of the Year award and I recalled the passion he had for greenkeeping. Although he had left the industry for a short period because of a family illness, he'd recently returned to greenkeeping and was currently working at the Forest of Arden. He convinced Alan McGregor and I that he would bring a more modern and business-like understanding of greenkeeping to St Andrews and help raise the standards. What Euan lacked in links experience he more than made up for in his enthusiasm; he was very much a people person and improved many of the individuals on his team through his leadership and encouragement. Although having experience of managing a links course can be helpful, I've never considered it to be absolutely vital as you're still trying to promote the same grasses whatever type of course you're managing in the UK, unless it has terrible soils or an exceptionally wet climate which makes that impossible. Euan was a quick learner, not one of those people who thought asking for advice was a sign of weakness. He was quickly able to pick up helpful tips from many of the staff, he just needed to determine if all of them were telling him the truth. The 'attention to detail' skill he learned through working at a high-end facility such as Forest of Arden quickly became apparent and he had a much better grasp of budgeting and financial planning than any of the others in the department through his experiences. With his arrival, and along with Gordon McKie, I was beginning to build a team willing to challenge the existing culture.

In October 2000, I was fortunate to meet Craig Courier, courses superintendent at Bethpage in New York which is a facility run by the City Authority and where there are five 18 hole courses, so it had a lot in common with St Andrews. Craig was over playing golf with friends who were also superintendents and had asked if we could meet up.

The Black Course was to stage the US Open in 2002, the first time the Championship had been played on a public course and it was Craig's suggestion that I come over as a volunteer and gain some insight to staging such an event. He had arranged accommodation for all the volunteers at a local agricultural college within walking distance of the course. Alan thought this would be worthwhile and that Niall Flanagan, the new golf manager, who started in his role at the Links the week before I did, should go with me. We flew out to America the Thursday before the tournament, as on the Friday I had arranged for us to play golf at Pine Valley with a member called John Ott, who happened to be the Mayor of Pine Valley no less. John was in his eighties then and had the strangest golf swing, worse than mine, but he could get the ball round. Pine Valley is still my favourite course in the world.

Then it was up to Bethpage ready for an early briefing on the Sunday with the other 100 plus volunteers. Rich Hurley was also working at the tournament as a volunteer and staying in our accommodation which we soon discovered was less than desirable, with damp rot in a lot of places and a mattress thinner than a wafer biscuit. Other than the Masters in April, it was the first major golf event after 9/11 and as such the security was extraordinary. There were snipers in the trees as we walked the fifteen minutes to the course each morning, even at 5am. The first morning was about familiarisation of the site and, along with Rich, my job for the week was to help with setting the pins on the back nine alongside Ryan Loudenslager, one of the full-time staff on the Black Course. Niall meanwhile, because he wasn't in the original plan, was down for divoting fairways which wasn't his scene and he only lasted one day! He was there to understand the other sides of the operation, not the golf course part. It was a great week, we had a ball and I took away a lot of good, and not so good ideas. The idea of having over one hundred volunteer staff was, to me, way over the top, perhaps not so much on a course like Bethpage but it's certainly not something you could justify on a Links course. Bethpage Black was like no course I'd seen before; I would describe it as 'big'. I've since been to Royal Melbourne and Sunningdale Old which although very different, have that same 'big' feel and look. A sign by the putting green (which has no holes cut in it) states, 'The Black Course is an extremely difficult course which we recommend only for highly skilled golfers'.

Craig and his team were well organised with a large crowd of volunteers on the bunkers which was much needed as there was a lot of sand. By Wednesday, after they had raked the bunkers, they were asked to rake up the grass around them as the players had instructed their caddies, coaches and anyone else going around with them in the practice rounds, to trample it down. With a lot of elevation on some holes and the rough being brutal it was a tough test.

The 2002 US Open at Bethpage Black. Probably the toughest course I've ever seen or played.

There was a lot of complaining from competitors as the distance to reach the fairways on some holes was over 230 yards and a lot of the field were struggling with that. We were in the era where tournament organisers were trying to 'Tiger Proof' their course, but how they were doing that played right into Tiger's hands. The greens ran between 14.5 and 15.5 on the Stimpmeter, the fastest I've ever experienced but they were all relatively flat with the exception of the 15th where, because of the slope, it was difficult to stop a ball on the back portion. I remember Craig's team talk on the Thursday morning before we went out. After giving all the other orders, he turned to the guys on the greens rollers and said, "Just keep rolling the greens until you run out of time, apart from the 15th, I guess we'd better leave it alone." Setting the cups was no great difficulty as neither Rich or I were getting anywhere near the hole cutter! Ryan and another member of staff did that while we repaired pitchmarks and, along with one of the tournament officials from the USGA, were looking at possible pin placings for the next day's play. This happened to involve a putter and three golf balls and we had good fun putting to potential locations to check they were fair. It was a two-tee start but there was no rush, completing the nine holes still took us over three hours. Then it was back for breakfast and watch the golf afterwards before getting back for the evening shift which was again repairing pitchmarks. All the staff clothing and food was sponsored by different industry-related companies which was something I took back to St Andrews for our future Opens. Craig's organisational charts and contingency plans were all well thought out and explained to everyone. Another idea I 'borrowed'.

Word got around that the person in charge of the St Andrews courses was in town and I received a request to do an interview for a local newspaper. I'd had some media training over the previous two years, so it didn't faze me. Niall came with me to listen and I kept it fairly general. One question was about the differences between managing golf courses in the UK and the US. I explained that due to the different climate and soil types, along with the harder ground conditions and generally stronger winds in the UK, it meant the game was played along the ground much more. We were lucky in the UK where it was cooler, generally less humid, and on the east coast in particular, drier. We didn't have as many types of diseases, or the same disease pressures or insects which could damage the turf. Likewise, on links courses, the grasses were suited to their environment, naturally slow growing and drought tolerant therefore we didn't need to fertilise or water them as much. I felt good and thought I'd done a decent job. Imagine my surprise when I walked in the following morning and someone said to me that I had better keep out of Craig's sight. The interviewer had turned my answer around and ran with the headline, "US GOLF COURSES USE FAR TOO MUCH WATER, FERTILISER AND PESTICIDES!" No one had briefed me she was a campaigner who was against using pesticides, in particular in the New York public parks which technically Bethpage was. Once I explained the situation to Craig and what I had said, he understood what had happened, (I think!).

We were able to sneak off and play at Winged Foot on the Tuesday between shifts and on the Saturday I had been offered a game at Shinnecock Hills. With it being at the other end of Long Island, Rich didn't fancy the drive on top of the early starts and late finishes. The weather forecast was poor for Saturday and we decided it was better to stay at Bethpage which was fortunate as heavy afternoon rain meant we were required to go out and 'squeegee' greens. I was sent up to the 18th green to sweep water off across the line of the golfers' putt when instructed by the Rules official. If there were no balls on the green then we could just get the water off as best we could. When I arrived, there was a quite a lot of water lying so I began sweeping, only for my squeegee to fall to pieces after three or four strokes as it hadn't been assembled properly. The New York crowd were raucous at the best of times but even worse once fuelled up with beer and I was greeted with loud cheers and calls of "Squeegee Boy, Squeegee Boy", which continued even after I got my squeegee repaired and started again. I had a laugh when a couple of people I knew arrived on the green and I greeted them with a, "Hi, how's it going?" followed by their name. Peter Dawson, Secretary to the R&A was first up. Then a few matches later, 1999 Open Champion Paul Lawrie.

It was great walking in each morning as, although there were snipers in the trees, they must have realised we weren't a threat and would shout "Hi" or "Good morning" to us. I was able to climb up a leaderboard and get the letters to put my name on top of the board with a score of three under par with Tiger underneath me at level par. The vendors didn't bother to lock their kiosks when they left the previous night so we often had a free ice cream to supplement our breakfast!

In July, once back home, I had the pleasure of playing with the highest ranked player I've ever played with, American Chad Campbell. He had been playing in the Scottish Open at Loch Lomond but had missed the cut and, before heading to St Georges for the Open, he called the Links to ask if there was any chance of him and his caddie getting a game on the Old Course. It so happened there were a lot of times available on the Saturday afternoon and the two of them were booked to play at 3pm. Being the only senior member of the management team around, I was dispatched to go and welcome them and tell them the championship tees were available if they wanted to play from them. I had already played, (very badly), on the Eden that morning and at the last minute I decided to take my clubs and ask if I could join them. Chad said I was more than welcome and in fact he asked another American who was waiting at the Starter's box if he wanted to make a fourball. Off we set along with my thirteen-year-old son Bruce caddying for me. It was Bruce who told me that Chad was currently well up on the PGA money list having already had eight top-ten finishes by then, including two runners-up places back in March. After a less than brilliant start I began to swing better just by watching the rhythm of Chad and his caddie who was also a professional golfer. Despite taking two shots to escape from the fairway bunker at the 2nd and another two to get out of the greenside bunker at the 12th following his drive, Chad was round in 76 while his caddie scored 75 and I had 78. When we were walking down 14, I discovered from his caddie that they met at college in Texas and I asked which one. When he replied it was Midland, I said I had a friend who went to that college, Steven Young, a three times Scottish Boys' Champion, Walker Cup player and who once beat Sergio Garcia 7&6. Steven lived just a few miles from me near Fraserburgh where I was born and his grandfather used to work on my family's farm. The caddie shouted over to Chad, "Hey, Gordon knows Steven Young." The three of them were at college together. It's a small world.

August 2003 saw the Links stage the British Mid-Amateur Championship which is run by the R&A and is open to players over 25 years old and who are supposed to 'work' rather than play full time amateur golf. It was to be played on the Jubilee and would be the first time the course had hosted a tournament of that size and prestige. The fact the tournament was coming to St Andrews was enough to draw a large entry, even though it was going to be played over the Jubilee rather than the Old. With so many entrants being exempt because they had won particular events, the R&A found themselves in the position there were hardly any places left in the field for many good players who would normally have entered. They approached the Links Trust to ask if they could have the use of the New course for a couple of days as this would allow them to increase the entries by introducing a 36-hole stroke-play qualifying event. The New already had numerous prepaid bookings so that wasn't possible, but the Links offered the Eden instead. Peter Dawson had never played the Eden since he came to St Andrews so we arranged a game for him where he could have a look at the course. On the day we played the wind strength could be described as average, but the direction was more easterly than normal and when we came to the 14th, I half-jokingly suggested he might be able to drive the green given his normal shot was a draw. At 350 yards and with a pond running up the left of the hole for the last 80 yards, it's not a shot you would normally attempt but with nothing at stake he gave it a try. He hit a beautiful tee shot down the right with a small draw and, between the helping wind and the fast-running fairway, his ball finished on the front edge of the green. In all my time at St Andrews I've only heard of one other person do that.

Peter was pleased with the course and was happy to have it used for qualifying along with the Jubilee. When that was announced, he received an email from an entrant from America who was most unhappy to, as he wrote, "Travel over to Scotland to play on a Mickey Mouse course measuring 6,200 yards." The first qualifying round was played in a howling gale with play close to being suspended. We kept an eye out for the person who had complained about the course being too easy. He scored 92.

The weather improved after that and there was some excellent golf played. The wind was again in an unusual direction as the opening seven holes on the Jubilee were playing directly downwind and players were regularly driving the first green. I went out to watch the final and saw some of the best golf I've ever witnessed. John Kemp from the John O'Gaunt Club in Bedfordshire, who was the holder and the 1999 winner, was playing Roger Roper from Yorkshire. Roper went to the turn in 33, three under par, and found himself four down. With the wind at their backs, they were driving close to many greens and the two par fives were easily reachable in two shots. On the 373yard 7th, Kemp drove it onto the green while Roper's 1-iron was only one yard short. Kemp actually missed short birdie putts on 10, 11 and 12 which would have seen him win out in the country but he still won the match by 4 & 3.

No sooner was the Mid-Amateur finished when there was another event taking place at the Links, this time of a completely different nature. The Links had been approached by a film company who were planning making a film on the life of Bobby Jones and they wanted to spend a week in St Andrews to record the historical visits he made here. There wasn't much warning this was taking place and when we first heard the timescale, we thought it would never happen even though the main characters had already been cast. However, the funding was already in place and the production company mobilised quickly. Within a matter of weeks, it was game on. The plan was to utilise two Sundays in August to film the main parts and to use the week between to film some other footage using the Eden course and those at neighbouring St Andrews Bay. Jim Caviezel was to play Jones and Claire Forlani his wife Mary, while Malcolm McDowell played his manager O.B Keeler and Aiden Quinn his adversary Harry Vardon. They also needed a cast of 300 extras, all dressed in 1920s period costume and many locals managed to pick up roles as extras, including yours truly who was playing a caddie. Alan McGregor landed a speaking part as the Old Course starter at the 1927 Open although he did make it sound as if he was introducing a boxing contest rather than a golf match! The way I looked at it, I was going to have to be around on the Sundays anyway to keep an eye on things, so I thought I may as well get paid for being there and I signed up at £60/day and a free 1920s style haircut. While they were doing some off-course filming on the Sunday morning, Malcolm McDowell arrived and was desperate to play the Old Course which of course he couldn't as it was closed. He went on and on about it until eventually I went to Alan McGregor with a suggestion that we let him play 1 and 18 while we were waiting. We told people the crew wanted to check the cameras and off the two of us went playing with his clubs in front of 300 spectators. Jim Caviezel was no golfer and Jamie Farmer, son of a local professional and an excellent golfer, was chosen to play Jones's swing double in long shots as he was of similar build and appearance to Caviezel.

If you ever see the film you have to be quick to spot me although in the poster used to advertise it, I was one of the largest people on it. Jones was being carried shoulder high from the 18th green after winning the 1927 Open and I'm right at the front, except I've got my best side to the camera, my back!

I also appeared very briefly coming over a mound in front of Jones when it was blowing a gale, for which they used a wind machine as it was flat calm all week. Then there are shots of Jones trying to play out of Hill bunker to the left of the 11th green on his first visit to St Andrews and when he famously walked off the course after that hole. There are numerous shots of a club hitting a ball which fails to get out of the bunker which were by me. They wanted these shots taken while they were filming another scene on the green and asked me if I would do them.

Bobby Jones and me. Not even Pauline recognised me!

I thought I was getting on reasonably well when they asked if I could make the ball hit the top row of turf on the revetted face to make it look as if the ball was almost going to get out. I told them if I was that good, I'd be on the European Tour, not messing around on a film set and if I got it wrong and hit the ball higher than intended, I was liable to take someone's head off as there was a crowd standing at the top of the bunker acting as spectators for the other scene. They persuaded me to give it a try and after three or four shots, I did clear the bunker face and fortunately the ball passed between the heads of two 'spectators'. I went back to making sure I thinned every shot after that. A few of us were invited to the 'wrap party' at St Andrews Bay after filming was complete on the second Sunday and we had a great time. I managed to blag Aidan Quinn's fleece which had the logo for the film embroidered on it and I still have the cloth cap I 'obtained' from wardrobe so all in, it was a good eight days.

While I kept the cap, they wouldn't let me have the car!

2004 brought a lot of changes to the department with two 'Heads' leaving. In March, Eddie Adams left to work for the European Tour where he would visit and advise at courses due to stage tour events later in the year. He had been at the Links since shortly after leaving school and had worked his way up through the ranks to become Head Greenkeeper of the Old Course at the end of 1991. There were more experienced and senior guys within the department but Eddie was a more rounded individual, better able to communicate with Committees, Tournament officials and the media. As well as struggling with parts of the role, most of the others wouldn't have enjoyed the position.

To replace him, I thought it best to move Euan Grant over from the New course where he had been performing well in the two years he had worked for the Trust. The Old Course was hosting the Amateur Championship in May and I thought Euan had more experience in hosting larger tournaments as the European Tour had often played events at Forest of Arden. Some of the other head greenkeepers felt they deserved the opportunity to get the post but Alan McGregor was content to go with my recommendation with the caveat that we write into Euan's contract the position would only be for a maximum of two Open Championships after which we had the right to move him to another course and give someone else the opportunity if we felt it would benefit the Links. Alan felt it was wrong that someone could tie the position up for as long as they wanted, particularly if it was thought they weren't carrying out their duties to the standard or in the manner the Links required. The idea was run past the Trust's lawyers to make sure it was legal and would stand up in court. It had long been regularly communicated by senior management and committees that each course was equal to the others and that budgets, equipment and staff salaries were all similar other than the Old having a few more staff and mowers. This was because the Old needed additional resources to get greens etc cut in front of golf each morning, which in the summer starts at 6.30am.

To minimise the disruption on other teams by having another internal move, I suggested to Alan McGregor we go back to the people we interviewed for the New Course in 2002 and ask one of them if they were still interested. As a result, I approached Dave Coull who was still the deputy at Luffness in East Lothian and Dave joined us in April. I was a little concerned that he mightn't stay as I knew his head greenkeeper at Luffness was approaching retirement and Dave would have loved that job but he assured me he wanted to stay at St Andrews. Watch this space!

It was around this time I persuaded the GSC and LMC to make two decisions which changed how golfers were allowed to play at St Andrews. One was to lengthen the Old Course for the club golfer by using the old championship tees for the measured course the Local Clubs played their competitions from. These would be at holes 3, 10, 13, 15 and 16, along with the championship tee at the 9th and was possible due to the new tees that were built for the 2010 Open at the aforementioned holes. The advancement in golfing equipment was now allowing regular golfers to hit the ball further and many Club players were regularly scoring 68 or better in various competitions. Interestingly, some 15 years on, this excellent scoring is again consistently being repeated.

The other decision was to allow golfers to choose which tee position they played from. Up until then, visiting golfers, or season tickets holders when not playing in a competition, had to play from the main play tees. This was standard procedure in most golf clubs across the UK at the time but was the most common complaint we received from visitors, particularly Americans, as they were used to having a choice of tees. I could relate to their frustration as many of them were exceptionally good players and, despite having paid a costly green fee, were getting what they considered less than the full experience. Kingsbarns Golf Links, a nearby course many of these same golfers would play on their trip, had allowed play from any tee since its opening in 2000. The only stipulation we put in place was, on the Old Course, three of the four golfers had to be single figure handicappers. There was resistance from some ticket holders but the better players were pleased with the change. There was a mixed reaction from some greenkeepers as they worried the additional play would cause excessive wear on the medal tees on the Par 3 holes.

As well as the Amateur Championship in May, the year 2004 was the R&A's 250th Anniversary and they were planning a week of celebrations to coincide with the tournament. There was a large marquee erected on the Bruce Embankment to host all the various dinners throughout the week with many famous people attending on different nights. It was quite a week and my wife and I were fortunate to be invited to a couple of the dinners. The first one was for representatives of the Local Golf clubs and we arranged for our eldest son to collect us at the end of the evening. His comment when he picked us up was that he had never seen so many drunk people together at one time.

The Amateur Championship was a great event, much less intense than an Open Championship and Euan handled things well, as did Davie Wilson and his team on the Jubilee course which was used for the two qualifying rounds along with the Old, before the competitors reverted to match play across the Old. The second qualifying round was disrupted by a heavy thurderstorm which delayed play for a couple of hours and softened the course up a little. Following the resumption of play, the course record on the Jubilee was broken when English internationalist James Heath came in with a 63. Then late in the day, Kevin McAlpine, from nearby Alyth and son of a former Dundee United goalkeeper, came in on the Old with a 62 which equalled the Old Course record set by Curtis Strange some 12 years earlier in the Dunhill Cup. The two of them led the qualifiers on a score of 135, nine under par. McAlpine incidentally went on to be a Scottish Amateur champion but is probably better known for caddying for Lexi Thomson on the LPGA Tour for a spell before marrying top Swedish professional Anna Nordqvist.

Two players who made the latter stages and went on to be notable names were Francesco Molinari and Spain's Gonzalo Fernandez Castano who both reached the quarter-finals. The final was between Scot Stuart Wilson and England's Lee Corfield and I recall an incident in the afternoon on the 14th green. Corfield was five holes down at one stage but was making a bit of a comeback when he reached the 14th green in two, or rather was on the 4th green which is shared with the 14th and he had Ginger Beer bunker between his ball and the pin. Electing to nip the ball off the turf with a sand iron, he was standing over his shot when the referee called him to stop. Technically, he was on the green and the referee realised if he hit the pin, he would be penalised so was asked if he'd like the pin attended. It turned out to be a good call as his chip finished only two inches short of the hole, a great shot under the circumstance but not enough to prevent Wilson winning the championship on the following green.

I had a similar incident on the same green a couple of years earlier although none of us thought of attending the pin that day. It was in the annual match held each September where the members of the R&A play against a team from the Local Clubs. The format is two-ball foursome and it uses all the courses apart from the Eden with some 800 players or more competing. My partner and I were playing against Past Captain Graeme Simmers and Immediate Past Captain Sir Michael Bonallack, both of whom I knew reasonably well. In his prime, Sir Michael was one of the best amateur golfers of all time to come out of the UK. He was still quite handy but after building up quite a lead, their putting deserted them and we began winning holes back when we reached the 14th. After their second shot Sir Michael found himself in the same position as Lee Corfield in that 2004 final, with the bunker between him and the pin. He had the option of putting across to the side and settling for a three-putt five, or chipping it over the bunker and trying to make a four which would have matched our likely score. He looked at me and said he needed to at least attempt the chip to try and make a four but was worried of taking a divot from the green. I agreed he had to at least try and that he go ahead and shouldn't worry. Then, when he was crouched over the ball I said, "If you do take a divot though, I'm going to call the News of the World newspaper." The ball was still rising as it passed the pin. We went on to win the match.

Just prior to the Amateur Championship, we had agreed that the Toro Company could make a DVD for advertising purposes as part of our agreement with them. This was going to be used the following year for the 2005 Open and as well as highlighting St Andrews Links it would also include another of their main clients, Pinehurst, who were to stage the 2005 US Open. This was a good match as both facilities have similarities with numerous courses and are part of a community. When undertaking something like this, it's always best to utilise a Sunday when the course is closed. We have to drive around asking people walking the course to wait where they are or move to the side for a minute so they're out of shot. Most people are okay with that but there's always someone who wants to be difficult and 'exercise their rights' to walk on the Links. I was more than happy to be there, to arrange anything extra they might require and which they hadn't thought of in advance, drive them around without damaging the course and be 'lookout' for the general public. We would supply a couple of greenkeepers to operate the equipment while the Toro company arranged the film crew. It's always an early start, around 5am, as that reduces the chances of interference from walkers and often it's the best part of the day for filming. After my experience of the Bobby Jones filming in 2003, this confirmed to me that filming can be incredibly boring if just looking on. I learned over the years not to make too many suggestions as they would be taken on board if there was time and the process would be prolonged. If the light changed there would be a retake or, if someone suggested it might be a better shot from a different direction, another retake. It could go on for what seemed forever. That Sunday of the Toro shoot, although it was early May, turned out to be the most glorious sunny day with only one real problem. I never even considered needing sunscreen and didn't notice as the day wore on, my face getting redder and redder until temperatures began to cool around 4pm, far too late to do anything about it. By the time I got home my face resembled what we refer to in Scotland as 'a skelpit a**e' (a smacked bottom). Lesson learned and note made for the future.

In July 2004 our long-time workshop manager George (Dod) McLaren retired after many years at the Links. I don't think he ever worked with Old Tom Morris but it felt like he had been there for a century and was a great servant over the years. He was an excellent mechanic and an absolutely brilliant problem solver. Because he was so 'hands-on' and was involved in all aspects of the installations of the irrigation and drainage systems, he was the man to go to when there was a problem. Dod knew far more about these systems than Walter, me, or any of the head greenkeepers ever did, although I made a point of trying to find out as much as I could. Fortunately, the new irrigation had excellent 'as laid' plans, as all the older stuff such as the drainage installation along with many other little things which had been carried out over the years was only stored in Dod's head. His skill, knowledge and dedication would be difficult to replace as he would be there and willing to help when there was a problem, any time of day or night. He never sought the limelight, that wasn't his scene, in fact he would get embarrassed any time he was thanked publicly by Alan McGregor. Many of the committee members were probably completely unaware of his input and how much he contributed to the success of the Trust.

In his deputy, Willie Redpath, we had a replacement who was capable of taking on the role. Willie had been with the Trust from the 1980s and had been steadily learning his trade and how the department worked. He still ran a small farm locally with his parents and as such, his knowledge of machinery in general and tractors in particular was a strong point. Someone new coming in could have been searching for years to get up to speed with everything but it was a lesson learned to make sure procedures and plans such as the irrigation, drainage and, in the future, fibre optic cables, were recorded for future reference. It wasn't easy to find an additional mechanic to fit into the workshop as it's a niche type of job, not necessarily suited to a car mechanic. There was a lot of competition in the turf industry locally and we had a few years of staff changes in the workshop for one reason or another before finding a settled team.

Before the year was finished, Dave Coull left to return to Luffness as head greenkeeper following the retirement of his old boss, despite saying at his interview he wouldn't do that. A short while after that job being advertised, there was no word who had been appointed which was unusual in the industry as various sales reps were always delighted to pass on that type of gossip. I was on the course with Dave one day and asked him if he'd heard who had got the job as I thought if anyone would know, Dave would. "Ah, he said meekly, I was going to speak to you about that, I have". It didn't come as a complete surprise to me as I knew how much he loved Luffness and while many people might have been disappointed that someone they employed would leave after only eight months, I was more philosophical. I had a good relationship with Dave who was an excellent greenkeeper and although I was sorry to see him go, his brief spell working at the Links did highlight a valuable lesson. His personality was different and he had his own way of doing things. This was fine because to an extent, each head greenkeeper needs the freedom to manage the course and their team as they see best. But there are certain things they need to comply with when being a manager within such a large and diverse organisation as the Links Trust. Dave could be very abrupt with his team and wasn't one to 'pussy foot' around when he wasn't best pleased. That was very different to how they had been treated by Euan and as such, most of them didn't take to him and probably weren't that bothered when they discovered he was leaving. While I was well aware of this, I didn't think it necessary to try to change how he managed. People are best when they are themselves and I was happy to let him manage as he saw fit, provided it didn't lead to any massive problem. Now being aware of the importance of appointing someone with a better understanding of how the Trust and the department operated, I decided on this occasion to go back in-house, moving Gordon McKie across from the Eden to fill the position on the New and promote his deputy, Graeme Taylor, to be head greenkeeper on the Eden. Gordon had another eight months of experience under his belt and the Eden had been a good 'breeding ground' for staff progressing in the past.

Chapter 13. Working with Nature

I F I'D been asked what the environment meant to me when I began my career as a greenkeeper at Fraserburgh back in 1976, I'd have probably said next to nothing. Even when I became head greenkeeper, looking after the environment wasn't on my radar, or at least not consciously. There was next to nothing in the way of gorse or any other shrubs and certainly no trees, it was purely dunes and grassland. I was only interested in presenting the course in as good condition as I could and my main challenges were weeds on the playing surfaces, worm casts on the greens and moles coming on to the course from the neighbouring farmland. It was an ongoing battle to eradicate these and the most successful methods were using pesticides. We cleared the greens of worm casts using chlordane, applying it through a watering can. To control the moles I would use strychnine, sprinkling it on worms before placing them in the mole run for the moles to eat. Both are brutal pesticides, which thankfully are now banned. I used to be petrified I would kill myself, especially when using strychnine. I was fixated about this and would wash my hands and all the equipment numerous times afterwards and still worry for a few hours. Even spraying selective herbicides to kill the weeds bothered me to an extent. Although I had my spraying qualifications, because I was still inexperienced, I was always worried about killing myself as well as the grass.

After moving to St Andrews things weren't much different initially although by then, there was increased talk in the greenkeeping industry that we should be more proactive in protecting the environment and providing habitat for different species. It was really through my involvement with BIGGA, the education they were providing and meeting other greenkeepers, which began to get me thinking more about the environment. To begin with, there were two areas which caught my attention, gorse management and the pond between holes 14 and 15 on the Eden Course.

Early in my time as head greenkeeper of the Eden, I was given permission to alter the look of the pond separating the 14th and 15th. These were two new holes at the far end of the course on land purchased at the same time as that bought for the Strathtyrum on the other side of the old railway line which was the previous boundary. The 14th and 15th are low lying and very silty as this area would have previously been a flood plain. The pond was created to collect drainage water from the surrounding area before escaping into the estuary at low tide through a large pipe with a non-return valve at the end. The extracted material was used to build up the surrounds of the newly-built Strathtryum course. The pond had been left looking like a boating pond when it was completed, with a stone wall edging the entire perimeter and no natural vegetation to provide habitat for any wildlife. I received a lot of advice on how to improve it from Les Hatton, the local Countryside Ranger who I dealt with in relation to the neighbouring Eden estuary, a SSSI and nature reserve. Working with Les further stoked my interest in environmental matters. The process itself was straightforward, driving soil from our composting area, tipping the material into the pond around the edges to build up the levels to just below the surface of the water. Les helped us source appropriate reeds from a nearby loch to transplant around the edges. It didn't take long for the reeds to establish and spread, or for the pond to attract moorhens, ducks and swans while there are always tadpoles in the spring. We even had fish which must have come up the pipe at high tide when the non-return valve had stuck open. Because I was on the board of BIGGA at the time, I was press-ganged into doing a presentation about the project at BTME afterwards, my first ever public speaking engagement. I was nervous as hell but survived the experience although most of the audience probably didn't understand a word I said because of my strong north-east accent and there were no subtitles.

In a follow up story about the pond, over time the reeds spread out and grew where the water is less than one metre deep, having to be cut back on a regular basis or the hole becomes a blind par three. The pond was slowly silting up and wasn't as deep as it used to be, although no one could tell me accurately how deep it was originally. At one point in the early 2010s I thought I would try and find out, borrowing a friend's kayak early one morning and going out on the pond.

My first substantial environmental project. Introducing new habitat around the edge of the pond on the Eden.

When I got to where I thought would be the deepest part, I tried to touch the bottom with my oar but once it went a certain depth the buoyancy of the oar pushed back against me and the force made me lose my balance and capsize. I thought I'd got off with it but Willie Redpath, the workshop manager, happened to be nearby and managed to take a picture on his mobile phone. I can confirm however, that day the pond was just under five feet deep.

Gorse management is another story all together and some golfers get very uptight about gorse being cut back, mostly because they don't understand how invasive it can be, the damage it does and how it can change a hole if left unchecked. An analogy I would use is to imagine your child growing up. Because you see them every day, the change in how they look is so slight you barely notice it, but if you compare your child with a nephew or niece you only see every three or four months, then the change in them is very noticeable. Talking with others in the industry I became aware how much gorse needed to be managed, something I never considered at Fraserburgh as I couldn't even get it to grow there.

Gorse encroaching onto a neighbouring stand of heather. If left unmanaged the heather would soon be lost forever.

What I didn't understand was, there was very little management taking place at St Andrews, only the tiniest amount in the odd place. There were tees on the Eden course where we could only use one half of the tee as gorse had grown up in front, blocking the line of site and it was similar on other courses. When I suggested to start cutting back some sizeable areas, I was met with resistance and negativity from my colleagues. After reading more about gorse management and talking to ecologists including Bob Taylor at STRI, I decided to go for it and began cutting down substantial areas. As predicted by colleagues, there were a lot of negative comments from golfers which I believe stemmed from a lack of understanding which wasn't helped by the lack of management carried out over the previous years. I also believe the reason for that was Walter and the other head greenkeepers didn't want to deal with any criticism it would attract, therefore it was easier to do nothing. I continued to cut back many areas each year on the Eden then, when I was promoted to Director of Greenkeeping, I contracted Bob Taylor to draw up a long-term gorse management plan for every hole on the Links which would continually roll over. We printed numerous articles in different publications explaining the reasons and used every opportunity we could to get the message across. Bob even visited and did a presentation to the committees as well as a public presentation to season ticket holders. And still many people don't get it! They'll say it has always been there but old aerial photographs from the 1930s and 40s show that isn't the case. Back then gorse was controlled by rabbits who would eat the young plants while they were still soft, but myxomatosis decimated the rabbit population allowing the gorse to gain a foothold. Gorse is an invasive species, it has a limited life cycle and will die off eventually and be replaced with other scrub, then trees, completely unsuitable for a Links course. It changes the grass species underneath its canopy as the needles enrich the soil, promoting coarser, undesirable grasses. As it ages, it loses its value as a habitat for nesting birds as the nests are more visible and accessible to predators, although it is beneficial to have stands of gorse at different stages of its life cycle around the courses. It was, and still is, a massive project, the largest part being to clear the gorse from the dunes which run through the Jubilee course and returning them to natural dune grassland.

Gorse clearing from the dunes on the Jubilee where it had smothered out all the fine duneland grasses. The grasses soon recolonised the dunes.

Shortly after becoming Links Superintendent, it became increasingly obvious that caring for the environment was starting to attract a lot of attention, both in the golf industry and society in general. With people and organisations constantly following what was happening at St Andrews and often looking to us for guidance, it was important we followed good practice and set good examples. With that in mind, I began working with different organisations to get the best advice and guidelines to ensure what we were doing was recorded and publicised. These included the Scottish Golf Environment Group, a subsidiary of the Scottish Golf Union, and the Committed to Green organisation headed by Jonathan Smith. It involved receiving awards for demonstrating the different practices the Links were doing but the awards were an aside. They allowed us to continually learn different things when going through the process. We were also putting information out there, showing other clubs around Scotland and the UK an environmental method of managing golf courses. By 2010, Jonathan Smith had moved and set up another initiative, entitled the Golf Environmental Organisation, (GEO), which was specific to golf but included all aspects of managing a golf facility. It wasn't just about the environmental projects undertaken but included fuel and energy usage, waste management, pesticide and fertiliser usage, water usage across the facility and how locally products were sourced. Although GEO found it difficult initially to gain recognition in the industry, it quickly evolved to prove itself the best, due partially to its independent verification system and the fact it was transferable and relevant in any country in the world. It began to receive golf industry support from the R&A and other Golf Federations or associations around the world along with plaudits from high profile environmental organisations.

I became involved with GEO in an effort to gain accreditation, working closely with Jonathan and his team along with other specialists in the golf industry. As well as benefitting the Links to gain accreditation, there was a benefit for GEO to have a famous complex like St Andrews involved in the programme through the world-wide publicity we would bring. It was a proud moment for me when, in 2011, we received accreditation. St Andrews Links were the third venue in Scotland, something like the 12th in the world and the first Open Championship venue to do so. It was hard work pulling everything together as initially I didn't get buy-in from many of the other departmental heads or senior management other than Alan McGregor. They didn't see the bigger picture, thinking anything regarding the environment was only related to the golf course and, as such, I had to find and extract a lot of the information myself. Fortunately, a couple of people, specifically in the accounts department and the course managers, were on hand to give support and provide the relevant information. The programme is about sustainability and showing continual improvement within the facility. To keep the accreditation, there is a requirement to reapply every three years and the Links Trust were reaccredited in 2014 and 2017. The process, while still time consuming, definitely became easier as others within the Trust became more understanding and supportive.

Receiving recognition for our first GEO certification in 2011.

The Links Trust had been working on protecting the courses from coastal erosion before I was promoted in 2000, with plans well underway for the beach nourishment work on the estuary adjacent to the 8th hole of the Jubilee course. Other areas of concern were along part of the Eden course where only a salt marsh protected it rather than gabion baskets and the dunes along the length of the West Sands beach. The West Sands runs from where the Swilcan burn comes out at the 1st hole of the Old Course to the 8th green of the Jubilee, a distance of between

2.5 and 3km. In the early 2000s, to ensure they kept their Blue Flag award for the beach, the Local Authority used a tractor and implement to clean the beach of rubbish which unfortunately collected all the seaweed at the same time. This is not good practice as seaweed traps the windblown sand and as the seaweed composts, it feeds the sea lyme and marram grasses spreading out from the existing dunes. This in turn catches more sand and begins the process of forming embryo dunes. The action of the local authority was breaking this natural cycle to the detriment of the dunes as they were being starved of new deposits. Both Ranald Strachan, FCCT[*] Ranger who had replaced Les Hatton, and myself would tell the local councillors, through a small advisory group, they needed to stop this practice. Eventually, Ranald and his manager managed to get an expert on dune management to visit and convince them to stop, although I suspect it was as much for financial reasons as environmental ones. This alone made a real difference but Ranald had a plan to further improve the health of the beach and the dunes which were becoming eroded by walkers, runners and cyclists, especially the dunes nearest the town. A storm in March 2010 caused severe damage to the dunes, persuading the different stakeholders that additional action was required. Ranald's suggestion was to fence off sections of the dunes to protect them and also to carry out a sand recharge on the first 100 yards of the worst affected area. He believed the fencing would also trap the windblown sand and allow the dunes to grow, giving further protection. Between us we managed to acquire funding from the local authority, the R&A and the Links Trust for the recharge which was the expensive part. FCCT had money in their budget for fencing, while I would use greenstaff to install it. We started slowly by fencing off areas nearest the town, leaving walkways at intervals for people to access the beach. We were expecting a considerable amount of criticism in the form of letters in the local press but there was very little. In fact, many people visiting the beach would ask the staff installing the fencing what they were doing and once it was explained, were very supportive. Over the course of a few years, we fenced off the entire length of West Sands, over 2km of dunes, leaving 12 access paths to the beach. Almost immediately the difference was immense and within the first year, embryo dunes began to appear outside the fenced areas, quickly extending some 10m or more down the beach. These embryo dunes may not last, they could

---

* Fife Coast and Countryside Trust, (FCCT), is an independent charity working with partners for a healthy environment that supports wellbeing and sustains the balance between people and nature.

even be wiped out in one storm, but at least they protect the older dunes behind and, if that is the case, then they'll have done their job and the process can start again.

The successful result of fencing off the dunes on the West Sands. Twelve metres of additional dune land formed over just a few years.

Technically, the boundary of land under management of the Links Trust extends to the high-water mark. As mentioned elsewhere, the Links are allowed to take sand from the beach to use for particular things which, provided we didn't take an excessive amount or do something such as sell it, was a historical 'right'. The situation changed around 2007 when Marine Scotland became responsible for all things pertaining to the coast instead of the local authority. We had to prove to them we weren't damaging the beach or causing coastal erosion which could be a significant problem if they were to stop us continuing with this practice. They requested a considerable amount of information and we needed assistance from many people to help with the application process and obtain a licence. Fortunately, we had an excellent relationship with

FCCT, the sedimentary group at St Andrews University and others, particularly Professor Jack Jarvis, who all assisted us. We were granted a licence but with a number of conditions which included limiting the amount of sand we took, monitoring the beach annually and having to reapply every three years, including submitting a report proving there was no detrimental effect to the beach. We still had to contact them every time we extracted sand, telling them when, from where and the amount taken.

At a later date, we applied for a licence to take additional sand from the same area to repair erosion within the dunes caused by the 2010 storms.

Restoring dunes on the West Sands damaged by a storm in 2010.

What followed highlights the inflexibility of government organisations and their lack of common sense for want of a better phrase. Part of the process was sending a sample of the sand from the extraction site to prove it wasn't contaminated, even though we were only going to be moving it a few hundred yards along the beach and onto the dune.

At first, I asked Marine Scotland if they could send someone down to look at the project, gain an understanding of all the good work we'd accomplished with FCCT, and how the beach and dunes were accruing. They replied they were too busy. The protocol they asked me to follow was to take four samples from across the site, (a sizeable area), therefore I headed down one day once the tide was well out. Rather than walk to different parts of the area, I decided to take a sample from only one place and split it into four. I thought at the time, this was an obvious weakness on the part of Marine Scotland in trusting me, or anyone, to follow their protocol. Imagine my surprise when they sent me notification showing two samples of the four were contaminated and we couldn't use that sand. How could that be since it was the same sample? Of course, I couldn't tell them what I'd done and called them to discuss the situation and what the next steps might be. They wanted me to provide further samples for testing but I established they still had some sand from the original ones and I asked them if they'd test them again. This time the results came back to say they were okay!

This type of inflexibility and the bureaucracy of different government agencies would frustrate me over the years, and it definitely became worse as time progressed. It seemed to become a tick-box exercise in most instances and when contacting them with a request or a change in a procedure, their default answer was always 'No'. I would always have to prove that what I was proposing would actually improve the environment or situation. Everything had to be explained by emails or telephone rather than someone visiting to look at the situation on the ground. Working at such a high-profile venue, I was always very conscious of doing things 'by the book' as the Links would have been a great story for any journalist if it was discovered we were doing something outside of the law. The last thing I wanted was to cause embarrassment to the Links Trust or the members of the different committees. As such, I would always do the right thing and contact the different organisations, SEPA, Marine Scotland or whoever before carrying out particular works. Then, something which should have been reasonably straightforward, would become a prolonged and over-complicated issue.

One example which really irritated me was regarding our water abstraction licence returns. We had to record the amount of water we abstracted from each borehole every day as they each had a limit on how much we could abstract per day, per month and per year. Each

November I had to return a form with this information to SEPA for their records. I was surprised therefore to receive an email from them one January to say they hadn't received them and be given a 'black mark' along with a warning that if it were to happen again then they might rescind our licence! I immediately phoned the person who emailed me to explain that I had returned the information in good time to the address I'd always sent it. They were adamant they hadn't received it and as such I was in breach of our licence. As I had the figures to hand on a spreadsheet, I was able to email them to the person straight away which I thought would show that I wasn't trying to mislead them or ignore the protocol. Despite that, they wouldn't remove the black mark against the Trust and there was no offer of an apology forthcoming. In future years I would send the information by post and email to several different people in SEPA, asking for a read receipt by return email!

A later project we undertook a few times with FCCT was to ask people to drop off their Christmas trees in January which we used to fill damaged hollows in the dunes, covering them in sand then transplanting marram grass on top.

As well as there being erosion on the West Sands beach, there has also been erosion within the estuary going back as far as the 1800s and Old Tom Morris's time. Part of the Eden course is only protected by a fragile salt marsh and, over the years, we have worked with Clare Maynard from the University of St Andrews, who leads the Green Shores Coastal Habitat Restoration Project. This involves transplanting saltmarsh grasses within the estuary to trap sediment, which while proving successful, is a very slow and long-term project. A large remaining section of the estuary on the golf courses' side is protected by gabion baskets dating back to the 1970s. Around 2006, many of these were beginning to collapse as the wire baskets became corroded and the stones within them spilled out. To replace or repair them using outside contractors would be a considerable cost, but we didn't have the expertise in-house. The solution was to hire contractors to repair a small section, arranging for a few of our more able staff to work alongside them, observing how it was done. Over the following three winters and working around the tide times, we would spend a few weeks repairing the remainder, a distance of over 1km.

At BTME in 2006 or 2007, I discovered a company who had developed a method of revetting bunker faces using recycled Astroturf, a process they went on to patent. Just as you would do when using turf,

Planting saltmarsh grasses on the Eden estuary to help reduce the power of the waves before the reach the coast.

Repairing gabion baskets at low tide on the Eden. estuary.

they stacked the Astroturf, (which was cut into strips the same size as the turf), on top of each other. Although the Astroturf strips were full of sand from the sports pitches they had come from, they were still thin in comparison to a strip of turf. I thought this was an interesting concept as the amount of turf used when rebuilding bunkers is considerable, plus, two inches of soil is being removed with each turf. Many golf clubs struggle to find enough suitable land on their premises to provide enough turf for revetting bunkers and buying it in for this type of work is hugely expensive.

Using recycled AstroTurf to revet bunker faces is a very sustainable practice.

The company was just starting out and was looking for some high-profile courses to market their idea. I offered to let them build a bunker on our practice area and, providing it looked and performed well, they could bring clients to see it and use it in marketing material. In return, they would allow us to build additional bunkers at the Links without having to pay for the patent. They agreed to this and the partnership has been very successful for everyone. That first bunker has lasted over ten years and the only maintenance required has been to replace the turf on the very top, as it builds up with sand splash over time. That's a huge saving on turf and labour from having to rebuild it every two years as expected if it's a practice bunker. Their initiative has also been very successful in Europe and America, including at some high-end clubs. Americans have never had much success with building revetted bunkers. I think the reason must be a mixture of the different grass types and climate to the UK, as the faces always seem to crumble. We went on to use Astroturf on all our practice bunkers and also on the bunkers on the Balgove course and a few on the Strathtyrum. We even pulled down some bunker faces and reshaped them using the same Astroturf strips when rebuilding the new ones. From a resources and environmental point of view this is brilliant, especially as the Astroturf would have been going to landfill. Will we ever see the bunkers on the Old Course built using this method? Never say never, it is possible, especially since the original idea has been developed, making the finished article look like real turf.

In 2014 I recruited our first environmental officer, employing James Hutchison from the greenkeeping team at Fairhaven and a previous winner of the BIGGA Environmental Greenkeeper of the Year award. While we were doing a lot of great work on the environmental front, I was very conscious neither I or any of the team had a great depth of knowledge on this subject and I could really use someone to lead on matters and coordinate things. I was also hoping that James, as well as educating the staff on environmental matters, would encourage some of them to focus more on the environment, so we could have a number of competent people on each team. Due to his home situation in Blackpool, James couldn't commit to moving to St Andrews and had to commute the five hours, (on a good day). He'd leave early on a Monday to get here for 8 or 9am then work his 40 hours before heading home on a Thursday evening or Friday lunchtime. Through summer it was easy for him to work on in an evening, while in the winter he would spend his time writing up reports or studying. That lifestyle however isn't sustainable and was particularly tough going through the winter. As a result, he left St Andrews to work for BIGGA at the end of 2015. It was an interesting experiment and difficult to quantify exactly how successful it was, but James produced some good reports and listed many different species of birds and well over 100 different plants he found on the golf course along with numerous fungi. More importantly, his enthusiasm rubbed off on many of the staff and I was able to identify at least one person on each team who had developed an interest in the environment and could continue the work. Although they didn't have the depth of knowledge James had, they had picked up a lot from him and I was confident each of them would continue with the good work he began.

There was always a lot of interest in what we were doing and we had many visits from various organisations, or individuals, wanting to learn or understand how we carried out different practices. I would also include details of our environmental work in any presentations I delivered at conferences. The downside was, when taking time during my working day to show groups around the Links to simply meet with them, I would often have to work on afterwards to catch up with my everyday things.

Working with partners is important. The Castle greenstaff helped FCCT remove bracken on the Braes adjacent the 7th hole. Every May this now provides a beautiful display of bluebells.

Along with other initiatives and collaborating with other groups and organisations, three things we were involved in annually were:

- Becoming involved in 'Operation Pollinator' where we would set aside areas on the course and develop wild flowers meadows.

- Giving a presentation on behalf of the St Andrews in Bloom group to the party who visited to judge the Scotland in Bloom competition.

- Give a talk to the Sustainable Environment class at St Andrews University. This involved an hour-long presentation to around 60 students. Then the following week, they would come in groups of 20 to walk the different areas of the courses to see in person what we were up to.

While I'm proud to have been involved and partially responsible for the success of numerous Opens and other tournaments, if pushed, I'd consider my involvement in the different environmental projects to be the most significant aspect of my time working at St Andrews Links.

Along with many different species of birds, hares are constantly seen on the courses.

Chapter 14. The 2005 Open, Another Tiger Win

2005 WAS a big year for me, the greenkeeping department and others in the Trust. Although both Euan Grant and I had been in our posts for the 2004 Amateur Championship this was going to a different level. As well as being the first Open I would be in overall charge, it was also going to be the first major tournament for Euan Grant.

Above that, having satisfied all the planning conditions and finalised the main details of the budget, the Links Trust was about to begin construction of another golf course which at that time was still being referred to as No. 7. By the time it was ready for opening in summer 2008 it had been renamed as The Castle course following a worldwide competition run by the Trust.

It was going to be a busy year with everything that was scheduled, although a lot of the groundwork in regard to the Open had been completed over previous winters. In truth, work for a St Andrews Open begins shortly after the previous one finishes as there is a debrief with the R&A where discussion centres on what went well and what could be better. Many people think St Andrews is on an automatic five-year rota for the Open but that isn't necessarily so, it's just been that way over the past twenty-five years but nothing is set in stone. It's fair to say, however, that it suits the R&A to stage it in St Andrews more frequently than other venues as it's always well supported and their staff have a lot less travelling to undertake in preparation for the event, especially between April and until the championship begins.

One of the things to come from the debrief are any course alterations which the R&A would like the Trust to consider and if agreeable, implement. To clarify, the R&A, don't own the course(s). For 2005 they requested that the Old Course be lengthened further by building additional tees on holes 2, 9, 12, 13 and 14 and extending the existing championship tee at the 4th. Given it wasn't going to affect the course for any local golfer as they wouldn't be playing from these new tees, there was no opposition from the Trustees or the LMC. There was no architect involved, it was merely a discussion between Peter Dawson representing the R&A Championship committee and Alan McGregor, Eddie Adams and me representing the Trust.

Not everyone in the golfing world was in agreement and one particular journalist made it his business to continually criticise both organisations, although the R&A took the brunt of his ire. For some reason the R&A are often in his firing line along with another two or three subjects. As a result, the majority of his articles tend to revert back to his opinion on one of these matters, those in authority, the golf ball and driving distances and course architecture in general. However, it does appear a couple of architects he favours can do no wrong. I used to enjoy reading his pieces but after a while I realised his angle and they all became rather boring. In my opinion he's become a bit of a one trick pony. I had a telephone conversation with him shortly before I retired when he called to ask why the fairway bunkers on the 6th of the Old Course were now in the rough rather than in the fairway as they used to be. I replied that in my twenty-seven years at the Links they had always been in the rough and I could send him aerial photographs to show they have been in the rough for at least forty years. (St Andrews is fortunate because, with the RAF base previously stationed at nearby Leuchars, there is a wealth of good aerial photographs). I also remembered when Eddie moved the maintenance road separating the Old and New courses further right to where it is today. Prior to that it actually ran between two of the bunkers and can still be seen as the grass type is slightly different. Although he accepted my account of things, it mattered not a jot and he still ran the article the following week, writing the fairway had recently been changed without anyone questioning it.

The new tees for the 2005 Open were built over the winters of 2002/03 and 2003/04 by Eddie and his team but to find the additional length, some of them encroached onto other courses. On the 2nd hole, the new tee was built on part of the 'Himalayas', or the Ladies Putting Club to give it its proper title. This added 40 yards to the hole as well as changing the line of the tee shot slightly. When in use, the out of bounds line has to be altered slightly to include the new tee as part of the golf course.

There was a small tee for the 9th hole built on the 8th fairway of the New Course immediately opposite the existing 9th tee. Built only a few inches above the level of the fairway it wasn't used and never has been as, at the last minute, the R&A thought it would make the hole easier for the right hander golfer who draws the ball. The outline of the tee can still be seen today.

On the 12th hole, a new tee was built on a mound immediately behind the 11th green. The mound itself had been man-made many years previously, probably as an obstacle to stop balls which went through the 11th green from finishing out of bounds in the estuary. The top of the mound was levelled to construct a tee smaller in area than considered ideal and it doesn't line up towards the 12th hole particularly well, but with limited room in that area it was as good as could be achieved. It added 34 yards to the hole, which meant to carry the two fairway bunkers, players would have to carry the ball at least 260 yards.

A new 12th tee was built for the 2005 Open. As seen here, it looks like it's lined up towards a hole on the Eden course.

The new tee on the 13th was built on the 3rd fairway of the Eden course and made the hole 465 yards, 35 yards longer than before. It was now 290 yards to pass the last fairway bunker on the left or to carry it for those players who preferred to try to go down the 6th fairway on that hole, as by doing this they are left with a better line to the pin for their approach shot.

For the 14th, a large depression near the 2nd green of the Eden course which had a couple of willow trees growing in it, was filled in with soil and sand until it formed a low mound. A new tee, some 50 yards behind the existing championship tee on 14 was constructed on top, making the hole the longest hole on the Open rota at the time, a mighty 618 yards. That meant it was now almost 230 yards to reach the fairway and 300 yards to pass the last of the Beardie bunkers on the left, with the out of bounds wall on the right. The people who were critical of the changes said this was another tee constructed on the Eden course which was incorrect. The hollow that was filled in had always been marked as out of bounds for those playing the 2nd of the Eden, even though it wasn't much further than 10 yards from the green.

The rationale for all the new tees was to bring the hazards, (bunkers mostly), back into play for the elite players given how much further they were now hitting the ball, a distance which had increased significantly since the Millennium Open. It was this aspect which caused the journalist to vent his anger at the R&A and, to a lesser extent, the Trust.

It can be debated what difference these changes made or if indeed, they actually favoured the bigger hitters. If you look at the history of golf and the Old Course in particular, then it could be said that the biggest hitters, provided they hit it reasonably straight, have always had an advantage. Irrespective of which tees golfers play from, there are certain bunkers or mounds some players will carry, while if they can hit it far enough on the fly, they will often land on a downslope as opposed to an upslope, further increasing their advantage.

How the changes would influence the championship would also be dependent on the weather conditions, especially the wind strength and direction. In a couple of the Patrons' days which the R&A hold for their main sponsors, the wind was particularly unkind, a strong breeze blowing in from the east, making it colder than average. I went out on both occasions to watch Retief Goosen and Jack Nicklaus playing. Neither of them could get past Hell bunker in two shots and Goosen ended up hitting a 4 iron for his third shot while Nicklaus had to hit a 3 iron for his, something uncommon for professionals to do. Of course, come the tournament itself, what little wind there was came more from the west and many players were getting up in two, only hitting an iron for their second shot.

Talking to Jack at a Patrons' Day prior to the 2005 Open.

Those of us on the greens staff who play golf had great fun on the practice days of Open week as, on our way round setting the course up in the early morning, we took our own drivers and balls to take on the challenge of hitting the fairway from the new tee on 14. For most of us, it was indeed a challenge and a number of balls were never seen again but that's why we're greenkeepers and not pro golfers.

With the construction of the Castle course due to begin in late March or early April we had advertised for a head greenkeeper at the end of 2004. We began interviews in January, with some taking place at BTME at Harrogate. It was important to me that we had a head greenkeeper appointed and involved from the beginning of construction. Not so much to be our 'eyes and ears' on site to check corners weren't being cut, but because they would take ownership of the project. Knowing and understanding so many aspects of the construction would be an advantage to them in time, once the course was open.

On completion of the interview process, we appointed Allan Patterson to the role of head greenkeeper of the Castle course. Allan had been the head greenkeeper of the Kings and Queens courses at Gleneagles Hotel for several years and was someone for whom I had a lot of respect. Whenever we met, I had been impressed by how he conducted himself. He was always interested in finding out what people were doing to improve their turf. Also, Allan was more than willing to discuss what he'd discovered, things which worked for him and things which didn't work so well. I liked this willingness to openly admit that things he'd tried hadn't worked out as he'd hoped, whether it was a product, a piece of equipment he'd purchased, or a different method of carrying out a particular task. It gives me trust in a person and a belief they will be open and honest. Along with these attributes, I knew Allan was someone who took a huge pride in his work and not someone who would be 'out of the door' at finishing time. I'd gleaned that not only by talking to him over the years but also through talking to others who knew him far better than I did. He would put his heart and soul into the role.

The construction of the Castle course began at the very end of March 2005 with Allan joining the Links the following week. A week later the contractors arrived to begin building the grandstands and tented village for the Open. With both projects running concurrently, I was constantly being torn between them but had every faith in both Euan on the Old and Allan at the Castle to ensure everything ran smoothly. Allan was the main point of contact with Paul Kimber, the on-site architect and they would discuss everything daily while I would try to get up to the site at least three or four times a week. To allow Euan to concentrate on the golf course, I would be the person to liaise with the contractors regarding their requirements. I would show them the routes to each site and where they could set down their materials to avoid or minimise any damage to the courses.

The weather from April until the end of June could be described as average. There was enough rain to keep the golf courses green but not enough to cause undue disruption to the construction work at the

Castle, other than the occasional very wet day when the shapers had to call a halt. If anything, there were a few negative comments about how green the Old Course was looking although the 1st and 18th fairways always tend to be greener than the others. At the beginning of July it all changed and became very dry. By the time the tournament began, the course, apart from some hollows, was completely brown and playing very firm and fast again. For the practice rounds of Open week itself, temperatures were as high as I have ever experienced at St Andrews; there was no wind and it was very humid. I was fortunate as I had decided to spend the week sleeping on a mattress in my office which had air-conditioning. Euan did the same in his office just along the corridor while a few of the staff had decided to pitch tents on the fairway of the 17th of the Jubilee course and use the showers and facilities at the maintenance facility. As well as wanting to be available at any time during the tournament, the other reason I was staying in my office was that we had decided to rent out our house. While this worked out great for me in the 25 degrees temperatures, it wasn't so good for Pauline who was in a caravan we borrowed from friends and pitched in a local caravan park. Plus, she had to share it with our three teenage children who had just returned from a weekend camping at T in the Park, a large Scottish music festival! I was particularly pleased I made the decision to sleep in my office.

We had a couple of guests join us, Cecil George and Jimmy Neilson, two stalwarts of Scottish greenkeeping and regular attendees at the Open. They had been involved with the Open since the association began providing bunker rakers for the championship in 1984 and although their involvement was now much reduced, they still came along every year and were always able to find a place for their caravan near the greenkeeping sheds at each venue. They would spend a lot of their day in the hospitality tent which BIGGA had within the tented village, meeting with both greenkeepers who were carrying out bunker raking duties as well as many visiting greenkeepers who attended the Open as spectators. There were always plenty of stories about the old days and how hard the two of them had things and although I'd heard most of them many times before, they were always entertaining. At night, they'd be back sitting outside their caravan with a dram or two, repeating the stories to the greenstaff who were staying on site.

That was after we came back from having a couple of beers in the Jigger Inn, as each night, once we had completed the evening shift, those of us staying on site would grab some buggies and drive across the courses to the little pub by the 17th fairway of the Old Course. We never had more than a couple of beers which were both well-deserved and much needed in the heat.

Having had the experience of being at Bethpage in 2002, I was able to introduce better facilities for our greenstaff for the 2005 Open. The R&A provided a marquee which was ideal for staff briefings but more importantly was somewhere we could all sit, relax and be fed. This was set up just outside the compound on the carry of the 18th of the Jubilee.

The catering tent in 2005 for staff to relax.

The Links Trust covered the cost of food for the early part of the week, while I was able to get four greenkeeping-related companies we dealt with to cover the cost of the food for each one of the tournament days. For that, they were able to put up banners and leave literature of their products while on the day they were sponsoring they could bring some of their staff or clients into the tent for some food and mix with the greenstaff. I hired a local outside caterer to do all the cooking and the staff were well fed with cereal etc from 4am, a cooked breakfast when everyone came in from the morning course set-up, soup and sandwiches for lunch and a hot meal before going out on the evening shift while tea and coffee was always available. My secretary would buy a selection of newspapers each morning and pin many of the golf related stories on notice boards for all the staff to read.

Toro, our machinery supplier, was kind enough to provide all the staff with uniforms for the week. They also supplied us with eight ride-on greens mowers for three weeks which, along with six of our own greens mowers, we used to cut the fairways.

Cutting the fairways with ride-on greens mowers.

This allowed us to achieve a tighter cut and get right into the base of the hollows. These different touches went down well with the greenstaff and, again, I tried to make sure everyone was included and that it wasn't just those working at the tournament which, by 2005, also included those constructing the Castle course.

Something we did for the first time in 2005 was to use turf irons to help reach the green speeds the R&A requested. Prior to the tournament we were able to get the extended use of a turf iron from one of the few companies in the UK who imported niche machinery for use on golf courses. That was fine but we needed more than one turf iron to prepare the course for the tournament each morning and were fortunate that we were able to borrow one from my friend John Philp at Carnoustie Golf Links for the week.

In all my experience around the Open and other large tournaments organised by the R&A, (I've attended numerous Opens either as part of the BIGGA greenkeeping support team, as a guest of the R&A, or as a spectator), the 'standard' requirement was usually to have the greens running around ten and a half feet on the Stimpmeter, (assuming a reasonable weather forecast). That would be a foot or even slightly more than we tried to achieve daily for everyday play as we find anything much faster than nine for the average golfer can have a dramatic effect on the pace of play, increasing the time for a round by up to an hour. We often received complaints from golfers, (generally those from the US), commenting that the greens were too slow, which could be a fair comment if it was a calm or damp day. But on another day when the wind was up and everything was dry, then nine feet or nine and a half feet was more than fast enough, as the wind could really affect the ball on the large green surfaces of the Old Course. This could be even worse on the greens at the far end of the course which are closer to the open expanse of the Eden estuary. Many caddies advise their golfers of these facts, which I'm sure reduced the number of letters or email complaints I received.

Greenkeeping isn't an exact science and procedures need to change with the conditions, therefore there is no 'standard' cutting height. As an average we would try to keep to a cutting height of 4.5mm through the summer to give us the desired speeds, but could lower it in 0.25mm increments to 4mm for short periods of a week or ten days for specific events. For a tournament such as the Open we have gone as low as 3.5mm if we really had to, but that would be a last resort and for as short a period as possible. The R&A, understandably, would always want the greens at tournament speed from Monday, the first day of practice. It wouldn't be fair on the players if they suddenly became six inches faster on the Thursday morning of the tournament. Therefore, we would always strive to get them up to speed for the beginning of the week and to maintain that speed throughout. It's also important to try to have the greens at the same speed for the late starters as they were for the groups going out early. That's not always an easy task to achieve as the weather can have a dramatic effect and the grass usually grows through the day! That's where keeping fertiliser amounts to a minimum is important, only applying any close to the tournament in exceptional circumstances. (These days however, the use of growth regulators, which basically almost stops the grass from growing, has become much more common practice but in 2005 it was only in its infancy and research of its effect was limited). On the other hand, on a sunny day with a drying breeze, the greens could actually speed up as the day progressed and the surfaces dried up. The use of the turf irons allowed us to add a few inches to the speed of the greens without having to reduce the height of cut which was healthier for the grass and the more that can be done to prevent the grass plant being stressed the better.

Being able to talk to many experienced superintendents and course managers to pick their brains and use that knowledge was a bonus I was fortunate to be able to call on to the advantage of the Links. Using turf irons was just one of the many practices that fall into that category. After the tournament I carried out more research on the various turf irons different manufacturers had developed. After reading a study conducted by Thomas Nikolai at Michigan State University, I chose the 'TruTurf' which was made in Australia by an independent manufacturer. It scored best in the research for the green speed being maintained for a longer period through the day. As well as being easy to operate, it was fast and one of the lightest. Weight was important as we didn't want to cause unnecessary compaction to the greens. The TruTurf company were looking for a UK distributor for their turf iron and I recommended Sandy Armit of DoubleA in Cupar. DoubleA is a progressive turf industry company who are distributors of a few niche machines used in the industry and do a very thorough job. They provide an excellent service and it seemed to me would be a great fit for TruTurf. Ray Duffy, the owner of TruTurf, and Sandy hit it off and DoubleA became their UK distributors. St Andrews Links was one of the first Scottish golf venues to buy the machines when we purchased two for the Old Course in 2006. We then went on to budget for two more each year for the other courses and reached a position where we had eight machines, replacing two each year. It became common practice to use them on the greens after mowing on four or more days per week through the main golfing season. In the winter when there was little growth, they might be rolled a couple of times per week rather than taking a heavier greensmower across them. They were also excellent for taking across the greens following vertidraining or any other aeration as they would settle the surfaces down.

Just as in 2000, the four days of the championship were played in ideal conditions with barely a breath of wind. Everyone was eager to see if Tiger could win at St Andrews again and if he could avoid all the bunkers just as he did in 2000. The latter part of that was beyond him when he found Shell bunker from the 7th tee on day one, not that it bothered him as his escape from the sand was close enough for him to get a birdie. He led from the moment he scored 66 on the first day and although he won by five shots eventually, it was a lot closer at one stage, particularly with only nine holes left to play. One of those closest challengers was home hope Colin Montgomerie, who started the final round three shots behind and had three birdies on the front nine holes before fading with three bogeys on his back nine to finish with a level par 72 and second place.

Of course, the tournament was also known as being Jack Nicklaus's final round of his professional career. Playing with great rival Tom Watson, he finished with a birdie on the 18th in the second round but that wasn't enough for him to make the cut. I'm ashamed to say I missed him playing his closing holes as I was so tired, I decided the time would be better spent trying to catch up on some sleep in my office rather than battle the large crowds watching him finish. Although I missed the occasion, there was a happy ending as in the evening, just as I was finishing tidying up at the 18th green with Euan, our golf manager came on the radio. Mr Nicklaus had booked the Links Clubhouse for a meal with his family and friends and he was asking if Euan and I could call in past to meet him and allow him to say thanks. When we arrived there some twenty minutes later, everyone was at dinner but he took the time to say thanks and tell us that the course was in great shape and how much he always liked to play the Old Course. We were both conscious he was eating and didn't want to hang around so we thanked him for his kind words and disappeared promptly.

Anyone who has watched the presentation ceremony of the Open will have noticed there are very few people in attendance although it does depend on the venue. Usually, the line-up consists of the Captain of the host Club, the Chairman of the Championship Committee, the Director of the Championship and the Course Manager, with the CEO of the R&A announcing the result. Therefore in 2005, I wasn't surprised when Alan McGregor told me it would only be Euan and himself representing the Links Trust attending the ceremony on the 1st tee. While some people might have seen that as a slur, I was neither surprised nor upset. I might have been disappointed for a short period, but it was Euan who had the responsibility for the course condition and I felt it would have been a lot more of a disappointment for him if it had been me up there taking the credit.

A couple of funnies from the week included one of the Old Course team falling asleep on his deck chair outside his tent one afternoon when only wearing shorts and getting his legs completely burnt in the sun. It was painful for us just watching him cut the 2nd and 16th green the next day.

The other one which comes to mind was another Old Course greenkeeper, Peter Stewart, whose job it was to cut the 7th and 11th green each morning. Anyone who has been to a St Andrews Open will know that the large grandstand behind that double green is one of the best viewing places as, with binoculars, you can see up to six different greens and holes. Peter was out there cutting his green on the Sunday morning, the last day, when at around 5.30am a spectator gets himself up into the back row of seats, sits down with his newspaper and makes himself comfy. Peter carries on cutting for a few minutes then when he gets reasonably close to the guy shouts, "Excuse me, excuse me." When the guy realises it's him Peter is calling to, as there's not another soul around, he asks, "Yes?" to which Peter replies, "You're sitting in someone's seat; he's just gone to the toilet!"

Although I wasn't on the 1st tee at the presentation ceremony, as a member of the Links Trust Championship Committee, I was able to use our small pavilion by the side of the 1st fairway during the week, which was also where we were to go before and after the presentation for some drinks. It's traditional the champion always comes into the pavilion for ten minutes or so after all the formalities, interviews and photographs are taken where the committee has a group photo taken with him and the opportunity to ask questions or just chat. I was looking forward to that and Tiger was barely through the door when I shoved my flag from 2000 in front of him and asked if he would autograph it, politely of course, and which he kindly did. The following week Alan McGregor told me sternly what I did was considered inappropriate. Oh well, it's often easier to apologise than ask for permission.

The fine weather continued well after the tournament which was a mixed blessing. It's great from the point of view of the contractors taking the infrastructure down as it reduces damage. They're in much more of a hurry when dismantling the grandstands and tents than they are when erecting them as they usually want to get them to the next venue ASAP.

And relax. The afterparty following the 2005 Open.

It would have been better if there had been a little moisture to aid recovery from the heavily trafficked routes or where we had to turf or seed areas. The drought continued all the way through to October and was great for building the Castle course, with all the earth moving being able to continue uninterrupted.

The season, and indeed the year, had an enjoyable finish for me. While I continued to be busy with my 'day job' such as planning and budgeting for 2006 along with other matters, there was still the Castle course being built and the Open contractors to get off site. They are normally clear by the end of August and the build for the Alfred Dunhill Links Championship, (ADLC), usually begins in early September. Many people might think it odd that we don't keep the same infrastructure but that wouldn't work. For one, the requirements at the Dunhill are minor in comparison to the Open. At the Open the grandstand behind the 18th green straddles the small shop there. In comparison, the Dunhill only has a small stand by the side of the shop which is the only grandstand on the course. Behind the 17th green, Dunhill have their hospitality pavilion rather than the huge stand used at the Open which seats over 3,000. There is only a very small 'tented village' at the Dunhill, located on the area known as the Bruce Embankment to the right of the 1st fairway, with a few other catering outlets around the course.

Alan McGregor had offered me the opportunity to play in the ADLC as the Trust's representative which I never expected, as normally the place goes to a Trustee or member of the LMC. I wasn't going to turn it down, what's not to like about having the opportunity to play Kingsbarns, Carnoustie and the Old Course? They are all places I love and have had the pleasure of playing many times. The format is an amateur is drawn with a professional and it's the best ball score of the two on each hole over each of the venues which would determine who made the final round on the Sunday over the Old Course. I just had to figure out how I could fit it in with making sure everything was going to run smoothly for the tournament. I had every faith that Euan would be able to handle anything that may crop up but I still thought it right that I be there each morning to make sure all was well, help out for as long as I could depending on my tee times, and make sure all the food was there for the staff barbeque.

The amateur doesn't find out who their professional playing partner is until the Tuesday evening reception, along with the order they play the courses in and each day's tee time. The reception is held in the Dunhill pavilion and while only a few of the pros attend, it's usual for many of the celebrities to be there, making for good people spotting. My pro was going to be Jason Knutson and yes, I had to look his name up as well. He's an American who was playing on the Asian Tour at the time, had won the Macau Open and had finished fifth on the Asian tour money list. The tournament was very popular in the Far East because of the Dunhill brand and as such, they always had places for a few players from that Tour in the field. The other two players on our fourball were the English professional Barry Lane and his wife. I managed to juggle everything around but didn't play particularly well though I did beat my pro in our first round which was over the Old Course. He'd never played links golf before and the greens, particularly on the Old Course, threw him a lot. By the time we got to Carnoustie on the Saturday, where my younger son Bruce was caddying, he was playing better but we missed the cut by a large margin. My highlight was a birdie at the 10th at Carnoustie which, due to it being a two-tee start we were playing as our first hole. The green is beside the Carnoustie greenkeeping facility and some of the greenkeepers came out to see me. That was more than Pauline, who decided to come and watch me play for one of the few times in her life but was late in getting there and missed my one moment of glory!

After the golf on the Saturday, there was a dinner and party in the Dunhill pavilion for all the competitors and their wives but most of the professionals gave it a miss. Mrs Moir, however, was really looking forward to the celebrity spotting. The entertainment was provided by ex-Eagles member, Don Felder and his band and through the evening they were joined on stage by some of the competitors such as Ronan Keating and Huey Lewis with Tico Torres on drums.

One of the gentlemen on our table was an Australian businessman called Alan Newcombe who had travelled over to play. We got to know him better as the evening wore on, especially when he began asking us the virtues of malt whisky! Alan had travelled over with the professional from his home club in Brisbane and had told his wife he won the trip through his business. He'd never been to St Andrews before and like many people he didn't know the set up and how things operated here. When he arrived, he just walked into the R&A Clubhouse and announced that he had come over to play in the Dunhill. He was quickly, and politely, put in his place and informed where registration was held. Not knowing the town and for simplicity, he arranged everything through the tournament organisers IMG, who, without offering alternatives, booked him into the Old Course Hotel for the week. He was lamenting how his caddy wasn't going to be able to play the Old Course as it was closed on Monday and they were flying back on Tuesday. As luck would have it, I said there was a possibility they could play on the Monday afternoon. If the tournament finished as planned on Sunday, then there is a small event for many of the volunteers on Monday morning which had a shotgun start.

With my son Bruce at the 2005 Dunhill

This means the course is clear by around 1pm and some of the greenkeepers and IMG staff are able to hold their own 'unofficial' shotgun game in the afternoon where there are usually spare places. I asked them to come to the JGC for 12.45 ready to play and we'd take it from there, no guarantees. I made a friend for life! I didn't hear from Alan again for something like eight years. Then he telephoned me one day to say he was in St Andrews and asked if I wanted a game. He had a close friend who had become a member of the R&A and Alan had travelled over with him for the R&A September Meeting. He has since come back most years in September either with his friend, or his wife and other friends.

There were no celebrities at our table but plenty of them at the neighbouring ones, including the great American 400m hurdler, Ed Moses, who wasn't a golfer but had come over to support some people he knew and help raise money for charity.

I happened to be wearing my kilt at the dinner and this fascinated Ed Moses' wife, who came from Watford, and we ended up chatting to them for a spell. They even asked us back to the hotel afterwards for a party but I was conscious, (barely, as the malt whisky had been flowing freely), that I was still working at 7am the next morning so we declined their offer. "Never mind," they said, "the party will still be going at 7 so just come up to the room." Well, the next morning everyone was in, the weather forecast was good and things were going to plan when I was driving down the 17th fairway around 7.30am. I wondered if the party was still going and parked my buggy at the edge of the fairway, jumped the small wall and made my way to their room. All was silent when I stood outside their door and I took a business card from my pocket and wrote on it, '7.30am, I'm here, where's the party?', signing it 'Gordon' before sliding it under the door.

All the senior managers and wives went to the pavilion for lunch on the Sunday to watch the golf finish before the presentation ceremony. We were sitting there when Mr and Mrs Moses came in, spotted me, and came over to say hello. When they left our golf manager at the time, who always wanted to be in the know, asked who it was. When I told him, he asked how the hell I knew Ed Moses to which I replied, "Oh, we go back years, I can't even remember when we first met."

Chapter 15. Building the Castle Course

B Y FAR the largest project I was involved with was the building of Course No.7 which went on to be named The Castle course. It's not everyone who has the opportunity to build a new course from scratch and it was an experience I thoroughly enjoyed, even though it added a considerable amount to my workload.

Thoughts of a seventh course began in 1998 as the Links were getting increasingly busy with more visiting golfers making the pilgrimage to the Home of Golf. Membership numbers in the Local Clubs were also expanding as this was required to obtain a season ticket if you weren't a resident of the town. Locals were finding it increasingly difficult to get times on the New and Jubilee courses as well as the Old. Therefore, the idea was to build another good quality course which would be aimed primarily at the visiting golfer, freeing up more times on the Links for ticket holders. One of the difficulties for Trustees was, following legal advice, any new development had to be contiguous with the town or the existing courses, which severely limited their options. At the far end of the Strathtyrum course, the land is extremely low lying with areas often lying under water. Plus, the proximity of the main A91 into town would have restricted what was possible from a health and safety perspective with the possibility of stray golf balls affecting traffic.

Across the A91 from the Strathtyrum course was Strathyrum estate and Balgove farm and this land was given serious consideration. The STRI was commissioned to carry out an assessment but their report suggested it was unsuitable due to a large, steep slope running through a section along with heavy ground conditions on another part of the site.

The process went on hold for a period until the Trust was approached by the owner of Kinkell Farm who had heard of our ambition. Kinkell Farm sits to the east of the town but another farm,

Brownhills, was between it and the caravan park which bordered the town. After negotiations between both farmers, the Trust was able to purchase over 95 hectares. It's a clifftop site with fantastic views over the bay, the East Sands, harbour and St Andrews. The soil was varied throughout with some areas of beautiful sandy soil while others were heavy clay, and every soil type in between. There was a large hill in one area while the wastewater treatment plant for St Andrews sat in a hollow on the clifftop with a road running through the centre of the site from the A917 to service it. In over ten years living in St Andrews, I'd never realised how much land there was between the main road and the sea as it falls away considerably from the road and most of it can't be seen.

This all happened in 2001/early 2002 and it was an exciting time to be part of the planning process. It's hard to remember the exact order of how things happened but one of the first things required was to appoint an architect and we made it be known that we were 'open for applications'. A considerable number of applications came from all over the world, including from 'big name' players. The Trust set up a working party consisting of committee members and some of the senior managers to oversee the entire project and I was tasked with drawing up a short list of six architects to be interviewed. We ruled out all the 'big name' players because of their likely fees while their visits to the site during construction are usually limited. We tried to keep it 'safe' to an extent and had well established, traditional, UK architects in the mix along with one American team, Dr Rich Hurley and Eric Bergstol, both members of the St Andrews Golf Club and frequent visitors. I'd experienced the high standard of courses they had built in the New York area, which Eric continued to manage as part of his business portfolio.

Even before we began looking for an architect, Rich Hurley walked the land with me on one of his regular golf trips and we identified some potential holes along the clifftop. At the end furthest from the town, the land we purchased became quite narrow and stopped just before a steep gulley. That section lent itself to a hole playing to the furthest point, followed by a Par 3 from the boundary wall down to the coast, with a steep fall on the right and behind the green. When we stood looking at that potential hole, Rich asked the possibility of purchasing an additional piece of land on the clifftop further to the east, just large enough to have a tee and a route wide enough for golfers and machinery to access. That would allow for a spectacular Par 3 of approx 200 yards over a ravine and looking back into town. The following week I took Alan McGregor out to look at this idea and we ended up buying an additional piece of land from the farmer.

Planning consultants were hired and the process stepped up a gear, with ecological and archaeological surveys commissioned. We had to find a water source to supply irrigation to the course, although everything at this stage was still subject to getting planning permission which we knew wouldn't be straightforward. During construction of the neighbouring St Andrews Bay Hotel and Golf Courses, some damage was caused to many minor roads around St Andrews by the construction traffic. The farmer also advised us of the difficulties when the wastewater treatment was built; he thought objectors planted some rare flowers called maiden pinks in an attempt to stop the process. Strangely enough, many golfers in the town didn't want the course to be built, despite the fact it would free up more times for them on the Links.

The interviews for the architect were duly held toward the end of 2002 and it was David McLay Kidd, (DMK Golf Design) who won the contract. He fulfilled the criteria for those whose decision it eventually was. He certainly had a good pedigree and was well known in the industry as a young, vibrant, up and coming architect, having made his name for designing Bandon Dunes in Oregon. I didn't know David although I had read and heard a lot about him, but did know his father well, as he was estates manager at Gleneagles for many years. His appointment would generate a lot of publicity and it would be great to highlight that we had hired a young Scottish, world-acclaimed, architect.

Each architect was given an hour to make their presentation and state their case for being selected. David was last to present, and he spoke for close on two hours! He presented a great vision and philosophy for the course, even though he had barely seen the land, other than a flying visit just prior to presenting. A point he pushed, which was going to be important for his growing reputation, was that it was always going to be compared to the Old Course and Kingsbarns Golf Links. A closer comparison perhaps might have been the 36 holes immediately next door at St Andrews Bay, (now Fairmont), as they were built on land which was comparable in soil type and views. It would have been important for him to create this expectation in the minds of the committee, that the course he would build was going to be up there with the Old Course and Kingsbarns, while also being different. His vision was that the entire site be shaped, then make the golf holes look as if they had been cut through the existing landscape. The ragged cliff-edge to the site, known as 'the Braes', and the rocky shoreline would be the inspiration for this look, which would work its way into the tees and bunkers. He would get the course to look as if it had been there for 100 years from the day it opened.

At an early stage when David and Paul were working on the routing, I explained to them about the additional small parcel of land we had bought at the eastern end and where we thought there might be the possibility of having a dramatic Par 3. David took it on board and shortly after, came back with the suggestion that in his preferred routing, if we could buy another small area beside it, they could improve what they were planning for the previous hole. They could build the previous green closer to the tee which would also give the golfer a shorter walk. We went back to the farmer again to purchase another small parcel of land, at a premium price! But it made sense and the result is the current 16th green and 17th tee.

An aerial of the Castle from 2007. Some roughs have still to be seeded.

The 17th at the bottom of the picture and 18th on the right.

The Clubhouse construction has still to begin.

How the Links Trust decided to build the Castle Course differed from the normal method where a main contractor would be appointed and given the project to build for his fee, working alongside the architect. Because we had experience in managing and maintaining courses, we thought we could carry out a lot of the work ourselves. Part of DMK's role was to be the project managers and David used his associate, Paul Kimber, to help with this and coordinate everything. Paul basically spent 2004 working with the consultants on the planning application and drawing up the tender documents for the contractors, once David and he had finalised the routing of the course.

DMK had their own shapers* they would use to add the finishing details and there were three subcontractors to carry out the other main tasks. Geddes of Arbroath were hired to do the bulk earthworks. John Meiklem was to do all the drainage while TIS Scotland were contracted to install the irrigation. We had worked with all three companies on various projects over the years and it was good to appoint companies who were all relatively local. We would use our own greenkeeping staff for all the intricate work required, the finishing touches, the seeding and grow in. I persuaded the committee we needed to have a course manager employed prior to the start of construction along with several other staff. The course manager would work alongside Paul Kimber representing our interests and he and his team would then have ownership of the course, acquiring knowledge of where drains and irrigation lines were located. The one regret I have was allowing David to persuade me to use his irrigation consultant to design the system rather than Adrian Mortram of Robin Hume Associates who had done all our previous work on the links.

Gaining planning permission dragged on and on until, eventually, full permission was granted in March 2004 but with 27 conditions, some more stringent than others. Many were instigated by the furore following St Andrews Bay being built next door. Amongst them were the following:

- No building to be seen from the historic centre of St Andrews, (the Castle, Cathedral or harbour area), or from the main A917 road.

---

* A 'shaper' is the person who carves out all the features and shapes of the golf course, the greens, tees, fairways and bunkers to the plans or instructions of the architect. Usually this is done with a bulldozer but some aspects can be shaped using a 360% swivel, tracked excavator.

- No heavy traffic movements to be allowed through St Andrews before 7am, between 8am and 9am, between 12 and 1pm or between 3 and 4pm. There was a designated route which vehicles had to use, keeping them off all the narrow back roads.

- Only twelve deliveries per day were permitted by vehicles over 7 tonnes. The Trust had to ensure that no vehicles would leave the site and deposit mud on the main A917. We had to record the registration number and details of all deliveries for fear of traffic breaching these conditions.

- The boundary of the site had to be secured prior to construction to prevent any damage from erosion or materials being washed onto the neighbouring land which was a SSSI.

- We would not be allowed to lay any new drains which would discharge water from the lower boundary of the site onto the Braes. We had to find and use existing drains and link into them without increasing the size of the outfall pipes.

- No materials, sand, soil, etc were to be taken off site during, or following, construction.

- A watching brief had to be undertaken in the event of finding anything which might prove to be of historical or architectural importance.

- The maiden pink flowers which were currently on site had to be transplanted to an area of the site which would not be disturbed during the construction process.

While it was only proper these conditions were imposed, they did cause us some concerns and much additional paperwork.

In regard to the buildings, the road which took the traffic from the A917 to the wastewater treatment plant dissected the course and we always imagined the clubhouse would just be off it. This would allow two loops of nine holes to go in opposite directions to either side of the property. It would also reduce costs as we wouldn't have to build or extend a road, while the utility services were already in place along its edge. However, that was going to be highly visible from the A917 and it was David who, when working on his routing, came up with the idea of the clubhouse being where it is today, looking out to sea with a double green for holes 9 and 18 in the foreground. It was a great location, but conditions stated it must not be seen from the historic centre of town and we had to put some mounding in place to fully achieve that. This was unfortunate as it would have been lovely to sit and look back towards the harbour and the town. I remember installing brightly coloured poles to represent the height of the finished clubhouse, then going down to the harbour area to check if we could see them. We couldn't, mostly because they were so far away and blended into the landscape. This was ironic as immediately above where the clubhouse would sit, all that could be seen on the horizon was the massive 209-bedroom Fairmont hotel. The maintenance facility would be just off this extended road, next to the wastewater treatment plant utilising the same hollow it is built in. It was a good position, giving easy access in both directions to the course and blended in well.

The traffic restrictions caused us no end of concern as we were paranoid some objectors would be hellbent on trying to catch us out and stop the project. We were so concerned that one member of staff, as part of his duties, had to record every delivery, date, time and registration of the vehicle. If anyone hadn't adhered to the conditions, and there was always the occasional one, we would contact the company asking them to ensure it wouldn't happen again. It wasn't too bad when we were constructing the course as we could easily manage to organise and spread out the deliveries of gravel, pipes and rootzone for the greens. It became slightly trickier once the clubhouse build began, although the course was nearing completion by then. Everything worked out in the end and we didn't have to delay any of the build waiting for materials.

We were able to locate numerous field drains across the site and where they discharged onto the Braes. Unfortunately, apart from three, the others were all small four-inch pipes and on the half of the site nearest the town, there were no significant drain outlets. Paul and David shaped the fairways in such a manner that in times of heavy rainfall, the water would run off them and into the deep roughs. They then built into their design, many areas which were well out of play and where water could be retained before being carried off-site through these existing small pipes. A benefit of this was it created a diversity of vegetation, providing different habitat for a variety of species.

Locating some of the drains was easy,
but could they cope with the additional flow!

Paul redirected the water coming from the A917 and the fields on the opposite side of that road, creating burns which ran through the course at holes 14, 5, 4, 2, 15 and 10. It was the plan from the outset to only install the main drains and to link into them once the course was complete and we established the wetter areas which would require additional drainage.

With no materials allowed to leave the site, it was up to Paul to devise a cut and fill* plan to make sure everything was used by the end of the construction. All the topsoil was stripped and stored, then the subsoil shaped up to resemble the finished levels before the topsoil was spread back on top once the drainage and irrigation was installed. Any excess topsoil at the finish was then shaped up to form more mounds in an area well out of play. At 95 hectares this was a large site so there was plenty of room between holes, even allowing for the steep slope

---

* Cut and Fill. Almost self-explanatory, where the contractors 'cut' into the surface and lower the ground level, using the material removed to heighten another area, or 'fill' it.

between what turned out to be holes 12 and 15 being unsuitable for golf. A private developer would have tried to build at least 27 holes into the area but the Trust were happy to only have 18 holes and a practice area, with the rest of the site being left to benefit the environment.

The archaeological survey had shown the only place where anything of significance might be found would have been in the area where it was planned to have the clubhouse, as that was the site of what was Kinkell Castle. Initially that was an area which David and Paul were planning to 'cut' but given this information it was changed and fill material was added to raise the existing levels. The last thing we needed was a delay to the project which would have cost money as well as time.

The maiden pinks which were to be found around the vicinity of the wastewater plant were transplanted to an area well out of the way and fenced off while our gardener at the Trust took some back to his greenhouse and propagated more plants for later use on all the courses although in reality, maiden pinks are not that rare in Fife.

An important consideration before beginning construction was finding a water source. Phil Langdon had been involved in golf course irrigation most of his career and although a consultant in his own right, was working alongside our consultants on this project. He had also learned the art of water divining from an old farmer. Watching someone water divining is fascinating. Having done his research, Phil turned up with his rods one day and began walking particular areas of the site.

Phil Langdon, with his rods,
water divining at the Castle course.

He found a few areas but reckoned the best one was just to the left of the roadway as you entered the site. He was even able to predict how deep we needed to dig and give an estimate of how much water we would manage to draw per hour. If you have little or no knowledge of water divining, would you invest upwards of £40K on sinking a borehole on the word of someone who walked across the ground with two rods and has told you to dig here, just because the rods they held in their hands crossed over? Probably not, and neither would the Trust, therefore they hired Raeburn Drilling and Geotechnical Ltd, Scotland's premier ground investigations and drilling company. They came on site and the result was we ended up with a borehole exactly where Phil Langdon had said to dig one. Not only that, but it went to the depth he said it should and supplied the water in the quantity he said! However, that didn't mean we could just go and abstract water. We first had to obtain permission from the Scottish Environment Protection Agency, who would only allow it after checking our abstraction didn't affect any neighbouring water supplies coming from the same aquifer. After a period of monitoring by SEPA we were granted our licence.

The more scientific method of finding water.

As mentioned in an earlier chapter, we had appointed Allan Patterson as course manager and he began the week after construction started in April 2005. We didn't require too many additional members of staff at that stage as most of the work was carried out by the contractors and shapers. There was next to no interest from existing greenkeepers working on the Links to move up and become involved in the project. In some respects this was surprising as it was a great opportunity to learn new skills and could lead to many different avenues opening in the future. I could understand the ones who had only been with us for a year or two and were still enjoying the novelty of working at St Andrews and looking forward to what would be their first Open, but felt there was a real opportunity for some of the others. At the end of the day, only one person 'jumped ship'. Gary Semple was a young Glaswegian who had been with us for around a year after coming back from the Ohio State programme. Gary went on to be third in charge and picked up a lot of construction skills. He eventually left to set up his own landscaping and gardening business, often helping Paul Kimber with projects on other golf courses.

In the end, it proved beneficial to start with what was practically a brand-new team. There was no looking 'over the wall' to see what another team were doing. With Allan leading by example and the positive way he conducted himself, it was a very different experience whenever I was up there meeting the staff. Two appointments which were to prove instrumental in the success of the finished product were employing a couple of local farmworkers, Dougie Brown and Willie Duncan. Without the specific skills they brought to the project, I don't know if we would have been as successful carrying out the finishing work and seeding of fairways. While greenkeepers can be talented in many aspects of the job, tractor operators they are not, especially when operating the larger, more complicated, pieces of equipment. Preparing all the fairways and roughs for seeding once the topsoil had been replaced was a huge job. The soil was tough to work with in most areas as, being clay, when it was wet it was sticky as hell. Then it would dry out over a couple of days and go as hard as a brick.

The slopes and mounds were numerous, as were the sprinkler heads for the irrigation which had to be avoided, while the tractors and equipment would have been far too big for any greenkeeper to handle competently. But those two guys did a tremendous job, which required great concentration as well as skill.

It was a fascinating project to be involved in and I felt I learned so much but it was an extremely busy period covering that, dealing with an Open and the routine things which were going on. By the time the course opened for play in June 2008, we had also staged the first ever Women's British Open to be held at St Andrews and the Curtis Cup. Plus, I had to find another course manager for the Old Course as Euan Grant left in 2007, going to work with Paul Kimber to build Machrihanish Dunes. Our appointment of Allan Patterson really proved its worth as I felt very comfortable delegating so much of the project to him.

I could write an entire book on building the Castle course and the process, indeed someone did. A friend of David McLay Kidd wrote one called 'The Seventh at St Andrews' but from David's perspective. While David spoke about his team a lot, the greenstaff, who had an integral part to play, rarely got a mention.

Paul Kimber was on site 24/7 for the best part of two years and put in significant hours there until the course opened. He did all the calculations, budgeting, and tendering while, along with Allan, scheduled and managed the contractors and other staff. He would have constantly been in contact with David, emailing pictures of what they had accomplished each day and discussing everything, but I very much feel the finished article has Paul's stamp on it. Once the course opened and we began making changes, which we did over each of the first few winters, David left Paul to work everything through with us.

What follows are some other key points including some of the more interesting things I can remember, along with my thoughts on the finished article.

Other than the initial routing plan, there was little else in the way of drawings provided. Instead, Paul worked with a box of sand in his office and would create shapes of each green. He would show these to Mick McShane, the lead shaper, who would go out and recreate that design on the site.

Paul's sandbox in which he designed the green shapes.

This allowed them maximum flexibility, as they could go to the area and make immediate changes. It gave them the freedom to find the best sites for views and what fitted the landscape best, relevant to each individual hole.

To say Mick McShane was an interesting character would be an understatement. He was employed by DMK, therefore we paid DMK who in turn paid Mick. Note to self: if there is such a thing as resurrection then I might want to consider coming back as a shaper in my second life. Not paid as well as a football player or a top golfer but liking the outdoor life, then this might be a good choice. Joking aside, it is a hugely skilled job. Mick, with his D5 Bulldozer, was like an artist with a blank canvas and could produce the most intricate details with that machine. As could Conor Walsh, the second shaper, who was mostly operating a 360, 12ton tracked excavator. Working from 7am until 7pm, they didn't have much of a break for lunch and would power their way through the work. Working those hours, or more, is normal during construction. When not on his machine, Mick could usually be found in the New Inn which was the nearest watering hole in St Andrews to the Castle course. He could be found there on most days after work, or if work had been suspended for wet weather. This probably explained why he could be a bit cranky a lot of the time! The New Inn was a favourite place for quite a few of the younger guys on the team after a long shift.

Early stages of construction on the Castle course.

As well as the entrance road bisecting the course, the main sewage pipelines, one from the town and one from the St Andrews Bay hotel, ran through the property to the WWTP. These, along with the entrance road split the course up into quarters. With the routes of these pipes marked, Paul and David thought it prudent to avoid moving heavy plant and materials from one quarter to another. This meant we basically worked in four different sections.

Ground conditions differed throughout the site and what finished up as the 9th fairway was a beautiful sandy soil. In other areas, we thought we'd struck gold by finding large sand deposits. Sadly, it turned out to be a very fine sand which held water rather than draining freely.

What we did find and which proved extremely useful, were areas of what is called locally, 'rotten rock'. This was great for using as road surfaces around the site and for building up areas before putting topsoil on top as it was a material which drained really well.

After the topsoil was stripped, David and Paul decided to begin at the highest point of the site and concentrate initially on what would be holes, 12, 13, 14, 16 and 17. These were all we were actually able to complete before the end of the growing season in 2005, although progress had also been made in other areas. When building the fairways on 12 and 16, Paul and David wanted to incorporate some 'ripples' to break up the sweeping expanse of fairway and give them a more natural look. As they explained, when looking at a new course the fairways don't have a huge amount of detail as they take on the form of the large 6m or 8m bulldozer blade which shaped them. This would be particularly relevant at the Castle course as the fairways would be a very generous width. To achieve this, once the fairways were considered ready for seeding, they had us tip dumper truckloads of topsoil on them. We then spread these out by hand to recreate some humps as would be found on older, established courses shaped by nature. The first attempts on the 12th and 16th fairway, both Allan and I thought too 'sharp'. We felt the angles created where the different mounds came together looked as if they might be difficult to cut because the cutting reels of the mowers wouldn't get down into the base of any hollow. Of course, it was difficult to confirm this as there was no grass to cut, so we came to a compromise with Paul. We'd soften these ones slightly and he wouldn't add any more mounds until the grass had grown and we were able to try cutting these. It turned out they were difficult to cut and although we softened them a little more, you can see still the ones on the 12th and 16th are different from those elsewhere on the course.

These are different from the other shapes which they incorporated into the fairways to make the course look 'windswept and rugged' and which came to be known as 'Don Kings'*. These were dotted at various places through fairways and roughs and although they weren't supposed to interfere with play, it was impossible to avoid them. In many cases the ball would come to rest at the base, or on the slope of one, and all the golfer could do was pitch out and accept they were probably going to drop a shot on that hole.

---

* Don King was a famous American boxing promoter with a distinct 'sticky-up' hairstyle. A golf writer, when reviewing the Castle course shortly after it opened for play, nicknamed the fairway mounds 'Don Kings' and the name has stuck. A bit like his hair!

One of the remaining 'Don Kings'.

Their argument was that, like a fairway bunker, the player should be able to avoid them but many of them were blind from the tee. Along with the different distances golfers hit the ball and changing wind condition, it was impossible to complete a round without encountering at least one. From the beginning, these received a lot of criticism from all quarters and at the end of the first season's play we began removing many of them. Something we would continue with over the following three or four winters.

The course took three years and three months from construction starting until actual opening, which was longer than we anticipated. Even then, some of the fairways which were seeded latterly didn't have much time to mature although all the greens and tees were completed mid-2007. An aspect which wasn't in the original plans, or at least something the architects never alluded to, was to shape up the vast expanses of rough between the holes. It was an idea they came to us with during the first winter where they suggested we retain Mick McShane for the winter to do this work. It was under the proviso he would be paid at 50% of his normal hourly rate, including no pay if he couldn't work due to poor weather or soil conditions. That was a good idea because it would look a little odd to have designed this 'moonscape' throughout the golf holes, then have these flat and wide-open areas between them. It also saved them having to transport their dozers away to another project and ensured Mick and the machines were there, ready to start again in the spring, when conditions were right. The finished product shows it was the correct thing to do.

The tee complexes at the Castle were an issue of debate. The architect's vision was to have numerous small tees which were common on courses built 100 years earlier rather than large teeing areas incorporating different sets of markers and resembling what is often described as 'landing strips'. The Trust had asked that each teeing complex should allow for five different measured courses, with the additional stipulation that on the Par 3 holes, the tees should be of a minimum area to allow for the sufficient spread of wear.

Building the tees on the 9th at the Castle course.

This concept was one which I fully agreed with and an example of how they made that work extremely well was on the Par 3 eighth hole. There, rather than the hole length varying hugely from front to back, the tees are built side by side and it's the angle which changes how the hole plays. The aspect I'm not so keen on is not having them level, (although most tees have a 1% or 2% fall for drainage which the golfer can't detect). Instead, some of the tees sloped significantly from one side to the other and often, a part of the tee would be rendered unusable as it rose or fell steeply to 'tie in' with the surrounding land. All these areas still require cutting, which means time and money. With all the individual pads being small, the tees can only be cut by pedestrian mowers, requiring additional staff. I would joke, partially tongue-in-cheek, that building the tees in this manner would give the greenkeepers plenty of work levelling them in the following years. But I do wish we'd insisted on having fewer pads, and having them slightly larger and level, just as we'd insisted on having the teeing areas on the Par 3s increased in size from the original ones they built.

In the early stages it was difficult to get either Paul or David to commit to what style the bunkers would be, or what they would look like. Eventually they produced ragged edged bunkers with big 'flash' faces which fit in well with the landscape and were the work of the second shaper, Conor Walsh. Many of them were placed for effect rather than being strategic, but they all required the same upkeep which was substantial on occasions. Following heavy rains there could be quite a bit of 'washout' as water from the surrounding ground ran into them, washing the sand from the face and down into the base, taking stones and some underlying soil with it.

The Castle bunkers are a very different style than those on the Links and they all required to have drainage installed.

Over time, the greenkeeping team would alter the surrounding land of the worst-affected bunkers to divert the flow of water away from them. Just before I retired, we began to install liners into some bunkers which would stop the washout and prevent the sand being contaminated.

When the Castle course is mentioned in any conversation, the topic discussed most is the greens and the large undulations which run through them. It's a controversial subject and many players dislike them as they can make a golfer look stupid at times. However, while I feel some of them may be too severe, for the main part I don't mind them. Having played golf around the world, I've experienced greens which have been harder to two-putt on. To me, the key is to hit the section of the green the pin is on as they are relatively large and there are often three, or even four, 'mini greens' within a green. In many ways it's similar to Augusta where, although the greens are much smaller, they are so much faster and if you don't finish in the correct section or stay below the hole, you're going to have to perform a miracle to get down in two more shots. Funnily enough, when the Castle first opened and the Trust were getting these negative comments about the greens, we came across a letter in our archives dated 1915 from a local golfer. He was complaining about the very same thing regarding the greens on the Eden course. Where David and Paul did make a mistake, and I think they'll admit to this, was not so much the sloping greens themselves but how they were all raised. This resulted in approach shots being deflected off in all directions unless they were perfectly hit. They wanted to ensure any water was going to shed off the greens but, as they were built to the USGA specification, that was unlikely to happen.

The grasses used on the greens, and indeed all other areas of the course, are the same fescues and bents which dominate the courses on the Links. The only difference between the greens and the tees, fairways and roughs is the percentage of fescue to bentgrass in the mixtures.

One thing I persuaded the committee to agree to was purchasing enough sand to allow all the approaches and surrounds to be capped with the same sandy rootzone the greens were built with. Having often played at nearby courses built on similar clay soil to the Castle, it could be frustrating hitting a nice shot which landed on the approach and if it had been wet, the ball would stop dead, or if it had been dry, take an uncontrollable bounce. On a windy site such as the Castle course there would be many occasions when a player would want to land the ball short of the green and allow it to roll to the pin. By sand capping 25 to 30 yards out from the front of the green, a ball would bounce more consistently, similar to how it would react if landing on the green itself. Likewise, if the five or six yards surrounding each green was sand capped, as well as a consistent bounce, there would also be a dry route for golfers to walk up either side of the green.

Even before the course opened for play, we received negative comments from people we had invited to play a few holes. Some of us involved in the project, including Paul, would often play the more mature holes and had similar thoughts, specifically regarding the penal result that could happen if a golfer just missed a green. Their ball could basically roll off the side of many of the greens and, because of the slopes, it would finish over twenty yards away. From there it was easy to either pitch the ball right across the green or find it back at their feet, even with a good shot. In other words, there was no bail-out to where players could hit their approach shot and leave themselves a more straightforward pitch or putt. Before the course even opened, we altered the area behind the 15th green by building a plateau to prevent balls running so far through. In some places, which could have been identified as the ideal place to land an approach shot, there was a hairy mound or 'Don King' which could screw up the shot completely. These were quickly removed and turned into softer mounds where a ball could be run over, using the slopes to get close to the pin.

A regular source of criticism came from the architectural website www.golfatlas.com, whose followers are mostly made up of people who like discussing and critiquing golf course design, past and present. While some are proper golf course architects, most are simply amateur enthusiasts. Once the early holes had taken shape, the criticism began and as is the case with online comments, some could be very barbed. There was obviously someone local who was posting pictures of the work progressing, adding their opinions. While initially I would look at the website most days, I eventually stopped following it as there was nothing which would alter people's opinions and I saw no point in getting frustrated or angry about something I couldn't control. I suggested to Allan he should do the same, telling him there's a saying in the North-East of Scotland which goes, 'fools and bairns shouldn't see half finished work'.

There were numerous calls for the greens to be altered or 'softened' once the course opened, but to alter the greens themselves and get them to blend into the surrounding ground would have been very difficult given they were built to the USGA specification. It would have meant stripping the entire green and surrounding complex out and starting again, resulting in the green being out of play for a substantial period until the turf knitted together. What was possible, and practical, was to look at altering the surrounds in many places and providing 'backstops' to prevent balls rolling so far away when missing a green. Paul would describe this as taking the double or triple bogey out of the equation so that, if you missed a green, you would at least be able to get down in a further two or three shots. Over the following five or six years we made alterations to something like 13 or 14 of the 18 greens surrounds. While we didn't rebuild any greens in their totality, on a few we were able to make small alterations to increase places where we could put the pin. At the 1st and the 3rd, we simply increased the size of the green.

One of the first full rounds I had on the course was just prior to its opening on the last Saturday of May in 2008, the second day of the Curtis Cup which was being held on the Old Course. I had been asked to take Peter Dawson of the R&A and David Fay of the USGA for a game and get their feedback. Peter did not enjoy the course, finding it far too penal in the areas we had already identified, namely the mounds on the fairways and the severity of the greens. What I remember most about the round though was the finish as, while coming up the 18th, I saw a car arrive which was unusual as there wasn't supposed to be anyone on site that day. From a distance I thought the person who emerged from the car looked like Herb Kohler, the owner of the Old Course Hotel, not someone I would have expected to be there. It transpired it had been Peter's 60th birthday the previous day and there had been a party in the Old Course Hotel. When mentioning he was playing the Castle in the morning, Herb said he would come up and greet him at the finish with a bottle of malt whisky and that's how we ended up with the four of us standing drinking a bottle of malt from crystal glasses, served on a silver tray by the 18th green.

As I've said, some of us would often play a few of the more mature holes in the months leading up to opening. Sometimes I'd go up and play on my own late in an afternoon if I had a spare hour after finishing work, while Alan McGregor was another regular player. He came back from one such game to tell us all he had a hole in one at the 10th but we discovered later he had hit two balls from the tee and it was the second ball he had holed, so we were insistent that it was only a three he scored. He still presented himself with a Links 'Hole in One' certificate signed by the CEO - him!

Another game of golf I enjoyed in the early days of the Castle course was with ex-Ryder Cup player Pierre Fulke and fellow Swedish professional Adam Mednickson. They were visiting with Petter Lindblad, the course manager at Visby Golf Club, and general manager Matz Bengtsson. Pierre and Adam had moved into the golf course architectural business and were undertaking a redesign of Visby GC. Surprisingly, Petter and I beat the two professionals and, as I recall, no strokes were received. Okay, Pierre and Adam were playing with hickory clubs, but a win is a win in my book! They went on to play the Old Course and Carnoustie in the following days where they scored under par playing with their hickories.

Periodically I would take committee members from the Local Clubs up for a tour at various stages of construction once there was something resembling a golf course to see. On one trip I was with a group consisting of members from the Ladies' Clubs. We were standing on the tee for the 18th and one of them asked me where the green was for that hole. I pointed 90 degrees away to our right at a peninsula which looked miles away, over rocks and water and said, "That's it over there," to which there was a deadly silence as they all thought I was joking. The 18th is a severe dogleg of 500 plus yards where there is a sharp right turn after a good tee shot.

View to the 18th green at the Castle from the landing area.

Allan did a great job during his time at St Andrews, developing a good team with many of them going on to good positions at other clubs or sectors of the industry. He also played an important part in the greenkeeping department overall and when he told me he was thinking of leaving, any disappointment I felt was purely selfish because I knew I would miss his input. When the opportunity to move to Turnberry came up in late 2014 his name was very much in the frame from the off. Being an Open venue, the R&A had a small interest and their agronomists at the STRI were asked for suggestions of possible candidates. Turnberry had been bought over by Donald Trump and the course was going to undergo comprehensive changes, therefore the experience Allan had gained at the Castle was another big plus. The only negative I saw was the fact he would be working for Trump given his reputation.

Allan would be a difficult act to follow but I'm very much of the mind that a person leaving to further their career is always to be embraced and it opens up an opportunity for someone else. Many people are worried by change, but it can be a good thing if channelled correctly. We decided on offering the job to a previous employee. Jon Wood had been deputy course manager on the Old Course from 2006 until 2011 before leaving to be course manager at Trevose GC where he received high praise for his work while gaining additional skills and knowledge. As expected, the staff at the Castle were apprehensive, especially those who had only ever worked for Allan in their greenkeeping career. It was pleasing that, after an initial period of adjustment to a slightly different way of working, everyone seemed to adapt really well to the change.

The course had played host to several smaller events and when it was chosen as the venue for Final Qualifier for the 2017 WBO which was being played at nearby Kingsbarns, it gave the greenstaff something substantial to prepare for. There were going to be some quality players in the field, including Paula Creamer, Christina Kim, Dame Laura Davies and Caroline Hedwall. It was going to be interesting to see how the course would perform when played by some of the best women players in the world. The tournament director decided on using a mixture of the men's medal and main play tees and the course would measure in the region of 6,400 yards with a par of 73 rather than the normal par of 71. The 7th and 12th holes would both be playing as par 5s even though they only measured around 430 yards. With reasonable weather conditions on the day, the scoring turned out to be very good with a couple of players posting 66s and a few 67s. The 7th hole proved particularly kind to the field with numerous eagle threes being recorded as it was easily reached in two shots by most competitors. The qualifying cut fell at two under par and there was a play-off between something like eleven players to determine the final five places. It was said that Laura Davies was in the Jigger Inn at the Old Course Hotel having a beer when she checked her phone and realised that she may be in a play-off so she went back up to the Castle and found it to be true. The play-off was sudden death beginning at the Par 3 10th before going on to holes 11, 15, 16, 17 and 18. Laura was actually the first person to tee off and promptly knocked a five iron to ten feet and holed the putt so she could relax and head back to the Jigger. The play-off continued until it was almost dark as it lasted 10 holes before the last player won through. I don't think they could have played another hole that evening because of the fading light.

At the end of the day, how would I rate the Castle course out of ten? As a golfing experience I'd give it an eight but with a few caveats. I enjoy going up there to play as it offers a completely different experience from playing the courses on the Links, but I don't know if I'd like to play all my medal golf there. I prefer playing from the main-play tees as opposed to the medal ones, which I generally only play from if I must, or if there's little in the way of wind. From the medal tees I have to hit long irons or woods into the greens on too many occasions, plus the landing areas are more visible from the main-play tees and the views are better. The fairways are generous once you know your way around, but as it's a course a high percentage of golfers will only play once, that's something which could be levelled against it. It's the scale of the undulations on the greens which mark it down for me and it's a tiring course. You really must give it your full concentration or a slack shot can quickly lead to a double bogey or worse. I don't buy the opinion that it's unplayable as there have been many good scores posted by visitors and locals alike, or at the WBO qualifying. As an example, one Australian amateur who missed the cut in the Links Trophy one year, scored 66 round the Castle the following day.

From a greenkeeping and maintenance point of view then I'd only give it a six, marking it down for the areas wasted on tees because of the slopes and the low number of pin positions available on the greens because of the undulations. While I still think Paul and David did a fantastic job in turning what was a relatively unexciting piece of land into what is there now, I just wish they hadn't pushed everything to the limit they did. The Trust, and me, have been criticised in allowing them to push things so far but I believe there are two reasons for that. Firstly, when you hire someone who is an expert in their field, then you should allow them to get on with things and not constantly interfere. Question things by all means, but you have to allow them freedom to get on with it. Secondly, if they had produced a course which was described as boring, they would have been criticised for a wasted opportunity. It was far better to build something dramatic like they did, but which could be reigned back in or 'softened' afterwards. There aren't many examples of courses which have started off as bland, then transformed into one people go on to consider a 'must play'. As time has moved on, the course continues to receive mixed reviews but the majority of visiting golfers appear to post very positive comments about their experience on social media. The verdict from local golfers is similar. Many of the ticket holders love the course and some play most of their golf there, while others hate it. Even those who have never played it!

Looking back in hindsight some fifteen years later, in my mind David himself probably regrets some of his decisions. Around the time he was building the Castle, he had another project going on in Oregon called Tetherow which I believe he also had to go back and soften, including removing numerous 'Don Kings' from the fairways. In 2018 at the opening of a new course in Wisconsin called Mammoth Dunes, he admitted in an interview that he went through a phase of pushing the envelope too far in his earlier days.

Chapter 16. The Women's British Open, Augusta and Leopard Creek

2006 BEGAN with me realising a long-time dream and something I'd wanted to achieve even more since 1998 when I attended the Masters; I was given the opportunity to play at Augusta National. The Golf Industry Show was going to be returning to Atlanta due to Storm Katrina destroying New Orleans back in August 2005, one week after I'd booked my flights for New Orleans!

I had already agreed with Alan McGregor I would attend with Euan Grant and Allan Patterson, then asked if I was successful in fixing up a game at Augusta for the three of us, would the Links cover the cost of the overnight accommodation and the green fees? I had no idea what the exact cost would be but had an inkling it wouldn't be too expensive. I thought it would be a just reward for all the additional hours both Euan and Allan had put in through 2005 for the Open and the early construction work at the Castle course respectively. As well as having to be signed on and play with a member, another of the requirements to playing Augusta is having to stay on the premises either the night before or after. Once I got Alan's agreement, I set to work on making arrangements.

After meeting Augusta member George Wislar at St Andrews in 2000, I was able to contact him through Rich Hurley and ask if he would host us. George was only too happy to help but he was over seventy years old and added the proviso that if the weather was bad then he wouldn't play, which meant we couldn't play! GIS was in February so it could have gone either way, but we decided to take the chance. We flew out on the Saturday to our rented house in Atlanta which we were sharing with Kerry Watkins from Canada and his friends as that was much cheaper than a hotel. The golf was set up for Monday which would allow us to come back and take in some education seminars on the Tuesday. The traffic was extremely busy around where we were staying and we later discovered it was the preparations for the funeral of the widow of Martin Luther King which would begin just around the corner from our house.

We met George at the clubhouse and went to Firestone cabin where we would be staying. After unloading our luggage, he showed us around Jones cabin where Bobby Jones used to always stay and then we went back to the clubhouse. Although I'd been to Augusta three times previously, I'd only ever seen around the course and the maintenance facility, therefore a tour of the clubhouse was fascinating.

At Augusta with Allan Patterson and Euan Grant.

George was a great storyteller and had many stories to tell, even how he became a member was something in itself. He was a scratch golfer when he was younger and back in 1971, had been invited along to Augusta for the weekend as a guest where he played on Saturday and Sunday and eagled the 13th on both occasions. Prior to leaving on the Sunday, he was introduced to Augusta Chairman Clifford Roberts where the feat of his two eagles was obviously mentioned. Little over a month later, on Christmas Day, George received a telephone call at his home in Georgia and it was Clifford Roberts. They spoke about his visit and his eagles and the call ended with Roberts offering him membership of Augusta. It was a special Christmas present and George had no hesitation in taking him up on his offer, spending a lot of time there where he used to play regularly with President Eisenhower and Byron Nelson. He was chairman of the practice tee committee at the Masters for over forty years and we spent a fantastic evening listening to all his stories of Augusta, although there's no doubt many of them had been embellished over time. The only slight disappointment was we ate in our cabin rather than the clubhouse because George wanted to watch the Superbowl on TV, which we never actually saw, as he was too busy telling stories while we hung on his every word.

Monday morning soon arrived and it was frosty which meant the tee times were delayed and as such, we had to miss playing the nine-hole Par 3 course. The forecast, which we'd been watching closely for two days wasn't promising as there was a heavy storm forecast to come through and it looked as if we were going to be right on the edge of it. After breakfast we set off for the practice range where we were introduced to our caddies and hit a few balls to loosen up. There was a very light shower just as we were starting but it never came to much and we were off. I'll not bore you with the all the golf details other than to say that Allan Patterson was round in a gross 74 which is a remarkable score by anyone's standard. He had two birdies, at the 2nd and at the 15th where he got up and down from the greenside bunker. Even more remarkable was the fact he went round without a three-putt, thanks to holing from twenty feet on both the 5th and 6th for his second putts on those two greens! My golf was terrible and I wouldn't have broken 90 as every part of my game was poor but the experience was amazing. I found the course difficult with many tee shots having to be threaded through narrow avenues of trees, sometimes with a draw, on other occasions with a fade. The other aspect people don't realise about the course is how hilly it is and if you hit an overhanging branch or simply don't hit the ball far enough, then it might finish on a downslope resulting in having to hit a long or medium iron to an elevated green. The ball has to be flown in since there's very little opportunity to run in a shot like on the Links. If you can hit it straight and long, then those approach shots from a flat lie and with a shorter iron, are so much easier. The greens themselves were perfect, not the fastest I've putted on but that might have been due to the light drizzle when we started. We certainly had to listen and believe in what our caddies told us about the line in particular, and for Allan to go round with no three putts was nothing short of a miracle.

When playing the 11th, there was a greenkeeper tidying up the banking of the pond with a hover mower who stood aside while we played our approach shots. It was only when we had walked twenty yards past him, I heard a call, "Gordon Moir, how did you get on here?". It was a Scottish greenkeeper I knew and for whom Rich Hurley had managed to arrange an internship. We chatted very briefly as we had to keep up with the pace of play. He came to meet us as we came off the 18th green for a better chat. I learned much later he was 'hauled over the coals' as employees are not supposed to mix with the guests. We were able to have a quick tour of the maintenance facility before we left as Euan and Allan had never visited before.

All in all, we had a great time and it was an amazing experience. When we returned to Atlanta, we discovered that it had been torrential rain there all day and all the courses in and around Atlanta were closed. Kerry and his friends were washed out at the Athletic Club so we were soooooo lucky. Even better, the bill wasn't anything like as steep as we'd thought it might be as the green-fees were complementary. In fact, it was extremely reasonable, and I say that from someone who doesn't like spending money, either my own or that of my employer.

At the show, we met up with Mark Stovall, an American who had previously worked at Augusta and had come to St Andrews to work at the 2005 Open. He was a superintendent in Chattanooga at a course called Lookout Mountain and he was adamant we must take the time to visit his course. We agreed to take in the trade show on the Wednesday and do all we needed to do, then headed off to his course on the Thursday morning which was around ninety minutes away. He called us in the morning to say that it had been snowing but the course would be open by the time we arrived. He was correct in that it opened by the time we ate but it was freezing and, of course, at that altitude and at that time of year, everything was dormant. When we ventured out to play, we discovered that the greens were like putting on glass and because we were on the side of a mountain, the three of us all found them impossible to read. We also suspected that Mark had one of his team out rolling them as soon as the snow cleared. Again, the golf was poor, but I did hit one decent shot onto a par 3 to around thirty feet but at no time did my putt for birdie ever get to within fifteen feet from the hole. Shortly after I hit it, the ball veered off in the opposite direction to what I thought it would, due to an optical illusion caused by the mountain. That's my excuse anyway! It was a good course though and Mark had it in nice shape given it was February.

Although things in general were going well across all the courses, we were always looking to continually improve. One of the weaknesses was the deputy head greenkeepers on some of the courses which could be traced back to their appointments in the mid-1990s. It wasn't they were bad or poor greenkeepers, in many aspects they were very good greenkeepers, but they weren't performing to the role of a deputy head greenkeeper. It could be argued that the head greenkeepers and I had failed in developing them, but we had invested in them over the years and provided plenty of training. At the beginning of 2006 Euan Grant approached me to discuss his deputy, who would do any job required on the course. He had a great history of the Links and especially the Old Course as he had worked on the Old since circa 1984 and was a great source of information. He was perfectly okay talking to another member of the team on a one-to-one basis, but he couldn't always talk to them in a group or direct them and would far rather do the tasks himself. When we said we wanted to talk to him about his role, we expected it to be a very difficult conversation, but it turned out he was relieved as he hadn't been enjoying the additional pressure.

We advertised the position and had a strong response with some excellent candidates, selecting a few internal candidates from the younger members of staff along with the external applicants. We appointed Jon Wood, an Englishman who had an impressive CV which included being on the Ohio student programme. At the time of the interview, Jon was at Portmarnock Links in Dublin working under Fintan Brennan who was well known to both myself and Euan. Fintan often came and volunteered at nearby Kingbarns for the ADLC and he could not have given Jon a higher recommendation. It was another step in the right direction to building a stronger team as he brought the various experiences he had picked up working at high end facilities during his travels. I had always been conscious many of the staff had little concept of how good golf courses could be maintained and presented as, since most of them didn't play golf, they had seldom visited any other courses. By the same token, many good local golfers don't play much away from the Links because they think, "Why should I travel to play there when I can play here?" I found that quite a strange mindset since it wasn't always like that. Back in the late 19th and early 20th centuries, many St Andreans travelled to introduce golf to the world and made their living from doing so. St Andrews can still appear quite insular at times, given the cosmopolitan influence from the large contingent of overseas students at the University.

Over the previous seven or eight years I'd become used to giving presentations to different audiences, large and small. There would be quite a few requests from different groups visiting St Andrews who wanted a tour of the facilities and learn about how we did things. These varied from members of different European greenkeeping associations to American college kids on study tours, or simply a group of visiting greenkeepers. Sometimes it might even be a just a single greenkeeper or superintendent who was in the area who would ask if they could call in. I'd also present to local organisations such as Rotary or Round Table which I felt was an excellent method of communicating with local season ticket holders. As the Links is a public facility, it was something we would always try to accommodate if we could and was encouraged by Alan McGregor. It also helped promote St Andrews while explaining to many people it was the Links Trust who managed the courses and that we were a different organisation from the R&A.

This often added an hour or more onto my day, but I enjoyed meeting all the different people and there was a feeling of satisfaction as they were so pleased someone had taken the time to meet with them. I was proud showing them the results of everyone's efforts, plus I often learned from them or it reiterated the fact we often shared the same problems. There were obvious subjects most people would want me to cover, preparing for an Open Championship being the most popular, along with what might be different in managing links courses. Other subjects could include how we managed the environment, maintained our bunkers, the challenges we faced and latterly, building the Castle course. If I had to travel any significant distance, I would suggest I did at least two different presentations, making it more worthwhile and adding value. I would always have in a slide or two of the main companies we had partnerships or relationships with, not in a blatantly advertising manner, but it was important to acknowledge them and what they did for us. If they were 'sponsoring' the talk then I would give them a slightly higher profile. Whether it was me or one of the head greenkeepers who were presenting, we never charged, only asking for our expenses to be covered.

I would use the picture of whatever was on the slide as my prompt rather than referring to notes. I hated reading from notes or headings as I never felt the talk flowed as well and always thought that was noticed by the audience. Reading from notes was something I had to do when presenting at our information evenings to the local stakeholders, particularly in Alan MacGregor's time, as we were paranoid we would say something wrong and people in the audience would make a note to use against us in the future. It also kept us on schedule as we would time ourselves in rehearsal and it was a good exercise in talking at a steady pace as I always had a habit of talking too quickly. Latterly, I used to drive my last CEO crazy when doing the information evenings as, while I was on time at rehearsal, I always went over on the night. I would throw additional comments into the talk and while that would only lengthen it by five or six minutes, it could be over 25% of my time. I did it on purpose as he always went over his allotted time whenever he spoke.

In March 2006 I was fortunate to be invited to South Africa for a week by the Toro company. Along with their South African distributor, they were staging a conference for all their top clients and on the back of the Links having renewed our deal, they asked me along to give some presentations on St Andrews. As those in the turf industry will know, the Toro Company don't do half measures, and this was one of those trips I'll never forget. It was a special trip as obviously, we weren't going all that distance just for a one-day seminar. We started off in Johannesburg, where their distributor Smith Turf was based. After a night in Jo'burg we were scheduled to go on a short safari, but the rains had been terrible where we were heading and the trip was cancelled because of flooding in the area. At short notice, Toro managed to arrange golf for us at The Royal Jo'burg and Kensington Club which was great and we had a second night in Jo'burg before heading to Leopard Creek a couple of days earlier than scheduled and where the conference was being held. It was an interesting two nights in Jo'burg for reasons not relating to turf.

On the first night when the group of us were at dinner, an argument started up between a husband and wife in the company. I don't even know who or what started it off (and the wife was sitting on my immediate right), but her husband who was sitting across from her threw a glass of water over her. She responded by throwing her glass of water over him. There was a delay of a few seconds when he then picked up his full glass of red wine and threw it, completely covering her. Everyone was eerily silent while she continued to eat, the wine dripping from her face. I found out later they had that type of relationship! On the second night some of us were enticed out by a couple of youngsters working with Smith Turf for the summer, although it would be fair to say I didn't need much enticing. We ended up in a club in Jo'burg where dripping wax and Flaming Lamborghinis, (which I didn't want), were involved and where I ended up being very unwell, (which I also didn't want!) They said the five hour drive up to Leopard Creek the next day was beautiful, but I wouldn't know. We took a longer and alternative route back, through an area where many of the top distance runners in the world go to train and it was lovely. As we now had additional days to fill, Toro had organised a few different safaris for all the delegates and inevitably each evening began with a sundowner. By the time it came to the day of the seminar my alcohol level gauge was showing full. I wasn't far into my presentation when I felt my mouth begin to get as dry as a duck's bottom and I had forgotten to pour myself a glass of water beforehand. Fortunately, there was a bottle sitting on the table for the speakers but when I went to pour it into my glass my hand was shaking like a lamb's tail and most of the water missed the glass. It was so obvious no one in the audience could have failed to notice and I blurted out, "My doctor asked me if I drank a lot but I told him no, I spill most of it!"

Leopard Creek is owned by Johann Rupert who basically runs the ADLC and it's an amazing course.

Leopard Creek is an amazing golf course.

There's a life size statue, in bronze, of a leopard on every tee and as you progress round the course it tells the story of the leopard's day. From wakening in the morning, stretching, stalking its prey, chasing, then catching and eating it, until on the 18th fairway there's another statue where it's going back to sleep. We were lucky enough to play there on our last day and it's a round I'll never forget as it's the only time in my life I never finished a round of golf because I ran out of golf balls. I was playing with the course manager and Andy Brown of the Toro company and we had hire clubs which weren't the best I'd played with but that's no excuse. The rough wasn't so much penal, more dangerous, as there were plenty of snakes around and we were advised not to go into it. We all played badly and the course manager was losing so many balls he called in at one stage on the back nine and asked his assistant to bring out more, which he also lost. On the 17th tee, I had to give them both a ball from my own ever-decreasing stock which only left me the one I was playing with. While they both lost their last ball from the 18th tee, I at least got to my approach shot to the green. I then hit it over the green where it fell into the lake which wrapped itself around the green. Game over!

This was shortly followed by one of my favourite moments of the trip. As we sat on the clubhouse veranda, Sue De Zwart, who was overall in charge of turf operation at Leopard Creek, suddenly sprang from her chair and took off down the steps and onto the course. Two giraffes had wandered onto the 18th fairway and Sue was running to stop them coming onto the green where they could have done some serious damage with their footprints. We followed quickly behind and were able to jump on some golf buggies and follow them into the bush. All in, the trip was one of the best experiences I had through my career.

The remainder of 2006 was fairly uneventful which wasn't a bad thing. The Castle course build was progressing well and I was spending a lot of time taking various groups ranging from Trustees, LMC and the Local Clubs up there to show them around.

A well-known American agronomist who was a regular visitor to St Andrews was Stan Zontek who would visit at least once a year with fellow agronomists from the USGA Greens Section or lecturers and professors from various universities which ran turf programmes. They would base themselves in St Andrews and either play golf or visit other courses around Scotland and were always willing to put on a short seminar to the staff or the local section of BIGGA. It was always interesting and educational to spend time in their company as there was always something I could learn from their experiences which would be relevant. I became good friends with Stan and also many of the people he brought with him and was saddened to hear of his sudden death in August 2012. We also began working with Frank Newberry to provide management training for the head greenkeepers, deputies and other staff who we felt had the potential to move into management. Frank had worked with BIGGA for several years and I'd always been impressed with his practical coaching when attending his workshops at BTME as he related things well to the greenkeeping profession. Whenever the Links organised this type of training it was always aimed at the staff working in the restaurants, shops or reception. Having Frank come to us for a couple of days was a much cheaper option than taking twelve or sixteen people to BTME and he could tailor the training to our requirements.

Before the end of 2006, as part of my continued professional development, I enrolled on the R&A's Rules Course which was a two-day course to be held in February at the Fairmont Hotel just outside town and attracted people from Golf Federations all around the world. The reason I was interested was to be more competent when marking hazards or GUR areas on the courses as it was something I felt was a weakness in the greenkeeping department. In the middle of December the R&A sent me a substantial amount of paperwork but with so much happening at home over the holiday period it wasn't something I looked at in any detail, barely opening the envelope. When I went back to work in January my focus was more on the greenkeeping show in Harrogate and it was only once I returned that I began to prepare. It was a shock when I found out I should really have been studying these papers since I received them as there was a lot of preparation required. I ended up having to cram everything in over the course of little more than a week. The course itself was good with mocked-up real life situations along with televised examples of breaches of the rules from tournament golf explaining what the player should have done. I struggled my way through the exam and passed with 75% which I was pleased with although you need over 80% to be allowed to referee at a R&A or tour event. I was able to tell people if they asked me for a ruling then three times out of four, I would get it correct!

2007 saw a first for St Andrews when we hosted the Ricoh Women's British Open, (WBO), which was to be the first time a women's professional tournament would be staged over the Old Course. That was something to look forward to but before then I had to find another head greenkeeper as, at the start of the season and out of the blue, Euan Grant handed in his notice. In hindsight it shouldn't have been such a surprise as Euan always had itchy feet and liked to move around, it was more the fact that he had only been head greenkeeper of the Old Course for under three years. Understandably, I anticipated him staying for at least another Open as everything was going well. He left to oversee and manage a new construction called Machrihanish Dunes on the west coast of Scotland for David McLay Kidd and Paul Kimber, our architects at the Castle course

If we had advertised the Old Course position externally there's no doubt we would have been inundated with applications given it's the most famous course in the world and trying to sort the wheat from the chaff would have been a mammoth task. I believe it would have been impossible to determine the reason why many people would want the position. For every genuine and excellent candidate who applied, there would have been one who thought if they were successful, they would use the position to promote themselves and plan on spending their time swanning around the world, telling everyone how good they were. As already mentioned, we had learned it's not easy to bring someone into the organisation and for them to fit in with our structure, irrespective of how good a greenkeeper they are. I've often reflected on what being course manager of the Old Course and indeed my own position does to people, even more so as I was getting towards the end of my career, and while it takes people with certain qualities to do it well, it does change them. It makes them much more confident and unless they have a strong sense of self-awareness, then they can become over-confident or over-bearing and begin believing the hype. To a large extent it's understandable why this should be, as people are always saying how good or special you are. Suddenly, you're being asked to do X, Y and Z, promote this product, talk at that conference or give an interview to some media organisation. As well as seeing how it changed others, I fell into this trap myself and it took Alan McGregor to point it out to me and, (hopefully), I changed my behaviour thereafter.

With that in mind, we decided to change things around internally as everyone had been progressing in their roles over the previous three years and there were signs that some of the training and ideas that I'd been slowly working to introduce were beginning to take effect. Gordon

McKie was given his opportunity and moved from the New course to take over the running of the Old. We moved Graeme Taylor from the Eden to the Jubilee, switching Davie Wilson across to the New course and promoted Kevin Muir from deputy on the Eden to head greenkeeper. It had been a quick learning curve for Kevin since he only left the Old in 2001. With a fresh start he had quickly moved up through the ranks and this was another example of the Eden and Strathtyrum being the best courses for developing staff.

Gordon had a few months to settle in before the WBO, which would be held at the beginning of August. It was nowhere near as large an event as the Open itself but the fact it was coming to the Old Course for the first time in its history was a big deal as it was classed as a Major and all the top players were in the field. IMG were the contractors responsible for putting the event on along with the Ladies Golf Union and assistance from the LPGA. As regards infrastructure, the build was very similar in size to the ADLC with disruption to the golf course(s) being minimal. It was going to be a busy month as Final Qualifying for the championship was being held over the New course on the Monday while immediately afterwards, we were straight into our own two weeks of annual tournaments. As with the Dunhill, Links Trophy, or R&A Medal week, the set-up of the golf course each day follows a similar pattern where we call on staff from the other courses and cut all areas each morning. Then the team are back at night to tidy up and if required, give the greens another cut. Morning set-up usually requires just over fifty staff depending on weather conditions while in the evening most of the work concerns divot repairs and bunker maintenance, especially if windy. Then staff would shovel the sand back in place before watering it to prevent it blowing out again overnight. On this occasion, unlike the Open, not all the courses were closed and we were able to keep the Jubilee course open. Normally at the Dunhill we use a composite course taking some holes on the Jubilee and a few on the New as the tournament practice area would be on the 1st and 18th holes of the Jubilee while players would use the 18th green of the New Course for short game practice. For this tournament, and with the New being required for Final Qualifying on the Monday, the organisers went back to using the old practice tee at the Old Course Hotel end of our Golf Academy. Being August, all the other courses were still requiring to be cut on a regular basis, therefore there was plenty to be done during the week, while the Castle course still had a few areas to be completed.

It wasn't feasible for the staff to camp in their 'normal' place on the Jubilee so I budgeted for a few Portacabins for accommodation. With no marquee provided by the R&A, there was no large gathering place other than within the main machinery shed and catering for the team had to be rethought. Fortunately, on the team we had two people who were former chefs and working with just the barbeque we used each Dunhill and a few extra pots and pans, they did a brilliant job preparing a variety of meals each evening. While one of them was local and a full -time member of staff, the other was the seasonal from New Zealand mentioned earlier who left a trail of debts behind. He had the balls to contact me when we were next staging the WBO in 2013, asking if I wanted him to come and work the tournament! Even though he was a damned good chef, the answer was No Way José!

I was fortunate that Alan McGregor gave me the opportunity to play in the Pro-Am along with himself and the Chairman of Trustees. It was a shotgun start on the Tuesday and our professional was Scotland's most successful lady golfer, Catriona Matthew. Although my golf wasn't great it was an enjoyable experience and throughout the round, I noticed that on the holes into the wind, I was hitting the ball around ten to fifteen yards further than Catriona. Then downwind, she would hit it that distance past me while her approach shots and short game were much superior. The pace of play was very slow, compounded by the double greens and shared fairways of the Old Course. It meant we were waiting on every tee where we would often be standing with the group in front and by the time we played, the group behind would join us. Playing behind was the Swedish professional Carin Koch and towards the end of the round when they joined us on a tee, she mentioned to Catriona that her husband, who was also her caddie, was desperate for a game somewhere. They asked me if there was somewhere he could play and I said the Jubilee was still open and did they want me to get him a time? They thought that would be great and I was able to book them 4pm as Carin said she might go back out for a few holes along with their children. I told her there would be no green fee but there was one condition, she couldn't tell anyone the greens on the Jubilee were better than those on the Old Course! She thanked me but I could tell that she thought I was talking rubbish and just kidding with her. By the time 4pm came, I was back in my office which was just over the banking from the 1st green of the Jubilee. At around 4.10 I took a walk out to see if they were playing. They had just played their approach shots and Carin had left herself a putt from around twenty feet which, when it was her turn, she knocked ten feet past the hole, saying, "I thought you were joking."

There was a bizarre situation at the beginning of the week when Reilley Rankin, an American player, introduced herself to Gordon McKie while he was changing the holes on the practice putting green one morning and asked him if he would caddy for her at the tournament.

With Carin Koch on the Jubilee course. She didn't believe me the greens on the Jubilee were better than those on the Old.

That was never going to happen, even though she was persistent but we offered to help her out by recommending a good local caddie. One of the greenkeepers had a relative who was an experienced caddie who I knew and we asked him if he wanted the job. He didn't have a bag that week so went out with her in the practice rounds and they got on well. The next time we saw her was on the Wednesday evening when we were setting up the course for the Thursday morning. We were at the far end of the course on the 12th green having just moved the hole to its position for the first round when she appeared from nowhere with some clubs and balls. The course was closed for practice by that time and we never saw her do anything illegal such as playing to any green or putting to where the next day's hole would be. We suggested to her that she had better get off the course in case someone did see her and might assume she had gained an unfair advantage. We kept an eye on her progress and she finished level par for the four rounds and in fourth place, winning over $100,000. Her decision to take a local caddie certainly paid dividends and he went to the States and caddied for her there for a spell afterwards.

As far as tournaments go, this was one I really enjoyed as I found it was more 'relaxed' than the Open. All the competitors were really friendly, partly I think because they were just so delighted to be there and have the opportunity to play their Open over the Old Course. Many of them had played it beforehand, especially the Europeans as they would come and play in the St Rule Trophy which is held every May with 18 holes over the New Course and 36 holes on the Old Course. Annika Sorenstam, Catriona Matthew and Maria Horjth, (who finished tied 2nd in the WBO), were all previous winners of the St Rule trophy. As is usual in St Andrews, many locals were negative towards the tournament and wouldn't come out to watch. I found this strange as they would have related more to how the ladies play than the male professionals, as the ladies hit the ball similar distances to the majority of low handicap men. They were playing the course at 6,638 yards, which is less than 100 yards the distance the local men's clubs play their medals over. I remember going to watch some golf on the Saturday morning and most players were hitting a seven or eight iron into the 1st green. When I went back in the afternoon as the leaders were going out, a strong wind had got up and, as it was into their face, they were all hitting rescue clubs for their second shot. I can relate to both those scenarios.

At the championship dinner on the Saturday evening, I was introduced to the president of the LPGA who was delighted with how well everything had gone. Many of the players had commented to her how they really enjoyed the course and thought it was in great condition. She wanted to come to our maintenance facility on the Sunday afternoon to thank all the team personally on the players behalf. I told her that would be deeply appreciated by the staff but there wouldn't be many there on Sunday afternoon, as apart from two people covering the duty rota, the others would be away shortly after 8am. Since that was going to be the case, she promised to be there for 8am to which I replied she would be welcome to join us for breakfast. True to her word, she turned up at the Jubilee sheds with another two officials just prior to 8am and while the staff were in the yard enjoying their BBQ burger or bacon roll, she climbed up on a chair and thanked everyone for all their hard work. It was a really nice touch and went down well with the team.

I went out to watch the leaders play the last nine holes on the Sunday from inside the ropes. Lorena Ochoa of Mexico, the number one player in the world at the time, had led from the time she scored 67 in the first round and being six shots clear at the beginning of the round, it was practically a procession. As she walked down the 17th fairway, fellow competitor Paula Creamer, (who's 21st birthday it was on the day), was cheering her on from the balcony of her room in the Old Course Hotel. Best of all though, with our new found friend Reilly Rankin also being a friend of Ochoa's, we were invited to the party afterwards in the Dunvegan Hotel which was where Ochoa was staying. A lot of the players were there and at one point Ochoa was up on the tables leading the singing, ra, ra, ra.

The week wasn't a complete success, however, as there was an unsavoury incident in the greenkeeping sheds on the Saturday night. Although it was Links policy not to bring drink onto the premises, we never placed a total ban on alcohol when guys were staying on site but remind them to be sensible and ask them to limit themselves to a couple of beers. A few of the people staying on-site ignored the advice, had way too much to drink and in the early hours of the morning a fight started up in the mess room.

Following a thorough investigation the following week, one member of staff was dismissed while others were fortunate not suffer the same fate. It put a dampener on the week and changed our rules and procedures at tournaments in the future.

Lorena Ochoa with some of the greenstaff.

My holiday in 2007 was a golf trip to the east coast of the USA in October after the Dunhill was finished. The catalyst for the trip was Eric Bergstol, who along with Rich Hurley, had been a candidate for building the Castle course. Eric had spent the previous nine years building a golf course on the shores of the Hudson River, within sight of the Statue of Liberty and which opened for play in 2006. He had already built and was managing eight or nine courses in the New York area along with one I'd played previously called Pine Hill just three miles from Pine Valley. Eric and Rich had been visiting Scotland for many years and the three of us made regular September trips around the UK where we'd played most of the better links courses. This latest course he had just completed, Bayonne GC, was the jewel in the crown and I was very keen to visit and play it.

With Eric Bergstol on the 16th tee at Bayonne GC and the Manhattan skyline back right. A little piece of the West of Ireland just a few miles from New York.

Between them they had sculpted this course from an old brown field site Eric had purchased many years previously. They used the dredging from where the Hudson River was being deepened for shipping to build the course, which looked like it belonged on the west coast of Ireland, next to Lahinch or Ballybunion. Rich had done the grassing plan which, other than creeping and velvet bentgrasses on the greens, consisted of mostly cool season grasses as found in the UK along with the plants found in the roughs on sandy sites. The big difference though was having the Manhattan skyline as a backdrop, (check out www. bayonnegolfclub.com).

I'd heard so many stories and seen all the pictures through the construction that I had to visit and play. I wasn't travelling all that distance for one game and I contacted a few superintendents I'd met over the years. Rich had organised the accommodation and was going to be my driver and playing companion for the week. Initially based at Rich's house in Pennsylvania we played Bayonne, which was every bit as good as I'd expected it to be, and Garden City GC, (home of the 1902 US Open and where Laurie Auchterlonie from St Andrews beat local favourite and Garden City member Walter Travis into second place).

We also played Baltusrol, courtesy of superintendent Mark Kuhns and took in a Rutgers College football game. We then moved out to Long Island to play National Golf Links, Sebonack and Shinnecock. Mark Michaud, the superintendent at Shinnecock, kindly drove me to Bethpage where I was staying with Craig Courier as I was playing the Black course the next morning. It was around this part of the trip I realised I had made a mistake when telling my wife when I would be returning. I had initially said Monday but then realised it wouldn't be until Tuesday, although it was worse than that. I wasn't scheduled to leave New York until Tuesday evening, therefore I wouldn't actually be home until Wednesday. Having that type of conversation by telephone when we were over 3000 miles apart was better than if we'd been face-to-face!

When I arrived at Craig's house, I was surprised he had another guest staying who I knew. Kevin Dawson was an Atlanta-based magician who I had met some years earlier at a GIS where I saw him do a card trick. I recognised this particular trick where he left a signed card and a dollar bill stuck to a ceiling by a drawing pin, exactly the same as was on the ceiling of the St Andrews Golf Club. I asked him after his show if he had ever been in the St Andrews Golf Club and he said he was a member. The next surprise was, it wasn't just any golf game we were playing on the Black Course; it was the final of the New York Metropolitan Area Superintendents Golf Championship which teams had to qualify to play in. Craig had organised for Kevin and I, along with an ex-NFL player and commentator, to play as part of his team although we couldn't win the competition, (little chance of that).

With Craig Courier, Kevin Dawson and an ex-NFL star and TV commentator at Bethpage Black.

He had also set the course up with the same Sunday hole positions as used for the 2002 US Open along with putting a pin and flag in the place where Tiger had driven the ball to on each hole of that final round. As we played, it was amazing to see how far ahead of our drives Tiger's were and we often had a 50- or 60-yard start on him! From memory, I think the only fairway Tiger missed that day was on the 16th. I also remember the course was brutally tough, one of the hardest I've ever played due to the elevation changes and the thickness of the rough, even just off the fairway.

Rich collected me from Bethpage after the round and we played Bayonne again on the Tuesday before I caught my evening flight home. Kevin Dawson came and stayed with us for a few nights the following summer and on one of the days, we went around the maintenance facilities where he did his magic show for the staff. In fact, he never stopped doing magic tricks all the time he was here, including entertaining Pauline over breakfast with flames coming from a wallet while she was trying to prepare to leave for work.

In November I'd been invited to go back to France by the French Association, (AGREF), to present at their trade show Green Expo, which was in Marseille. The only cost to my employers was the time away from work although I often used part of my holiday allowance, or some of the days might include the weekend. Latterly, because of technology, I was still able to reply to emails etc when I was away. I was happy to be going back as I'd made friends with a few of their committee, in particular, Remy Dorbeau from the Chantilly GC and Emilio Vichera from the Sperone Golf Club in Corsica. The show was held over three days with dedicated times throughout the day for seminars and presentations, while at other times the focus was on visiting the trade stands. I especially liked the relationship AGREF had built up with the French Golf Federation and they seemed to be held in much higher regard than BIGGA is with the UK Home Unions. I suspect this was testament to the work Remy, Emilio and their president at the time Patrice Bernard, had done with Jérome Paris of the FGF over the years and the respect they had for one another. This gave them a good relationship with the government, particularly in environmental stewardship and it was something I thought they were more advanced in than we were in the UK. I sometimes feel there are too many organisations involved in UK golf, each one looking out for their own interests rather than all pulling together for the good of the game. I've never felt the home unions have shown much interest in supporting the golf course side of the industry other than the Scottish Golf Environment Group. From the fee they receive from each individual club member annually, they contribute pennies towards formal greenkeeping education while the vast majority goes on elite amateur golf and covering committee attendance at events, something which only represents and benefits a tiny proportion of the country's golfers. I think they could support the turf industry so much more than they do, not only financially, but by promoting the professional work that course managers do and how they are integral to the success of a golf club. Course managers should be a key member of a clubs' organisation and decision-making process. Unlike their European counterparts, too many course managers in the UK are still regarded as nothing more than grass cutters by their club.

Although it wasn't something we did every year, 2008 began with a trip to the GIS which this year was in Orlando, at the end of January immediately after Harrogate. This year I went with Jon Wood, deputy from the Old Course and Trevor Harris, deputy on the Castle. As well as being an educational event it was also in some regards a small reward for their efforts along with an opportunity for me to find out a little more about the individuals I travelled with. We would rent a house some thirty minutes from the convention centre which was a cheaper option than a hotel, it just meant taking turns to drive. I'd arranged for us to play TPC Sawgrass the day before the education seminars started as I knew a member who stayed there in the winter and who was also a member of the R&A. We travelled up on the Saturday and booked into a motel near the course at our own expense. That was our first mistake as the barmaid in the motel knew Peter Stewart who used to work with us before spending a few years working at Sawgrass. The second one was it was 25th January, Burns Night in Scotland, where we celebrate the birth of our National Bard, (poet). We celebrated to such an extent I barely remember playing the front nine. The friend who took us on, Jim Raitt, still reminds me that I began with a Titleist golf ball which had a different number on one side than on the other, telling me I should keep it as a collector's item. I can't remember that and didn't listen to him, predictably hitting it into a pond somewhere and losing it. I do remember Jon, who didn't play much golf, reducing the 18th to a drive and wedge to 15 feet from the pin, then three putting to lose us the match.

One evening during the show we were invited out by friends to celebrate one of them winning the GSCAA Distinguished Service Award for his services to the industry. Jim Loke had been a superintendent for over thirty-five years and held the top position at various clubs which had hosted tour events and other high profile amateur ones. He also had sat on different GCSAA boards in his time and mentored many young Superintendents. I had first met him when he and some colleagues visited St Andrews to play and we had kept in touch. One of his industry colleagues on that St Andrews trip was covering the cost of the meal, or his company was, so off we went for an enjoyable evening. There was a large magnum of wine with the hors d'oeuvres but it was finished by the time the main course arrived. Considering we weren't paying for a meal that evening, I thought it a nice touch if I bought a second bottle for the company and asked the waiter to bring a second bottle, then, when he brought the bill, to make sure there was a separate one for the wine which I would pay. When he brought the bills, our host asked why there were two and although the waiter explained the situation, the host wasn't for having any of it and insisted that he pay them both. Despite putting up a strong resistance I reluctantly had to concede. It was only after we left the venue and were walking back to the car Trevor asked me if I knew how much the bottle of wine cost. I didn't have a clue as I just ordered another of what we had and never saw the bill, but Trevor had clocked the wine menu and it was selling at $400 a bottle. Bloody Hell I thought, that would have been a tricky one to explain to our finance manager.

2008 was another special year as the Old Course staged the Curtis Cup at the end of May and the Castle course was due to open in July. The Curtis Cup is an amateur team event played between GB&I and America every second year and although it had been played since 1932 this was the first time it would be played at St Andrews.

One of the joys of staging an event such as the Curtis Cup is the crowds are quite small and everyone coming to watch is an avid golf supporter. They're not there because it's the 'place to be seen' or because they're on a corporate hospitably package, they're there because they love to see good golf, or they have a friend or family member in one of the teams. With the smaller crowds, everything is much more relaxed and most of the time you can get close to the players as not all fairways are roped off. An added bonus was there were four Scots in the GB&I team and one of them, Krystle Caithness, was a local member of the St Regulus Golf Club in St Andrews while another two of the four regularly used the courses and facilities here.

Unfortunately for the home team, the Americans opened up a

small lead on the first morning which they gradually increased at each session other than one which was drawn. Krystle Caithness put in a gutsy performance winning all three games in which she competed. I watched her come down the closing stretch in her singles match on the closing day where she played outstanding golf to win 2&1. The best performer in either team however was the American Stacey Lewis who had a 100% record, winning all five of her matches.

In 2007 came the financial crisis and as it continued through 2008, the management team was looking at redundancies and asked if any staff would be interested in taking voluntary redundancy across the departments. Only one person in the greenkeeping department was interested and it was one of the head greenkeepers. Roddy Barron from the Strathtyrum course had worked at the Links since 1974 and as such, had built up a considerable pension fund. Roddy also had other interests to pursue such as teaching the bagpipes and the St Andrews Pipe Band and felt this was a good time for him to bow out. Having shared an office with Roddy for over four years I enjoyed hearing his stories from when he started work, how things were organised, the practices employed and what he and some others used to get up to. As I've alluded to elsewhere, although he didn't play golf, Roddy had a great eye for detail in construction jobs and was very knowledgeable in flora and fauna and his experience of teaching the pipes made him a natural teacher to younger staff. He had worked on all the courses over his thirty-five years and from 1990 it was his job to paint the holes[*] at the Open and Dunhill which as well as a deft touch, requires a great deal of patience. It's the one job which, if messed up, everyone sees!

During his sixteen years on the Strathtyrum he made many improvements, including to the Golf Academy, where he introduced numerous different greens for chipping and putting, with bunkers of varying degrees of difficulty around them. He even built raised greens on the landing area of the Golf Academy as targets but the hassle of removing them for the tented village at the Open, then rebuilding them afterwards, was too much as the work had all to be done at night when the range was closed. One thing I remember him getting wrong was when he tried to deter crows from damaging the turf at certain times of the year when they searched for larvae in the turf.

---

[*] Once the hole cup is put into the new hole, an inch below the surface, the soil between the top of the cup and the surface is painted white, helping show the hole better for television and the players. There is a special tool for doing this and we only did it for televised events.

Roddy Barron overseeing the irrigation installation on the Strathtyrum course.

He copied an old trick many farmers used and, having obtained a dead crow, he hung it on a metal post as this kept other crows away from the area. His mistake was to put the post on the 1st fairway of the Balgove which is the course the children played. It wasn't long before Ian Forbes was fielding calls from all the angry mothers whose children had been traumatised by the sight of a dead crow hanging from a post.

Replacing Roddy with another head greenkeeper wasn't going to reduce the payroll budget to the extent we hoped, or that several people taking redundancy would. For some time I'd been thinking of how we could improve efficiency within the department and I saw this as an opportunity to implement an idea I had, as I thought we now had the personnel where it would work. It was to amalgamate two teams into one where they would share resources, both staff and equipment, which was something that already happened at tournaments. It was the complete opposite direction to the one we'd always taken where each course (with the exception of the 9-hole Balgove) had its own head greenkeeper, team and everyday equipment. As I saw it, the obvious teams to amalgamate were the New and Jubilee ones as the two courses sat side-by-side and above the 18 holes, only had a practice putting green each, the tournament practice tee and a redundant fairway which local golfers used as a practice strip. That was a better option than trying to use one team to oversee the three courses on the Eden side along with the Golf Academy. Above that, Kevin Muir had only been in charge of the Eden for a little over 18 months and was by far my least experienced head greenkeeper. It was a challenge which Graeme Taylor on the Jubilee would relish and although it was only to be a trial initially, I was confident it would be a success. It meant Davie Wilson was having to move again and he went across to the Strathtyrum and Balgove as I decided to switch responsibility of the Balgove to the person looking after the Strathtyrum rather than the Eden. That made sense as the greens were constructed of the same material and therefore required the same maintenance programmes and practices. In turn, the person responsible for the Eden took over the maintenance of the Golf Academy.

Near to St Andrews sits a mansion house called Hill of Tarvit which was once owned by the Sharp family but is now in the ownership of the National Trust for Scotland (NTS). The Sharp family were jute merchants and Frederick Sharp was a keen golfer and member of the R&A who built his own nine-hole course in land beside the house. The course fell into disrepair until staff from the NTS discovered a map of the course dated 1924 along with the golf bag and clubs of Fredrick Sharp. A retired businessman called David Anderson became involved and decided to resurrect the course and bring hickory golf back to Hill of Tarvit. It wasn't possible to restore the course to its original route and while some holes were recreated, a new layout was built and opened in June 2008. David was the real driver behind the project and to bring the NTS on board and help them understand the concept and the opportunity of providing something different, David spoke to the R&A, the Links Trust and Elmwood College to ask for their support. As a result, I was invited to be a 'Trustee' along with Peter McEvoy, (ex-amateur champion golfer), Steve Isaac from the R&A and Paul Miller who was a lecturer in greenkeeping at Elmwood. The term 'trustee' is very loose, but his idea was to show the NTS that three major organisations were supportive to give the project some gravitas. Our role was to consider and advise how the course would have been maintained in 1924, with minimal inputs of fertiliser, no chemicals and using only the basic equipment that would have been available at the time. The grass was cut to the heights it would have been back in 1924, there was minimal watering while topdressing was prepared and applied by hand and any weeds on the greens were removed by hand. A parasitic plant called yellow rattle was introduced to thin out the roughs, (latterly they have sheep keeping the rough down). We met twice a year on site and David would report what work had been carried out and what was planned. David and his wife Michelle were the face of Kingarrock when it opened, where they would greet players as if they were a guest of the family in the 1920s and would give a little presentation on the history of the family and the course along with a small dram before they set off to play. He had sourced dozens of hickory clubs and old canvas bags and found someone who manufactured golf balls which went the distance the ball would have travelled in 1924, (there was also the option of playing an 1898 ball). For the green fee, players chose their clubs, were given three balls and off they went. On returning, a glass of ginger beer and a piece of shortbread were provided. Tee time intervals were well spread out so no one ever felt rushed. David was such an enthusiast we couldn't help but assist when he asked and it never felt onerous to do so; he was always very generous in return. Paul Miller and David did a lot of research on the family which had an amazing history. For anyone who hasn't visited I would highly recommend a trip there and enjoy playing a game with hickories.

Chapter 17. Rain and Wind, the 2010 Open

W E WOULD often say the Old Course could host an Open at a week's notice (without all the infrastructure in place) but it's not quite as simple as that to reach the precise standards the R&A consider ideal. A challenge many golfers don't consider, and I include local golfers in this, is the fine balancing act between setting the golf course up for staging an event such as The Open and for 'normal' play. This is particularly relevant on the Old Course as it hosts the championship twice as often as the other venues and it is much more accessible to the everyday golfer, with over 50,000 rounds of golf played over the course each year. The course has to be prepared to challenge the greatest golfers in the world but it also has to be playable for those of all abilities in the weeks and months either side of the tournament. The severity of the rough and the width, or narrowness, of the fairways is always a concern. No one enjoys searching for golf balls at every hole and taking five hours for a round. Changing the width of a fairway or growing rough takes months, if not years, for them to perform properly and blend in to look natural. Likewise, the firmness of the fairways and greens, along with green speeds, can make the course too difficult for the average golfer if they become too hard and fast.

As already mentioned, preparations for a St Andrews Open begin almost immediately the previous one finishes when there's a debrief with the R&A to discuss what went well and what could be improved upon. In regard to the golf course, the new tees on holes 2, 12, 13 and 14 were well received while the only aspect which could be considered disappointing was the fact many players chose to hit irons from the tee on the 17th, a hole considered one of the most challenging in the world. This was partly due to the weather conditions as the wind direction through the tournament was helping. The bigger reason was the severity of the rough which increased the further the hole progressed, becoming very penal after 200 yards from the tee. This was especially true on the right-hand side of the hole next to the Jigger Inn where there was an area where players could easily lose a ball. With the ground firm and fast running, it was easy to run out of fairway if using a driver as the fairway became very narrow around 240 yards. This meant many players selected to hit a three or four iron from the tee on the 455 yard hole, leaving themselves a shot of around 150 yards to get onto the top level of the green. To have one of the most feared holes in championship golf reduced to a 4-iron followed by an 8-iron due to the distances the professionals were now hitting the ball, was a major talking point. There was no mention of finding a solution discussed at the debrief, but it wasn't long afterwards before I casually mentioned to Peter Dawson that it wouldn't be too difficult to lengthen the 17th. I would often meet Peter at Local Club events, or when he walked the course with his dog and I don't think he took my suggestion seriously initially but I continued to mention it any time we met. Eventually I asked him to come and have a look at the hole as I thought there were a couple of possibilities depending on how much length required to be added. We both thought any new tee had to come back on the same line as the existing tee, as moving it to the right would mean the Old Course Hotel would be too much in line with the drive while taking it left would result in it interfering with the 16th hole. When going back on the same line, immediately behind the existing tee was a tarred pathway. This was well-used by greenkeepers and their equipment or by people walking to the Golf Academy, while it was also a major spectator route at tournaments. It actually used to be the route of the old railway line from Leuchars to St Andrews. Beyond the road was the Golf Academy, although balls hit from the academy wouldn't be a huge problem. A new tee could affect spectator movement if it went ahead and potentially affect TV towers and a grandstand which was usually in that area. It's likely there would also have to be an alteration to the out of bounds line as it affected the 16th; any new tee would be to the right of the existing boundary. The ground on the Golf Academy was considerably lower than the roadway which, depending on what was decided with the tee, might have to be moved. I parked a tractor and trailer in the area of the academy where I thought the tee should be and, with a couple of wooden pallets placed on the trailer to stand on, the hole from the height and place where the tee might go could be visualised. This was going to increase the length of the hole by around 50 yards making it just under 500 yards in total and Peter Dawson was impressed enough to consider the idea further. This took place towards the end of the summer and Peter wanted feedback from people whose opinions he valued and therefore, at the Dunhill that October, I set the trailer and pallets up again. During practice on the Tuesday, it was arranged I meet with Padraig Harrington when he got to the 17th tee, while Peter arranged to take Ernie Els out to look at the idea later in the day. Both players thought it was a sensible and appropriate change to make, bringing the challenge back into the drive without compromising the integrity of the hole. Although the change was straightforward, following the positive vibes from Harrington and Els, the R&A asked golf course architect Martin Hawtree to draw up some plans. Martin was the R&A's architect of choice for the Old Course and some of the others on the Open rota, while they work with Martin Ebert on others. After the plan was passed by the Links Trust, it was a reasonably quick task for the greenkeepers to build the tee, bringing material in to raise the ground to the required level and move the fence line so the new tee was incorporated into being part of the golf course. Of course, as is normal with anything regarding the Old Course, not everyone was happy about the change and the usual suspects whipped up a small media frenzy about lengthening the course further. Through their access to players, many journalists managed to get some critical quotes but these were predominately from players who hadn't actually seen the changes or even the plans and I imagine any questions would have been framed in such a manner as to lead the player into giving a negative response. I found it amusing when some of the European Tour officials, in perhaps some subtle protest, initially said they wouldn't use the new tee in the following ADLC. However, when it came to the event they did, albeit not over the first three rounds as any change in the weather could have led to the field playing on any one of the days having a significant advantage. By the week of the Open, while there were a few negative comments from the same journalists trying to make a story out of nothing, the vast majority of the players were understanding, particularly after having seen and played the hole.

The other change for the 2010 Open wasn't to the actual golf course but to the infrastructure, as the R&A were installing fibre-optic cabling to all the Open venues to improve pictures in the television coverage for HD TV. That meant installing fibre-optic cables all around the golf course and also to the TV Compound, the practice area, the tented village and the sites of the pay gates as these were all linked.

The cables were all underground, but every so often they came to the surface to what was called a 'node box', to which small overground cables could be connected just prior to the tournament and lead to the TV towers. (By 2015, the node boxes also connected to the electronic screens situated around the course which provide all the scoring information). The cost of installing this was met by the R&A and as such they would 'own' the cable and the boxes but, of course, it was laid on land owned by the Links Trust and we would be responsible for making sure it wasn't damaged in the intervening years. They 'sold it' to us that the cables would all be laid in ducts at a depth similar to our irrigation system, a minimum of 450mm, and we would be provided with 'as laid' plans showing the exact location. They also confidently predicted this would reduce the size of the TV compound in the future as there wouldn't be the requirement for so many vehicles, but that turned out not to be the case as, over the following years, the TV Compound actually increased in size!

The R&A arranged for the contractor they used for all the Open preparations at that time to carry out the work. Grant Smith was fairly local to St Andrews and our team had been well used to working with him over many years, at previous Opens, Dunhills and some of our own projects. He knew the golf courses well and we were comfortable that he would do an excellent job with minimal disturbance to the ground, avoid damage to any existing underground pipes or cables and be respectful to any golfers. Even though the work would be taking place between November and April, all our courses would still have full tee sheets most days. Despite a terrible winter the work went well, the only disappointment being the size of the node boxes as many of them were larger than expected and while they were reasonably well screened by gorse bushes, the department of the R&A delivering the project didn't realise gorse requires to be managed and occasionally needs to be cut back completely. The one other problem, which didn't come to light until the winter after the Open, was a section of cable which was installed at the very last minute. Rather than being trenched in at the agreed depth, it was laid using a mole plough immediately prior to the tournament and we were never made aware of it going in. (With everything else going on in the weeks leading up to an Open and with different contractors working everywhere, it's impossible to know everything that's going on). In November 2010, when one of the staff was deep aerating a traffic route to the side of the 2nd hole, we discovered the cable when he accidently caught it and brought it to the surface. I use the words 'brought it to the surface' loosely, as it was only a couple of inches below the turf where he hit it. It's expensive when you hit a fibre optic cable but there was no way the person responsible was to blame. Neither he, nor us, were aware it was even there, let alone at such a shallow depth. What really annoyed me about the incident was the person leading on the project for the R&A refused to accept any responsibility, despite there being two factors which laid the blame firmly at the R&A's door. My mood didn't improve when Alan McGregor, for whatever reason, agreed with the R&A to claim on the Links Trust insurers to cover the repair cost as I felt that by doing so, he was inferring it was our fault.

To say the winter before the 2010 Open was tough would be a bit of an understatement and there were two incidents in particular that caused concerns at the time. The first began the week before Christmas 2009 when, on 17th December, a reasonable amount of snow fell on the courses. It's not unusual for us to have snow at any time between late November and the end of March but it seldom lies for more than a few days because of our proximity to the sea. The snow had fallen on ground which was slightly frozen, an unusual occurrence, and on Christmas Eve, as temperatures rose and some rain fell, the snow suddenly melted. Because the surface was still frozen it just lay there and overnight the temperature dropped dramatically to well below freezing. It was my job to always check the courses on Christmas morning and when I went in that day, there were pools of frozen water everywhere. Almost every hollow where the water had gathered and had been trapped was like a skating rink. Most greens across all the courses were affected to some degree or other and some, like the 8th and 10th double green on the Old, had as much as 50% of the surface under ice.

The temperature dropped even further over the coming days and nothing had changed by the 4th or 5th of January when most staff were coming back to work after the festive break. After a few more days and with no prospect of any change in the weather, both Gordon McKie and myself began contacting people we knew in Canada and Scandinavia to find out how they dealt with these conditions and what they thought we should do. The consensus of opinion was, provided it didn't go on for more than thirty days, then there shouldn't be too much of a problem given the grass species we had. Where things could get difficult was if the sun came out, the ice would act like a magnifying glass and the grass underneath could burn. I'd experienced that once in my fifteen years at Fraserburgh GC but on a much smaller scale and remember spending days breaking ice on greens. It's amazing how much room broken ice takes up when trying to move it in a wheelbarrow!

A Christmas Day 2010. The 8th and 10th greens covered in ice.

The other problem people warned us about was if we went through a process of the ice thawing and freezing again for a few consecutive days. With this information in mind, we tentatively tried to break some ice on an area at the front of the 17th green of the Eden using a Vertidrain. It wasn't too successful, since as well as damaging the machine, it was difficult to gauge how deep to go without punching into the surface. Even though we didn't go as deep as the grass, the action of the tines was pushing ice into the surface so we only did a small area before stopping. We also had the notion of laying straw or something similar over the ice to block the sun but eventually decided to leave things alone and rely on nature to run its course. In the end, after something like twenty-five or twenty-six days, the thaw came and other than trying to remove as much of the melting water as we could before it froze again, we didn't take any other action, the courses finally opening again on 17th January. As is often the case, leaving things up to nature proved best. Throughout all the courses, the only greens which showed any ill effects were the 16th of the Eden and the 17th of the Strathtyrum, both of which were dominated by annual meadow grass. Of course, with everything being frozen for such a prolonged period, other preparations including bunker repair work and laying the fibre optic cables were held up to an extent.

The next scare came on the 30th of March, again in the form of extreme weather and it was a perfect storm. A deep low-pressure system in the North Sea caused gale force winds and coincided with high spring tides. The wind ferocity was such that in mid-afternoon at high tide, the entire length of the West Sands took a battering with the waves crashing through many of the lower dunes. Waves were also flowing up the Swilcan burn, which had burst its banks and sea water spilled over onto the 1st fairway and 1st green. Other than myself, all the greenstaff had gone for the day and I was concerned the salt water would severely damage the 1st green.

Waves coming up the Swilcan burn, flooding the 1st green and fairway.
30th March 2010.

By 3.30pm, the tide had turned and the water was receding from the green but I was still worried, so connected a hose to the irrigation system and began watering the front of the green where the water had been lying. (I couldn't use the sprinklers on the irrigation system as, in the wind, most of the water would have missed the target). Despite the absolutely horrendous conditions, two golfers came down the 17th and while I was thinking they must be completely mad playing golf in that weather, they were probably looking at me thinking I was the mad one watering the green when it had been pouring with rain most of the day. Just as I was finishing, one of the players' assistants, who was just going off shift appeared and said that there was some flooding on the holes near the Eden Estuary at the far end of the Eden course. That news didn't surprise me as the pond there had occasionally burst its banks in the past under certain conditions. Before I went home for the day, I decided to take a drive past those holes to see how bad it was, thinking the players' assistant had likely exaggerated the situation. When I got there, I had the shock of my life as holes 14 and 15 of the Eden along with 12 and 13 of the Strathtyrum were under five feet of water while other holes were partially flooded. The sea wall protecting the courses from the Estuary at high tide had been breached some 200 yards beyond the golf courses. The fields in that area are so flat, like those holes on the courses, there was nothing to stop the water flowing up and over the courses. As it was getting dark there was absolutely nothing I could do other than talk to the farmer on whose land the breach had been. While he was aware of what had happened, he was unable to do anything immediately due to the conditions. When the tide went out most of the water went with it, then when the tide came back in, the water came back flooding those holes again. After the second or third day, when most of the water had receded at low tide, we were able to dam the narrow section where it was coming through onto the courses. We then pumped any remaining water off but the entire area was left under a thin film of silt which had been carried up from the fields by the incoming tide. It took the Eden and Strathtyrum greenstaff a few days to get as much cleared as was possible. To clear the silt from the greens they connected hoses to the irrigation system, using them like a power washer. On any low points of the fairways where most silt had lain, they again used hoses to get the silt into a solution and pump it off with hover pumps.

They did a great job in getting all the holes open again in less than a week. Surprisingly, and fortunately, there was next to no damage done by the salt water on either the 1st green of the Old or any of the holes on the Eden and Strathtyrum other than a couple of small out-of-play areas where it had lain for a few days. This would have been because of the grass species and how they had become acclimatised and reasonably salt tolerant over many years.

They say bad things come in threes and the third one came on the opening morning of the Open itself, or it began the preceding morning to be precise, when heavy rain caused the four-hole challenge featuring the past champions to be cancelled. First staged for the Millennium Open where it proved very successful, the R&A brought it back as this was going to be 150 years since the first playing of the Open and many players including Lee Trevino, Arnold Palmer, Bob Charles, Gary Player and Tom Weiskopf had flown in especially for the event. It had been heavy rain and strong winds through most of the morning and early afternoon and the event would have been no fun for the spectators, or indeed any of the players. As luck would have it and as is often the case, less than thirty minutes after the R&A reluctantly, and correctly, decided to call the event off, the wind dropped, the sun came out and by the time it had been due to begin, it turned out to be a beautiful afternoon.

That didn't last however and the rain returned with a vengeance through the night and as such we had to alter our plans on the Thursday morning, dropping the fairway cutting along with a few other jobs. Staff scheduled for those tasks were sent to clear water lying on the 1st fairway just short of the Swilcan Burn and from the carry on 18 between the tee and the burn. These are the lowest lying areas on the Old Course and if water is going to lie anywhere, it'll be there. Fortunately, the staff are well used to carrying out this operation and were able to clear the water some thirty minutes prior to play starting at 6.30am. I recall doing a couple of interviews about the weather on the Thursday morning, one for Radio Five Live and one for South Korean TV. I hope the Koreans had subtitles!

Staff are well used to having to cope with flooding at tournaments. This picture is from a Dunhill tournament.

As anticipated, the controversy surrounding the new tee at 17 grew in prominence before most of the players even arrived with many Sunday paper journalists trying to stir things up. While a few players were critical, once they had played from the new tee the vast majority understood why the hole had been lengthened and didn't have a problem. (Like the 14th tee in 2005, some of us tried it out early on the Sunday and Monday mornings and I can confirm that for the average golfer, it's a beast). What became more of an issue was the condition of the rough on the left of the hole which was growing thicker by the day. It had been an area both we and the R&A had been keeping a close eye on from the beginning of the growing season. Through April and May everything was looking as it should be and come the Open, it should be tall and wispy. This would make it easy to find a ball and tempt the player into a heroic shot where the grass might turn the shaft causing a big hook or it might take the backspin off the ball causing it to shoot through the green and onto the roadway. Unfortunately, the wet summer caused a late spurt of growth and the week prior to the tournament it became exceptionally thick. At the beginning of tournament week, we could swear it was growing in front of our eyes and as practice rounds continued, the protests from the players became more vocal. Eventually at 5am on the Wednesday morning, Grant Moir, (no relation), who along with Peter Dawson is the R&A Director responsible for how the course is set up, met with Gordon McKie and myself at the 17th to look at the area in question. There are generally three or four paces of semi-rough either side of each fairway before it changes to uncut rough. It will vary in density and height depending on a variety of factors such as the soil conditions and grass species. That morning, just a foot beyond the semi rough in this area, we were dropping a golf ball from waist height and struggling to find it, let alone be able to hit it back onto the fairway. The growth in that area over the previous five to seven days was hard to believe but there was little we could have done to change things beforehand. Now we were at a critical stage, little more than twenty-four hours away from the start of the championship and we had to do something. Grant called Peter to join us and discuss the situation although our options were limited to say the least. In the end, we did the only thing we could which was to extend the width of the semi rough in that area by a further three paces to allow the players a little more leeway.

Following the tournament, we had a discussion with our agronomists on how to improve the rough in that area to make it more 'linksy' in style with tall seed heads blowing in the breeze. The land in that area is low lying and has a slightly higher silt and soil content, making the grasses it supports coarser than the traditional fescues, sweet vernal and crested dogstail species typically found on a links course. Instead, there was a lot of rye grass with clumps of cocksfoot and Yorkshire fog, all of which are very dense. We did consider killing off the existing vegetation with glysophate and stripping the turf from the area before adding sand to reduce the fertility. While affecting the numerous competitions staged over the Old Course, it would have also caused a huge disruption to all the golfers playing for the best part of a year until the area recovered sufficiently. Because the new grass species would have been so different from those on the fairway, it would have been quite noticeable, even at ground level. It would have been even more distinct from the high TV towers or the balconies of the

Old Course Hotel. Also, most modern-day sports grasses are bred more for in-play areas rather than roughs so we would have had to inter-seed it with species such as sweet vernal and crested dogstail. In the end we decided to try a programme of cutting it back each winter and removing the clippings.

Scarifying the rough on 17 after the 2010 Open to try and thin out the base.

This would be supplemented with scarifying the area to remove some of the thatch which had built up, adding sand and using a new product containing a graminicide which kills the coarser grasses while not affecting the finer ones.

This programme would take longer but would be less disruptive. We ended up doing this for a number of years with limited success as initially, the area became quite open and easy to play from. For the visitor or the Local Club member playing a medal, this was a bonus but it needs to be more challenging for any elite golf tournaments. We would rope it off through the winter to reduce people trampling through it as much as possible which helped, but a lot of the coarser grasses came back. With hindsight we should have continued with the graminicide products for a longer period but on a more selective basis using hand-held applicators to spray specific areas. On the other hand, there's an opinion that the area between the 2nd and 17th should be more open to allow golfers the opportunity to hit the green. Many golfers aren't aware the front nine is relatively new in comparison to the back nine. It's been said most of the areas between the front and back nines used to be cut as fairway but it must have been well before I arrived at the Links, if indeed it's correct. The idea of allowing players to go for the green from the left is based on the risk and reward element that introduces, as it brings Road Bunker much more into play. While I understand the concept, I'm not convinced it would necessarily be the case now given the distance the top players hit the ball along with the height they can hit it and the control they have. The days of them having to run a four, five or six iron into the 17th green are more or less gone as most of them can launch the ball up into the air, land it on the top shelf and still stop it.

While it's an objective to get things just right and one should strive for that, it's a difficult balance. There's a large part of me which thinks that when dealing with nature, there has to be an acceptance of what that brings and things can be completely different from one year to the next depending on the weather in the preceding months. As an example, a cool dry spring and early summer will leave the roughs much more open than if there had been a wet and warm one. If it's the latter then by early June, every second member in the golf club is usually on my back about the thickness of the rough and how many balls they're losing. Fortunately, it's relatively short lived and by the second half of July, things are beginning to die back and it's mostly a case of being patient and letting nature run its course, as to intervene can lead to greater problems in the long run.

In 2010 we had our marquee with full catering just outside the compound. The Toro Company once again provided the greenstaff with a jacket and four golf shirts each while four other companies we dealt with regularly, (Aitkens Seedsmen, Greentech, Aquatrols and Barenbrug), covered the food costs each day. Although the forecast for the week was mixed with strong winds and heavy bursts of rain, everything started off on a good footing. Toro had again loaned us six ride-on greens mowers and while there weren't so many pictures in the press as in 2005, they were still very happy with the coverage they received. Once again, they booked out the four days at the Eden clubhouse for customer hospitality from around the world. Some

Australian superintendents they had invited followed the staff around during the morning shift.

With everything in the world advancing quickly in these technological times, the Open and the greenkeeping industry were no exception. As well as the fibre-optic cabling for improving the pictures for HD coverage on TV, management of the grass and golf course had become much more scientific and performance based, using data to assist in making decisions on what was required to get the greens to optimum condition. The STRI along with Hallam University, Sheffield, had developed a computer to measure the smoothness and trueness of greens which they had been trialling for over a year. St Andrews was one of the venues they had used and as such we had a reasonable amount of data relevant to our venue which gave more accurate figures to the ongoing study and from which we could benefit.

Being such a prominent organisation is a bonus, but it can also be a hindrance as we were always receiving requests to try different equipment, products, trials, etc, or to be involved in research for them. Of course, if a company or organisation could link their product or machine to St Andrews that would be a huge benefit to them and as such, we always had to be careful of what we became involved with. We certainly wouldn't give an endorsement for anything unless we had used it for a considerable time and were happy with its performance before reaching agreement with the company. There were a few occasions over the years where it was brought to my attention that certain companies were openly mentioning items which they claimed we used or had endorsed. We had to contact them and ask them to remove our name from their advertising as their claims were false, occasionally having to take legal advice. On the flip side, because we understood the worldwide interest in St Andrews and how other golf venues would look to us for leadership and best practice (and I say that as a factual statement and not because we thought we were better than anyone else or did things better) we felt we had a responsibility to promote good practice. We're also aware we're a public body and feel we should be seen to be supportive of good causes, in particular environmental research or similar.

But back to the Open and STRI with their new gizmo called a Trueness meter but affectionately nicknamed a Bobble-meter. It consisted of a free-rolling metal sphere the size of a golf ball, linked by wires to a computer which was pushed along the surface of a green at a slow, steady pace for around ten metres. How the sphere reacted would measure the vertical deviation, (smoothness) and the horizontal deviation, (trueness), and the numbers given would relate to what was deemed reasonable, good or very good, based on data accumulated since research began. The figures from that earlier research, taken before and after different mechanical practices such as cutting, rolling or verticutting, provided us and the STRI to base decisions on what maintenance was required to get the greens in the best possible condition and the standard required by the R&A for the championship.

As well as smoothness and trueness, we were also trying to get consistency between greens in firmness and speed. Firmness was done using an implement called a Clegg hammer, a piece of equipment adapted from a tool used to measure the firmness of tarmacadam roads. Again, following a couple of years of collecting data, we knew we were looking to get the greens to a position where they were giving a figure of between 120 and 130 gravitas, (the measurement used). The figure was reached from studies monitoring a crisply hit seven-iron from a fairway and how it reacted when hitting what was considered a good, firm, golf green, where it would bounce twice, checking on the second bounce before running out. This information in conjunction with the weather forecast would help decide how much irrigation the green might require each night. While it was important to keep the grass healthy and not stress it too much by letting it become too dry, it was important not to overwater and make the greens too soft and holding, whereby players could stop the ball easily, even when coming from the semi-rough. Of course, if there was substantial rainfall then, to a certain extent it became irrelevant. As more data and research has been carried out, we've been able to work towards lessening the effect heavy rain would have on surface firmness.

By measuring and tracking the organic matter[*] in the top 20mm of the green, we would work towards keeping it at around three percent volume of a sample. While keeping the organic matter to a minimum won't stop the rain lowering the firmness, it reduces the time taken for the greens to firm up again.

---

[*] Organic matter. This is a thin layer of decaying grass blades and roots at the surface of the turf. If allowed to become too thick it will hold too much moisture, making the surface soft. This in turn can lead to shallow rooting, increased possibility of disease, foot-printing, ball marks, (pitchmarks) and other issues. It also allows the player to have greater control of their golf ball from the rough or semi-rough. A small amount of organic matter is beneficial in protecting the crown of the plant.

Measuring moisture and firmness levels on the 17th green.

Because we only began collecting data in 2009, we were still at an early stage and the control of firmness could not be completely managed. The amount of rain there was in the days preceding the tournament made it irrelevant. Over time this approach would also provide consistency between greens as regards firmness which in itself is an interesting concept, especially as it was later extended to greens approaches. Being 'old school', I'm not totally convinced this is the best way to determine the best golfer. While I accept there has to be a minimum standard of presentation and playability, to have every aspect of the course play the same is not something found in nature. Take the 9th hole on the Old Course for example, because at least 90% of golfers walk to the right of the green to get to the 10th tee, the approach from the right is much firmer than from the left where there is also the smallest of hollows immediately in front of the green. So why should they be equally as firm? Similarly, the approach on a raised green is likely to be firmer than one which has a hollow at the front. To my mind, having them the same reduces the skill required. As an old greenkeeper once said when a player complained about the greens all being different speeds, "That's why you get practice rounds."

That takes me back to green speed which I do believe should be as consistent between greens as possible but where research has shown that even a professional golfer will find it difficult to tell the difference in green speeds if it's less than six inches. The average golfer struggles to tell the difference when it's less than a foot and that becomes even more difficult in the wind. The R&A requirement was for 10½ feet on the Stimpmeter from the Monday, the first day of practice, and the STRI agronomy team were on site ten days before the tournament began, to get to where we wanted them to be. They had been involved in a smaller capacity at previous Opens and felt that sometimes the greenstaff, when measuring green speeds had not always been as precise as they could have been, something I had often thought in my own mind. I'd seen it myself, including at St Andrews, where the head greenkeeper had been asked to get the greens to a particular speed for an event. Yet when I checked them myself for my own curiosity, I got a lower reading. It's the easiest thing in the world to give the Stimpmeter a little 'help' by nudging it up just as the ball begins to roll, gaining a few extra inches on the final numbers. Then they can report to the tournament organiser that they are meeting the requirement. Greenkeepers always like to be able to tell their peers how fast their greens are and are prone to exaggerate, which I have done myself on occasion. I've also been asked by regular golfers at what speed the greens are running when they saw me measuring them. I would usually ask them what speed they thought they were and reply they were correct, irrespective of what they answered. Then they would say to their playing partners, "I told you!"

To achieve as accurate a reading as they could, they used a cloche, (a cover you would use to protect your vegetables in the garden), to take any effect the wind would have out of the equation and that took a bit of work to move around the green and set up. This all took time as they had the practice putting greens to measure first before getting onto the course itself. They would measure the green speed before the staff would cut it and then again afterwards to determine if we needed to cut it again or roll it to reach the desired speed. Even though they went out fifteen minutes before the greenstaff to begin this, it seemed to take ages before we really got into our stride, even with two teams from the STRI measuring. However, once they did get past the first few greens it flowed well and we were always well ahead of any golf.

Using a cloche when measuring the green speed on the 11th at the 2010 Open.

There would be a daily briefing each afternoon with Peter Dawson, the STRI, Gordon McKie and myself, where we would share feedback on the course, then discuss and agree what work was required that evening and the next morning. The Met Office would also be represented as they were on site to give an up-to-date weather forecast throughout the week. That led for some interesting exchanges as they were often inaccurate with their forecasts. At one meeting, Peter Dawson informed them he'd received a more accurate forecast from Tom Watson's personal weather forecaster than they had provided. And he was based in the USA!

One further thing, which demonstrates the attention to detail the R&A put into the event and also the skill the players possess, was the accuracy required for the course guides they produce, even though many of the caddies will draw up their own. The Links have yardages on every sprinkler giving the distance to the front of the green, but the R&A would arrange for a company to come and measure the course. This would include taking a measurement from each fairway sprinkler to the front of the green and they'd log these in the booklet they produced. When they came and did this a few months before the tournament, over 200 of our sprinkler lids were different from the measurements they recorded. The vast majority of them were only one yard out but it meant we had to replace the lids on every sprinkler that was different. They joke on television when Bernhard Langer's caddie tells him the pin is xxx yards from this sprinkler he asks, "Is that from the front of the sprinkler or the back?" Having to change over 200 plus sprinkler lids the week before the tournament was just something else to add to the list of things to do.

Another area the STRI is involved in is the environment side. Like the Links, the R&A are very conscious of their responsibility towards protecting the environment and minimising any negative effect staging such a large event has on the course and surrounding areas. It's important we all promote this and the general benefits to the environment golf offers. There are many groups and organisations who still believe golf is bad for the environment, claiming it destroys habitat as well as being a poor use of land and resources. To this end and along with the help of the Links Trust and Fife Coast and Countryside Trust, the R&A produced a small booklet to raise awareness of the work we undertake to protect and enhance the wildlife and habitats. They had produced a similar booklet every Open from the late 1990s and this was the third one they had done for a St Andrews Open, highlighting the different work programmes in place for managing the gorse, grassland and heather, focusing on the wildlife values of each. There were also sections on the work we had carried out on coastal protection and how we met the requirements of the Environment Impact Assessment when building the Castle course. The Links had worked closely with Bob Taylor, the environmental officer at the STRI for many years, both directly and through his role as advisor to the R&A. One of the standard duties we would have to carry out was to prepare routes through the roughs and gorse to allow easy access for spectators around the venue, ensuring any potential trip hazards were removed. This is a winter project and has to be completed before any birds began nesting in the spring. As we approached the breeding season we had to regularly walk or drive these routes to prevent the ground-nesting birds from building their nests in the closer cut grass. However, there was one situation we had never thought of and by the time it was discovered it was too late to change. When Bob arrived at the beginning of Open week to have a close look around, he found the scoreboard by the 17th green had a swallows' nest with young chicks in it. This scoreboard informed the 3,000 spectators on the grandstand there which players were approaching the green as well as showing the leading eight or ten players. With the discovery of the nest and chicks in one corner, Bob insisted that only the other half of the scoreboard could be used to prevent them being disturbed. This wasn't an ideal situation but until the chicks flew the nest there was no other solution and the week progressed with only half the scoreboard in operation. It was an important learning curve and noted for future Opens that structures such as leader boards, TV towers and grandstands required regular inspections after being built.

Friends and other people I talk to often ask me about players and what they are like, thinking that I'm always meeting them when they are out practising but the fact is, unless there is something specific to look at, I was seldom out on the course through the practice days other than when helping first thing in the morning or with the evening tidy-up. Even though there's a tournament taking place, the normal everyday things continue and there are numerous other things to attend to. There are often course managers, superintendents and other industry professionals from around the world attending the tournament and looking to either catch up or be shown around the maintenance facility. I felt it important to try and set aside some time to meet with them, even if it's just a case of providing them with a coffee and letting them relax in our catering tent. I always saw my role as looking after all the other aspects to prevent them becoming a distraction, allowing the course manager and the team to focus on the golf course as getting everything right with it was the main objective. They were the ones who looked after it throughout the year and where their strengths lay. I was quite happy just helping out through morning set-up whether it was directing people after the STRI had carried out their measuring, putting the tee markers out or simply sweeping the course behind everyone to see things were as they should be. It was the same in the evening where I might collect the tee markers before they went missing as 'souvenirs', or assist with the fairway divoting, something I enjoyed as it gave me an opportunity to talk with many of the staff. The evening shift would be the only time I was liable to meet any of the players when those practising late would still be on the course. I never bothered trying to enter into a conversation with them unless they instigated it as this was their job and they should be allowed to focus on what they were doing. Pleasantries would be exchanged but unless they asked a question, then a, "Hi, are you enjoying the course?" or something similar would be the extent of it.

I did manage to catch Tiger Woods on the practice chipping green and get my 2005 Open flag signed, although he didn't sign my flag from the 2002 US Open at Bethpage, as he said he would sign only one. There are often stories about Tiger being unwilling to sign autographs but that's not my experience. Following the third round in 2005 when, even though he was leading, he headed back to the practice ground until it closed as he was unhappy with a particular aspect of his game. As he left the area there was a sizeable group of children waiting for him and while it would have been easy for him to walk past them after a tough day, he stopped and diligently signed autographs for them for a good ten minutes.

Other golfers can be less accommodating. I also had a flag from the 2004 Masters which I had been given and which I wanted Phil Mickleson to sign as he won that year, but that wasn't so easy. While I was putting the tee markers out early on one of the practice days, Phil was out playing with Jim Furyk who had long-time friend Paul Kirkcaldy, the manager of our Golf Academy, carrying his bag. While they were putting on the 9th green, I spoke with Paul on the 10th tee as I also had a flag from Harbour Town where Furyk had won. Paul said that Furyk would sign but doubted Phil would and he was correct. I was told by his caddie that Phil didn't sign autographs during his practice round. The next day I was at the 17th green where Tom Weiskopf was giving an interview and the reporter had asked for me to be there to check the historical accuracy. While I was waiting, who happened to come along from the Old Course Hotel to begin his practice round but Phil Mickleson. I still had the flag in my pocket, so I asked again only to get the same answer. He then proceeded to begin his practice round from the 18th tee and I heard later he complained to the R&A because there was no crowd control on 18 when he was playing his practice round. He was referring to the spectators in general and not me I hasten to add. I was a bit hacked off with him by then, but I did make the effort to go and catch him later when he completed his 19-hole practice round and had my flag signed, eventually.

The 2010 Open was a very different and more difficult Open from our perspective than the previous two, simply due to the weather. The guys camping out had to deal with wet or damp clothing for most of the week, even though we had reasonably good drying facilities within the maintenance facility. There was also no Jigger Inn to nip down to and quench our thirst after the evening shift, as a management company had rented it out for the week and entry was by invitation only. That meant we had to take the buggies and head up to the first tee and grab a quick beer in the Dunvegan Hotel or No. 1 Golf Place.

The rain at the beginning of the week made conditions softer than the R&A, or we, would have liked which led to some excellent scoring on the Thursday as the greens were holding and there was little wind. A lot of those on the staff were hoping Rory McIlroy would win his first Major and it looked promising after an opening 63 but things changed quickly on the Friday when the wind got up and he scored 80. It was so strong at one point, play had to be suspended for over an hour as balls were moving on the greens at the far end of the course which is more exposed due to its proximity to the Eden Estuary. While McIlroy had to come in off the course because of the wind after his 3rd hole, Louis Oosthuizen was safely in the clubhouse after taking advantage of the early calm conditions, adding a 67 on the Friday morning to his opening 65. That gave him a six-shot lead which he was never to relinquish, eventually winning by seven shots from Lee Westwood and a resurgent McIlroy who recovered to score 69 and 68 over the weekend.

Louis Oosthuizen, a popular winner, with some of the greenstaff.

Oosthuizen turned out a popular winner in town as he's a regular supporter of the ADLC each October and comes across as a genuinely nice guy. Unlike 2005, along with Gordon McKie the course manager, I was invited to be part of the presentation party at the end of play which was a privilege. I was also more relaxed about getting my flag signed as I knew I'd have plenty of opportunities to see Oosthuizen at future ADLC tournaments.

Of course, a variety of things are continually taking place across the Links other than just on the Old. On the Eden course, we began using a relatively new product called 'Rescue' to resolve the problem with ryegrass infestation on the greens, which had been affecting the surfaces since long before I arrived at the Links.

Ryegrass is a broadleaved grass compared to the fescues and bents which are the preferred grasses for golf greens. It begins growing earlier in the spring and is difficult to cut, no matter how sharp the mower blades are, as it tends to fold down under the bottom blade then spring up once the blades have passed over. It makes the greens bumpy, slower and ugly to look at, especially from March through until late May, when the finer grasses aren't growing strongly. This product, a graminicide, had been in development for several years and had the ability to kill off the ryegrass without affecting the finer grasses in a way similar to how a selective weedkiller works, as the larger surface area of the leaf will absorb more product. Not all the greens on the Eden were affected, only the eleven original ones built before 1987. The plan was to spray the product then, after a couple of weeks as the ryegrass began to die off, overseed the greens with a fescue and bent mixture to fill the gaps. The results weren't as good as we expected. As well as the ryegrass, some of the greens treated had a high percentage of Highland bent which was also killed off while the success of overseeding wasn't as good as we'd hoped for. It left the greens bare and bumpy in places and we had to overseed again later in the year. If there's one thing you can be sure of in St Andrews, it's that the local golfers aren't slow in telling you there's a problem with the greens on a golf course! Despite constantly communicating what we were doing and why, by numerous different methods, people would constantly ask me what had happened to the greens on the Eden. They didn't seem to notice it was only some of the greens on the front nine holes which were affected and that the greens on the back nine were as good as any on the Links. The Eden suddenly had this reputation locally that the greens were poor. Other problems we experienced was the ryegrass wasn't killed off completely and in areas where it was worst, it began returning, while in some of the hollows on greens such at the 8th, the dominant grass was annual meadow grass which would look yellow and sickly in the spring. Kevin Muir and his team had to repeat the process of spraying for three or four years, along with overseeding the greens as often as was practical, to get on top of it. Strangely, when the greens on the Eden were back to being as good as ever, the message took much longer to spread round the local golfing community. It's difficult to explain what went wrong, if indeed anything did, as I've seen and played other links courses who carried out the same work but didn't run into the problems we did although many did lose a lot of grass cover initially. I was certain there was nothing wrong with how the team carried out the work and we were in close correspondence with the company who manufactured the product, but they couldn't give us a definitive answer why we experienced what we did. It could have been purely down to timing and the weather immediately afterwards, or the amount of play on the Links making it difficult to get really good results from any overseeding we undertook.

Graeme Taylor tried the same product on the 18th green of the New course the following year, fertilising the green heavily beforehand to get the grass growing strongly. We thought this would lead to a good recovery afterwards but the result was worse. When the coarse grasses died off, the bare areas were filled with annual meadow grass. Some ten years later and after numerous overseedings, the green can still be very mottled in spring as there's still a lot of annual meadow grass throughout although the percentage of bent grass is increasing year on year. Rescue was a product which was much anticipated prior to its release on the market as greenkeepers had constantly looked for a method of controlling ryegrass but it never quite lived up to its expectations and was withdrawn from sale by 2016.

A similar product called Laser became available at the same time. It was agricultural-based and more potent and therefore considered risky to try on greens. Along with a few other golf clubs, the Links funded trials to get approval from the environmental agencies for its use on golf courses. We used it to control coarse grasses in semi-roughs and roughs and had spectacular results as they left the bands we sprayed very 'open'. It's great to see the tall seedheads blowing in these areas but still be able to go in and find a golf ball relatively easily.

December 2010 saw a significant change in the organisation

as Alan McGregor, CEO since 1998 retired from the Trust and Euan Loudon was appointed as his successor. Alan was a popular leader with most of the staff and knew many of them by their first name, including some of the seasonal staff as he would regularly go on 'walkabout' where he would stop and chat. He was very much a team builder and there would be regular get-togethers of the managers from all the different departments. Sometimes these involved an overnight stay off-site where we would discuss a particular subject, carry out team building exercises and receive training on different subjects. I built up a good relationship with Alan following my promotion but even before then he always came across as being genuinely interested in all that was happening, wanting to help in any way he could. That's not to say we could do whatever we wanted as he would often disagree with us or our suggestions and the idea would finish there, or together we would come up with another method to reach a similar result. That was very different to the two Secretaries to the Trust who went before him as they tended to remain near their office, seldom seen by the staff and I doubt I saw either of them more than once a month. Through our regular Directors' meetings and his observations, Alan knew a lot about many of the staff, good and bad. He was a huge influence on my life and career, as well as promoting me to manage the greenkeeping department, he was always there to offer advice and encouragement, sometimes directing me while on other occasions allowing me to come up with my own answers. I would often go with a situation or problem along with my solution to get his thoughts before proceeding. I also found him very open when we had management team meetings and if there was a difference of opinion over a particular course of action which affected us all, he would talk it through with us before reaching a conclusion.

There were a couple of things Alan changed in the two years prior to his retirement. He made it one of his objectives before he retired to change the titles of the senior managers, including his own. Up until then his position had always been Secretary to the Links Trust while those leading departments had been golf manager, finance manager etc and from 2011, I had been referred to as Links Superintendent. The Trustees agreed to change his title to Chief Executive while the rest of us became Directors of our departments and I became Director of Greenkeeping. It was a change which affected me in name only but allowed the head greenkeepers to become course managers which was something much more reflective of the role they carried out, and important in how they were perceived externally, giving them a more professional persona. This filtered down to their deputies and overall was a positive step other than the fact it didn't lead to any increase in salaries, or not one I was aware of!

The other change he introduced was some of the senior managers were to stop attending Trustees meetings apart from the director of finance and the commercial director. I'd been attending these meetings, of which there were eight per year since 2001, and while I seldom had anything major to report on, there were generally some questions about the courses or events taking place which I could accurately answer. While it was nice to meet the Trustees and understand their thinking, as well as building a relationship with many of them, this change reduced my workload.

While talking about Alan's time at the Links I think it would be good to throw in a couple of stories about him. One of the first things he had to deal with when he started in January 1998 was the aftermath of the Christmas party of 1997 as it ended up in a bit of a free for all. Fortunately, and for once, it wasn't the greenkeepers who were involved!

In the early 2000s around 5pm on a Friday through the winter, the other senior managers and I would sometimes meet in the boardroom at Pilmour House where we would sit and chew the fat, taking it in turns to bring along a bottle of wine. Once finished, we would leave the empty bottle in the litter bin under the desk in Alans's office for the cleaner to find!

Chapter 18. People I've met and places I've visited

THIS CHAPTER is simply a collection of different stories of some of the characters I've met, things I've done and places I've been fortunate to visit in the course of my work.

Although I seldom had conversations with professionals during the course of a tournament, I did have the opportunity to meet a few of them on other occasions. One player I met a number of times over the years was Gary Player. The first time was when he and Jasper Parnevik came to play with their sponsors the day after the 1997 Open at Royal Troon. I can imagine that would have been the last thing Parnevik wanted to do as he may have felt that was the Open he really let slip from his grasp. When I discovered they were playing the Old Course, I collected my two boys and took them down to watch. Andrew was eleven, Bruce seven, and when we arrived at the course, Player was on the 17th fairway waiting for the green to clear. I sent the boys over to him to get his autograph, Andrew arriving slightly ahead of his little brother. When Bruce got there, I heard Player asking Bruce to show him his hands. Bruce obliged then Player asked him to turn his hands over which he again did. Then to his amazement he said, "Your name's Bruce." You can imagine how that seemed to a seven-year-old. He was completely confused but desperately tried to figure out how Player knew. He had lots of theories but the fact Player had asked Andrew before Bruce arrived on the scene wasn't one of them. Just then, a young lad was cycling past on his way from the Golf Academy when Player shouted to him to stop. The boy was taken by surprise but stopped his bike non-the-less. Player then asked him to get off and show him his swing. Again, the boy obliged and Player complemented him on his fine swing before he got back on his bike and cycled off, probably wondering what the hell had just happened. We followed Player up the 18th where he almost drove the green, not bad for someone already in his 60s. He was very proud of his drive, telling everyone standing behind the green watching, carefully omitting the fact his ball landed on the roadway crossing the fairway on its first bounce. On another occasion when he was playing the Old, the last hole was playing into a stiff breeze and his drive came up short of the road. There was a crowd watching and ever the showman, in a loud voice he said to his caddie, "Give me a seven iron," while reaching over and pulling a four iron from his bag!

I was fortunate to be invited to Gleneagles on the Saturday of the 2014 Ryder Cup by the Toro company. When I first arrived, I headed to their hospitality pavilion for some breakfast. While sitting there, two American guests came and sat beside me but we made the big mistake of not introducing ourselves. In the course of conversation, it became obvious they knew who I was, (I've no idea how but suspect they asked someone before they came over), but by then it was too late for me to ask who they were. Early in the conversation, I picked up on the fact one was quite a good golfer and he'd played the Old Course, then as it went on, I figured out he'd played in an Open at St Andrews but which one and who was he? It was only when they left and I had the opportunity to ask on of the Toro staff I discovered it was Jerry Pate, 1976 US Open Champion who has a number of Toro dealerships in the southern US.

Another major champion I met is Paul Azinger, and again, coincidently, Toro were involved. I was on a trip to the Toro HQ in Minneapolis with another two dozen course managers from the UK and Europe on a feedback session. We were in a bar-cum-restaurant one evening when one of our party spotted Azinger come in with a couple of his friends. Andy Brown, our host from Toro, approached him and explained who we were and he came up and chatted to us and we had some pictures taken. The bizarre part of this story is what happened next. A group of around ten girls came into the restaurant and one of them was celebrating her birthday. One of her friends came and asked our group, and Paul Azingers, if we could form a line, standing with our legs apart, and the birthday girl had to crawl through our legs. The twist was, her skirt was hitched up and each of us had to spank her as she crawled through. Andy Brown met Azinger in an airport lounge a few years later where he introduced himself by saying, "Mr Azinger, you probably don't remember me but we met in a restaurant in Minnieapolis a few years ago when I was with a group of British golf course managers". "Oh yes, I don't think I can ever forget that evening," replied Azinger smiling.

At a GIS show in America one year, I was walking with my friend Joe O'Donnell when we met an older gentleman who Joe introduced to me as 'Speedy', aka Jim Limpari, who gave me his business card for Speedy Enterprises with a three of diamonds on it. After introductory pleasantries, he immediately produced a pack of playing cards and took us over to a nearby table where he performed a card trick based on the story of a Mr Fixit, called Speedy, who was represented by the three of diamonds. 'Speedy' lived in New York and was tasked to find different things for a Mr Big for his new venture, namely 'dancing girls', 'gentlemen', alcohol etc with the trick finishing in a story about playing poker, having used every single card. As I love card tricks and used to do a few of my own for our kids, I was hooked. I eventually persuaded 'Speedy' to show me how to do the trick which he very kindly did on the proviso I would never do it at any turf shows. It took me a little while but I mastered it and used to do it on a regular basis at parties, especially when our kids, (who were young adults by then) had their friends round and would join in the fun. I met Jim on a number of subsequent shows where he would always perform the trick to all and sundry, everyone knowing him as Speedy.

My friend Speedy, aka Jim Limpari.

My secretary sent through a call one day from someone whose name I recognised although I didn't know him personally. I was aware he had often contacted Alan McGregor about his concerns with dog-eared lichen which would occasionally appear on some fairways. This wasn't a concern I shared as it would disappear on its own once growth commenced. This day, he was concerned with dog-eared lichen on his lawn rather than on the courses and wanted to know if I could sell, (probably give), him something to eradicate it. This wasn't something we did at the Links and I politely tried to explain to him some fertiliser and perhaps aeration once the weather improved would cure it, but he was insistent that we sell him something. Eventually I said "I'm sorry but we don't sell products to the general public," to which he replied, "I'm not a member of the general public, I'm a member of the R&A!"

I was contacted by one of the R&A secretarial staff regarding a request on behalf of a wife of one of their members. She explained it was the member's birthday shortly, a big birthday to be exact, and his wife wanted to give him a set of cuff links in the form of two glass phials, inside which would be some sand from Road Bunker. I said this wouldn't be a problem and I'd drop a small amount of sand off with the porter in the R&A clubhouse over the coming days. I was very tempted to simply go out into the yard and collect a handful of beach sand from one of the storage bays but something got inside my head which prevented me doing this. For some irrational reason, I convinced myself the member concerned was Johan Rupert, the businessman behind the Dunhill. As a result, the next time I passed the 17th I stopped my car and walked to Road Bunker to collect a small container of sand and hand it into the R&A.

Sitting at the bay window of the St Andrews Golf Club one September, Rich Hurley said to me, "See the person standing at the fence by the 18th green, that's Howdy Giles, Arnold Palmer's dentist." Rich knew him through his association with Palmer in the seed business, part of which was attending the Arnold Palmer Invitational tournament at Bay Hill every year. We went out to meet said Howdy and chatted to him for a while. As well as being Arnie's dentist, he was a personal friend and, at various tournaments where Palmer was playing, Howdy would get a press pass to go inside the ropes with his camera. Except, to the best of my knowledge, he only ever took pictures of Arnie. Afterwards, he often sent me pictures of Arnie, or him and Arnie. The following summer, an email arrived in my inbox from a Randy Jefferies, someone

I'd never heard of. It went on to explain he was a friend of Howdy Giles and was going to be visiting St Andrews with his two sons and could I get them a game on the Old Course, stating they were quite happy to pay the green fees. With enough things going on, I replied to say I was sorry but there was little I could do. The next day, another email arrived saying he was a member at Isleworth, Tiger's home club, and was I sure there was nothing I could do? Maybe I was too rash in my first reply. I went back the second time with my normal response to people I knew. Firstly, I can only enter the ballot for them with me as one of the players. This allowed me to apply for a local preferential time which gave us a better chance of getting a time. Secondly, it would have to be a Thursday afternoon or one of the last six times each day as these were the local times when I could play. Failing that, I could ask to go out with them at the end of the field, which might mean we'd have to play the closing holes in the dark depending on the weather and the pace of play. Finally, I couldn't help with the green fees in any way. He was happy with that and we proceeded on that basis. Come the day, we got an afternoon time on Thursday. Only, when they arrived to meet me at the tee, there were four of them as Randy had invited his best friend along. I was in a panic as I needed to be one of the four players but the crisis was averted when Randy explained he had played the Old Course in a previous visit and was standing aside to allow his sons and friend to play. It turned out a beneficial move for me as when we went on holiday to Orlando a couple of years later, Randy took my son and I on to Isleworth as his guests. He drove us around the gated community and showed us where Tiger lived. Unfortunately, Tiger was away playing in an event on this occasion but was there practising when I went back, again as guest of Randy's, on a subsequent visit with a couple of Links' staff when we were over at the Golf Industry Show. It pays to be helpful.

We often get requests from families asking if they can scatter their loved one's ashes on the course, something we always say yes to, generally advising them to do so in the area between the 18th tee and the Swilcan bridge and asking they be aware of golfers. If they could do it on a Sunday, that would be even better. On many occasions, people don't ask and the first we know about it is when we notice a grey substance on the turf in a morning, which can be in a number of locations. But that's fine, we don't mind. However, one family requested to scatter them on a mound behind the 8th tee of the Old Course, overlooking the estuary.

They also wanted to do it on a particular Saturday as some of the family had travelled from abroad and would only be there that day, only the particular Saturday they chose happened to be during the Dunhill. We came to an arrangement where it could take place in the evening as soon as the last competitors were finished and before it became dark. Hence, that's why one particularly dreich Saturday at dusk and as soon as the players finished their last hole, the ninth, I found myself leading a convoy of cars through the Links road network to the 8th tee. Once there, the family did the needful and we sang a hymn before returning to town. The varied life of being Director of Greenkeeping.

My wife and I, along with another couple, were at the preview night of the nearby Pittenweem Art Festival one Friday in August. While on the harbour front enjoying our fish suppers, I heard someone shout my name and it happened to be Jim Leishman. Jim is a larger-than-life character, an ex-footballer and manager before going on to being general manager of his beloved Dunfermline FC. He had recently gone into local politics and was currently the Provost of Fife which entitled him to sit on the Board of Trustees at the Links.

With Trustee Jim Leishman, the Provost of Fife. I'm pleased he spoke up for me at the Trustees' meeting!

I'd known Jim for a number of years, we'd shared the top table at a couple of dinners where we were speaking. I had also been invited to dinners hosted by Scottish Grass Machinery which were held at Dunfermline FC's ground and where Jim was the master of ceremonies. With a photographer in tow and wearing his chain of office as Provost, he approached us to ask if he could have his picture taken with us for the local newspaper, all while he ate my chips. With the pictures duly taken he left, in typical Jim Leishman fashion, shouting loud enough for everyone nearby to hear, "They tried to fire you at the Trustees meeting this afternoon Gordon, but I spoke up for you, telling them you weren't a bad lad and they should give you another chance."

From around 2002 or 2003 until I retired, I worked every Christmas morning. Until then, there was always one Starter and one Ranger on duty on the Old Course, simply to collect green fees and ensure everything ran smoothly. One member of the greenkeeping staff, usually a head greenkeeper or deputy, would come in first thing in the morning to check the courses for frost. It was then decided it wasn't worth the difficulty trying to find staff willing to come in when weighed against the few green fees that were taken. Although the courses, especially the Old Course, might be busy if it was a nice day, it was predominately local ticket holders who would play. Living close by, I hastily said I would come and check over the courses myself on Christmas morning to ensure they were playable. That was fine provided there was no frost, but when there was, it became a bit of a pain as I would have to constantly come back at various times until the frost had lifted. Then, once people realised there was no Starter and they could play the Old Course for free, it became a bit of a nightmare as they would come from over forty miles away to play. We could have left the courses alone and let people play irrespective of the condition but I knew I'd get a lot of stick afterwards from local golfers if we allowed that. I would generally go down around 7.45am, (official daylight wouldn't be until after 8.30), where I'd find a group on the first fairway waiting for those on the green to finish putting and with over twenty people standing patiently at the tee. If it was frosty, I would go and ask them to leave until the frost lifted. I'd then take a run round the internal road network in my car and discover others who had parked up somewhere and begun their round at different holes. It was much simpler if it was a nice day, a really horrible day, or if the courses were covered in snow. When Christmas Day fell on a Sunday, when the Old

Course is traditionally closed, it could still be a challenge as people would still turn up to play. On those occasions I'd go down at dusk on the Saturday and remove the markers and pins from the opening and closing four holes, using an Astroturf plug to cover the hole on the greens. Despite that, I could still come across some people playing at 8am on Christmas morning.

In my early years on the Eden, one of the staff members on another course suffered from diabetes which he didn't always keep under control and had 'hypos' on a few occasions. The only one I personally experienced was when we were collecting some long rough which had been cut down and were stacking it on a trailer to take away for composting. He was up on the trailer when some of us realised he was in the early stages of a 'hypo' as he began staggering and slurring his words as if he was drunk, a typical sign of very low sugar levels. We knew he carried sweets with him for such an occasion but he was at the stage where he was like an aggressive 'drunk' and refused to take them. We were worried he would fall off the trailer while, at the same time, he wouldn't allow us onto the trailer to administer the sweets. Eventually, we managed to get him to the front of the trailer while someone jumped on to it at the back and grabbed him, before pinning him down and forcing the sugary sweets into his mouth. There were two other occasions when he had 'hypos' which both resulted in him having to go to hospital. One was when he was on his own, removing tall weeds from the deep roughs. He had a 'hypo' and lay down in the rough where it took his colleagues ages to find him. That was once they realised he was 'missing'! The other occasion was when he was raking bunkers, again on his own, and he lay down in a bunker where he became unconscious. He was noticed by a couple of golfers who, rather than wake him or check he was okay, simply reported to reception that a greenkeeper was lying drunk in a bunker.

Although I'm a Type one diabetic myself, I've never allowed my sugar levels to drop as low as that. Luckily, I've recognised the signs in time and taken the sweets or whatever else I carry with me. When I was working on the Eden, I would often carry my lunchbox with me. Cutting the ninth green with a pedestrian mower one morning, I saw a crow fly past with a sandwich in its mouth and thought it really funny. Then I realised it was my sandwich!

A very nice gentleman who contacted me was a Swede by the name of Tomas Svensson who was travelling over to St Andrews and asked to meet me. Tomas applied for a summer job on the greenstaff way back in 1965 when he was a student, by writing to the then Town Clerk, who was Secretary to the Joint Links Committee. He received a positive response from John Campbell, the Links Supervisor and after obtaining a work permit, began as a student trainee on £5/week. In those days, Tomas worked from the 'black sheds', which are the green ones golfers drive over now when playing the 17th of the Old Course. Tomas has been a regular visitor to St Andrews and Scotland since and although he didn't pursue a career in greenkeeping we share many friends in common. He went on to write a short essay on his time working on the Links and is an enjoyable golf companion. He may have been the first overseas seasonal greenkeeper at St Andrews.

Another Scandinavian I became friendly with was Carsten Brandt, the MD of Reesink Denmark, the Toro distributors for Denmark. Carsten contacted me as he wanted to run a competition, not a golf one, for young Danish greenkeepers with the winner getting a trip to St Andrews to work for one or two weeks. Initially they came in November and one greenkeeper soon became two and the date moved to coincide with the Dunhill. This allowed them a week experiencing setting the course up for a tournament while the second week, depending on what was taking place at the time, they would participate in various projects across all the courses. I would spend a small amount of time with them, even if it was on an evening, explaining about St Andrews and if they were fortunate there might have been someone from outside the Links giving a seminar for BIGGA while they were here. The programme ran for around ten years until I retired and there were some outstanding students, many of whom went on to become course managers or acquire other good positions in the turf industry. Carsten and I remain good friends and only Covid has prevented us from playing golf together or seeing each other as much as we'd have liked to since I retired.

Sometimes, because St Andrews is a relatively small community and I'm reasonably well known within town, I'm asked to assist with the oddest requests. A friend from the Rotary Club of Kilrymont St Andrews, a club of which I'm now a member, approached me asking if a fund raising idea they had was possible and if so, could I help. Their plan was to sell 300 plastic ducks to members of the public, release them in the Swilcan Burn by the 1st green of the Old Course, and the first duck to reach the sea won a prize for its 'owner'. Everything is possible. Unless it's a dreadful summer, the burn would only have a few inches of water in the base but we still had the ability to dam it if required. One Sunday in July 2017, I arranged for the burn to be dammed by the staff when they arrived at work at 5am to allow a build-up of water along with adding additional water from the irrigation system. At 3pm we released the ducks and opened the floodgates! There was wasn't a great flow but with the help of high-pressure jets of water from the irrigation hoses, we were able to wash the ducks to the finish line. Try as I might, I still couldn't get my duck to the front! Who says life as a greenkeeper is boring?

Helping at the Rotary duck race and trying hard to propel my duck to the front.

The Links has been fortunate over the years, having hardly ever suffered much in the way of vandalism or damage to the turf. Remarkable really, given the vast area it covers, most of which is a considerable distance from town. The only serious incident I recall was during a Dunhill weekend in 1997. It preceded a meeting of the Commonwealth Leaders in Scotland being held the following week which may have been a factor. On the Saturday night, a number of greens on the Balgove course had the CND logo written on them with a chemical which killed the grass. Perhaps it wasn't related to the Commonwealth meeting but it was a bit of a coincidence.

A less serious one, but it could have been embarrassing, occurred a few weeks prior to the 1995 Open when three feet high letters spelling the word C**T appeared on the 7th green of the Old Course. This would have appeared very obvious when viewed from a high TV camera tower, or even from a grandstand. Fortunately, it had only been written using fertiliser or sulphate of iron which had greened up the grass. Additional sulphate of iron was applied to green up the area surrounding the letters so all that remained visible was a green rectangle. At subsequent Opens, guards were on duty at every green for the week. Initially they were from the Gurka regiment and I don't think you would have wanted to mess with them. Latterly it was one of the usual security companies who weren't best pleased one year when we forgot to tell them the irrigation sprinklers would come on in the middle of the night.

By far the most common problem we have is the theft of pins and flags, usually from the 17th and 18th of the Old Course, and it's not uncommon to lose over forty each year. That's the reason nothing has a logo on it other than the flag on the 18th which the Starter replaces with a plain white flag when he finishes each evening. We always get a good number of them back when the students leave their accommodation at the end of term. Over the years, we have found the odd condom in Road Bunker and on a couple of occasions, someone has even done a poo in the cup on the 17th green!

When Donald Trump opened his new, (controversial), golf course on the outskirts of Aberdeen in 2012, I was fortunate to be invited to play there during the opening week. Course designer Martin Hawtree was granted use of the course on two days in recognition of his work and to celebrate 100 years of the Hawtree design business. He invited people from many of the businesses and Clubs he worked with, of which St Andrews was one. When Rich Hurley and Eric Bergstol were setting up their golf trip for later that year, Rich emailed me to tell me the courses they wanted to play, culminating in the Bing Crosby tournament and Town Match at St Andrews. Then, on their last day they wanted to play the Trump course. Pauline happened to see my email and asked, "What does that last part mean?" as Rich had written, 'Eric will call Donald'. I explained Eric knew Donald Trump through business and that it meant what it read. Joined by Iain MacLeod from Tain, we had an enjoyable game though modesty prevents me from saying who won. Interestingly, while driving home the course manager called me to ask what we thought of the course. He'd been messaged from America to get our feedback.

Not all the characters I've met are overseas based, we have our share in the UK as well. One such person I came to know is John Hunter, a past captain of Wick golf club in the very north of Scotland. John could even be called Mr Wick GC given everything he's contributed to the club. I first met John when we were selling off the old sprinklers when changing over the system in 1999. We were offering them to small golf clubs for £5 each and would give away the broken ones for free as parts of them could prove useful for spare parts. After agreeing quantities etc over the telephone, John turned up in a large van to collect the sprinklers and we've been friends ever since. In the days before smart phones, he would call me and disguise his voice. Pretending to be a sound engineer, he'd have me whistling down the telephone to try to repair a fault. That was one of the kinder things he did to me, and to many others, and he'd always finish the conversation with a joke. Although he's now in the golf industry, manufacturing bespoke course furniture for many top golf courses around the world, back in 1999 he had a very successful record company. As well as being an excellent golfer, in 1986 he qualified for the Scottish clay pigeon Olympic trap team, a significant achievement given where he lived and the distances he had to travel to compete in competitions.

Another character was the late George Brown, the estates manager at Turnberry before he retired shortly after the 2009 Open. George was previously at Princes GC where he was greenkeeper/professional, a common occurrence back in the day. He moved to Turnberry only a few months before the 1986 Open was held there, taking over from the head greenkeeper who died suddenly and was also called George Brown. Late into his 60s he was still an excellent golfer and would regularly post good scores despite claiming to having numerous ailments; either his back, leg, shoulder, and sometimes all three! George was often asked to play with celebrities who visited and was a brilliant storyteller. One of the few I can repeat is regarding an interview he gave just prior to his retirement. The interviewer, looking out of the Turnberry clubhouse window to Ailsa Craig, asked, "How old is that rock?" George told him it was two million and 24 years old. The journalist asked how he could be so precise to which George replied, "Well, when I came here 24 years ago, they told me then it was two million years old."

When I was still working on the Eden course, I played in the Town Match against the R&A with my regular golfing partner when we scored the best sequence of holes I've played, even though the format was a 2-ball foursome. On the Old Course, after starting with two pars and a bogey, we went 3,4,3,3,3,3,3,3,3. Seven birdies in nine holes and every birdie putt was a short one. We were six holes up with six to play but went in a fairway bunker on the 13th and took three to get out! We won on the 14th green. One of our opponents that day was John Salvesen, a past R&A Captain. At one point he asked me what I thought of the new holes on the Eden course. I didn't hold back, telling him, with the exception of the 17th, I thought they were bland and featureless in comparison to the original holes. There were no fairway bunkers and every green was flat. In fact, I felt the course wasn't properly finished and thought the architect, Donald Steel, hadn't put much effort into the design. "We didn't have much of a budget to work with,"was John's reply. Oops, I didn't realise he was involved in golf course design and had worked with Donald Steel on the project! However, I was forgiven for being outspoken and we were invited into the R&A clubhouse for lunch after the game. By the time we arrived, our opponents had told their fellow members about our round and several people came up to say hello. One of them was Sean Connery, (he wasn't yet Sir Sean), a regular competitor in the R&A Autumn Meeting in those days. After chatting for a few minutes, he said his goodbyes, to which my partner said, "See you later Sean." Almost exactly a year later, my friend was given four tickets to a performance at the local Byre Theatre by a work colleague who was in the amateur dramatic group there. When we arrived at our seats, who was sitting immediately next to us but Sean Connery, as he was a patron of the Byre. He blanked us!

While my wife had the pleasure of driving Seve at the Open, the occasion when I met with him was slightly different, but it could have ended a whole lot worse. I was driving round the Bruce Embankment early one morning when I saw someone putting on the 18th green of the Old Course. That shouldn't have been as there was no way the first golfers would have been on the 18th by then and I assumed it must be someone practising. I thought to myself, "I'll soon have them off there," as I drew into the R&A car park. Fortunately, I had learned not to jump in with both feet by then because, as I was heading down the steps to the green, I suddenly recognised it was Seve. He was filming a documentary on his life and was recreating the winning putt from his victory in the 1984 Open, even though the hole wasn't in the same position. He was wearing the same-coloured clothes as he wore that Sunday, with the white shoes. Seconds after I arrived, a helicopter appeared to film the scenes of him holing the putt and doing his celebratory fist pump and I didn't get the opportunity to talk to him. It was unusual for something like this to happen and the Links not to be informed beforehand.

Seve back in St Andrews for a documentary of his life.
It could have all gone very wrong for me!

I've tried to avoid too many stories of golf trips in my book as every golfer who's been on a golf trip will have numerous stories of their own, but the following one had a few funny twists during it. It was 2004 and Rich and Eric wanted to play Royal Troon when they came over in September, as the Open had been held there in July. The trip began when I met them at Glasgow airport and we caught the Loganair morning flight to Machrihanish, part of a fly and golf deal. In those days, Eric was a scratch golfer, Rich played off two or three, while I was a four handicapper and we asked if we could play from the white, (medal), tees. We were told we couldn't as they were for competitions. Undeterred, we set off playing from the main play tees until, on the third green, we met head greenkeeper Peter McVicar. I didn't know Peter but we introduced ourselves and got chatting. As we left, he asked why we were playing from the main play tees and after relaying the story, he said it would be okay to play from the whites. As we came down the 17th, a member from a group of golfers who had caught us up came running across and berated us for playing from the white tees, which we continued to do on the 18th, thinking "What can they do now we're finished?" I was in the locker room when the same member came storming in, demanding to know why we played from the whites and who gave us permission. I stupidly told him, to which he stormed off again muttering, "He has no right, I'll see to this!" Oops, sorry Peter.

Next day, we were at Powfoot GC, just outside Dumfries and were delighted, and surprised, to get a 10am tee time at a private members' club on a Saturday. The tee was reserved for an hour in front of us for a junior medal where these kids, no taller than my driver but as keen as mustard, were playing from the medal tees, many of them not hitting their drive past the main play one. We again asked if we could play the medal tees but were given the same answer, "Sorry, competitions only." After three or four holes we decided just to move back to the whites. Rich, in a book he wrote about his life in golf a few years later, dedicated a snippet in the book to this entitled, 'When in Scotland, don't ask to play the medal tees.' We went on to play The Pines course in Dumfries in the afternoon, (from the medal tees), as we were guests of course owner Duncan Gray. Sadly, The Pines is no longer there.

Sunday morning, we played an open competition at Southerness GC, where Rich picked up third scratch prize. Then we drove to Royal Troon where we had a 4pm tee time and Billy McLachlan, the course manager, had said we could play from the championship tees! A thunder and lightning storm delayed us for thirty minutes or more while we were playing the 7th, but luckily there was a shelter off the left of the fairway to give us protection. This delay meant we played the last couple of holes in the dark and the rain made the course play exceptionally long, especially from the 'tips'. Too long for me, especially as we were playing £1 'skins' from the time we started at Machrihanish, and by the end of the day I was over double figures in skins down to both of them.

The last day was to be 36 holes at Glasgow Gailes and Western Gailes and the forecast was horrendous. So much so, Stuart Taylor, who was course manager at Glasgow Golf Club and was going to partner us, turned up but said he couldn't play as he had something to attend to. We weren't twenty yards off the first tee before the rain started and it didn't let up until we were on the 18th tee. Eric and Rich were despondent, trudging down each fairway like 'drookit dugs'. On the other hand, my golf had taken a turn for the better and I was playing well, even chipping in for a birdie on the 15th, where the hole was completely submerged. By the finish I had turned the skins deficit into a lead. The afternoon round at Western was played in brilliant sunshine and my golf was almost as sparkling, finishing something like fifteen skins up on both of them.

Being the keen golfer I am (read "obsessive" - Pauline) my job made it possible to play some of the greatest courses across the world. From Royal Melbourne and others in Australia, to several in Europe and America as well as the best the UK and Ireland has to offer. In that regard, I've been extremely fortunate. Some years ago, I was gifted a pin board showing America's top 100 courses at that time. Going through the list, I've played 25 of the 100 and 12 of the top 25, including the top five. If I was to be really pushed, then I'd say Pine Valley is my favourite, closely followed by Cypress Point. Did how I play influence my decision? Perhaps. Both times I played Pine Valley, I played well although I played badly at Cypress Point. I've already mentioned many of the others in America I've had the privilege to play. Others worthy of a mention are: Seminole, the San Francisco GC, Kiawah Island and Harbour Town. If talking about UK and Irish courses, then I find it too difficult to name one as my favourite but, in no particular order, here are ten I love. Royal Birkdale, Royal County Down, Portrush, the redesigned Turnberry, North Berwick, Western Gailes, Ganton, Royal Aberdeen, Elie and the Old Course. But you could replace any of these with a selection from another 50. I've spoken to many Americans over on golf trips who spend a lot of their time on the road. They'll constantly be criss-crossing the country ticking off the trophy courses, going from Ayrshire to the Highlands, down to East Lothian, back to the west coast before finishing at St Andrews. Most would be far better spending the time in one location, playing the championship courses in that area along with the neighbouring ones. Then, when they return, they could do the same in another area. They often associate the price with quality but would find numerous fun, yet challenging, courses all around the UK at half the cost and perhaps even more suited to their game. There's barely a course from Aberdeen, up the northeast coast to Fraserburgh and along the Moray Firth to Inverness I don't enjoy playing. From there, I'd equally happily head north again to Dornoch then Wick and along to Durness. The same could be said for so many other coastal areas around the UK and Ireland.

George Frye, who assisted me when looking at purchasing our sulphur burner, was always asking me to come and play at Kiawah Island. He was the superintendent there when it was built and through the early years, but had since moved on although he still lived in the area. Three of us decided to go one year when the GIS was in Orlando and drive to the show afterwards. Even though it was a distance away, we felt we could pick up some tips on how they dealt with their challenges of rough weather amongst other things. We were diverted to Savannah due to a thunderstorm but made it to Charleston where George met us and had the golf organised and, although he didn't play himself, he talked with us about the different situations they faced during construction and grow in. The cost for this? His wife's church group were having a chilli cooking competition and we were chosen to be the independent judges. We didn't require dinner that evening.

The next day we set off for Orlando, via Harbour Town, where I'd previously visited on a golfing holiday and where I knew the superintendent. Over the years we'd often spoken regarding seasonal staff. Harbour Town often had Europeans on their staff and I'd been able to convince some to come and work at St Andrews for a summer before they returned home. When we set out to play golf, the rain was just beginning to fall and by the time we reached the back nine, it was becoming torrential. We were the only people to complete 18 holes (our fore-caddie wasn't impressed) and when we eventually putted out on the 18th, a member of the greenstaff collected the pin. Course closed.

An aside. When I played at Harbour Town on that earlier holiday, it was only a few weeks before their regular tournament on the PGA Tour. While the greens were okay, the group I was with were surprised they weren't as good as they thought they might be with the tournament so close. All except the 17th and 18th that was. I was able to demonstrate the effect trees have on golf greens as the last two greens were out in the open, whereas the other 16 were all heavily shaded by the trees surrounding them.

The R&A often assist Golf Federations in many different ways in countries where golf is a minority sport. One of these is subsidising or supplying greenkeeping machinery and, in fact, the R&A purchased a number of mowers from the Links Trust back in 2001 when we signed our first commercial deal with Toro. Most of these were shipped to golf clubs around the world while some were supplied to small clubs on the Scottish Hebrides. As a result, they had built a relationship with a Kenyan Indian based in England who, through his company, exported equipment to Kenya and a few other African countries. As his 50th birthday approached, they asked if I could take him for a game on the Old Course and they would cover the green fee. That is how I met Sunny Thethy, who could be described as extrovert, and Pauline and I became good friends with him and his wife Alison over the years. So much so, that he invited us to Kenya for a holiday one year, with a pre-condition. We were to visit several golf clubs he dealt with and I had to meet with the course managers/head greenkeepers and discuss the courses, even though I explained I had little knowledge of warm season grasses. However, Sunny was very persistent and off we went one October for a 10-day trip which proved both fascinating and interesting.

The one thing which amazed me was the passion and dedication of the greenkeepers I met and their thirst for knowledge, most of which they had learnt from American websites. That and the skills they had, working with old and primitive machinery which was continually breaking down and which they would repair in the most innovative fashion as budgets were minimal. Interestingly, the course I found to be in the poorest condition was the one which was the best resourced, partially because the committee thought they had superior knowledge to the greenkeeper and insisted they knew best. Their biggest fault was simply to keep applying too much water to the course.

The holiday involved a few rounds of golf for me, including a competition at the club where Sunny was a member, and where there was a memorial tournament taking place. Only Sunny never told me

I was to present the prizes until after we played! It was a surreal day, something akin to a throwback to many UK golf clubs I experienced in the 1970s and 80s. It seemed like everyone who played stayed after their round until the prize presentation, and they didn't just sit around drinking Coke or coffee - beers and spirits were the order of the day. The winner, an elderly gentleman with only half his teeth remaining, proudly announced to everyone that he was heading for downtown Nairobi to spend his winnings on a whore, (to great applause!). Then, despite all the alcohol which had been consumed, everyone jumped in their cars and headed home, us included, although neither Sunny, Pauline or I were driving. The scariest part was, at the end of the golf club road was a dual carriageway where cars had to go left, (as in the UK, people drive on the left in Kenya). Except, we wanted to turn right and by going left we would have had to drive a mile or more before there was an opportunity to change direction. The solution, our driver simply turned right and drove against the flow of traffic for 100 yards until he reached a gap and could cross onto the correct carriageway!

All in all, it was a wonderful trip, visiting Nairobi (horrendous traffic) and Mombasa, experiencing the culture and taking in an overnight stay in a small safari retreat. The highlight however, was visiting the elephant sanctuary in Nairobi and seeing the baby orphaned elephants being fed, then going on to a giraffe house where we climbed stairs taking us up to the height of the giraffes. If you've never kissed a giraffe, then I promise it's something you should try before you die!

In the spring and autumn, I would often leave my office just as it was turning dark between 5pm and 6pm. Sometimes I would drive around the courses on the internal road network and leave by the exit at the Eden side of the complex, just to be nosy and see who, if anyone, was going around. One evening I was flagged down by a cyclist who told me that just around the corner, there was a car head first in a bunker! Sure enough, two minutes later I saw this car in one of the cross-bunkers, fifty yards short of the 7th green of the New course, with a bewildered owner standing looking at it. On stopping, I recognised the owner as he was a member of the same golf club as me, the St Andrews GC. He gave me a story about how he was out practicing his golf and when finished, decided he would go to the nearby toilet before going home. Then, rather than reverse, he decided to take a 'short-cut' across some holes on the New course and re-join the roadway at a different point. I explained that there was nothing that could be done immediately but if he left me his car key I would arrange for some of the team to lift his car out in the morning, adding the proviso that we wouldn't accept any liability if we damaged it. I offered him a lift home but he insisted on walking. It was only when I was back home, I began to wonder if he may have been concussed and worried that he might collapse somewhere in the middle of the golf courses. I was able to get his telephone number from the golf club directory and called to explain the situation to his wife. She didn't seem to be the least concerned and referred to him in a less than complimentary manner! He had obviously called her before I did. My team had the car lifted from the bunker by 7am the following morning, using our digger to do so, and I thought that was the end of the matter. It was quite a surprise to see a story about it in a national newspaper a couple of days later with a picture. I have absolutely no idea how that happened given it was nearly dark and my team had removed the car so early the following morning. What made it more interesting was his job. He was the Health and Safety Officer at a fairly large local business!

I've always said the bunkers on the Links are proper hazards!

My friend Rich Hurley wrote a book in the 2000s about his experiences in golf and asked me to provide some stories for it. One of the stories I told him was about a local golfer who, every time he had a good score going when playing the Old Course, he would drive out of bounds on the 17th. Having a very odd sense of humour he left instructions that, when he died, he wanted his ashes scattered on the 17th tee. The family gathered on the tee one day to carry out the request but when they threw his ashes up, in a cruel twist of fate, a gust of wind blew them out of bounds! It was a complete fabrication, based on a joke I'd once heard. It made the book.

I can assure you, dear reader, that there are no fictional stories like the one above in this book!

Chapter 19. Controversy. What ARE
They Doing to the Old Course?

W.E.B. LOUDON, CBE, was Alan McGregor's replacement and began his tenure in January 2011. A former Commander of the 2nd Division of the British Army, he then had four years as Chief Executive and Producer of the Royal Edinburgh Military Tattoo before joining the Links Trust. Although both Alan and Euan had military backgrounds, their style of leadership and personalities were very different. While Alan was very much involved in the everyday business of the different departments and knew everything that was going on, Euan delegated more responsibility to each of his directors. He was very interested in the commercial side of the business and building up a sound financial base from other areas rather than simply relying on golfers visiting St Andrews and paying a green fee. The Trust had been exploring this since before the catastrophe of 9/11 and the subsequent disruption to air travel which brought their financial vulnerability more into focus. While there had been some success with this, Euan's objective came across as being to raise it to another level without compromising on the good traditions of the Links or impinging on the rights enjoyed by the residents of the town and local golfers. It's the non-golf part of the Trust which raises any surplus the Trust makes, rather than income from green fees and season tickets. This is partly due to the fact around 50% of the golf played across the courses each year is by season ticket holders who pay a relatively small annual fee. In 2021, a resident of the town paid £240 for a yearly ticket; surely the best deal in world golf?

When any CEO changes within an organisation, it's inevitable there will be a period of uncertainty and anxiety in the workforce. I found the change unsettling myself as, although Euan was always pleasant, I found him difficult, if not impossible, to read and it was a different leadership style to what I'd been accustomed to for the previous ten years.

In 2011, the Scottish Open moved to a new venue, Castle Stuart Golf Links on the outskirts of Inverness which only opened in 2009 to great acclaim. With its fine grasses and fast running surfaces it would be good preparation for the following weeks Open Championship. Jacobsen were the equipment suppliers to Castle Stuart and purchased hospitality packages for the tournament days, inviting me along with some other Scottish course managers. After a hospitable evening on the Friday, we were having breakfast in our hotel early on Saturday when we were told the start of the golf was delayed. There had been a tremendous amount of rain that morning, which was on top of thunderstorms on Friday that caused a suspension of play. We arrived at the maintenance facility and met with course manager Chris Haspell who told us over 80mm of rain had fallen and caused two landslides on holes 1 and 12. The course is built on two levels with some holes down at sea level, some twenty or thirty metres below the others. There was little likelihood of golf starting any time soon and Chris asked if we'd be prepared to help his team clear up the damage to which everyone agreed, even though most weren't exactly feeling in the mood for some physical work. Wearing dress clothes and golf shoes, we soon found ourselves on the first fairway shovelling the displaced sand and soil into Cushman vehicles to get carted away. By now the sun was shining and soon afterwards a TV crew from the BBC appeared, headed by lead presenter Hazel Irvine. Hazel had interviewed me the previous summer when the Open was at St Andrews and recognised me straight away. With next to no notice, I had a microphone shoved in my face and I was being broadcast live on national television. The damage to the course was such that there was no further play that day and the event was reduced to 54 holes. We all headed off home in the afternoon having had no champagne, no nice lunch and without a seeing a shot played!

2011 also saw me visit a country which isn't exactly renowned for golf, Poland. I had received an invitation to visit and play at Gradi Golf Club which is situated some three hours' drive from Katowice. Some years earlier I had met the owner when he visited St Andrews and had arranged for him to play the Old Course as my guest. He had built a course and was staging a tournament called The Retro Cup in which he asked me to play. This seemed like a fun thing to try and the fact it was taking place over a weekend meant that I wouldn't need to take time off work. The only snag was, along with Gordon McKie, I had already booked flights to attend a Toro event in London which began on the

Monday and which I didn't want to miss. I worked out I could fly out on the Friday evening and then back to Gatwick on the Sunday. It was a great weekend in Poland where the weather was superb. The golf course was still relatively new and while it needed time to mature, was in reasonable shape and has gone on to stage professional tournaments. The trees which bordered many of the holes were still quite small and I thought to myself, 'This course is going to be very tight once they grow'. It was an invitation event and I got the feeling a lot of the people attending were from the upper echelons of Polish golf, if not indeed Polish society, and I felt very honoured to be invited. The competition was 18 holes each day and each player had to hit their opening shot with an old John Letters persimmon driver. Most of the competitors were dressed in 1920s clothing, hence the name, Retro Cup. I went partially prepared in that I wore golf clothes which didn't have any logos and my cap from the Bobby Jones film in 2003, (I knew it would come in handy), and went on to win the over 50s section, just. I did take my kilt and all the accessories for the evening dinner which was a tremendous affair, heavily sponsored with different bands playing, stylish old cars to ride in and many other things going on. I was really glad I went even though it was hectic. On the Monday morning I met up with Gordon McKie for the Toro event which was at Goodwood, where we had the opportunity to drive three different sports cars round the race circuit. We then went onto the Grove where, after some presentations by the Toro staff, we played golf on the Tuesday. You can understand why I didn't want to miss it!

At the end of 2011 I was given the opportunity to play some of the best courses in the Philadelphia area when a friend in the industry invited me to his annual 'Retreat'. I first met Dan Meersman some years earlier when he visited St Andrews on honeymoon with wife Carrie and we had kept in touch. When we first met, he was based in Indiana where he organised a weekend to which he would invite the top superintendents from around the US to come for a few days to play golf, then three or four of them would give a talk on some of the practices or projects they were involved in. He would organise some sponsors to pick up the costs so the only expense was getting there and because it was over a weekend, participants didn't have to take much time off work. He had invited me a few times on the understanding I would give a talk, but to get from St Andrews to Indiana would involve three or four flight changes so I'd always turned him down. However, once he moved to the Philadelphia Cricket Club it was much more practical although it would still be expensive. After some discussions, Dan managed to find a company to not only pay my flights but collect me from Newark airport and drive me the two hours down to Philadelphia and back. Obviously, it wasn't practical for me to go just for the weekend and I took a couple of days holiday to allow me time to travel out earlier. I asked Dan if he could help get me on to Merion GC which was nearby and was going to host the US Open in 2013. Leaving on the Thursday morning gave me the day to travel and on the Friday, Dan gave me a tour of the original Philadelphia Cricket Club course which was a 9-hole course with small square greens, built in 1895 and extended to 18 holes two years later. In the afternoon I was playing at Merion, a course which had long been on my bucket list. Preparations were well under way for the upcoming Open and work was taking place on several holes. A few greens were having areas changed to accommodate more pin placings while the entire green at the 12th was out of play as it was being completely recontoured. Disappointingly, because the 2nd December was off-season, they had taken in the wicker baskets they use on the pins instead of flags and what the club is known for. However, it was still a brilliant experience. That evening, the other guests from some of the top courses all over the US arrived and it felt surreal to be there with them. On Saturday we played the Militia Hills at PCC which had just undergone a reconstruction under Dan's supervision and on Sunday, we played at Aronimink GC, another excellent, traditional golf course which has hosted PGA Tour events and some national championships. It was all very relaxed with the talks fitted in before or after dinner, or in the morning before we headed for golf. Coming from so far, I gave a couple of different presentations which went down well with the audience. Many of the guys headed off soon after the golf on Sunday while I had Monday to travel back to New York for an evening flight.

As mentioned previously, planning for an Open begins fairly soon after the previous one finishes, or it did for us at St Andrews, but then we had been in a cycle of hosting the Open every five or six years since 1978. Historically, other than adding a number of new tees to create more length, there had been no significant changes to the Old Course since the 1920s. Fairway lines had been tweaked and bunker sizes changed but these were things which had happened without much direct committee or R&A involvement. Bunker changes didn't happen by accident but were more a result of greenkeepers, not necessarily the head greenkeeper even, simply deciding when repairing a bunker what looked right and how it fitted into the surrounding area. They seldom took into consideration how the land around the bunker had changed in the previous few years with sand splash or wind blow. In an ideal scenario, it would be better to strip back the turf over a much larger area and remove the sand which had accumulated but which is a much bigger job. That requires more aftercare as the newly returfed area needs to be protected for a considerable time afterwards and there was always pressure to get bunkers back into play a.s.a.p. This was especially true of the more famous 'named' bunkers such as Road, Hell, Shell and Strath for example. Visiting golfers often felt short-changed if those bunkers were out of play, even though it was the depth of winter and they had paid a much-reduced green fee. It was such that we had to plan to only do a couple of these more famous bunkers each year to avoid too many of them being roped off as GUR at the same time. It was a similar problem with the Swilcan bridge as it was nigh impossible to keep grass cover around it given the number of people who walked in that area. Staff would turf these areas at least once a year but even putting ropes up to protect the new turf was almost futile as everyone wanted their picture taken on the bridge and, invariably, the posts and rope would be lying on the ground each morning. This was something which became worse in the time I was at St Andrews as more and more non-golfers would want 'that' picture and the advent of smart phones made it easier. Some years we would use crowd barriers in winter but often would have to take them down to allow wedding photographs to be taken on the bridge. Relative to its size, it has to be one of the most photographed bridges in the world.

Peter Dawson of the R&A approached the Links Trust in 2011 to ask if they would consider changes to the Old Course. There might be a presumption in many people's minds it's wrong to make alterations to the course given its history, but there are no legally binding restrictions to prevent it being altered, although a large part of the Links is a designated landscape. The initial request was simply to explore whether the Trustees would consider making a number of alterations other than simply adding more tees, or if they felt the matter was taboo. The original request was in relation to Road Bunker guarding the 17th green, how it gathered the ball and the degree of difficulty it presented. Also in the mix, were suggestions to move the greenside bunkers at the 2nd and to introduce a fairway bunker at the

9th. The Trustees understood the course wasn't a museum and many aspects of it had evolved and changed over the years, (sometimes naturally by sand movements), and agreed the idea should at least be explored. Following a discussion between the parties it was agreed the R&A would appoint Martin Hawtree to visit and review the course and submit his recommendations. The R&A were already using Martin to work with them on other Open venues while we had just begun a conversation with him regarding changes for the Jubilee course.

In July 2012, a course walk was arranged with representatives of the R&A, The Links Trust and Martin Hawtree, after which Martin drew up a number of suggested improvements. Peter Dawson already had an idea of things he wanted considered which Martin took on board while other than a small hollow in the centre of the 7th fairway which constantly gave us a challenge, the Trust were more content to wait and see what would be proposed. Measuring no more than 10 yards square and only a couple of feet in depth, this hollow collected a large number of golf balls and as a result was always heavily divotted. The damage was so severe it would be roped off and marked as GUR for large parts of the season as it was often more sand and divots than grass.

When Martin came back with his proposals, the R&A discounted a number of them before approaching the Links Trust with the remainder which included filling in the hollow on the 7th fairway as requested. This number of changes and the difference they would make to the course compared to simply adding tees was significant and would need sensitive consideration and handling. Everyone was well aware of the number of people, locally, nationally and internationally, who had great affection for the Old, believing it should be preserved as if it were an artefact in a museum, despite the fact it had constantly changed over the centuries. All these changes have been well documented.

In my opinion, all the changes presented to us and the reasoning behind each one made perfect sense. They were practical, relatively straightforward and didn't affect the integrity of the course. I viewed them all as improvements and felt my role, although an employee of the Trust, was to support them and help get them approved by the GSC, LMC and Trustees, as well as gather support from the St Andrews golfing community.

For the record, here is the list of proposed changes:

Hole 2. There were four bunkers short and to the right of the 2nd green which were so far from the green they really only caught a very poor shot and even the average local golfer seldom worried about landing in one. When the pin was on the lower right-hand half of the green, then any shot finishing green-high left a simple putt over an area which had previously been levelled to increase the size of the 3rd tee. The plan was to fill in all four bunkers and build two new ones immediately next to the front right of the green to provide some tighter hole positions. Prior to this, there would only be one pin placing on the lower left of the green where mounds protected it. This meant on the other three days it would be on the top left tier, closer to the 16th flag, causing disruption to the pace of play if the two flags were too close to one another. In addition to the new bunker, the flat area to the right of the green would be redesigned. A series of hollows and undulations would be introduced so any player whose ball finished there would face a slightly more challenging shot. It was a change which would be replicated around other greens and became something we would refer to as 'broken ground'.

The two new bunkers guarding the 2nd green of the Old Course.

Hole 3. There were three fairway bunkers along the right-hand edge of the fairway. The distance even average players were now hitting the ball meant the first of them, at 215 yards, was redundant. The proposal was to fill the first one in and introduce a new bunker at 285 yards.

Hole 4. Similar to the 2nd, the two bunkers protecting the right of the green were some distance away and seldom troubled the better player. It was proposed to fill them both in and introduce a new one immediately next to the green at the front right corner. Immediately behind the new bunker, more 'broken ground' would be introduced into the hollow which was already there. The objective was to increase the penalty for less than perfectly executed approach shots coming from the left to a front right pin. Many players preferred to boom their drives well left on the 4th as the right side of the fairway was very narrow with sharp mounds and pot bunkers. This makes the hole very tight for those players who can't carry the ball 290 yards.

Hole 6. This is a relatively short hole although the tee shot is blind, with three bunkers on the left separating the 6th fairway from the 13th. The proposal was to introduce a fourth bunker on a similar line to the existing three to tighten the tee shot up. There was a natural slope at the proposed area which was always pock marked with divots and, at around 300 yards from the tee, would have been the ideal place. As with the 2nd hole, the walk off to the right of the green had previously been levelled to increase the size of the 7th tee. The tee had subsequently been moved further right and away from the green but the surround had been left completely flat. The plan was to again introduce a hollow with some 'broken ground' to increase the challenge if any ball missed on the right.

Hole 7. Martin had included in his plans our request to fill in the depression in the middle of the 7th fairway. As well as solving the divot problem, balls would be more likely to run out further and some would even reach Shell bunker. And as at some of the earlier holes,' 'broken ground' would be introduced between the 7th green and 8th tee.

Hole 9. Often a driveable par four for many of the players in calm conditions or in the prevailing wind. The hole had become easier over the years as the heather which ran up the left of the fairway had become increasingly weak and thin. Old aerial photographs show how it had receded back some five yards or more from the edge of the fairway. Heather is a very fragile plant and doesn't cope well with the pressure of golfers trampling through it therefore, as play has increased over time, a lot of the heather has died out. In past tournaments spectators were allowed to walk over this area which would have had a negative effect on the heather. The heather across all the St Andrews courses has suffered and reduced in health due to the increase in play and being exposed to irrigation water of high alkalinity. To tighten the hole up it was proposed to build a new bunker on the left side of the fairway, some twenty-five to thirty yards short of the green, just encroaching into the fairway. This would reduce the gap players had to run the ball through to the green to twenty-five yards and would be far enough back from the green to leave a challenging shot if it caught their drive.

The new bunker on the 9th which makes the fairway just a little narrower.

Hole 11. The proposed change to the 11th hole would be the most difficult to carry out and likely to attract the most comment as it involved making an alteration to a section of the green itself. Over time, green speeds have increased due to a combination of improved maintenance practices and finer varieties of grasses being inter-seeded into the surface. This made it impractical to use the back left section of the green for a hole position as we were worried a ball might not come to rest when close to the hole if there was more than a gentle breeze. It was also possible the green itself had become steeper over time through constant topdressing and sand splash from Hill Bunker. The 11th green is the most exposed one on the course and always the one which gives the most concern. As a result, during tournaments it was common to have three of the hole locations on the flat area immediately behind Strath Bunker, with the other one on a small shelf at the back right of the green. This meant the nearest pin to the famous Hill Bunker to the left of the green, which Bobby Jones took numerous shots to escape from when he first played the Old Course in 1921, was over thirty yards from the nearest hole location and never came into play for the best players in the world. The plan was to reduce the slope in that small, back-left portion of the green to make it level enough to allow one hole placement there over the four days. This would tempt the players to take on Hill Bunker, which is one of the most penal on the course and also risk going over the green into the deep swale behind, leaving them with an almost impossible chip back.

Hill bunker on the 11th where Bobby Jones became a cropper in 1921.
The slope on the green just above it was softened slightly
to create an additional pin position.

Hole 15. This was a very minor change. Some further 'broken ground' was to be introduced to a flat area immediately behind the green as currently, any shot going long to a back pin, left a straightforward return putt.

Hole 17. As far back as I can remember, Peter Dawson had never been completely happy with how Road Bunker played. As well as the size and steepness of the face constantly altering over the years, the bunker wasn't 'gathering' the ball like it used to. Other than anecdotal evidence there was no measurable proof of this but it's something with which most people, myself included, would concur. The change wasn't the result of a decision passed by a committee, but simply by sand being blown out of the bunker or being carried out on players' feet as they exited, raising the entry point. I don't think golfers have any idea the amount of sand which can quickly accumulate by these two methods and rapidly change the ground level around a bunker. There had been discussions regarding Road Bunker, its shape, size, how penal it was or should be, and its gathering effect ever since I was appointed Director of Greenkeeping. Peter Dawson had previously commissioned some research into the bunker which showed that from every Open between 1970 and the present day, there were some huge differences and variations in how it looked, its size and the height of the face. Video footage from the 1970 Open showed Doug Saunders could clearly see the bottom of the pin. In 1978 when Tommy Nakajima couldn't extract himself from the sands in the third round, the bunker again didn't have a particularly high face while in 2000, David Duval looked lost in a cavernous bunker and would have been fortunate to see the flag, let alone the base of the pin.

Road Bunker has changed size and shape numerous times, even over the past five decades.

The plan for the 2015 Open was to completely rebuild the bunker to a size, shape and height that everyone agreed with, and to shape the surrounding ground, including a small section of the green, so the contours would direct a ball ever so slightly off line into the sand. After the work was completed, the bunker and surrounding area would be digitally mapped so it could be rebuilt to be the same for future Opens. This was a technique seldom used in the UK but was a common occurrence at some of the larger venues in the US, particularly Augusta.

We didn't receive confirmation of the proposals from the architect until late August 2012 and intended to begin phase one of the work, which would be done over two winters, in November. It was a tight schedule to try to seek all the necessary approvals, especially when dealing with committees as in my general experience, many committee members see themselves as budding golf course architects. And so it proved, as immediately there were members who didn't like a particular aspect or suggestion based on that most important of criteria, "That's where my ball finishes on that hole."

Given these alterations were going to be scrutinised throughout the golfing world, the final decision rested with the Trustees, (under normal circumstances it would be an LMC decision following detailed discussion with the GSC). The different committees were supportive but felt we should meet with the committees of the Local Clubs before they gave final approval.

The proposed change questioned most by the LMC was the additional fairway bunker on the left of the 6th. The main grounds being the aforementioned, "That's where I often finish," or, "My playing partners always land there," coupled with the fact it would be blind from the tee. When we subsequently went to present the plans to the Local Clubs, and it was a presentation for information only rather than seeking their blessing or approval, I formed the impression Euan Loudon used the bunker at the 6th as a sacrificial lamb to secure full support for the other changes. It was a classic political move, in by conceding this point, they would feel they had more of a contribution than they actually did. I might have read that wrong but it's how it came across to me at the time. If it was planned, it worked perfectly as all the Clubs were fully behind the changes and certainly, the lower handicap golfers we spoke with felt the alterations were much needed to strengthen the challenge of the course. I would have liked to have seen the bunker at the 6th included and I know Peter Dawson was disappointed when it was left out and has reminded me ever since, as has his successor Martin Slumbers!

After visiting and talking to all six of the main Local Clubs including the R&A (The R&A Golf Club is a separate entity to R&A Ltd which is the organisation that stages the Open) we then reported the positive responses back to the different committees. All these steps take time as the LMC and Trustees only meet approximately every alternate month and we were beginning to head into the winter season, which was when we would carry out the work.

While waiting for final approval from Trustees, we agreed some basics with the R&A based on everything getting the go ahead. The work would be carried out over two winters and the 11th green alteration would be included in the first phase to allow the maximum amount of time for it to heal. The architect or an associate would be on site throughout to monitor and advise as work progressed and, along with the architect, we agreed on a contractor to carry out the detailed shaping work. The Old Course greenkeeping team would be responsible for all the preparatory work, material movements and finishing work. The Trustees' meeting to agree the alterations was scheduled for the last Friday in November and we took a calculated gamble that everything would be passed and arranged for the equipment to be delivered on that day. The architect and the 'shaper' would be on site on the Saturday in readiness for a Sunday start, (the Old Course is closed on a Sunday and also closed on Mondays through November). At the meeting the Trustees agreed to all the changes other than the aforementioned bunker on the 6th, therefore on Sunday 25th November we started phase one – and then the fun began!

Beginning on the 11th hole, while greenstaff stripped the turf from the area of the green which was to be altered, the shaper and some other greenstaff spent the time filling in the hollow on the 7th fairway as it was only fifty yards away and a task which we could complete in two days.

What no one had considered was the media explosion which erupted on the Monday and continued for weeks. A student at St Andrews University who had a significant interest in golf course architecture had been walking the Old Course on Sunday afternoon, had seen the work taking place and took some pictures on his mobile phone. He then sent them to various people and organisations around the world along with his own comments and opinions rather than any official explanation.

One of the main places these were picked up was on the website called golfclubatlas.com where architects and golfers discuss and comment on course architecture around the world. It also includes many golf writers and commentators who provide a direct link to major media outlets. While we had press releases on all the details ready to send to the golfing press on Monday (they couldn't go out earlier as the final agreement hadn't been reached until Friday afternoon) social media had exploded and not in a particularly positive way. Before we knew it, both the Links and the R&A were inundated with queries and comments from golfers, or those associated with the golf industry, from all around the world. While both organisations anticipated some negative publicity, neither expected the amount we received, some of which was pretty vitriolic. We were well aware there are numerous people who make it their job to constantly criticise both the Trust and the R&A on various subjects or how they run their respective organisations and there's no doubt some of them were behind whipping up this particular storm. They even managed to find some top Tour players, past and present, to say they were against the changes, no doubt phrasing any question in a manner to obtain the answer they desired. People were wanting to link it to the distance the golf ball travels so they could bash the R&A, while others were wanting to treat the Old Course as if it was a historical painting or sculpture which could never be changed and these alterations were an open goal as far as they were concerned. Of course, there might have also been a certain amount of jealousy at play, such as the response of an architect who wasn't given the opportunity to put forward their proposals. One person started a petition which might have been linked to golfclubatlas.com called 'Why I Signed'. As a result, in the following weeks I had over 3,000 emails from people around the world with that heading. After opening the first twenty or so I started putting them in a folder unopened which I deleted prior to retiring, still unopened. Journalists and architects I knew would call me to ask what the process was in regards of the decision-making, the timeline and who made the decisions. Even though I explained it all as I've done here, because it wasn't necessarily what they wanted to hear, they continued to write their own opinions. I even saw it written a number of times that we (the Trust and the R&A) planned everything to start on Thanksgiving weekend as we thought America wouldn't notice! Really?

There were a number of people who supported the changes, including golf course architect Scott McPherson, who wrote the book 'The Evolution of the Old Course', which charts all the changes on the course from the first Open to be held here in 1873. It's a book I often used to research information for presentations or reports. Another supporter was David Joy, a fourth generation St Andrews golf historian who, as well as writing about Old Tom Morris, would dress up in period costume and play Old Tom in the theatre or at small gatherings. As David would say, "Old Tom lived through a period where he would have seen more changes in the world of golf than anyone."

Most importantly, the vast majority of local golfers were supportive, an unlikely scenario when it comes to the relationship between them and the Trust as, at the end of the day, it's their course. It was rumoured Sky Sports sent a news crew to St Andrews to find some opposition but, despite visiting bars and talking to numerous local golfers, they couldn't find anyone to comment negatively about the changes.

At the end of the day, phase one of the changes was completed in just over two weeks and would have been finished in under that time, but frost delayed staff relaying the last of the turf on the 11th green. The 11th green was by far the biggest project of that phase as it had to be the most precise, while lifting and relaying the turf was a time-consuming task given how fragile it was. After removing the turf, the sandy topsoil was scraped off and stored on boards on the 12th tee. Then the 'dirty' sand underneath was altered to replicate the new shape before the topsoil was returned, creating the smallest of shelves at the back-left corner suitable for a hole placing. This shelf still has a small slope to it and still depends on a favourable forecast with the wind coming from a particular direction before a pin could confidently be placed there. It was a surreal thought that we were doing all this work and come 2015, which would be the first 'test', the new position might not even be used. Interestingly, once we removed the top 10-12 inches of sandy topsoil, there was the thinnest of layers of what appeared to be ash. It was common practice in the early days of golf course construction, that a thin layer of fine clay or ash was used as a means of retaining moisture before irrigation was available. We had found this on greens on other courses but in my opinion, the layer found on the 11th of the Old was too thin for that.

Phase two, which included Road Bunker, was done the following autumn/winter. We didn't bother with a big announcement that we were about to begin the second phase and there was little publicity generated. We were able to start earlier in November and again completed the work in little over two weeks. In fact, after a very short time it became difficult to see what had been done and remember what areas looked like previously. I challenge anyone to go to the 7th fairway and tell me with any accuracy where that original hollow was.

Prior to all the mayhem kicking off, I had my annual holiday and in 2012, my wife and I were heading for America with another couple for two weeks which included visiting friends in Chicago. It was common for us to have our main holiday during the school holidays in October as it was away from the main golfing season and the ADLC was over. The second week would be in Tampa so there were going to be good opportunities to play golf at both places. In Chicago I arranged games for us at the Chicago GC and at Olympia Fields. The Chicago GC is one of the oldest golf clubs in the US and one of the most exclusive with less than 150 members but fortunately the Links had formed a relationship there through the Walker Cup. It's a tremendous course, designed by CB MacDonald and redesigned by Seth Raynor and is steeped in history. The day we played was particularly cold and it played really tough with a cold wind. My friend found the greens particularly challenging, putting off some of them as they were so slick in the conditions. Or perhaps it was the fact we found ourselves driving on the wrong side of the road in downtown Chicago on our way there which unsettled him! Up next was Olympia Fields, which had previously hosted of the US Open and which we travelled to by train, being dropped off right at the entrance gate to the course.

The following week we went down to Tampa where I'd arranged a game at Old Memorial, a club where some St Andrews caddies go to work over the winter. My contact there was the course architect Steve Smyers whom I'd met previously at St Andrews. The first question I was asked by my caddie was did I know so-and-so as he rattled off names of St Andrews caddies who were due to arrive over the following weeks. After the game, while we were grabbing a bite to eat, I heard a voice say, "Gordon Moir, what are you doing here?" This was an old friend from Scotland who had left greenkeeping some time back. He was currently caddying at National Golf Links on Long Island and happened to be in Tampa on a golf break. Small world. In Tampa, we were staying in an apartment on a little-known golf course. Every time we drove in or out, we passed this hole which I couldn't decide if it was a tough par three over water, or a short par four where you would hit a five iron off the tee then wedge it onto the green. Wakening at greenkeeper hours, I decided to go for a walk to investigate this hole one morning. When on the course I met in with the superintendent who was spraying greens and we stood and chatted for ten minutes. After establishing the hole was a short par four, I left him to get on with his work and I headed back to the apartment. I was literally five yards from leaving the course when, from behind some bushes, I heard golfers arriving on buggies. I stood to the side and when the first cart came round the corner I said, "Good morning." Silence. The next one came round and I gave the same greeting to which the driver stopped his cart and simply said, "Please get off the golf course." I thought to myself, 'I hope you never come to St Andrews, you'll get a hell of a shock with people walking everywhere.'

It was a great trip but for me it wasn't quite over and was going to get a whole lot better. Long after we booked our holiday, Euan Loudon asked me if I would like to visit the Jacobsen factory in Charlotte N.C, then play at Augusta. Yes, please! He had been invited by David Withers, President of Jacobsen who, although he knew we were in a contract with Toro for our machinery, also knew the contract was shortly due for renewal. He thought it worthwhile getting to know Euan and show him what Jacobsen had to offer. I'd known David for many years as he came up through the ranks at Ransomes in Ipswich to his present position, Jacobsen having bought over the Ransomes brand a few years earlier.

At the end of our two weeks and after dropping Pauline and our friends at the airport in Orlando for their flight home, I jumped on an internal flight to Charlotte to meet up with Euan, David and some of the other key personnel at Jacobsen. Staying at a corporate lodge Jacobsen had at Sage Valley, we had a tour of the production depot at their headquarters in Charlotte before golfing at Sage Valley, which was another excellent course and very similar to Augusta. Jacobsen is a subsidiary of the Textron group and this was how David managed to get us a game at Augusta as another subsidiary is Ez-E-Go buggies. The VP of Ez-E-Go was a member of Augusta as was his son, Frank Dolan, who was going to be our host. Surprisingly, we didn't have to stay on the premises overnight, something I thought was mandatory. Come the day, the three of us set off for the course along with our driver, Nick Brown, the key account manager for Jacobsen. Nick was another person I knew well and he was sick as a parrot because he wasn't going to be playing.

David had arranged for a quick visit with superintendent Brad Owens beforehand and we turned up at the main entrance well before our tee time where we were met by an armed guard. Things had changed since I'd last been there in 2006. When the guard approached the car, David introduced everyone but we were told our host wasn't 'on the property' yet so we couldn't enter. David explained we had an appointment with Brad but the guard had no record of that on his notes so David asked him to call Brad to confirm our appointment. Off he went to check and when he came back, he confirmed the meeting was in order but we weren't allowed in the main gate and to turn around and use another entrance. We found the correct entrance and Brad was the perfect host, showing us around the facility and answering many of the questions we asked. There was still a lot of, "I'm sorry but I can't disclose that," even regarding greenkeeping, which was fine by me. Brad soon got a call to say our host was 'on the property' and Nick dropped us at the clubhouse before leaving the site.

The Par 3 course at Augusta is no walk in the park.

The plan for the day was to play the Par 3 course first which I was really looking forward to, having missed out on that previously, then have a light lunch before playing the main course. The Par 3 is a great little course with most, if not all the holes, under 150 yards.

With tiny greens it's no walk in the park, especially towards the finish where numerous water hazards come into play. Frank made a comment on the first tee which I went on to use myself when taking people onto the Old Course. He told us, "Don't treat this as if it might be the only time you'll ever play here. Always think it's just another game and that you'll be back in the future." It helped put us at ease and although I didn't play particularly well, I played much better than on my first visit. Frank was a tidy player and helped us enjoy the round. Although he wasn't the story teller George Wislar was, he had his own little stories, such as the relatively new member who was constantly complaining about things he thought could be better. He received a letter with a cheque for the same total as his fees enclosed, along with a note saying if he thought so many things were wrong with the club, he perhaps would be happier if he was a member elsewhere.

Augusta only has two sets of tees, the ones for the championship (7435 yards), then those further forward at 6365 yards for the members. The members tees are only a matter of inches higher than the surrounding ground and really blend into the landscape. There's just a single plaque sunk into the ground with the hole number and yardage and, when the tournament comes along in April, those members tees aren't cut for a few days prior. A green cover matching the colour of the grass goes over the plaques and you can't tell the forward tees are even there. Shortly prior to us visiting, Augusta had admitted their first female members and we asked Frank where they played from and he confirmed they played off the same tees as everyone else. He said he wasn't going to suggest there should be additional tees to accommodate them as there was a member who once commented about one of the bridges looking weather beaten and a little worse for wear. The club had the bridge dismantled, the stone cleaned and the bridge rebuilt, before sending him a bill for the work!

It was another great experience but different from my first visit with George Wislar, who coincidently was in the clubhouse having lunch and with whom I spoke briefly. Our host was most hospitable and afterwards we ended up in the company of his father and a few other members. At times I felt uncomfortable with how they spoke and the comments they made about particular things. To be talking as they did in front of people, who to them were complete strangers, all three of us thought very surprising. I was particularly glad I didn't wear my 'I love Obama' cap. Equally surprising was when on a tour of the clubhouse, there appeared to be another bar pop up everywhere we went. It was a good job we had a driver.

Following a visit to the Pro shop to purchase some clothing, I realised I'd forgotten to buy the cap I'd promised Nick our driver. I excused myself and went back to the shop, but Frank noticed when I returned I was still empty handed. Between my two visits, the shop had closed for the day and when I explained my story, Frank ushered me to go with him to the locker room where he began to open various member's lockers, none of which were locked. Eventually he found one with a cap in it, simply handing it to me with the explanation, "It's ok, I know him!"

I left for home the following evening on my own, as Euan was heading to Minneapolis to have a similar tour of the Toro HQ and facilities. Unfortunately for me, because I had booked my flights as part of my holiday, I was in my normal standard class as opposed to business class. But hey, it was worth it to get another game at Augusta, although by then I was beginning to question myself whether I really liked America. The allure and thrill of visiting the States from those early trips was beginning to wear off as I became less 'star struck' and more aware of different aspects. I still have a lot of friends in the States whose company I enjoy but from that visit on, I began noticing things which, when I first went, had passed me by. Or perhaps they were a little less obvious to a lad from Fraserburgh. Certainly, any time I went back after then, I found a week was more than enough.

Before the changes to the Old Course took place, the three preceding years saw some changes and large projects to the Jubilee, Eden and Strathtyrum courses along with rebuilding the 1st tee of the Old and a number of changes in staff at the top of the department.

Beginning with the Jubilee, the team completely changed the 9th and 10th greens which were two new greens from the course changes back in the mid-80s. They had both been problematic over the years for various reasons and remedial work had already been carried out on the 9th a few years earlier to improve the drainage. The biggest issue was, both were built on top of what had been part of the old town dump, which had been capped with a clay soil to seal it. The soil profile of both greens had a high percentage of fine sized particles in the rootzone rather than being of a sandy nature. I persuaded the GSC we could do this in-house, the 10th green would remain in the same place but be raised to the same height as the ground on its left, while we would move the 9th green some twenty yards right, down into a sandy area. The changes were met with mixed reactions from the local golfers, mostly for no other reason than it was a change to what they were accustomed. What wasn't in question was the greens performed much better than the previous ones, especially in wet weather. With some people on the LMC not fully on board with the changes, it was agreed that we bring in a golf course architect to look at other aspects of the Jubilee I thought could be improved upon and approached Martin Hawtree to come up with some ideas and plans.

Discussing the changes to the 10th green on the Jubilee course with members of the GSC.

In March 2012 we brought contractors in to carry out extensive drainage work on the holes at the furthest away points of the Eden and Strathtyrum courses which had suffered from the flooding back in March 2010. They carried out 'sand banding' at metre intervals across the fairways on holes 12, 13 and the lower part of 14 of the

Strathtyrum and the 14th of the Eden. These six-inch wide channels removed old river silt which these fairways were built on. Backfilling the channels with fine gravel topped with sand, this allowed surface water to link with the sandy soil and the main drains underneath. It was the last project Davie Wilson would be involved in as he retired shortly afterwards at the age of sixty.

Davie, who was from St Andrews, had begun at the Links way back in 1968 but left after a couple of years only to return in 1972, making him the longest serving member of staff by some years. He was one of the first greenkeepers to attend Elmwood college and sit the City and Guilds qualifications in turf management and rose up through the ranks. In 1987, he became head greenkeeper of the newly redesigned Jubilee course. In his time at the Links, he had worked on every course at some point other than the Castle and had been involved in eight Open Championships which is probably more than any other greenkeeper in the modern age. He was very much a creature of habit which included numerous cups of strong black coffee each day from the minute he arrived in the morning. He was reliable, always on time and could usually accurately fill in the details of things which happened in the past. One episode which took him by surprise was when he asked one of his staff to begin cutting fairways for the last hour of the working day, telling him he could work on for a short while after finishing time. The following morning, he asked the lad to cut the remaining fairways and was given the answer there were none left to cut. He had worked on until after 9pm, at time and a half rates! At his retirement, Davie spoke well of his time at the Links, recounting many memories of what it was like back in the 70s and how he was looking forward to transforming his garden. It was very sad, and quite a shock to everyone he had worked with, that he died less than two years after retiring.

With the different team structure we introduced on the New and Jubilee some years earlier working successfully, this was an opportunity to do the same over at the Eden side of the complex without having to go through any difficult redundancy process. The idea was always in the back of my mind from the time I saw the benefits on the New and Jubilee team. It was just a case of waiting until the opportunity presented itself which I knew wouldn't be too long as Davie had made it known he'd be retiring when he reached 60. The toughest decision to make was who was the best candidate for the role and who was capable of it. With 45 holes and all the different facilities at the Golf Academy, it was arguably the biggest job in the department. Okay, there wasn't the pressure of maintaining the Old Course with the big tournaments, TV coverage and the expectations which comes with that, but the Eden and Strathtyrum are the favoured courses played most by the local golfers, which brings its own pressures. The area of those three courses and the practice ground which includes seven additional greens is half the total area of the Links, therefore maintaining it with a team not much larger than the Old Course team required serious consideration. I had a choice between going external or giving the position to Kevin Muir who had done well on the Eden over the previous four years. While I'm sure there would have been a large response if we'd advertised the job, it would be good to keep it in-house as we had been encouraging internal opportunities as a policy across the Trust. The only concern I had in appointing Kevin was the fact he didn't play golf and how that would affect his ability, not to do the actual job, but in communicating with the Local Clubs and their members. I've always thought it important and a benefit to be seen and known to that section of our customers so they can identify with us. One method of getting around that situation and filling the gap, was by trying to ensure the people directly below Kevin were golfers. That was the route I followed and, as on the New and Jubilee, it worked extremely well.

On the Old Course, while the medal tee on the 1st was always in excellent condition for the amount of play it received, the area of the main play tee was never quite as good and wasn't particularly level as, over the years, it incorporated an area of the fairway. The GSC agreed to raise and level the main play tee, fitting it in with the surrounding land so it wouldn't just resemble a large square. I thought it prudent to ask for professional advice and we asked Martin Hawtree to work with us on the project while he was advising on proposed changes to the Jubilee course. The tee was completed in late 2011 and the new area was considerably larger. Some extremely wet weather during the project damaged the soil structure a little, as did another common problem we encounter on the Old Course. No sooner is work finished than people want to play off the area without giving the turf an opportunity to establish. It's normal to have over a dozen people on that 1st tee (caddies, spouses of the golfer, tour operators, etc) making it a challenge to retain a strong grass cover.

The Ricoh British Women's Open, (WBO), returned to the Old Course for a second time in August 2013 and the event had grown considerably since it was in St Andrews in 2007. One change from 2007 was that Final Qualifying would be held at nearby Kingsbarns Golf Links rather than on the New course. This was due to more infrastructure being in place and the players using the same practice area as the men use on the 1st and 18th holes of the Jubilee. As in 2007, the greenkeeping team looked forward to the event which was the beginning of a busy month with the annual Boys', Junior Ladies' and Eden Tournaments taking place immediately afterwards. It didn't run without some difficulties when, during round three and in a repeat of the 2010 Open, play had to be suspended due to high winds causing balls to oscillate and move on the 11th green. The local golfers were less than impressed as golf for them continued on the nearby composite course of the New and Jubilee and also at the more exposed Castle course but it was the correct decision to stop play for the day. As the leaders had still to begin their third round this meant they had to play 36 holes on Sunday for the championship to finish on time. That led to a tough shift for the greenstaff as the wind left the bunkers requiring a lot of work to get them back into a suitable condition, resulting in us having to drop some other routine tasks.

Although we had tightened up procedures on behaviour for the staff following the 2007 tournament, there was one incident which came to light as the Sunday morning shift progressed. It became apparent a few of the staff who had camped on site for the week may have over indulged on the Saturday night. When checking how things were going it was noticeable that a couple of them were well behind schedule cutting their greens. On closer inspection you could see small strips of grass had been missed, although in the main they had been erring on the side of caution and overlapping their lines in an effort to prevent missing bits. We tidied things up so they weren't noticeable and the individuals involved were left in no doubt they were out of order.

The eventual winner was American Stacey Lewis, star of the 2008 Curtis Cup and the 2012 Player of the Year. It was a close-run affair as, although lying second at the beginning of the final round, she fell three shots behind with six holes left. Playing in the fifth last group as the final day's pairings were based on the halfway leaderboard, she birdied the final two holes following a magnificent approach to three feet at 17 and a two-putt birdie from some 40 yards short of the last green. Na Yeon Choi of South Korea, who was leading, fell away with bogeys at 13, 14 and 17 allowing Lewis to win by two.

In another coincidence with the 2007 winner, Lewis was also staying in the Dunvegan Hotel for the week and I managed to get my flag signed on the Sunday night although there was no repeat of the party Ochoa had afterwards. I really enjoyed both Women's Opens held at St Andrews in my time there. It was less intense than the Open and the competitors and tournament officials were more relaxed although that's not to suggest things didn't have to be just right. As regards the standard of golf, I feel I can relate more to the distance they hit the ball. At 6,672 yards, (34 yards longer than 2007), it is basically the length of course I face when playing in a Club medal. I only wish I could finish eight under par for four rounds as Stacey Lewis did!

While Martin Hawtree was visiting to oversee the changes on the Old and possible changes to the Jubilee, we asked his advice on a redesign of the 5th green on the Eden. A short Par 3, this was the smallest green on the course and which also had two tiers. There had always been wear issues and difficulties with pin placing due to its size, causing us to rest it for a couple of months in the winter. In recent years there had been increasing problems with drainage, even through the summer. As one of Colt's original holes, it had such a lot of character I felt it was important we retained as much of that as we could. Martin's suggestion was to increase the size of each tier and make both a little more level as it appeared the back half had sunk in areas over the previous ten years. He also proposed adding a bunker on the right and changing the banking at the rear to prevent balls running back down onto the green. When the Eden team were carrying out the work, they discovered a layer of silt and ash at approximately fifteen inches below the surface which had been preventing water draining through the profile. When the green was built in 1914, this would have been put in place to help retain moisture though the summer as there wouldn't have been irrigation available. With continual topdressing applications over the years, this layer was now deeper than the depth we could aerate. This meant we were no longer able to punch holes through it and allow the water to escape into the sand beneath.

One of the largest and most important projects I was involved in began in 2014 and lasted until early 2017. We were tasked by Trustees to carry out a comprehensive evaluation of our equipment fleet to determine whether we were still getting the most suitable equipment and the best 'deal'. This would include discussions with Toro, the equipment provider we had dealt with since 2001, along with trialling machinery and checking on the services provided by the other two major manufacturers, Jacobsen and John Deere. We prepared a document explaining our vision and requirements for each of the three companies. As well as assessing the different mowers and other equipment they could supply, it took into consideration the support they would provide, future training for greenstaff and our workshop engineers, their investment in innovation and willingness to have the Links Trust involved in new technology as well the obvious aspect of cost. For the successful company there would be an opportunity to partner with the Links Trust which could bring benefits to both parties rather than them simply being suppliers of machinery.

The course managers were to carry out a detailed and honest assessment of each trial piece of equipment the three companies supplied, recording our findings on a spreadsheet using a scoring matrix. They would use their deputies and supervisors to help and while the other greenstaff could, and would, try out some of the new mowers etc, we tried to keep the comments and opinions to the three senior members of each team along with our workshop team. Certain staff would often dismiss a different mower as being 'rubbish' while some were biased towards certain manufacturers and wouldn't give an accurate assessment, so we wanted to keep it tight. It was my job to arrange with each manufacturer when and what they would send in. Given the number of pieces of equipment we were talking about, that wasn't as simple as it sounds. As each piece of kit had to be assessed by four different teams and by up to three people in each team, it wasn't a case of just getting a machine in for a day or two. We needed each item for a minimum of eight weeks to allow a reasonable amount of time to try it in varying conditions. To have a piece of equipment from each manufacturer for that period of time was a big ask, but all three companies responded magnificently to try and accommodate us as best they could. It might appear obvious to try and have the same machines from all three companies in at the same time to allow us to compare them directly against each other, but that would have been more or less impossible. From the company's perspective, they have a business to run, with other customers looking to buy their equipment to consider. From our point of view, we have different things going on across our courses each week which might prevent one team having the time to assess a machine at that precise moment. Add the fact the machine had to be with us at a time which was appropriate and when it could be used. No point in sending mowers in the winter or when there was little growth, or sending aeration equipment in summer. There was also the problem of space, since we simply didn't have the room for too many extra pieces of kit. Everything had to be coordinated through the local dealerships for each company, fitting in with their schedules, as they would require to be on hand when the machines arrived to provide the basic operational procedures and record all health and safety protocols had been explained and understood. The first items to arrive towards the end of 2014 were some utility vehicles from John Deere and the number of different ones they had in their range started to make the process very complicated, as you weren't always comparing apples with apples. There was the complication of the 2015 Open when, out of respect to the Toro company, we didn't want to have other manufacturers' kit on site. However, we did get through it and towards the second half of 2016 we finished up by bringing some items back, either because one team didn't have the opportunity to assess a machine properly, or some people simply wanted a second look.

Throughout the process we were in regular dialogue with each company while a group of us visited the Toro base at St Ives, Jacobsen's base at Ipswich and John Deere's European headquarters in Germany to see different aspects of each company's production and distribution services and continue the conversations.

Finally, with the assessments complete, we had to make a decision. The greenkeeping department was clear we had a preferred company in mind although it was very a very close-run thing. No single company had the best piece of kit in every field and in an ideal world we would have liked to pick and choose the best machines from each, but commercially that was never going to get us the best deal. In the end we looked at what are the most important aspects of the golf course, which are the fine turf areas, (greens, surrounds, fairways and tees), and what would give us the best results in these areas. That made Toro the clear winner in our minds but it was now out of our hands and I wasn't 100% confident the Trust would sign with Toro unless they also put forward the best financial package. If they went with what might appear on paper to simply be the cheapest option, the team would feel deflated, given all the work they had put into the project. Of course, we understood the deal Toro brought to the table had to match, or come close to matching those from the other two companies, either from a straight financial viewpoint, or bring other benefits of some type. We wouldn't have expected the Trust to simply follow our recommendation at any cost, but it led to a nervous few weeks.

Each company visited St Andrews to present their proposals to the senior management team, the course managers, the chairman of Trustees and others representing the different committees. Each company focused on different aspects of any future deal or partnership, making it difficult to compare them financially and be exact in an overall cost.

To the greenkeeping department's pleasant surprise, the result was to go into further negotiations with the Toro company to reach an agreement which would satisfy both parties. This was thrashed, out and we finally signed a fifteen year partnership deal in early 2017. The length of the contract took many people by surprise, but given its detail and the work involved in the entire process, it made perfect sense for it to be a lengthy agreement.

Toro introduced a new design for their delivery vehicles in the US and also produced model trucks to mark the new partnership.

A couple of large projects appeared on the horizon before the end of 2014 and, fortunately for the greenkeeping teams and the local golfers, we managed to literally divert one of them. The University were building a Biomass heating plant at nearby Guardbridge and were looking to lay a pipeline carrying the hot water it produced into many of their buildings on campus. The route they were considering came right through the 12th and 11th holes of the Strathtyrum course then through some holes of the Balgove. Even though the route of the pipe was going to be tight against our boundary fence, because they needed between 20m and 30m working space, it would have caused huge disruption on these holes, resulting in them having to be closed to allow a safe area to work in. There was a much easier route on the other side of the A91 but I suspect initially the farmer who owned those fields was looking for too much in compensation and the University thought we might be a cheaper option. Once I pointed out the amount of revenue lost to the Trust if these holes were closed for an extended period, along with all the irrigation and drainage pipes we had in the area which would have to be either protected or replaced at the finish, they quickly reopened negotiations with the farmer and chose that route.

The other project which appeared out of the blue concerned the R&A and the broadcasting companies who cover the Open. Previously the TV compound for the Open and the other televised tournaments, was located off-course on a narrow strip of land adjacent to the 3rd hole on the Jubilee course. We had previously built a road to the site which allowed vehicles back to the Links clubhouse in one direction and the far end of the Old Course in the other. Prior to the 2015 Open the R&A had signed a new deal with the broadcasting companies, moving from the traditional terrestrial BBC to Sky TV and in America, from ESPN providing the coverage to NBC. However, even though it was going to be their last year, the BBC, ESPN and TV Asahi who provide the Far East coverage wanted bigger, better facilities. (Remember back in 2009, a large selling point of installing fibre optic cabling was being told the size of the TV compound would be reduced?). In discussions for 2015, the size, shape and condition of the TV compound had been raised but all involved had concluded, though not ideal, it would have to suffice. However, during the WBO in 2013, some of the main people involved with the broadcasters came across an area next to the 15th of the New course. This was where we stored all our sand and materials for construction jobs on the courses along with our grass clippings, which we turned to compost and gave away free to anyone who wanted it. They thought this area would make an ideal location for a new TV compound as it was much more central and nearer the Old Course. Immediately next to it was a grass strip which used to be a hole on the Jubilee pre-1987 and which local golfers now used as a practice area, and the broadcasting companies began working on the idea of this area as an alternative site. The R&A approached me in late 2014 regarding the possibility of developing this area into what was required as, after taking relevant measurements, the area wasn't going to be quite large enough as it stood. The entire plan wasn't ideal from my perspective as there was a huge pile of material requiring to be moved, once I identified a suitable site, and we would have to find another area for storing and mixing material in the future. I would also have to obtain approval from various committees as there would be an impact on the 15th and 16th holes of the New course since, to make the area the required size, towards them was the only direction in which it could be extended. The idea was problematic but I put my support behind it and concentrated my efforts into what could be done to reduce the impact to the greenkeeping department. The R&A agreed to extend the concrete area already within the site which we used when mixing materials. When not in use as a TV compound, we could continue to use the area although any material stored there would have to be removed prior to an event. They would contribute to the cost of removing the 80,000 cubic metres of soil and composted material which was currently there, but it was where to put it which was the dilemma. The Links has been developed so much over the past fifty years there were few 'spare' areas. The most suitable one, which was also by far the handiest, was basically just on the other side of the practice strip next to the site. There is a spine of dunes separating the outward and inward holes on the Jubilee course and at one point there was a gap which went down into a hollow and was somewhere we could lose most, if not all of, the material. After due discussion with committees, we began moving the material in February 2015, transporting it with six-tonne dumpers and turning what was once a hollow into a mound which we shaped up at the completion to look like another dune. Ideally, I would have liked to have had the ability to 'sand cap' it so the vegetation matched the surrounding dunes but lack of suitable sand and time constraints prevented that. To screen the compound from the New course, as it was basically just a large flat area topped with gravel, some of the material was used to form a bund alongside part of the 15th and 16th holes which again, would have benefitted from sand capping and more appropriate shaping to make it more like a dune but lack of room prevented the latter. Between Grant Smith and ourselves, the staff performed a heroic task to complete the work in a little over three weeks, in what, at times, was horrendous weather. Especially if you were one of the people on the dumpers!

Over the course of the winter of 2014/15, I asked Kevin Muir, course manager on the Eden side, to use a different type of sand in any bunkers they rebuilt over that winter. The Eden had always used the same sand from the beach as the Old and New courses, while the Jubilee and Strathtyrum had a much heavier grained sand which wasn't as prone to wind blow.

The new TV compound between the New and Jubilee courses.
The 9th green of the Old is on the bottom right.

The process we went through when deciding to change the sand in the Jubilee bunkers to a heavier grained sand back in the early 90s, just after I started at the Links, was still etched in my mind. Walter had to get five different sands and fill a number of bunkers with different ones, then get feedback on which sand the golfers preferred. Well, guess what? Everyone had a different opinion on which sand was the best therefore, whichever one we went with, it was a lose/lose situation as those golfers who didn't like it would constantly complain. I didn't want a repeat of that scenario so asked Kevin to just do it and not tell anyone. We went with a sand specifically put together by our supplier Hugh King, called Bunker8. It was the same sand used in a number of the Open Championship venues and other top links courses. It was the same colour as our beach sand but had a slightly larger grain size, its only fault being if there was too much sand in the bunker, a ball might plug. My plan was to add it to the twenty-five or so bunkers rebuilt on the Eden that winter then wait and see what feedback we received, if any. There was nothing, apart from a few golfers I knew who said to me they were finding the bunkers on the Eden better to play from, but I never let on. It wasn't until around September or October, after asking the question at a GSC meeting if the members had noticed anything different about the Eden bunkers and they replied, "No," that I came clean and told them. We continued to add Bunker8 to any bunkers on the Eden as we rebuilt them over the following two or three winters, eventually doing the same to the New, Jubilee and Strathtyrum courses. To change the sand in the Old Course however was a step too far for me!

Chapter 20. Terrorist or Bodyguard? The 2015 Open

U NLIKE THE winter prior to the 2010 Open, where we had over twenty-five consecutive days of ice covering the courses and a storm in March when sea water came up the Swilcan burn before bursting over onto the 1st green and fairway of the Old, the 2014/15 winter was much more normal with no dramas. The work to provide a new TV compound on the site of our composting area was completed before the beginning of the season. Likewise, the programme of replacing divots on the Old Course fairways with plugs of turf was finished by the end of 2014. Replacing approximately 40,000 divots with plugs of turf was something we'd done every winter on the Old Course since 2000, (we also did it the winter before the 1995 Open). Basically, staff took the tool used for changing holes and used it to collect 4" deep plugs, which they would then use to replace the deepest divots.

Replacing divots with plugs of turf prior to the 2015 Open.

This would make a tremendous difference to the condition of the fairways by April, as from November until the end of March, golfers playing the Old Course carry a piece of Astroturf matting with them and hit their ball from the mat if it is on the fairway. Due to the low temperatures, there's no recovery from divot damage through the winter as there's no growth. Normally we would take the replacement plugs from one of the on-course turf nurseries we cultivate each year where the grass is over 90% fine fescue. This causes a small visual problem as the turf on the fairways is a mixture of fescue, bent, ryegrass and crested hair grass, some of which are quite broad leafed, making the new plugs stand out. This particular winter we took the plugs from a strip down the right-hand side of the 1st fairway, under where the large grandstand would be and where the grass was identical in species composition. This was one of the first stands to be built and one of the last to come down, therefore, as the turf would be covered from early April until late August, it would need extensive renovation or even to be returfed afterwards.

A change of maintenance practice to the fairways from previous years was applying a monthly application of a wetting agent to help retain some moisture, reducing stress on the grass. Gordon McKie, the Old Course manager, had carried out an experiment with this on parts of the 9th and 10th fairways in 2014 and the difference between the two areas was remarkable. The treated area remained green through the driest part of the summer, while the untreated one suffered from dry patch and loss of grass cover. There was no difference in firmness between the two areas but the treated one looked so much healthier throughout, while the untreated one took weeks longer to recover in the autumn.

Following the success of this on the Old in 2015, we did another comparison in 2016 where we applied wetting agent to the fairways on the Eden and the New courses but not the Strathtyrum or Jubilee. The result at the end of the summer was the Eden and New course fairways, despite only receiving half the amount of irrigation, kept their colour better and were healthier than those on the other two courses.

As well as the new TV compound, the R&A required a new, larger site for the contractors who build the infrastructure. With the scale of the tournament having grown since 2010, the original site the contractors used for their cabins and some equipment had become too small and the R&A had asked for an area on the Balgove course, which reduced the course from nine holes down to seven from late April until the end of September and leaving us with a considerable amount of reinstatement work once they were off-site. The Balgove course is always used for car parking at the larger tournaments. The greens and tees are roped off for protection and because the ground is sandy and firm, vehicles cause minimum damage to the fairways, even if it's wet.

There were other requests which came along late in the proceedings, since there's always something new each Open as the R&A try to improve the experience for the spectators and television viewers. One was to build a replica of Road Bunker inside a marquee in the tented village and the other was to install a tiny camera at ground level at the very front of the 1st tee, directly in front of the markers to give a 'worm's-eye' view of the players teeing off. The bunker was straightforward other than having to leave it until the last minute to ensure the turf wouldn't dry out. The Eden team who built it made a good job and during the week spectators had the opportunity to play from 'Road Bunker' and win a prize for getting nearest the hole. The camera installation was going to be more problematic and with the camera being incredibly small, there was the concern it might be damaged by a mower. We ran a cable between the medal and main play tees and put the camera in a small box before laying turf back on top with only the lens, which was the diameter of a pencil, protruding by a centimetre. We marked it with a small irrigation flag until golf was ready to begin, and informed all the staff to be careful when cutting in that area. Only the medal tee is cut with a pedestrian mower, the main play tee being incorporated in the areas cut by the surrounds and fairways team on their ride-on mowers. This worked well until the extra day's play on the Monday when, because one of the team had booked holidays, he was replaced by another member of staff. Unfortunately, the team leader hadn't told the new member about the camera and by sheer bad luck, it happened to be on his line when they went about their work. That was the end of the camera.

Other than being a relatively wet summer, there was nothing remarkable or out of the ordinary in the lead up to the Open. There was the usual last-minute rush to install cameras in bunkers as the TV companies decided they wanted to put them in different bunkers than those they'd initially asked for. Then there were the obligatory sprinkler lids to be changed over again to correspond with the numbers on the yardage books.

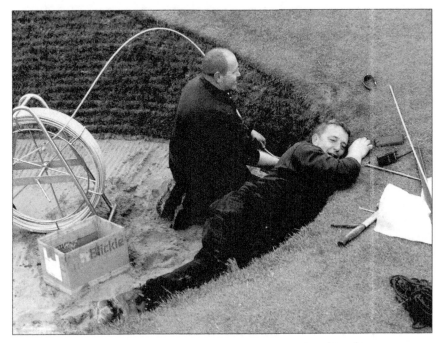

The workshop staff repairing the camera in Road Bunker.

Since 2010 we'd replaced all the sprinkler lids with ones which were easier to read the yardage on, but the R&A required the yardages to be in metres as well as yards. It was a time-consuming task to replace between 300 and 400 lids, making sure they were all correct. We changed them back afterwards as the tournament lids had so much information on them they might have confused our regular golfers. In the spring of every Open year, we have to remove several sprinklers by blocking them off and turfing over where they were. This is because some of them, to give accurate irrigation coverage, are actually on the large double greens and, because they're close to where a hole might be placed, they could interfere with the line of a putt. A couple of others are on approaches and again, when the pin is in a particular location, might be in the exact area a player would want to land his shot. This means these areas have to be hand-watered using hoses until after the Open when the sprinklers are reinstated.

The week before the tournament one of the greenstaff saw a bird fly out of the short rough immediately behind the mound on the 5th championship tee. He asked James Hutchison, our environmental officer, to have a look and James discovered a nest with four or five eggs in it belonging to a meadow pipit. This meant we had to cordon off an area to prevent spectators disturbing the nest until the young chicks had hatched and fledged. This wasn't ideal as it was a popular mound where spectators would have been able to stand immediately behind the players as they drove, while it was also next to a buggy route which had to be redirected. Once Bob Taylor the R&A's ecologist arrived at the very beginning of Open week, he asked the cordon be increased in size. Although we had been very careful to monitor areas to try to prevent this type of thing happening, it's difficult to be everywhere on such a large site and this was an unexpected place for a bird to choose given it was in a busy area where vehicles constantly passed. This might not seem like a big deal but it's against the law to disturb nesting birds. The R&A's actions help highlight the importance the R&A and the greenkeeping industry place on the environmental aspect of golf. The chicks hatched just before the tournament began and fledged the week after. Great timing!

By then I was beginning to think it might be my last Open, even though it was expected to return to St Andrews in 2021 for the 150th playing of the tournament. Although I was only fifty-six, I couldn't see myself working much past the age of sixty, mostly due to my health as I've suffered from rheumatoid arthritis and diabetes for thirty and twenty-five years respectively and wanted to stop work while I would still be able and fit enough to enjoy life. From when I first contracted rheumatoid arthritis there's hardly been a day when I don't have pain to some extent in one joint or another. Over the years I've lost most of the movement in both wrists, while joints such as my ankles, toes and fingers are all fairly restricted. Having also been diabetic since 1994, it's a miracle I was only absent twice in the 27 years I worked at the Links, notwithstanding hospital appointments. One absence was in the late 1990s when I suffered a back spasm and was off work for three weeks, which happened to coincide with a Dunhill Cup. The other was when I suffered food poisoning on the Sunday of the 2010 Ryder Cup and was unable to go to work on Monday. The fact the Ryder Cup went to a Monday finish because of atrocious weather meant I was given an extremely hard time when I went back to work on Tuesday!

It was also going to be Peter Dawson's last Open as he was retiring as CEO of the R&A and his replacement, Martin Slumbers, was appointed early which would allow him to shadow Peter through the tournament.

Why is it that, when we are busy, something totally unrelated to the tournament crops up? Normally it's just something like a greenkeeping group wanting to arrange a visit or an equipment company wanting to demonstrate their latest all-singing all-dancing machine. The extra media interest and everything which comes with an Open we expect, but often we receive the most bizarre requests. In 2005 the Golf Channel wanted to film an episode of their show 'Big Break' in the period the course was closed prior to the tournament. In June 2015, it was a film production company wanting assistance.

Jason Connery, (son of Sir Sean), was going to be making a film based on the book Tommy's Honour about the relationship between Old Tom and Young Tom Morris. Jason Connery came to see me to explain what he was looking for and because it was a period drama, using the backdrop of the 'Home End' and the R&A Clubhouse wasn't practical as so many things had changed between the 1870s and the present day. He had found a couple of places which he thought might be more suitable, one was at the Castle course and the other at a site further down the coast where he was looking for help to transform it into something he could use. The Castle course request was relatively straightforward as he found a location on a fairway where all he required was for us to cut out a green and put a hole and flag in. As it was on the 16th, they had time to film in the early morning before golf reached that point. For the other area, he took me down to an area of links land near Lower Largo that someone had recommended. Once there, it was obvious some parts of the site would make natural golf holes, in character with the period in which the film would be set. The only thing was, he wanted me to organise getting it shaped up a little more and build a green in a particular location to replicate the 18th green of the Old Course as they had a mock-up of the R&A clubhouse to site behind it as if it was the real deal. As much as I was intrigued and keen to help, there was no way I was going to be able to get a group of people and equipment together to get this done at short notice with the Open less than a month away. Fortunately, I knew a man who could and put him in contact with Willie Baird of Turffit, a nearby turf supplier who had the equipment and materials required and was able to get the job done. The area they used went on to be the site of one of Fife and Scotland's best new golf courses, Dumbarnie Links, which was constructed in 2018 and opened for play in summer 2020. As for the film, as films based around sport go it's better than many and it received good reviews. When released it was chosen to open the Edinburgh International Film Festival, to which my wife and I were lucky enough to be invited. People must have wondered who we were as by coincidence, we arrived at the venue at exactly the same moment as Jason Connery and spent some time talking to him on the red carpet.

A month before the Open I was involved in something which fortunately ended well other than embarrassment and the fact my wife became aware of it before I was able to tell her. Occasionally on the courses we have a problem with rabbits causing a nuisance by burrowing in the semi-roughs, weak areas of the fairways and in bunkers. It isn't widespread but there are particular areas where they constantly dig and can make a real mess before myxomatosis, (which is a horrible disease), reduces their numbers again. To tackle this, we would allocate some hours to a couple of staff to go around and either put gas tablets into their burrows before blocking them up, or destroy the burrows completely by collapsing them. Most of the burrows are located within the stands of gorse around the courses therefore it's a time-consuming task. Above that we contract a company who send in a couple of people to go shooting which, because the courses are on public land, has to be managed in such a way as reducing any risk. They can only use a high-powered air rifle and in the summer, they have to start at 4am and finish up by 6am while in the winter it would usually be in an evening between 7pm and 9pm, using a searchlight to locate the rabbits when they're out feeding. The rabbits can get wise to this irrespective of whether it's in daylight or darkness and because they have to get within thirty or forty yards of the rabbits, it's difficult for them to shoot more than eight or nine rabbits over a two-hour period. Through the spring and early summer of 2015 there were a couple of particularly bad areas on the New and Jubilee courses which I thought would benefit from more attention. With the staff busy with preparations for the Open, I decided to come in earlier than normal and do a small amount of shooting myself before the staff reached the far end of those courses where the worst problems were. Another area off the courses which was getting a lot of rabbit damage was the dunes on the West Sands, the worst section being the 100m nearest the town. After speaking to the Countryside Ranger, I agreed to try and tackle that area before the situation got worse and the rabbits spread along the entire dune system. I would take the air rifle home overnight, then on my way into work at 5am, I'd stop off at the dunes where I'd be able to get up to ten shots off from behind the wooden fencing before the rabbits realised what was happening. Then I'd jump the fence and make sure any I had hit were dead before collecting them and disposing of them appropriately back at the sheds and head out onto the courses in a utility vehicle. I'd been doing this on two or three mornings for a couple of weeks and getting good results when one morning, while I was out at the far end of the Jubilee, my mobile phone rang. I noticed the caller was one of the guys who came in shooting for us which was unusual, especially as he wasn't due in that week and when I answered, the conversation went something like this: "Hi Gordon, what are you up to this morning?" "Well funnily enough, I'm actually out doing some shooting," I replied. "I wondered if you were, I've just had a phone call from the police asking if we were out shooting today." It was normal for them to contact the police prior to going out each time, wherever they were shooting, then call back to say they were finished for the day. "The car description and licence plate they gave me didn't match your car but I told them it might still be you and that I would check." "That's because I have my wife's car today", I replied. That day my wife, who was deputy head teacher at a local primary school, had to transport some children who were transitioning from primary to secondary school and needed a larger car so we had swapped cars for the day. "Do you think I should call them?" I asked. "Probably better, just to make them aware." I was heading in anyway and thought I'd wait until I got back to the office before calling in, but five minutes later my mobile rang again and it showed 'number withheld'. This was the police who were at my office by that time and I told them I was heading there but was still around five minutes away. It transpired someone had seen me down at the dunes with the gun earlier and although they saw I was shooting rabbits, they called the police. The police were fine about it as I had a licence, but told me I should always call in beforehand to confirm who I was, the type of gun, what I would be using it for and where I would be shooting. I would get a case number and call it in again when I was finished, allowing them to know if a member of the public called in to report someone with a gun. That was fair enough and good advice and I thought that would be the end of it.

Then, around 10am I got a call from my wife which was unusual when we were both at work. Her opening line was, "Has shooting those bloody rabbits got you in trouble then?" Damn, I thought, how did she find out about that? It just so happened that a couple of weeks previously, her car was badly scratched outside the school and the police were only now following up on it. They had gone to see her to have a look at the damage and get a statement, only Pauline had my car that day. It was when they were noting her name and address, the same officer I had spoken to earlier realised we were husband and wife and said, "Oh, I was talking to your husband earlier." He didn't need to explain, Pauline knew exactly what it had been about! When we were both home, Pauline said the officer told her the hierarchy in the command centre were getting excited about someone going around with a gun just a few weeks before the Open and were considering sending out a helicopter and S.W.A.T. team. One of the local policemen said, "Look, at 5am, there will likely be a simple explanation, give us a bit of time to investigate." I don't know how much truth there is in that last part, if the officer even said it or if Pauline is only getting me back for all the times I've wound her up over the years. She's never confirmed or denied it!

The 2015 Open was going to be my third as Director of Greenkeeping and Gordon McKie's second in charge of the Old Course, while we had both overseen two WBOs, a Curtis Cup and hosted the Dunhill every year. While the Open is much larger than these other events, the actual set up and managing of the golf course and how the main playing surfaces require to be presented isn't hugely different. Once again, our partners at Toro were excellent in providing us with eight new ride-on greens mowers from three weeks prior to the tournament to supplement our own fleet and allow us to cut the fairways as tight as we possibly could.

Fairway mowing at the 2015 Open.

We had the usual marquee and caterers in place to feed the sixty-four staff plus our workshop team. Of the six volunteers, some had worked at the Links previously in their careers therefore had the relevant knowledge of what was required and the 'newbies' would always be shadowing an experienced member of staff. Plus, we had three full practice days to iron out any unforeseen circumstances. As in 2010, the STRI team worked with us collecting and providing data from ten days before the first shot was struck. They had carried out this role at every Open since 2010 and knew the Old Course well, so everyone was very relaxed without being complacent. A question I'm often asked is, "How do you cope with the pressure of staging an Open?" With all the experience around me, knowing all of the staff, the skills they possess and their awareness of the importance of the event, it gave me a lot of confidence that whatever might be thrown at us, the team would cope. I'd far rather have it that way than having forty or more people I didn't know arriving to assist and not being sure of their motives for volunteering, albeit the vast majority would be there to improve their knowledge and help their career. They may not know the site, perhaps aren't accustomed to the equipment we operate and we could never be sure of their skills despite what they might say in their applications. By the time they arrive on site for the first practice day, it's too late if they're not all they claimed to be. We're all nervous to an extent which is no bad thing, but knowing everything is covered certainly reduces a lot of the pressure.

The course was going to play very differently to 2000 and 2005 as the summer had been relatively wet, especially since the beginning of July when the course was flooded following a downpour. It proved to be a tough week with the weather and I was grateful to have a team who would rise to the occasion. It began with great anticipation as Jordan Spieth was going for his third straight major, Louis Oosthuizen was looking to regain the trophy he won here in 2010 while it would be the last Open for former champions Nick Faldo and Tom Watson. Unlike 2010, the Past Champions challenge was able to go ahead on the Wednesday afternoon where the legends Arnold Palmer, Gary Player, Peter Thomson and Tiger were among the players who took part.

It didn't take long for the weather to make an impact although Day One went extremely well, with the soft and benign conditions leading to some excellent scoring, especially from the morning players. Friday, however, was a different story as before the staff had completed their morning set up tasks and immediately the first group of players teed off 6.30am, the heavens opened. I was driving back through the course carrying out a final check while those cutting the fairways and raking the bunkers were finishing up at holes 9 and 10 when the rain started. I was passing the 3rd green and literally, within two minutes, the green was completely submerged. With 12mm of rain falling in thirty minutes, no amount of greenstaff would have been able to keep greens clear and play was immediately suspended. This allowed the staff to grab some breakfast back at base as, until the rain eased, there was little point in attempting to begin the clear-up. It began to lessen by 8 o'clock and around 25mm in total fell between 6.30 and 8.30. All the wet weather equipment required was ready to go. While we abandoned the idea of trying to cut the few remaining fairways and some staff went to repair the damage done to the bunkers, most went to clearing the water.

Some of the team clearing water from the 1st fairway at the 2015 Open.

Experience had shown us this would take about an hour with the worst areas being around the 1st green and 18th tee as usual, although such was the ferocity of the deluge that the Valley of Sin in front of the 18th green was completely full of water. As play had only just begun, it wasn't as if we had numerous areas to attend to immediately. While we were concentrating on getting the 1st fairway and green cleared along with the Valley of Sin, most of the other areas further out on the course cleared themselves, only leaving the occasional hollow which we needed to either pump or squeegee clear. Our experience allowed us to inform the R&A from the outset that once the rain eased, we would have the course playable within an hour. This in turn let them plan for a resumption of play as they knew the players required around forty-five minutes to prepare and warm up. Eventually play restarted by 10am and the morning starters again got the best of the weather as the wind gradually grew in strength through the day. With over three hours lost to the delay, many players had still to finish, the last group only being on the 8th tee. When play is suspended like this, it often means players choose to mark their balls where they lie rather than finishing the hole they're on, which causes a challenge for the staff the following morning. Although we'll get a list of where tee pegs or coins have been left, we still have to find them to prevent cutting or moving them and while it's bad enough on greens, it's worse if on a fairway. On greens we normally have another person there to stand by the coin and as the mower approaches it, they lift the coin and place it back in the exact same spot immediately the mower passes.

The outlook for Saturday wasn't good with high winds forecast and indeed, the wind had never subsided much through the night as it usually does. Knowing the forecast, we had already agreed our work programme with the R&A and STRI. We decided against cutting the greens at the far end of the course from holes seven through to eleven and would make a decision on cutting the 6th and 12th green in the morning although that isn't a green which historically gave us problems with balls rolling in the wind. What transpired on Saturday morning caused a lot of controversy and complaints but here's my take on it as an observer who was present, along with what I saw on television later.

I was at the 11th green prior to play starting and where all three players had marked their balls the previous day. They had probably thought the wind would be less in the morning and that the green would be smoother having just been cut, which of course didn't happen. The pin, which was still in Friday's position, was on the flattest and 'safest' part of the green which was behind Strath bunker. (On the Thursday, it had been in the 'new' position which caused the furore in 2012 when the green was altered). Grant Moir, from the R&A Rules and the person responsible for the course set-up, turned up to assess whether the course was playable and had his putter with him. Although it was very windy, he putted a ball from each marker, which varied from three feet to twelve feet from the hole, and holed each one. After a discussion between a number of us, he decided it was playable even though the wind was strong. That message was conveyed back and the players were sent out to complete their 2nd round, but in the intervening thirty minutes, and by the time they got to the green, the wind had increased significantly. It had increased to the extent that none of the three players would putt, as they claimed the balls were oscillating when they addressed them. They were calling for a further suspension. Eventually Brooks Koepka tried, but couldn't replace his ball without it moving. They waited so long for a lull in the wind which never materialised, that the players who had begun on the 8th hole and all those between them and the 11th, were now waiting on the 11th tee. Eventually, the R&A called for a suspension in play some thirty-two minutes after it had started.

The controversy came from the fact that while those on the 11th green hadn't played a shot, those behind and those in front of them had played anything from one to three holes. I was fully in support of the R&A in their initial assessment as, prior to the players arriving at the 11th green, the course was playable. It was unfortunate the wind increased while the players travelled out and it was something which was difficult to detect with accuracy when we were out there exposed to it through that period. Those players who had been on the 12th, 13th and 14th and who played on, dropped shots which they may not have done under better conditions. Jordan Spieth and Dustin Johnson, both on good scores, took three and four shots respectively from the front edge of the green on 14 when they would have normally expected to get down in two. Oosthuizen had one putt from around three feet on the 13th which, after he touched it, proceeded to roll some eight feet past. Researching weather data after the Open showed that historically, that week in July often had strong winds from the same direction as we had in 2015. There was the normal debate about green speeds in the media and between players but the greens weren't that fast. Ideally the R&A would be looking for them to be around 10½ feet on the Stimpmeter with a minimum requirement of 10 feet but on this occasion with the winds we had forecast, most weren't even as fast as 9½ and remember, we hadn't cut the greens from the 6th through to the 12th that morning. I can't give a number as to what speed they were running on the Stimpmeter on that Saturday morning as the wind would not have allowed for any accurate measurement.

It transpired that play ended up being suspended for over 10½ hours, not resuming until nearly 6pm which led to its own problems. The team from the Met Office said at first it would begin easing at noon, then 2pm, then 3pm and so on. Therefore, we had to have the entire team on standby as we would need everyone to be available to get the bunkers back into a reasonable condition as the wind would have played absolute havoc with them, blowing most of the sand along to one area, leaving the rest of the bunker bereft. It also confirmed what we already suspected, the tournament wouldn't conclude until the Monday which, with staff already tiring, was an additional day of early starts. As a precaution for scenarios like these, the Old, New and Eden courses are held in reserve for the day after the Open with any bookings made on the understanding that, if the tournament runs over, they are lost. The Old is normally given over to the R&A on the Monday where they use the day for their main Patrons and guests. First tee time on the New and Eden courses would usually be 9am on that Monday but now the Open was a Monday finish, first tee times on the New and Eden would revert to the normal 6am on Tuesday, requiring yet another early start for the team. The suspension in play also left some 40,000 plus spectators with little to do for the day which proved a bonus for many of the shops and bars in St Andrews. They often complain they don't benefit a great deal the week of the tournament as most of the spectators are day travellers and only spend their time at the golf course, using the food and beverage facilities which are on site. Not this particular day as most people headed up town to pass the time. By the time play resumed, you could say they were more animated than the usual St Andrews golf spectators. It was said both beer supplies and cash machines ran out of their respective commodities!

The staff were able to take a short break from the time play was suspended if they wanted to go anywhere or do anything but given most of them travel from outside St Andrews to work, it was hardly worth their while. Those on site in tents were unable to catch up on sleep as the wind was howling, even though the tents were in a sheltered place. There were newspapers to read and we had a table football game to help pass the time but other than spending time on their mobile phones, it was just a case of sitting around and waiting. It was different for me as I always had things to attend to in the office although I never felt inclined to get on with office paperwork around the buzz of a tournament.

Our marquee which we used for meals, relaxing and staff briefings.

In the late-afternoon I was sitting in my office when I saw a couple of policemen come into the yard on their bicycles and approach the front door so I nipped downstairs to see if I could help. They explained they were only calling round out of courtesy to check there were no problems. I said everything was fine and asked if they wanted a coffee which they thought would be a good idea and I asked them to follow me over to the catering tent where it was readily available. On the way across I suggested playing a practical joke at someone's expense and asked if I went into the tent and pointed one of the staff out to them, would they pretend they were going to arrest him? They were happy to play along but I had no idea who I was going to pick on, I only knew it would be someone towards the back of the tent for maximum effect. I entered with the two policemen and looked around before pointing to a tall lad with ginger hair who was a young seasonal greenkeeper and said, "That's him." There was silence as the two policemen walked across the room, all eyes following them as they approached the lad. Once they reached him, one policeman reached out to shake hands and said, "Everything okay son?" It was a mischievous thing to do but it broke the monotony of sitting waiting and the young lad in question took it in good spirit. He left to get a full-time greenkeeping position at Royal Aberdeen GC at the end of the season and at the time of writing is, by all accounts, doing well in his career there.

When we got the nod that the winds were abating enough to allow play to begin again, then it was all hands on deck to get the bunkers into a playable condition although the strength of the wind remained high enough to continue moving the sand in them, despite staff dampening it down with water from the irrigation system. As I missed Jack Nicklaus's last round in 2005, I was keen to see Tom Watson make his last walk up 18, which looked as if it would be late on Saturday as he was unlikely to make the cut. Unfortunately, I thought I'd miss it as I'd been invited to dinner with a Chinese film crew who were looking to work with the Links Trust. What made it worse was I was driving and missed out on sampling some rare whisky they had bought. However, because I was starting work at 4.30am I made my excuses and left early. As I was driving back into town, I realised by the crowds that Watson hadn't yet finished. I was able to make it to the 18th just in time to see him hole out, even though it was almost completely dark.

Sunday proved to be a more 'normal' day for us although there was still some nervousness regarding the weather forecast which prevented us chasing green speeds and doing anything other than cut them. Most of our efforts were directed to the bunkers and redistributing the sand to where it should be. It turned out to be the best day of the week with little in the way of wind and with soft, holding greens which weren't running overly fast. The players took advantage with many of them scoring under 70 and by the end of the day sixty-three players from the eighty who made the cut were under par for their three rounds. It was close at the top with twelve players within three shots of the lead, and shaping up to be an exciting final day.

Monday saw a return to poorer weather with squally showers and a breeze making the 16th and 17th holes play the toughest on the course. Spectator numbers on the Monday were good as anyone could turn up and buy their entry ticket at the gate. After setting the course up in the morning, the staff went back to their own courses for a spell or went home for the day, with a few Old Course staff on a duty rota if anything should be required. For Gordon McKie and myself it was an opportunity to rest up as best we could and even watch some golf before the finish and presentation ceremony. My wife and I were fortunate to watch the closing groups come up 18 from the front of the

R&A Clubhouse. It then went to a three-man playoff between Zach Johnson, Louis Oosthuizen and Marc Leishman with Johnson winning by playing the four holes in one under par. While Pauline went back to the Links Trust hospitality tent to watch the playoff on television, I went inside the R&A Clubhouse and watched it on television there as I had to be ready to leave from the clubhouse with the rest of the presentation party at the completion of play.

I can vividly recall Peter Dawson's words to us just before we set off, "Check your mobile phones are switched off and your zips are pulled up". It proved valuable advice because as soon as we walked to our positions on the 1st tee, I realised that I was going to be standing immediately behind where the Champion Golfer of the Year would be presented with the Claret Jug and from where he would be making his thank-you speech. As soon as Zach Johnson began talking, I could feel my mobile phone vibrating in my pocket as 'friends' from around the world were sending me text messages and pictures of Zach standing there with the trophy while Gordon McKie and myself were standing either side and slightly behind him in our blazers and ties, looking like his bodyguards!

Zach Johnson and his 'minders', Gordon McKie and me!

After the ceremony we were fortunate to have some pictures taken with Zach and the greenstaff, who had been chosen to form a 'Guard of Honour' for the presentation party as we walked on to the course. However, I didn't have time to organise a flag for Zach to sign when he came to our hospitality cabin later but I did have a plan. My friend Rich Hurley goes to the Masters at Augusta every year, where he rents a house for the week and latterly he had been renting a room to Damon Green, who was Zach Johnson's caddie. After the tournament I got my own flag and Gordon McKie's one and gave them to Rich to take to the 2016 Masters. I thought that was easier than trying to get Zach to sign them before he left St Andrews or trying to track him down at a future Open. It all went well apart from one small thing, Damon Green, who was a good player in his own right, also signed the flags.

It was quite a quiet affair after the presentation ceremony, I think we were all tired and knew we had an early start the next morning, or maybe we were just getting a little older and wiser.

As I've said elsewhere, there's no real time to rest and relax after the tournament as the courses are all incredibly busy and we're straight into events such as the Boyd Quaich, a 72-hole international student event held over the Old and New Courses. It's normally held earlier in the year but when the Open is here it's held the week after and they play to the Sunday Open hole positions in their first round. Then we're straight into the Boys', Junior Ladies' and Eden Tournament events, while the contractors are working like crazy dismantling the infrastructure.

This year, I decided to take my wife's advice and have a break after the tournament, so in August we headed to Majorca for a week in the sun before she returned to school. We were staying in an hotel in Port de Pollenca and were on the beach one afternoon when I decided to go for a swim. When in the water, a guy approached me and, in a strong Glaswegian accent asked, "Did I see you on television the other week at the Open Championship?" How bizarre is that? As we got talking, I realised we'd met on the Sunday at the beginning of Open week. He was walking the Old Course with his wife and another couple while I was putting protective nets onto the 11th tee to stop the players destroying the tee during their practice rounds. They had stopped and asked me a few questions about the course and the Open.

Just to put the icing on the cake, at the greenkeeper exhibition at Harrogate the next January, there was a new award at the opening ceremony for the best Greenkeeping Team Performance of the Year. Someone had nominated us and we had been shortlisted for the award by the judges. It was an honour to discover we won and to go up with the other St Andrews staff present at the show to collect the award from BBC presenter Naga Munchetty.

Being presented with the 'Greenkeeping Team Performance of the Year' award at BTME in 2016.

Chapter 21. The British and International Golf Greenkeepers Association

A GREAT DEAL of what I achieved in my career is down to the help and advice I gained from being a member of BIGGA, I have absolutely no doubt about that. As well as giving me the opportunity to access a great variety of education, it was through membership of the Association I met so many people who went on to be good friends.

It was back in 1980 through Elmwood College that I first became aware of the Association, which at that time was the Scottish and International Golf Greenkeepers Association, as England had their own two versions. I was encouraged to join by Bill Forsyth, the head greenkeeper at Duff House Royal GC, one of the nearest courses to Fraserburgh and someone I often went to ask for advice when I first became a head greenkeeper. Bill was an active member and on the committee of the North section at that time. On a rotten day in winter, I would sometimes visit Bill or Harry Forrest at Cruden Bay GC to see what they were doing or find out what products or machinery they preferred. When I first joined BIGGA, I only attended the two golf outings the North section staged each spring and autumn and I remember vividly travelling up to Dornoch in May 1981 to play in an outing. That was a long haul from Fraserburgh back then, taking over four hours each way as the Kessock Bridge at Inverness hadn't been built and we had to go via the Beauly Firth. I travelled up with one of the greenstaff at Fraserburgh, Tommy Trigg, who in his day was a scratch golfer and though he had played most of his golf at Nairn when he was younger, he had never been to Dornoch. We arrived in time to get in an evening round and as we were playing the closing holes, I don't think I'd ever seen so many rabbits on a course. We finished just in time for a drink in the clubhouse before it closed; it was still 10pm closing back in 1981. I said to the barman I couldn't believe the bars in

Dornoch all closed at 10pm and he suggested we try a hotel called the Burghfield. We finished our drink and walked up there where we were greeted by the barman who, I went on to discover was the joint owner with his brother. We asked when he closed and he replied, "Around October!" before asking us if we were residents. When we said we weren't, he told us that we could get one drink. As we sat drinking, three young ladies who the barman knew came in and sat at the next table. When they went up to get another drink I asked if they could get drinks for us and I'd give them the money, explaining the barman said he would only give us one. "He says that to everyone," one replied and it turned out the five of us sat there drinking well into the early hours. In fact, the barman eventually said he was going to bed and if we wanted any more drinks then we could help ourselves and just leave the money on the counter. He trusted us because the three girls were local police officers and when we did call it a day, they gave us a lift back to our B&B! In a mini!

When I went to the BIGGA outings I would always try to be paired with a head greenkeeper and I'd spend a lot of the day asking questions about how they managed their courses rather than concentrating on my golf as I knew I had so much to learn. They must have loved that! It wasn't very long before I joined the committee and shortly after became secretary and treasurer, taking over that role from my good friend Iain MacLeod from Tain. That position allowed me to join the Scottish board and attend the meetings usually held at Haggs Castle Golf Club in Glasgow, quite a trek from Fraserburgh. After lunch in the clubhouse, we'd hold the meetings in course manager Chris Kennedy's sheds and that was where I met such luminaries in Scottish greenkeeping circles as Walter Woods, Cecil George, Jimmy Neilson, Jimmy Kidd and Elliott Small as well as Chris Kennedy, who went on to manage Wentworth for many years, and Joe McKean, the secretary of SIGGA at the time, a member at Haggs, past President of the Scottish Golf Union and a great supporter of the Association. All these people would go on to have a significant influence in my career.

While Secretary/Treasurer of the North section, I was heavily involved in organising a couple of conferences in Aberdeen which were attended by over 100 people from as far afield as Brora in the North to Perth and Dundee in the South, such was the eagerness of greenkeepers to improve their knowledge. The first big conference I attended was actually in St Andrews in the autumn of 1985 and it was staged to coincide with an international tournament for greenkeepers sponsored by the machinery company, Ransomes. The tournament was over the Old Course and there were teams from America, Canada, Europe and the four Home Nations while there was a one round event over the Eden course for those attending the seminars. The conference attracted international speakers as Ransomes covered their travel costs. Golf over the Old Course was also arranged for them, (it was much easier, and cheaper, to get a game on the Old Course back then). I travelled down with Pauline and we stayed in a B&B along with Harry Diamond, another legend in the history of Scottish greenkeeping. Harry was the head greenkeeper at Ayr Belleisle and a fantastic Robert Burns speaker as well as a great story teller. He was a real advocate for greenkeeper education and improving our working conditions. Other than the par three holes and the 18th, I don't remember much of the Eden course which was the old layout back then and this was the only time I ever played it. When I came to work at St Andrews, people couldn't believe I didn't remember some of the other holes.

It was Walter Woods who first thought of using external greenkeepers to work at the Open, having them rake the bunkers after a player went into one during their round. Walter's close relationship with Sir Michael Bonallack made this possible and first began in 1984 when the Open was at St Andrews, using members of SIGGA. The R&A provided a tent as a base for the greenkeepers within the tented village and this opportunity for greenkeepers to be involved has gone from strength to strength with BIGGA members also helping out with divoting fairways and other tasks if the host club is low on staff numbers. It was a role I undertook on a number of occasions with my first experience being at Muirfield in 1987.

I was only able to attend for the weekend that year and I drove down from Fraserburgh in the early morning leaving at 3am. With the roads being so quiet I overestimated the time it would take me and turned up at Muirfield far earlier than anticipated, getting there shortly after 5.30am. We had to arrange our own accommodation back then and the volunteers were all gathered in cars and tents in an area over the wall from the 1st fairway. It was a horrible morning when I arrived, strong winds and squally showers. I had been parked up in my car beside a reasonably large marquee some greenkeepers were sharing. I was there for no more than ten minutes when the marquee blew down, but no one crawled out! Eventually a few bodies surfaced, I think they'd had a good night.

By 1989 at Troon, the R&A had arranged for everyone to stay in proper accommodation, normally at nearby colleges, and hired mini buses which BIGGA members would use to drive everyone to the venue and back. We were kitted out with shirts and waterproofs in case of inclement weather and provided with food vouchers for during the day. Some members would attend every year although I only ever put myself forward for the Scottish venues.

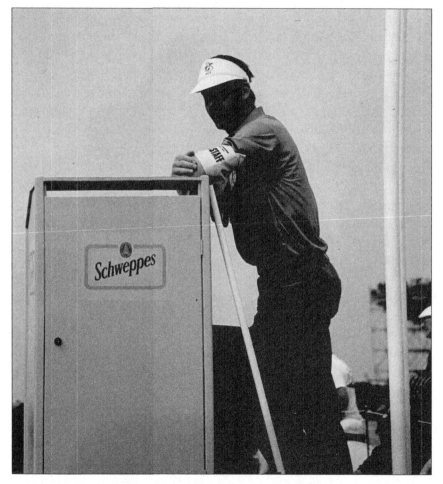

Catching a good view of the golf when on bunker raking duty, Troon 1989.

I worked at St Andrews in 1990, Muirfield in '92 and Turnberry in '94 where I remember raking in the group which included Tom Watson, who went into the lead when he birdied the 11th hole in round three. As he walked to the 12th tee, I was close enough to hear him say to his caddie something like, "This will surprise a lot of people that I'm back challenging, let's go show them I still have it." Unfortunately, on the following holes he missed a couple of short putts and fell away but who would have thought he would go on to almost win there some fifteen years later? My abiding memory of that year came after the presentation ceremony when a few of us were tidying up our base by the 1st tee. The champion, Nick Price, came in with the claret jug and asked to use the toilet. He had just left the press tent and was heading for the Championship committee tent when he was caught short. Someone jokingly said it would cost him a case of champagne and around fifteen minutes after he left, a steward came in with a case of champagne. Those of us there took a bottle each away with us and the remainder we passed on to be used as prizes at future section golf events.

In the early to mid-1980s there were moves for the three different UK greenkeepers associations to amalgamate and form one association. After much discussion and deliberation this eventually happened towards the end of 1986 and BIGGA was formed with a new CEO, Neil Thomas, and based at Aldwark Manor Hotel and Golf Course just outside York. The people I mentioned earlier, namely Walter, Cecil George, Elliott Small, Jimmy Neilson and others were hugely influential in establishing this, in particular Walter, who again used his relationship at St Andrews to persuade Sir Michael Bonallack and the R&A to support the new Association. Walter went on to be the first Chairman. I still believe this was one of Walter's greatest achievements along with working with Elmwood college to develop greenkeeper education.

When I moved to St Andrews in 1991, I initially retained my membership of the North section rather than transfer to the Central section and remained as secretary/treasurer for a short time until the section found a replacement. This allowed me to stay in touch with people who had become friends and I would take days off to attend the North outings and have some time away from St Andrews. It was the North sections turn in the 'rota' to put forward a candidate to be Scottish chairman. Walter, who by then was off the main board of BIGGA, suggested to me that I should take on the role of Vice Chairman of the

Scottish Region which was a two-year post, followed by two years as Chairman. This meant during my four years in office I would be one of the Scottish representatives on the main BIGGA Board, such was the process at the time. It was another new situation I found myself in and although I enjoyed my time on both the Scottish and National boards, looking back it probably came too soon as I was lacking in experience, especially as it was still a new association trying to find its way.

The main objectives of the association were to improve greenkeeping education, publish a monthly magazine and stage an annual exhibition incorporating both education seminars and a show highlighting machinery and other industry items. Today you can add raising the awareness of greenkeeping as a professional occupation and improving the working conditions, salary and wellbeing of the members. The magazine was up and running almost immediately while the first show was held in Harrogate in January 1989 and ran for a week, Monday to Friday. Harrogate was chosen as the venue as it had a great exhibition centre and was central for everyone in the country with good road and rail links while it also had Leeds/Bradford airport nearby for those people from Ireland or Europe who attended. January was the obvious month to choose as it's a quiet time on the golf course although there's always the worry of getting to Harrogate because of snow at that time of year. Fortunately, in all the years it's been running there have only been two or three occasions where it's proved a real challenge. From the first year, the show has gone from strength to strength, attracting thousands of industry professionals over the course of the five days. The BIGGA staff organising it do a tremendous job and it has always been well supported by those in the trade, the members and the rest of the industry. Many people make it a 'must go to' event and have never missed a year, myself included. As well as the varied education on offer, (everything from growing grass to managing staff or committees), and seeing the latest equipment or products, attendees treat it as a social event, meeting old friends or colleagues, making new ones and networking. The small, tight centre of Harrogate makes it impossible to go into a bar or restaurant and not meet a familiar face.

In the early years, with the education conference starting on a Monday morning, I had to make my way down on the Sunday. Many a time I caught the train from Aberdeen with fellow greenkeepers from that area, then we would meet up with others we knew at Edinburgh.

Delegates at a BTME conference.

Of course, you couldn't travel all that distance without a beer or two as a refreshment. On the Thursday evening there would always be a dinner followed by some entertainment and BIGGA used to get some household names from the world of UK entertainment, albeit many of them were reaching the later stages of their career while some may not have been so well received now in this more politically correct world. There were regular TV comedians such as Tom O'Conner and Stan Boardman. Stan was a Liverpudlian who appeared on a programme called The Comedians and a regular part of his routine was to poke fun at the Germans and the war in his Liverpool/German accent. Unfortunately, the night he appeared, Neil Thomas and some board members were hosting a delegation from the German Greenkeepers Association at the top table. When Stan Boardman asked if there were any Germans in the audience and found out there were some sitting at the table closest to him, he must have thought his Christmas had come again! Other acts I remember performing were the Bootleg Beatles and Showaddywaddy, while there were individuals such as Lynn Paul from the New Seekers and Linda Nolan, one of the Nolan sisters. Harrogate week was around the 25th January, Burns Night, and on a couple of occasions we Scots organised a Burns Supper for between forty and fifty of us. Or at least Cecil George and I did, with the pair of us and Harry Diamond being the speakers, as if there wasn't enough happening.

Pre-dinner drinks at an early BTME.

In my early years at St Andrews, it would only be some of the head greenkeepers who would go down with Walter although I went every year. We normally shared a B&B while Walter would stay in a small hotel but we would travel together and socialise some of the time we were there and that was when Walter was at his best, sharing stories and his experiences.

Over the years, the format has changed slightly with the education starting at 9am on a Sunday with a mixture of one- or two-day workshops and half-day or full-day seminars alongside shorter seminars from Monday to Wednesday. The exhibition itself begins on the Tuesday morning and closes at lunchtime on Thursday while the grand dinner on the last night has been replaced with a Welcome Celebration on the Tuesday evening where various awards are given out in different fields. It is still an incredibly successful show and is the main contributor towards financing the organisation.

The number of staff attending from the Links grew over the years. Shortly after I was promoted, we began renting a house or houses for the week rather than staying in hotels or B&Bs. This proved a much cheaper option, allowing us to send more staff to take advantage of the different education programmes and packages. We'd plan the transport so vehicles were going down and back full, using the Links minibus, my own vehicle and the workshop truck. It's not just about the education, it's a great week for helping with staff morale and showing they feel valued, along with broadening their horizons and providing opportunities to advance their careers.

If I was to sum up attending BTME in one sentence it would be the following: A greenkeeper could turn up at BTME with a lot of problems, but they would always leave with a lot of solutions.

Exhibitors and attendees in one of the halls at BTME.

I've always tried to support the association in as many ways as I can, whether personally or through my position at St Andrews. I became Secretary/Treasurer of the Central section in 2010 until shortly before I retired. Being Director of Greenkeeping provided me with the opportunity to meet with many people who could help in different ways. I would be asked regularly by agronomists, superintendents or college professors, (mostly Americans), visiting St Andrews if I could get them a game on the Old. I wasn't always able to help and would tell them I couldn't help with the green fee but I would try for an afternoon ballot time. At worst I'd get them out at the end of the field in what is termed a 'dark time' and we'd hopefully get round before dark. In return, I'd ask them to put on an evening seminar for either our staff or for section members as we had the use of a room at Elmwood which would open it up to more than just the St Andrews staff. Most would be more than happy with this, the only down side being it ate into my time as I'd often have to fit in additional hours at work to make up for the time I was away playing golf. Still, it meant I met many clever and interesting people over the years who I could call on for assistance if required.

I've never fully understood why every greenkeeper in the UK doesn't join the association, or at least why those in promoted posts don't. There are so many different benefits available for everyone, e.g., insurances and helplines. There's also the fact the association is continually striving to improve salaries and working conditions for all greenkeepers, regardless of their status or the size of their golf club. The advantages for those who want to make a career in greenkeeping are endless with the range of education BIGGA provides for all levels. Since its inception some thirty-five years ago, the opportunities and benefits have increased for members who now have the chance to participate as volunteers at the Players Championship at TPC Sawgrass or visit GIS each February as part of a delegation. Once there, they'll participate in education seminars along with visiting some high-end courses and the trade exhibition. There are also scholarships available along with a fairly intense training week where attendees are mentored in taking the step up from deputy to course manager. The Association works closely with other organisations e.g., the R&A, the Home Golf Unions, the Club Managers to name but a few, promoting the importance of greenkeepers and sustainability. At the other end of the scale, a benevolent fund is available to help any member finding themselves in financial difficulty while the awareness, assistance and support to those struggling with mental health problems has increased significantly.

Over the past few years BIGGA's professionalism has increasingly been recognised and accepted by the different bodies within the golf industry, (R&A, Home Golf Unions, PGA, etc), with our advice sought on a variety of topics. This has been made possible with the guidance provided by the many volunteers who have served on the different boards and committees over the years, most of them working course managers or head greenkeepers. Their vision has given clear direction to current CEO Jim Croxton and through his leadership and the enthusiasm of his dedicated staff, past and present, I'm certain BIGGA will drive further improvements for its members. Our influence in the industry would be even greater if all or most course managers were members as there is no doubt there is strength in numbers.

The BIGGA staff work tirelessly throughout the year on behalf of the members.

Chapter 22. Heading for Retirement

THE WINTER of 2015/16 was wetter than average and convinced me to move forward with a couple of drainage schemes about which I had been procrastinating. We'd had a full survey carried out on the existing drainage on the Old and New Courses by the STRI back in 2013/2014 but had never acted on it for various reasons. It might surprise many people the amount of drainage there is across the Links since most people would consider the sandy soil would mean it is a free and fast draining site. The fact is, it's so low lying with many areas barely above sea level, the water table in the winter gets high enough that many bunkers across the Links often lie full of water from December until March.

With the high water table, many bunkers can lie full of water from November until March on the Old, New, Jubilee and Eden courses.

371

As well as an extensive pumped drainage system installed on the Strathtyrum and some holes of the Eden, there are two pumped drainage systems on the New and Old which were installed in the 1980s, complementing gravity systems from earlier times. One collects water from the 14th fairway of the New course and the 9th and 10th of the Old, pumping it from behind the 9th green of the Old across the New, Old and Eden into the estuary just in front of the 4th tee of the Eden course. Another large scheme runs from the 15th tee of the New course, through between the New and Jubilee courses to a holding tank to the left of the 1st fairway of the Jubilee, from where it's pumped out to sea. The survey showed an old drain ran up the first few holes of the New course with tails going across to take water from the 2nd, 3rd and 4th of the Old, but they had all been shattered when installing different irrigation systems over the years. This drain also finished in the sea via the Swilcan burn, but when the water level is up in the burn or at high tides it wouldn't run efficiently. The lowest lying area on the Old Course is the fairway on the 1st and the carry between the 18th tee and the Swilcan Bridge. Pipes from the 1st fairway run into the burn but of course, when the water level in the burn is high, the non-return valves in the outlets close and the water can't escape. New drains were installed in the 1980s on the carry of 18, along the left of the 17th green with a tail to the approach of 17. From a manhole in the left rough opposite the 17th green, they go across to the front of the 2nd tee and feed into the drain coming down from the 1st of the New course, going into the sea at the Bruce Embankment. I'd investigated putting new drains in this area before, including a pumped system, but to install this the Links Trust would have had to increase the size of the nearby power supply at a cost of over £100,000 so the idea was dropped. Following the wet winter, we decided to tackle two areas in particular. On the drain taking water from the 1st of the New and beyond we installed a pump in a chamber near the Swilcan burn. Taking power from the new Caddie pavilion this would allow the drain to discharge water whenever levels were high, rather than being restricted to when the tide was out. The other area we targeted was to put in a new drain on the 1st fairway of the New course and link it into the existing one near the 1st tee. This fairway often had standing water, or lay saturated, because the old drains had been shattered by different irrigation installations.

Willie Redpath, who had been with the Trust for over thirty years in total and workshop manager since 2004 approached me regarding his future. Willie was a very capable mechanic with great knowledge of the irrigation, drainage and fibre optic systems and was the 'go to' person when anyone wanted information on these things. After some discussion regarding his role, he left to work for the local Jacobsen dealer. While I knew it would present us with some short-term problems, I again saw it as an opportunity for others to shine. His deputy Lani Togi had been doing a good job in the workshop, was a good mechanic and could turn his hand to manufacturing many different things, while he'd already been dealing with the staff appraisals. Although he initially found it daunting, he willingly took advice and learned new skills to assist him with that process. The one aspect of the role he wasn't keen on was the irrigation system, which had just undergone a significant audit and was requiring a considerable amount of repair. The system was over sixteen years old and although still working adequately, was beginning to give some problems. While it hadn't been neglected, we should have invested more time and resources on it over the years[*]. Particular electrical components were beginning to fail along with corrosion in some of the valves. The pump system, which must be the largest of any golf complex in Europe, had recently been replaced but was also causing problems.

We had often considered employing a dedicated irrigation specialist and here was the perfect opportunity, only we didn't think we had anyone on the staff with that skill-set. Like environmental work, many of the staff saw working on irrigation as an easy option and few of them had approached it with the seriousness it required. You had to enjoy problem solving, have the determination to see the task through and be prepared to work additional or odd hours to get things fixed in an emergency. And not be afraid to get wet or cold as you'd be working with water which was usually freezing. Most staff would give up when something became difficult and would revert to taking it to the workshop to get it resolved. To be fair to Willie, when it was his responsibility, whenever there was a problem with the system he would be there, any time of day or night, to get everything operating again. He had set up alarms and cameras to monitor the pumps and flow rates

---

[*] Once I retired, I noticed this was becoming a common problem in many golf clubs around Scotland. Many irrigation systems had originally been installed in the 70s and 80s and were coming to the end of their lives, with the old PVC pipes failing at the joints which were only glued together, while the wiring was suffering corrosion. Clubs are shocked at the cost of installing a new system but had spent next to nothing since the system went in the ground and had never considered putting some money aside each year in preparation to replace the system at a future date.

from home or on his phone and I don't recall him ever letting us down in that regard. My first course of action was to approach specialists in the industry to find out if there was anyone interested. One of the Toro irrigation specialists then suggested to me he thought we had a capable person on our staff who, although he would need to acquire a lot of knowledge quickly, had the right attitude. Craig Wilson was the 3-Ic on the Eden team and was also from a farming background. He loved problem solving and had that desire to look at a problem and try different things to fix it along with a willingness to learn new skills. Tony Barnett at Toro promised he would work closely with Craig and pass on all the knowledge Craig could take on board, while he would always be on hand to answer any questions on the phone if he couldn't make it to St Andrews personally. This was important as we were about to upgrade all our computer systems over the coming years, changing from the existing software programme to a new one called Lynx and Craig would be integral to this along with Tony and Toro. To support Craig and also benefit the staff, we selected one member per team to work closely with Craig and get a better understanding of the system. We'd invest in them by providing more in-depth training, allowing them to problem solve many of the smaller faults themselves, quickly and more efficiently. They would be heavily involved in the changeover to the new Lynx system which would further enhance their knowledge and skill set. I was pleased for Craig and this organisational change worked really well.

Hiring seasonal staff was becoming more problematic, particularly finding people to carry out divot filling as their sole role. Using people who came mostly from eastern Europe, as we'd been doing since 2005, wasn't working as well as it did initially. As a department we agreed to change tack and undertake the divot filling role as part of the duties of the full and part-time staff rather than have a dedicated team. Provided there was no comeback from committee that divots were becoming an issue, then I was more than happy to make this change.

We had a new chairman of the GSC in January 2016 with Ian Marshall replacing Dottie Kennedy as her term of office on the LMC was over. Dottie had been my chairperson for four or five years and had been good to work with, as indeed had all the chair people throughout my time as Director of Greenkeeping. Ian was a member of the R&A and a good golfer and had already served on the GSC for a few years so there was no huge change other than a new member taking Dottie's place.

Steve Race, the chairman of LMC also usually attended our meetings which gave us five members of the eight on the LMC attending. This was great from my perspective as any proposals passed unanimously at GSC meant we could begin implementing them without having to wait to have them 'rubber stamped' by LMC.

One of the proposals which came forward from the ICLC, not for the first time, was for the increased use of trollies on the Old Course. These had always been restricted to after 12 noon in the summer and no trollies were allowed at all from October until April unless a Local Club had the course for the day, a concession granted to them in the 1990s. Or, if a club had a competition which straddled 12 noon their members could take a trolley from their first tee time. No one is absolutely sure when or why the 'no trollies' rule came in but my belief is that it's two-fold. One reason was to ensure adequate work for the caddies who earn their livelihood working at St Andrews. The other was to prevent wear, not because of the trolley wheels but because everyone takes the same route which, because of the large double greens on the Old Course, everyone with a trolley would go along the same side of the green to get to the next tee. On a 'normal' course, golfers would pass up both sides of a green on many occasions. It's the feet of the golfers taking the same route which cause the wear rather than the trolly per se. It's difficult to get the message across to golfers the extent of how this pattern affected the turf. To try and highlight this, I requested the help of Steve Otto from the R&A who provided 50 GPS tracking devices. Over the course of a week, we gave some of these to golfers with trollies and asked them to clip them to the trolley. Those carrying their clubs, or using caddies, had to clip them to their bag or carry them on their person. The trackers were set up to plot the route in different colours, yellow if they were being carried or blue if on trollies. The results were quite striking, as the lines created by those on the trollies could be clearly seen to merge and track around the side of every green to the next tee. The ones being carried came on to, and left, the green at different points, mostly avoiding walking on the green surrounds at all. There was the odd caddy who forgot to hand their tracker back at the end of their round and we could see everywhere they went afterwards until it ran out of battery! We presented the evidence to the members of the ICLC but it didn't lead to the matter being dropped entirely and eventually the GSC and LMC succumbed to further trials and trollies were allowed all year round after 12 noon.

The winter programme in 2016/17 saw us return to implement part of the plan Martin Hawtree drew up for the Jubilee course, in particular his proposed change to the 4th and 15th holes which ran adjacent to each other. The 15th at 356 yards and the number two stroke index hole was one golfers either loved or hated. A tight driving hole with a large dune on the right and which, from the right half of the fairway, left a blind shot to a small plateau green. Even though we had removed the gorse from the right-hand dune and around the green years earlier, many golfers still preferred to hit their ball down the neighbouring 4th fairway and approach the green from that angle. Due to the 4th fairway being at a lower level, along with some mounding and gorse, golfers couldn't be seen on that fairway from the 15th tee and it was always a concern someone would be hit with a golf ball. Martin's plan was to move the 4th fairway to the right and nearer the out-of-bounds fence which would allow more space between the holes. At the same time, a large part of the dune on the right of the 15th would be cut away to allow golfers to see the green better from the fairway. Having seen the skilled work his shaper from SOL Golf had done at the other Open venues moving whole slabs of marram grass from dune systems and re-laying them, I was confident that this would be an improvement to both holes and improve safety.

Altering the 15th hole on the Jubilee course, October 2016.

Around that time, something else which I had seen a lot of on Open Championship venues and other top links courses was the introduction of large sandy waste areas. The mastermind behind this initiative was Bob Taylor, the environmental officer with the STRI and it was to create more diversity of habitat across the course as, in general, gorse was beginning to dominate golf courses more than ever. This was leading to the loss of many other species, be it heather or different wild flowers, as the gorse would suffocate them. By removing the gorse and other vegetation, burying it to a depth where it won't regrow and returning the ground to a 'dirty' sand, the natural species found on links land will gradually return to colonise the ground. There were numerous areas across the Links which would be perfect for this and therefore, when the contractors were working on the Jubilee, we asked them to create some of these large 'sand scrapes' in different areas on the New course where gorse removal over the previous winters had left ugly scars on the landscape as weeds had invaded the areas. Before beginning, I visited both Royal Troon and Turnberry where the contractors had carried out this type of work the previous year. We published information advising our ticket holders and visitors of the work and the reasons behind it. The areas selected weren't directly in play but you can never assume where a golfer's ball will finish and many people weren't happy landing in one of the areas and having a less than perfect lie.

Introducing 'sand scrapes' in place of gorse.

They had quickly forgotten that the previous year it would have been a lost ball, or at least a penalty drop, whereas now they could at least find and hit their ball.

Over the years, I had always worked closely with Fife Council and the Fife Coast and Countryside Trust, (FCCT). This was mainly in regards to the West Sands beach, the dunes and the area between these and the Jubilee course. The area was used for car parking and the grass was cut by the Local Authority, while at tournaments it was a public car park and the TV compound. Prior to the 2015 Open, the R&A asked Fife Council if they could improve the area as it had become very uneven but Fife Council told them we were the landowners and they should ask us. Technically we were, as the Links Trust 'owned' everything down to the High-Water Mark, although Fife Council had always managed and maintained the area. There was even a period where the Council erected a barrier and charged people to park there, but in recent times their involvement was becoming less as they were looking to reduce costs. One thing which was increasing however was the number of motorhomes using the area to park up overnight, sometimes for a week or more. Some nights there might be over thirty motorhomes parked up, such was the power of social media. Given there were no facilities to dispose of their waste, we became aware a small minority would simply empty it over the fence onto the roughs of the Jubilee course. We began receiving an increasing number of complaints from committee members and golfers asking us to resolve the problem.

The Local Authority weren't interested in dealing with the situation, while the police were powerless to do anything unless they caught the owners in the act. We sought legal advice and erected numerous signs asking people not to camp overnight but essentially there was little we could do other than take them to court and get an injunction against them. As well as proving expensive, in reality it was impractical as the time this process took, they would have moved on. Many afternoons I would drive along the West Sands, asking people if they knew they weren't allowed to stay overnight. While most wanted to do the correct thing and were understanding, a few could be rude and some would be downright aggressive. A common excuse was they'd had a drink, which prevented them leaving and they generally moved on the following day but there were always those who 'knew their rights'. Although they were actually wrong, they probably knew or suspected there was little we could, or were willing to do. There was no point in saying I'd get the police as the police either wouldn't come or, if they did, were unable to do anything as it wasn't a criminal offence.

The best, or worst case, depending on how you looked at it, involved a family from a nearby town who rocked up one April at the beginning of the school holidays. By the time I was aware of them, their caravan had been unhitched and the car which had delivered it was gone. I spoke to the woman and heard her story of how she was recuperating from an operation and just wanted a quiet break with her two young children while her husband was still having to work, and would come back for her in two weeks. She laid it on thick and was very polite. She really needed this break and there would be no problem with noise etc. While showing sympathy I continued to say that they weren't allowed to stay overnight, let alone for two weeks. She suddenly changed her demeanour and threatened that she could make one phone call and by tomorrow, 100 travelling people would be parked up in the area. I was helpless to do anything immediately although I was able to get the local authority access officer to come down the following day to try and explain the situation to her. That fell on deaf ears and in the end, I had to instruct the Trust's solicitors to go to court and obtain an order to move her on. By then it was Good Friday and the courts were on holiday for Easter therefore it was later the following week before we could get anything done. By the time the order was signed and officers came to deliver it, it was the following Friday and she had left that morning. To cap it all, and I had to laugh, she somehow managed to get my email address and the following week sent me an email thanking me for allowing her to stay and that she'd had a wonderful two weeks!

After much consideration and negotiations with FFCT we agreed to pay the salaries of a full-time and part-time Ranger to manage the West Sands which included the beach itself. In return, they would help us with some projects on the golf courses which included bird and butterfly counts, along with recording wild flowers. Because they were present into the evenings, they took on the responsibility of talking to the motorhome owners. By then, we had erected a height barrier to prevent higher vehicles accessing the far end of the area. This massively reduced the problem as it was less attractive to stop over nearer the town end of West Sands than the quieter far end.

The other issue with that area were the 'boy racers' who would congregate there, especially in winter evenings and rip up the grass by doing 'donuts' and leaving their take-away cartons lying everywhere. I'd sometimes talk to them or simply just hang around and observe them if they happened to be there before I left work. Again, there was little I could do to stop it and if the police did make an appearance, the culprits would simply stop until the police left. After my retirement, my successor had a run in with one and got in touch to ask if I knew who it was but I didn't recognise the car or the person who had said to him, "F***'s sake, you're a grumpier b***** than Gordon."

There were a few events on the horizon, some of which had still to be confirmed or weren't yet in the public domain. The Senior Open in 2018 would be the first time it was played on the Old Course. Then the Open would be returning in 2021 which would be the 150th playing of the Open while there were also discussions regarding the Walker Cup coming in 2023. Following the 2015 Open debrief, there was only the one change to the golf course which would affect the yardage. The R&A had asked to extend the tee at the 8th to lengthen the hole by around twelve yards. This involved removing a mound which had been built previously to provide a good viewpoint for spectators. Since it didn't affect the golf course for everyday golf, then the different committees had no difficulties in agreeing to this and once passed, the actual work didn't take long. The other areas of the course the R&A were looking at were regarding spectator movement and improving the facilities for them. These included putting in some mounding for better viewing and removing gorse in areas, including on other courses, to give more room for catering facilities. The Open has grown hugely since I first attended as a spectator at Carnoustie back in 1975. It's almost unrecognisable from then and even the Opens I've been involved in since coming to St Andrews in 1991 have grown considerably. The Millenium Open was the largest ever at that time and, reflecting back, the infrastructure at the 2015 Open dwarfed the 2000 tournament in every way.

Even though I knew these events were coming up, by the beginning of 2018 I was almost certain in my own mind that I was going to retire at the end of the year. At my annual appraisal with Euan Loudon, I mentioned this to him, but I didn't want it leaked as I hadn't completely decided and said I would confirm with him by the end of August. There was no specific or over-riding reason, just a variety of different ones which together made me feel retiring was the best option for me. Increasingly, whenever I was on holiday, although I would spend an hour on my phone each day answering emails, I would still have to go into the office at weekends on my return to catch up with paperwork. In the years immediately before Pauline retired, she was seldom home before 6pm in the winter therefore I would often stay in the office until then. That led for a long day as I generally went in at 7 or 7.30am. Pauline had been retired for over 18 months and was enjoying the freedom and the reduced stress this brought, while we had become grandparents in March 2018. And I could see her spending our money and having a good time while I continued to work! If said quickly, working for another five years until the Walker Cup was played didn't seem too long. There were a few things happening in other departments which I didn't agree with, but I had reached the stage when I didn't feel inclined to become involved. Perhaps over forty years in the industry was beginning to wear me down. Also, in the background was my aforementioned rheumatoid arthritis and diabetes which would leave me sore and tired on many occasions.

In April, well before the Senior Open, we had some unexpected visitors to the Old Course when a number of sand martins set up home in the face of Hell bunker.

Greenstaff have now to install netting on the face of Hell bunker each spring to prevent sand martins from nesting.

For over ten years we had always prepared areas for them to nest in, usually a vertical face of soil in our composting area or elsewhere on the links. They can be very fussy about what the material consists of, too sandy and it'll collapse or too stony they can't dig into it, (one year they chose our divot filling material causing us to find other material until they left at the end of the summer). They arrive without warning, the first we know is they've burrowed into a banking somewhere. It has to be vertical to protect them from predators and from March we would try to ensure we didn't leave a vertical bank on any material we would be using. This year they obviously didn't fancy the areas we'd set aside and instead chose the face of Hell bunker underneath the top row of turf where there was just enough depth of soil between the turves for them to dig into. Their burrow, as that's what it basically is, can go over two feet into the face. Once established, the birds are protected as it's illegal to disturb them. We had no option but to rope the bunker off and mark it as ground under repair. Having to take one of the iconic bunkers out of play didn't go down too well with a number of people but we couldn't have golfers continually walking around the bunker playing their shots. If they had a second brood this would keep them there until September. Come the Senior Open, I reluctantly agreed the bunker could come back into play for the tournament days. I agreed this on the basis it would be unlikely any player would go into it as that would have been a serious miscalculation or mistake on their part. The staff had to rake it each morning and I don't believe any player did go into the bunker. It was September before they literally 'flew the nest' and in future years, netting has been pinned to the face of the bunker to prevent them returning.

The Senior Open is a much smaller event than an Open, more in line with a WBO or Dunhill, despite being classed as a major on the Senior circuit and having a stellar field which included many previous Major champions. In 2018 we set the course up exactly as we would for any other event and it was an enjoyable tournament to be part of. During the tournament we still had golf available on the Castle and composite courses and, after the Senior Open, we were straight into the Boys, Junior Ladies and Eden tournaments again.

The tournament attracted good crowds and ran smoothly on the whole with decent weather and little drama although there was a serious incident one day involving a referee and a buggy. The referee had been parked up by the 4th tee when he was called to give a ruling on the 12th or 13th hole. He decided the fastest route was to cut across the front of the 3rd green and get to that side of the course where he could head out on the tarmac road to the incident. Only, he hadn't realised there was a large bunker (Cartgate) protecting the front of the 3rd green and he didn't see it until he drove over the mound behind it, by which time it was too late. His buggy went over the eight-foot face of the bunker and head first into the sand at the bottom, the steering wheel going into his chest where, if I remember correctly, it broke a number of ribs. Given the height of the bunker face he went over, I think that was probably a good result as it could have been a lot worse. The incident highlighted a danger we, the greenstaff, have been telling people about for years but many still think we exaggerate the problem in an attempt to reduce the number of buggies on the golf course, or keep them off altogether. That's not the case and our fears have always been based on the fact people would be driving in places they didn't know, with steep slopes and where bunkers were situated in unexpected areas. Often the golfers wouldn't be concentrating as they were excited to be playing golf at St Andrews. This is at its worst on the Old Course as many of the bunkers date back to when the course was played in the opposite direction. Therefore, when the golfer is driving down a fairway in the direction the hole is played, the bunkers are hidden from their view by mounds. In my time at the Links, the fact staff have only accidently driven into a bunker on a handful of occasions, is a minor miracle. There have been a few other occasions when mowers or tractors have landed in bunkers, but these were the results of tyres slipping or mechanical failures rather than a lack of awareness.

Accidents can, and do, happen. Fortunately, the greenkeeper in this instance escaped unhurt.

The tournament finished with Miguel Angel Jimenez winning by one shot from three-times previous champion Bernhard Langer and three other players a further shot back. I was fortunate to collect a flag and have Jimenez sign it after his press conference. The European Tour had organised an event on the Bruce Embankment with a band, drinks and snacks for after the presentation ceremony. This was mostly for the volunteers and staff although anyone could attend and Tom Lehman came along.

There were a few things I was keen to do before I retired and one was to attend the Masters for a second time, exactly twenty years after my first ever trip to America. I thought I could do something similar to then but needed a golfing partner and asked Sandy Reid who held a similar position to me at Carnoustie. Sandy is an excellent golfer but surprisingly, had never visited Augusta, so when I made the suggestion to him, he was keen as mustard. I knew I'd be able to arrange the accommodation with Rich Hurley while I'd also talk to Joe O'Donnell in Atlanta about the possibility of staying with him for a few days to play golf in the Atlanta area. Tickets for the golf weren't as easy though, as Augusta had stopped granting tickets to international members of the GCSAA, but through contacts we succeeded. Sandy needed to be back in Carnoustie the day after the Masters finished as that was when the contractors arrived to begin the Open build. We went out early and managed to play at Atlanta Athletic Club, Peachtree, East Lake and nine holes at Joe's Club at Berkeley. At Peachtree we played with the superintendent William Shirley, just as I'd done twenty years earlier. His golf had really gone downhill in the intervening years, as this time he only hit his drive at the 360 yards opening hole onto the approach rather than the green!

We went to Augusta on the Wednesday for the Par 3 competition and were fortunate to be standing on the path to see Nicklaus's grandson have a hole in one at the ninth. On our way out we stopped to have a look at the 18th green from just inside the rope line which prevented 'patrons' stepping onto the green. There wasn't another soul around and as we left, we simply ducked under the other ropes to get back to the area behind the green. Suddenly a marshal appeared and called us over and give us a severe ticking off for not exiting the roped area at the appropriate place, warning that if it happened again, we'd be removed from the premises.

Back at the Masters in 2018 with Sandy Reid who succeeded me as Director of Greenkeeping at St Andrews.

We spent Thursday and Friday at the tournament before golfing at Reynolds Plantation on the way back to Atlanta.

Another trip I set up was a final visit to Barenbrug and their seed research station at Arnhem with a mix of course managers and deputies along with David Greenshields of Barenbrug. I kept it deliberately short, catching an early morning flight and spending one night only in Holland so there was no overnight stay in Amsterdam on the final night. We first headed to a golf club which was one of a group of over twenty where the greenkeeping was contracted out to a company. We were there to meet William Boogaarts, a Dutch greenkeeper who had worked with us for two weeks one October. This was through our arrangement with Reesink Turfcare, the main Toro distributors for Europe and who are based in the Netherlands. William was keen to show us a driverless fairway mower this company were using. The mower itself was a Toro, similar to the ones we used at St Andrews, but a Dutch company had developed software they fitted to it which allowed it to be used without an operator.

Back at the Barenbrug seed research station.

The contracting company had a mower like this working on every course they maintained apart from one. Guided by satellite links, we watched as it cut a fairway as precisely as any operator could. Meanwhile the 'operator' went around raking nearby bunkers and trimming sprinkler heads, keeping a close watch on the mower. Prior to retiring, Toro had developed this further and we had a prototype autonomous mower delivered for a trial at St Andrews. As I was finishing this book in February 2022, Toro were displaying their latest version at the GIS Show in San Diego which they will be field testing at select venues through the remainder of the year. We spent the remainder of our first day at Barenbrug HQ, listening to a presentation before looking at their trial site and new developments. On day two we visited two courses, the Dutch and one which was due to open in 2019 called Bernadus GC. Trips such as these were always worthwhile for a variety of reasons. When people are receptive to new ideas there's always something they will learn to help them in the future, while it is also beneficial to spend time away from the workplace with colleagues.

Michigan State University is home to one of the largest turf schools in the US and Kevin Frank who is a lecturer there, had often asked me to talk at their annual turf conference but the stumbling block was it was always held at the very beginning of January. Finally, I agreed to go one year and in December 2017 Pauline and I went to New York for New Year which would let us head to East Lansing on 2nd January in readiness for the conference beginning on the 3rd. We had a great four days in New York visiting the sights, apart from the fact the temperature never got above minus 13 Celsius at any point and it was even colder once we got to East Lansing. When at BTME later in January, John Kaminski at Penn State University, which has an even larger turf school, asked why I had never come to talk at their conference. My reply was because I had never been asked, so he suggested I should come over to their conference in November. I couldn't tell him I would probably be retiring shortly after that and bought some time by saying I would think about it. After some thoughts and discussions, I agreed to go and due to the distance involved I would give two talks, one of them being a joint presentation with Pauline on managing change through leadership! I took holidays rather than time off work and we went to New Orleans beforehand for the weekend, then flew up to New York and drove to Penn State which is in the middle of nowhere. We rehearsed our presentation numerous times and initially I tried to do my part without referring to our notes but went a bit off script. Pauline began to wonder what was happening, thinking I might have been taking a diabetic hypo when I decided it best to go back to what we'd prepared. The feedback we received was good with many in the audience telling us the content was relevant which was a relief. However, by mutual agreement, we decided we wouldn't do another one! As soon as I finished my presentation the following morning, we were back in the car and off to Newark for our flight home, hitting the NJ Turnpike in the rain and darkness at rush hour.

Before I formally confirmed my retirement with Euan, I accepted a request from the Finnish greenkeepers to present at their conference in Helsinki in December. The following week, the Norwegian greenkeepers asked for the same and their conference was immediately after the Finnish one, but in Alicante, Spain. I was reluctant to attend both but the chairman of the Norwegian association was a friend, a fellow Scot who came from my home town of Fraserburgh where I played golf with his father. Fortunately, their conference began on the

Saturday so, again, by using up some more of my holidays I decided I could do both. Then the Finns told me they'd switched venue to a place in the Artic Circle, a three-hour train journey from Helsinki. On the Thursday afternoon I flew to Helsinki where I spent the night, before catching the 7am train in the morning. I arrived, gave my presentation, which included a brief history of St Andrews Links, managing a links course and preparing for an Open Championship, then had lunch before catching the train back in time for my flight home. I can't tell you much about Finland as it was dark most of the time I was there. On Saturday I flew to Alicante and picked up a hire car for another three-hour drive to the venue. The Norwegians were all chilled out and my first presentation, similar to the one in Finland, was more informal and scheduled after the golf on the Sunday morning. I had another talk on renewing the irrigation system at the Castle on Monday, before participating in a course walk with Fanny Sunneson, who spoke on how the players would expect a course to be set up for a Tour event. At that conference I met Peter Guterstam who worked in the irrigation sector for the Toro company in Scandinavia. He asked if I'd like to visit Sweden to give some presentations in the spring which I agreed to, going to Stockholm and Halmstad in March 2019. After Sweden I called time on any further presentations as I didn't feel comfortable talking about what happens at St Andrews once I had moved on and I didn't feel inclined to present on any other subjects.

Shortly before the Senior Open I confirmed with Euan Loudon I was going to retire, giving six months' notice as per my contract although we agreed to keep it to ourselves for a few weeks until the next meeting of the GSC. Just before the meeting I asked the course managers to meet me beforehand under the pretence I wanted to discuss something about the meeting and this would allow me to tell them first before announcing it to the committee. Afterwards I called a few friends to tell them, including Sandy Reid at Carnoustie, as I felt bad about attending the Masters with him and saying nothing.

I was pleased to be involved in finding my successor, vetting the applications, writing up some of the interview questions and having an input into selecting the candidates for interview. I also sat in on the interviews but had no say in the final decision. The applications were interesting, with the first one arriving the day after the position was advertised, addressed to Martin Slumbers who of course is CEO of the R&A. On paper it was a good candidate but the fact it was addressed to the wrong person along with it arriving so quickly suggested they were sitting with applications ready to be sent out for any vacancy. It was quickly filed under B for bin. It might surprise people to know there were less than thirty applications for the position and I discovered a couple of reasons for that. I spoke to a few people who I thought might be possible candidates and for various different reasons, the timing didn't work for them. Quite a few people I knew called me to ask about the position but misunderstood the role. Once I explained they'd be in the office most of the time and the course managers ran the courses, they realised the job wasn't what they thought and decided it wasn't for them.

Once the news of my impending retirement was public, I was overwhelmed by the messages of kindness and congratulations I received from so many people and different sections of the industry. Pauline soon put my gas at a peep by saying, "You're never more popular than when you announce you're retiring!" But the industry was amazing, as were the Links Trust and many of the staff. John Grant, the Director of Golf would go on to say, "No one has ever had so many retirement parties!" David Withers, who had left Jacobson and was now back in the UK as CEO of Iseki, contacted Euan Loudon to suggest the industry should have something official for me and I was asked to come up with eighty names of people to invite for drinks in the Links clubhouse. It was a tough ask to keep the numbers to eighty even though I didn't expect people to travel in midweek from all over the UK for a couple of hours and I was astounded when practically everyone invited came along. This included Barry Beckett of Toro who was based in America, although he happened to be in the UK at the time. Barry and Andy Brown had been in St Andrews earlier that week and I had no idea they had stayed for an extra day.

The Links Trust had commissioned a painting of a person tending the 18th green of the Old Course by a well-known and respected local artist, which I received at the annual Trustees dinner. Meanwhile, the ICLC had also commissioned a sketch by David Joy which had me sitting on the Swilcan Bridge with Old Tom and Daw Anderson standing behind me. Martin Slumbers invited me to the R&A Clubhouse, where I was presented with a beautifully bound book containing photographs from all the Majors held at St Andrews from 1995. There were numerous lunches and dinners through December and into January where I was overwhelmed by the number of gifts I was given by different people, companies and organisations.

The final surprise came at BTME in January where I attended the STRI Environmental awards one evening. I'd entered the Links for this the previous summer and we'd made the short list and was hopeful we might win. We'd won previously and had either made the final or been highly commended on a few occasions over recent years. Alas, it wasn't to be and the different winners were well deserved. I thought that was the end of the evening when Bob Taylor, the host and the person who organised the competition, announced he had one other duty to perform. This was to recognise someone who had supported the awards over the years. He then preceded to run a slide show with various pictures of me, most of which he took when he was up at St Andrews in the autumn carrying out the judging! He did me up like a kipper and I was completely surprised and embarrassed.

I consider myself very fortunate to have had the career I've had, working in golf, a game I love. It was something, to a certain extent I fell into, never setting out with a goal of reaching a particular level. I was never particularly motivated by money and it was only because I wanted to provide a better standard of living for my family than that which Fraserburgh Golf Club could provide that I left there. In many ways I was lucky how things unfolded, often being in the right place at the right time.

If the opportunities arose today as they did back in 1991, or more specifically 2000, would I have been as fortunate? While I had the experience and a good work ethic, I had very little in the way of formal education. Other than the original qualifications I achieved as an apprentice, I only had a few short courses on supervisory skills and other relevant subjects to my name. It was only after being promoted in 2000 that I gained my SVQ Level 3 certificate in management. After then, between work and home life, it was difficult to commit time to progress on that route. In saying that, before 1995, there wasn't much further education available in the UK relevant to the greenkeeping industry and by then I was already in a well-recognised position. I remained committed to improving my knowledge but preferred the continued professional development opportunities one-or-two-day courses provided, as I enjoyed the interactions between the lecturer, others in the class and myself. As my career progressed, I discovered that people learn in different ways and while some like to absorb knowledge through the internet or by reading, that wasn't necessarily my style.

Although not impossible, it would certainly be more difficult to reach the position I did without having some more advanced qualifications. I would always encourage those starting out on their career today to look at obtaining qualifications alongside gaining different experiences, such as volunteering at tournaments or participating in something like the Ohio State programme. Also, attending different events or conferences to allow networking can provide enormous advantages, which, if applied correctly, will assist them to advance in the profession.

I would never have achieved as much as I did without the help and support of so many people. From the CEOs and fellow Directors I worked with, to the different course managers, committee members and many greenkeeping staff at the Links, not to mention numerous others in the greenkeeping industry, in particular the different companies and organisations I dealt with. Far too many people to mention individually.

I would have achieved nothing without a good team behind me.
This is only some of the greenstaff from the 2015 Open.

Could I have done things differently or better? Almost certainly, but I always felt I gave my best. This was often at a price, whether that was time not spent with Pauline and my family when they were growing up, or it was detrimental to my health. At the same time, I had a fantastic twenty-seven years meeting so many wonderful people and visiting amazing places. As the great professional, Walter Hagen said, "You have to take time to smell the roses." It might not have always felt like it, but I think I did that.

I was always conscious of the legacy of Old Tom Morris during my time at St Andrews Links.

Acronyms

ADLC - The Alfred Dunhill Links Championship. The European Tour event held over the Old Course, Carnoustie and Kingsbarns each year since 2001. Prior to then it was the Alfred Dunhill Cup, a team competition held over the Old Course, featuring international teams. Referred to simply as the Dunhill.

BIGGA – The British and International Golf Greenkeepers Association.

BTME- The British Turf Management Exhibition.

GCSAA – The Golf Course Superintendents Association of America.

GIS – The Golf Industry Show. An annual conference and show held by GSCAA in America.

GSC – The Green Sub-Committee.

LMC – The Links Management Committee.

PGA – The Professional Golfers Association.

R&A – The Royal and Ancient Golf Club of St Andrews. A private member's golf club. From 2004 it can also mean the organisation (R&A Ltd) which stages many tournaments, including the Open Championship, and is one of the governing authorities of golf along with the USGA.

SALT – The St Andrews Links Trust.

SEPA – The Scottish Environment Protection Agency

WBO – The Women's British Open.

USGA – The United States Golf Association.

Printed in Great Britain
by Amazon

22197350R00225